THE AMORTIZATION HANDBOOK

covering
Monthly Payment Schedules
Loan Amounts
Real Estate

Longmeadow Press

THE UTMOST CARE HAS BEEN TAKEN IN ORDER TO ENSURE THAT ALL FIGURES USED IN THIS BOOK ARE ACCURATE. BUT DUE TO THE COMPLEXITY OF PUBLISHING THIS TYPE OF HANDBOOK, NO WARRANTY OF ABSOLUTE ACCURACY IS GIVEN BY THE AUTHORS OR PUBLISHERS.

THE AMORTIZATION HANDBOOK

PUBLISHED BY LONGMEADOW PRESS, 201 HIGH RIDGE ROAD, STAMFORD, CONNECTICUT 06904.
ISBN: 0–681–40053–6
PRINTED IN THE UNITED STATES OF AMERICA

0 9 8 7 6 5 4

TABLE OF CONTENTS

SECTION ONE

Monthly Payment Schedule

MONTHLY PAYMENT TO AMORTIZE A LOAN

These tables represent the regular and equal payment necessary to be made at the end of each period that will repay both the interest on a loan and the original loan amount.

EXAMPLE: You have a loan for $75,000 at 10% interest for 30 years. What is the monthly payment?

Turn to the page where the interest entry is 10% and find the term—30 years on the horizontal line at the top of the chart. Then follow the 30 year column down the page to the $75,000 line. At this point you will find the figure $658.18. This is the monthly payment necessary to repay the principal and interest on a $75,000 loan for 30 years at 10% interest.

5%

MONTHLY PAYMENT

Necessary to amortize a loan

TERM / AMOUNT	1 YEARS	2 YEARS	3 YEARS	4 YEARS	5 YEARS	6 YEARS
500	42.80	21.94	14.99	11.51	9.44	8.05
600	51.36	26.32	17.98	13.82	11.32	9.66
700	59.93	30.71	20.98	16.12	13.21	11.27
800	68.49	35.10	23.98	18.42	15.10	12.88
900	77.05	39.48	26.97	20.73	16.98	14.49
1000	85.61	43.87	29.97	23.03	18.87	16.10
2000	171.21	87.74	59.94	46.06	37.74	32.21
3000	256.82	131.61	89.91	69.09	56.61	48.31
4000	342.43	175.49	119.88	92.12	75.48	64.42
5000	428.04	219.36	149.85	115.15	94.36	80.52
6000	513.64	263.23	179.83	138.18	113.23	96.63
7000	599.25	307.10	209.80	161.21	132.10	112.73
8000	684.86	350.97	239.77	184.23	150.97	128.84
9000	770.47	394.84	269.74	207.26	169.84	144.94
10000	856.07	438.71	299.71	230.29	188.71	161.05
11000	941.68	482.59	329.68	253.32	207.58	177.15
12000	1027.29	526.46	359.65	276.35	226.45	193.26
13000	1112.90	570.33	389.62	299.38	245.33	209.36
14000	1198.50	614.20	419.59	322.41	264.20	225.47
15000	1284.11	658.07	449.56	345.44	283.07	241.57
16000	1369.72	701.94	479.53	368.47	301.94	257.68
17000	1455.33	745.81	509.51	391.50	320.81	273.78
18000	1540.93	789.69	539.48	414.53	339.68	289.89
19000	1626.54	833.56	569.45	437.56	358.55	305.99
20000	1712.15	877.43	599.42	460.59	377.42	322.10
21000	1797.76	921.30	629.39	483.62	396.30	338.20
22000	1883.36	965.17	659.36	506.64	415.17	354.31
23000	1968.97	1009.04	689.33	529.67	434.04	370.41
24000	2054.58	1052.91	719.30	552.70	452.91	386.52
25000	2140.19	1096.78	749.27	575.73	471.78	402.62
30000	2568.22	1316.14	899.13	690.88	566.14	483.15
35000	2996.26	1535.50	1048.98	806.03	660.49	563.67
40000	3424.30	1754.86	1198.84	921.17	754.85	644.20
45000	3852.34	1974.21	1348.69	1036.32	849.21	724.72
50000	4280.37	2193.57	1498.54	1151.46	943.56	805.25
55000	4708.41	2412.93	1648.40	1266.61	1037.92	885.77
60000	5136.45	2632.28	1798.25	1381.76	1132.27	966.30
65000	5564.49	2851.64	1948.11	1496.90	1226.63	1046.82
70000	5992.52	3071.00	2097.96	1612.05	1320.99	1127.35
75000	6420.56	3290.35	2247.82	1727.20	1415.34	1207.87
80000	6848.60	3509.71	2397.67	1842.34	1509.70	1288.39
85000	7276.64	3729.07	2547.53	1957.49	1604.05	1368.92
90000	7704.67	3948.43	2697.38	2072.64	1698.41	1449.44
95000	8132.71	4167.78	2847.24	2187.78	1792.77	1529.97
100000	8560.75	4387.14	2997.09	2302.93	1887.12	1610.49
200000	17121.50	8774.28	5994.18	4605.86	3774.25	3220.99
300000	25682.24	13161.42	8991.27	6908.79	5661.37	4831.48
400000	34242.99	17548.56	11988.36	9211.72	7548.49	6441.97
500000	42803.74	21935.69	14985.45	11514.65	9435.62	8052.47

MONTHLY PAYMENT

Necessary to amortize a loan

5%

TERM / AMOUNT	7 YEARS	8 YEARS	9 YEARS	10 YEARS	11 YEARS	12 YEARS
500	7.07	6.33	5.76	5.30	4.93	4.62
600	8.48	7.60	6.91	6.36	5.92	5.55
700	9.89	8.86	8.06	7.42	6.91	6.47
800	11.31	10.13	9.21	8.49	7.89	7.40
900	12.72	11.39	10.37	9.55	8.88	8.32
1000	14.13	12.66	11.52	10.61	9.86	9.25
2000	28.27	25.32	23.03	21.21	19.73	18.50
3000	42.40	37.98	34.55	31.82	29.59	27.75
4000	56.54	50.64	46.07	42.43	39.46	37.00
5000	70.67	63.30	57.59	53.03	49.32	46.24
6000	84.80	75.96	69.10	63.64	59.19	55.49
7000	98.94	88.62	80.62	74.25	69.05	64.74
8000	113.07	101.28	92.14	84.85	78.92	73.99
9000	127.21	113.94	103.66	95.46	88.78	83.24
10000	141.34	126.60	115.17	106.07	98.64	92.49
11000	155.47	139.26	126.69	116.67	108.51	101.74
12000	169.61	151.92	138.21	127.28	118.37	110.99
13000	183.74	164.58	149.72	137.89	128.24	120.24
14000	197.87	177.24	161.24	148.49	138.10	129.48
15000	212.01	189.90	172.76	159.10	147.97	138.73
16000	226.14	202.56	184.28	169.70	157.83	147.98
17000	240.28	215.22	195.79	180.31	167.70	157.23
18000	254.41	227.88	207.31	190.92	177.56	166.48
19000	268.54	240.54	218.83	201.52	187.43	175.73
20000	282.68	253.20	230.35	212.13	197.29	184.98
21000	296.81	265.86	241.86	222.74	207.15	194.23
22000	310.95	278.52	253.38	233.34	217.02	203.48
23000	325.08	291.18	264.90	243.95	226.88	212.72
24000	339.21	303.84	276.41	254.56	236.75	221.97
25000	353.35	316.50	287.93	265.16	246.61	231.22
30000	424.02	379.80	345.52	318.20	295.93	277.47
35000	494.69	443.10	403.10	371.23	345.26	323.71
40000	565.36	506.40	460.69	424.26	394.58	369.96
45000	636.03	569.70	518.28	477.29	443.90	416.20
50000	706.70	633.00	575.86	530.33	493.22	462.45
55000	777.36	696.30	633.45	583.36	542.55	508.69
60000	848.03	759.60	691.04	636.39	591.87	554.93
65000	918.70	822.89	748.62	689.43	641.19	601.18
70000	989.37	886.19	806.21	742.46	690.51	647.42
75000	1060.04	949.49	863.80	795.49	739.84	693.67
80000	1130.71	1012.79	921.38	848.52	789.16	739.91
85000	1201.38	1076.09	978.97	901.56	838.48	786.16
90000	1272.05	1139.39	1036.55	954.59	887.80	832.40
95000	1342.72	1202.69	1094.14	1007.62	937.13	878.65
100000	1413.39	1265.99	1151.73	1060.66	986.45	924.89
200000	2826.78	2531.98	2303.45	2121.31	1972.90	1849.78
300000	4240.17	3797.98	3455.18	3181.97	2959.35	2774.67
400000	5653.56	5063.97	4606.91	4242.62	3945.80	3699.56
500000	7066.95	6329.96	5758.64	5303.28	4932.24	4624.45

5%

MONTHLY PAYMENT

Necessary to amortize a loan

TERM / AMOUNT	15 YEARS	20 YEARS	25 YEARS	30 YEARS	35 YEARS	40 YEARS
500	3.95	3.30	2.92	2.68	2.52	2.41
600	4.74	3.96	3.51	3.22	3.03	2.89
700	5.54	4.62	4.09	3.76	3.53	3.38
800	6.33	5.28	4.68	4.29	4.04	3.86
900	7.12	5.94	5.26	4.83	4.54	4.34
1000	7.91	6.60	5.85	5.37	5.05	4.82
2000	15.82	13.20	11.69	10.74	10.09	9.64
3000	23.72	19.80	17.54	16.10	15.14	14.47
4000	31.63	26.40	23.38	21.47	20.19	19.29
5000	39.54	33.00	29.23	26.84	25.23	24.11
6000	47.45	39.60	35.08	32.21	30.28	28.93
7000	55.36	46.20	40.92	37.58	35.33	33.75
8000	63.26	52.80	46.77	42.95	40.38	38.58
9000	71.17	59.40	52.61	48.31	45.42	43.40
10000	79.08	66.00	58.46	53.68	50.47	48.22
11000	86.99	72.60	64.30	59.05	55.52	53.04
12000	94.90	79.19	70.15	64.42	60.56	57.86
13000	102.80	85.79	76.00	69.79	65.61	62.69
14000	110.71	92.39	81.84	75.16	70.66	67.51
15000	118.62	98.99	87.69	80.52	75.70	72.33
16000	126.53	105.59	93.53	85.89	80.75	77.15
17000	134.43	112.19	99.38	91.26	85.80	81.97
18000	142.34	118.79	105.23	96.63	90.84	86.80
19000	150.25	125.39	111.07	102.00	95.89	91.62
20000	158.16	131.99	116.92	107.36	100.94	96.44
21000	166.07	138.59	122.76	112.73	105.98	101.26
22000	173.97	145.19	128.61	118.10	111.03	106.08
23000	181.88	151.79	134.46	123.47	116.08	110.91
24000	189.79	158.39	140.30	128.84	121.13	115.73
25000	197.70	164.99	146.15	134.21	126.17	120.55
30000	237.24	197.99	175.38	161.05	151.41	144.66
35000	276.78	230.98	204.61	187.89	176.64	168.77
40000	316.32	263.98	233.84	214.73	201.88	192.88
45000	355.86	296.98	263.07	241.57	227.11	216.99
50000	395.40	329.98	292.30	268.41	252.34	241.10
55000	434.94	362.98	321.52	295.25	277.58	265.21
60000	474.48	395.97	350.75	322.09	302.81	289.32
65000	514.02	428.97	379.98	348.93	328.05	313.43
70000	553.56	461.97	409.21	375.78	353.28	337.54
75000	593.10	494.97	438.44	402.62	378.52	361.65
80000	632.63	527.96	467.67	429.46	403.75	385.76
85000	672.17	560.96	496.90	456.30	428.98	409.87
90000	711.71	593.96	526.13	483.14	454.22	433.98
95000	751.25	626.96	555.36	509.98	479.45	458.09
100000	790.79	659.96	584.59	536.82	504.69	482.20
200000	1581.59	1319.91	1169.18	1073.64	1009.38	964.39
300000	2372.38	1979.87	1753.77	1610.46	1514.06	1446.59
400000	3163.17	2639.82	2338.36	2147.29	2018.75	1928.79
500000	3953.97	3299.78	2922.95	2684.11	2523.44	2410.98

MONTHLY PAYMENT

Necessary to amortize a loan

5.5%

TERM / AMOUNT	1 YEARS	2 YEARS	3 YEARS	4 YEARS	5 YEARS	6 YEARS
500	42.92	22.05	15.10	11.63	9.55	8.17
600	51.50	26.46	18.12	13.95	11.46	9.80
700	60.09	30.87	21.14	16.28	13.37	11.44
800	68.67	35.28	24.16	18.61	15.28	13.07
900	77.25	39.69	27.18	20.93	17.19	14.70
1000	85.84	44.10	30.20	23.26	19.10	16.34
2000	171.67	88.19	60.39	46.51	38.20	32.68
3000	257.51	132.29	90.59	69.77	57.30	49.01
4000	343.35	176.38	120.78	93.03	76.40	65.35
5000	429.18	220.48	150.98	116.28	95.51	81.69
6000	515.02	264.57	181.18	139.54	114.61	98.03
7000	600.86	308.67	211.37	162.80	133.71	114.37
8000	686.69	352.77	241.57	186.05	152.81	130.70
9000	772.53	396.86	271.76	209.31	171.91	147.04
10000	858.37	440.96	301.96	232.56	191.01	163.38
11000	944.20	485.05	332.15	255.82	210.11	179.72
12000	1030.04	529.15	362.35	279.08	229.21	196.05
13000	1115.88	573.24	392.55	302.33	248.32	212.39
14000	1201.71	617.34	422.74	325.59	267.42	228.73
15000	1287.55	661.43	452.94	348.85	286.52	245.07
16000	1373.39	705.53	483.13	372.10	305.62	261.41
17000	1459.23	749.63	513.33	395.36	324.72	277.74
18000	1545.06	793.72	543.53	418.62	343.82	294.08
19000	1630.90	837.82	573.72	441.87	362.92	310.42
20000	1716.74	881.91	603.92	465.13	382.02	326.76
21000	1802.57	926.01	634.11	488.39	401.12	343.10
22000	1888.41	970.10	664.31	511.64	420.23	359.43
23000	1974.25	1014.20	694.51	534.90	439.33	375.77
24000	2060.08	1058.30	724.70	558.16	458.43	392.11
25000	2145.92	1102.39	754.90	581.41	477.53	408.45
30000	2575.10	1322.87	905.88	697.69	573.03	490.14
35000	3004.29	1543.35	1056.86	813.98	668.54	571.83
40000	3433.47	1763.83	1207.84	930.26	764.05	653.52
45000	3862.66	1984.30	1358.82	1046.54	859.55	735.20
50000	4291.84	2204.78	1509.80	1162.82	955.06	816.89
55000	4721.02	2425.26	1660.77	1279.11	1050.56	898.58
60000	5150.21	2645.74	1811.75	1395.39	1146.07	980.27
65000	5579.39	2866.22	1962.73	1511.67	1241.58	1061.96
70000	6008.57	3086.70	2113.71	1627.95	1337.08	1143.65
75000	6437.76	3307.17	2264.69	1744.24	1432.59	1225.34
80000	6866.94	3527.65	2415.67	1860.52	1528.09	1307.03
85000	7296.13	3748.13	2566.65	1976.80	1623.60	1388.72
90000	7725.31	3968.61	2717.63	2093.08	1719.10	1470.41
95000	8154.49	4189.09	2868.61	2209.37	1814.61	1552.10
100000	8583.68	4409.57	3019.59	2325.65	1910.12	1633.79
200000	17167.36	8819.13	6039.18	4651.30	3820.23	3267.58
300000	25751.04	13228.70	9058.77	6976.94	5730.35	4901.37
400000	34334.71	17638.26	12078.36	9302.59	7640.46	6535.15
500000	42918.39	22047.83	15097.95	11628.24	9550.58	8168.94

5.5%

MONTHLY PAYMENT

Necessary to amortize a loan

TERM / AMOUNT	7 YEARS	8 YEARS	9 YEARS	10 YEARS	11 YEARS	12 YEARS
500	7.19	6.45	5.88	5.43	5.06	4.75
600	8.62	7.74	7.06	6.51	6.07	5.70
700	10.06	9.03	8.23	7.60	7.08	6.65
800	11.50	10.32	9.41	8.68	8.09	7.60
900	12.93	11.61	10.58	9.77	9.10	8.55
1000	14.37	12.90	11.76	10.85	10.11	9.50
2000	28.74	25.80	23.52	21.71	20.23	19.00
3000	43.11	38.70	35.28	32.56	30.34	28.51
4000	57.48	51.60	47.04	43.41	40.46	38.01
5000	71.85	64.50	58.80	54.26	50.57	47.51
6000	86.22	77.40	70.56	65.12	60.68	57.01
7000	100.59	90.30	82.32	75.97	70.80	66.51
8000	114.96	103.19	94.08	86.82	80.91	76.01
9000	129.33	116.09	105.84	97.67	91.03	85.52
10000	143.70	128.99	117.60	108.53	101.14	95.02
11000	158.07	141.89	129.36	119.38	111.25	104.52
12000	172.44	154.79	141.12	130.23	121.37	114.02
13000	186.81	167.69	152.88	141.08	131.48	123.52
14000	201.18	180.59	164.64	151.94	141.60	133.02
15000	215.55	193.49	176.40	162.79	151.71	142.53
16000	229.92	206.39	188.16	173.64	161.82	152.03
17000	244.29	219.29	199.92	184.49	171.94	161.53
18000	258.66	232.19	211.68	195.35	182.05	171.03
19000	273.03	245.09	223.44	206.20	192.16	180.53
20000	287.40	257.99	235.20	217.05	202.28	190.03
21000	301.77	270.89	246.96	227.91	212.39	199.54
22000	316.14	283.79	258.72	238.76	222.51	209.04
23000	330.51	296.68	270.48	249.61	232.62	218.54
24000	344.88	309.58	282.24	260.46	242.73	228.04
25000	359.25	322.48	294.00	271.32	252.85	237.54
30000	431.10	386.98	352.80	325.58	303.42	285.05
35000	502.95	451.48	411.60	379.84	353.99	332.56
40000	574.80	515.97	470.40	434.11	404.56	380.07
45000	646.65	580.47	529.20	488.37	455.13	427.58
50000	718.50	644.97	588.00	542.63	505.70	475.09
55000	790.35	709.46	646.80	596.89	556.27	522.59
60000	862.20	773.96	705.60	651.16	606.84	570.10
65000	934.05	838.46	764.40	705.42	657.41	617.61
70000	1005.90	902.95	823.20	759.68	707.98	665.12
75000	1077.75	967.45	882.00	813.95	758.54	712.63
80000	1149.60	1031.95	940.80	868.21	809.11	760.14
85000	1221.45	1096.44	999.60	922.47	859.68	807.65
90000	1293.30	1160.94	1058.40	976.74	910.25	855.15
95000	1365.15	1225.44	1117.20	1031.00	960.82	902.66
100000	1437.00	1289.93	1176.00	1085.26	1011.39	950.17
200000	2874.01	2579.86	2352.00	2170.53	2022.79	1900.34
300000	4311.01	3869.80	3528.00	3255.79	3034.18	2850.52
400000	5748.02	5159.73	4704.00	4341.05	4045.57	3800.69
500000	7185.02	6449.66	5880.00	5426.31	5056.97	4750.86

MONTHLY PAYMENT

Necessary to amortize a loan

5.5%

TERM / AMOUNT	15 YEARS	20 YEARS	25 YEARS	30 YEARS	35 YEARS	40 YEARS
500	4.09	3.44	3.07	2.84	2.69	2.58
600	4.90	4.13	3.68	3.41	3.22	3.09
700	5.72	4.82	4.30	3.97	3.76	3.61
800	6.54	5.50	4.91	4.54	4.30	4.13
900	7.35	6.19	5.53	5.11	4.83	4.64
1000	8.17	6.88	6.14	5.68	5.37	5.16
2000	16.34	13.76	12.28	11.36	10.74	10.32
3000	24.51	20.64	18.42	17.03	16.11	15.47
4000	32.68	27.52	24.56	22.71	21.48	20.63
5000	40.85	34.39	30.70	28.39	26.85	25.79
6000	49.03	41.27	36.85	34.07	32.22	30.95
7000	57.20	48.15	42.99	39.75	37.59	36.10
8000	65.37	55.03	49.13	45.42	42.96	41.26
9000	73.54	61.91	55.27	51.10	48.33	46.42
10000	81.71	68.79	61.41	56.78	53.70	51.58
11000	89.88	75.67	67.55	62.46	59.07	56.73
12000	98.05	82.55	73.69	68.13	64.44	61.89
13000	106.22	89.43	79.83	73.81	69.81	67.05
14000	114.39	96.30	85.97	79.49	75.18	72.21
15000	122.56	103.18	92.11	85.17	80.55	77.37
16000	130.73	110.06	98.25	90.85	85.92	82.52
17000	138.90	116.94	104.39	96.52	91.29	87.68
18000	147.08	123.82	110.54	102.20	96.66	92.84
19000	155.25	130.70	116.68	107.88	102.03	98.00
20000	163.42	137.58	122.82	113.56	107.40	103.15
21000	171.59	144.46	128.96	119.24	112.77	108.31
22000	179.76	151.34	135.10	124.91	118.14	113.47
23000	187.93	158.21	141.24	130.59	123.51	118.63
24000	196.10	165.09	147.38	136.27	128.88	123.78
25000	204.27	171.97	153.52	141.95	134.25	128.94
30000	245.13	206.37	184.23	170.34	161.10	154.73
35000	285.98	240.76	214.93	198.73	187.96	180.52
40000	326.83	275.15	245.63	227.12	214.81	206.31
45000	367.69	309.55	276.34	255.51	241.66	232.10
50000	408.54	343.94	307.04	283.89	268.51	257.89
55000	449.40	378.34	337.75	312.28	295.36	283.67
60000	490.25	412.73	368.45	340.67	322.21	309.46
65000	531.10	447.13	399.16	369.06	349.06	335.25
70000	571.96	481.52	429.86	397.45	375.91	361.04
75000	612.81	515.92	460.57	425.84	402.76	386.83
80000	653.67	550.31	491.27	454.23	429.61	412.62
85000	694.52	584.70	521.97	482.62	456.46	438.40
90000	735.38	619.10	552.68	511.01	483.31	464.19
95000	776.23	653.49	583.38	539.40	510.17	489.98
100000	817.08	687.89	614.09	567.79	537.02	515.77
200000	1634.17	1375.77	1228.17	1135.58	1074.03	1031.54
300000	2451.25	2063.66	1842.26	1703.37	1611.05	1547.31
400000	3268.33	2751.55	2456.35	2271.16	2148.07	2063.08
500000	4085.42	3439.44	3070.44	2838.95	2685.08	2578.85

6%

MONTHLY PAYMENT

Necessary to amortize a loan

TERM AMOUNT	1 YEARS	2 YEARS	3 YEARS	4 YEARS	5 YEARS	6 YEARS
500	43.03	22.16	15.21	11.74	9.67	8.29
600	51.64	26.59	18.25	14.09	11.60	9.94
700	60.25	31.02	21.30	16.44	13.53	11.60
800	68.85	35.46	24.34	18.79	15.47	13.26
900	77.46	39.89	27.38	21.14	17.40	14.92
1000	86.07	44.32	30.42	23.49	19.33	16.57
2000	172.13	88.64	60.84	46.97	38.67	33.15
3000	258.20	132.96	91.27	70.46	58.00	49.72
4000	344.27	177.28	121.69	93.94	77.33	66.29
5000	430.33	221.60	152.11	117.43	96.66	82.86
6000	516.40	265.92	182.53	140.91	116.00	99.44
7000	602.47	310.24	212.95	164.40	135.33	116.01
8000	688.53	354.56	243.38	187.88	154.66	132.58
9000	774.60	398.89	273.80	211.37	174.00	149.16
10000	860.66	443.21	304.22	234.85	193.33	165.73
11000	946.73	487.53	334.64	258.34	212.66	182.30
12000	1032.80	531.85	365.06	281.82	231.99	198.87
13000	1118.86	576.17	395.49	305.31	251.33	215.45
14000	1204.93	620.49	425.91	328.79	270.66	232.02
15000	1291.00	664.81	456.33	352.28	289.99	248.59
16000	1377.06	709.13	486.75	375.76	309.32	265.17
17000	1463.13	753.45	517.17	399.25	328.66	281.74
18000	1549.20	797.77	547.59	422.73	347.99	298.31
19000	1635.26	842.09	578.02	446.22	367.32	314.88
20000	1721.33	886.41	608.44	469.70	386.66	331.46
21000	1807.40	930.73	638.86	493.19	405.99	348.03
22000	1893.46	975.05	669.28	516.67	425.32	364.60
23000	1979.53	1019.37	699.70	540.16	444.65	381.18
24000	2065.59	1063.69	730.13	563.64	463.99	397.75
25000	2151.66	1108.02	760.55	587.13	483.32	414.32
30000	2581.99	1329.62	912.66	704.55	579.98	497.19
35000	3012.33	1551.22	1064.77	821.98	676.65	580.05
40000	3442.66	1772.82	1216.88	939.40	773.31	662.92
45000	3872.99	1994.43	1368.99	1056.83	869.98	745.78
50000	4303.32	2216.03	1521.10	1174.25	966.64	828.64
55000	4733.65	2437.63	1673.21	1291.68	1063.30	911.51
60000	5163.99	2659.24	1825.32	1409.10	1159.97	994.37
65000	5594.32	2880.84	1977.43	1526.53	1256.63	1077.24
70000	6024.65	3102.44	2129.54	1643.95	1353.30	1160.10
75000	6454.98	3324.05	2281.65	1761.38	1449.96	1242.97
80000	6885.31	3545.65	2433.75	1878.80	1546.62	1325.83
85000	7315.65	3767.25	2585.86	1996.23	1643.29	1408.70
90000	7745.98	3988.85	2737.97	2113.65	1739.95	1491.56
95000	8176.31	4210.46	2890.08	2231.08	1836.62	1574.42
100000	8606.64	4432.06	3042.19	2348.50	1933.28	1657.29
200000	17213.29	8864.12	6084.39	4697.01	3866.56	3314.58
300000	25819.93	13296.18	9126.58	7045.51	5799.84	4971.87
400000	34426.57	17728.24	12168.77	9394.01	7733.12	6629.16
500000	43033.21	22160.31	15210.97	11742.51	9666.40	8286.44

MONTHLY PAYMENT

Necessary to amortize a loan

6%

TERM / AMOUNT	7 YEARS	8 YEARS	9 YEARS	10 YEARS	11 YEARS	12 YEARS
500	7.30	6.57	6.00	5.55	5.18	4.88
600	8.77	7.88	7.20	6.66	6.22	5.86
700	10.23	9.20	8.40	7.77	7.26	6.83
800	11.69	10.51	9.60	8.88	8.29	7.81
900	13.15	11.83	10.81	9.99	9.33	8.78
1000	14.61	13.14	12.01	11.10	10.37	9.76
2000	29.22	26.28	24.01	22.20	20.73	19.52
3000	43.83	39.42	36.02	33.31	31.10	29.28
4000	58.43	52.57	48.02	44.41	41.47	39.03
5000	73.04	65.71	60.03	55.51	51.84	48.79
6000	87.65	78.85	72.03	66.61	62.20	58.55
7000	102.26	91.99	84.04	77.71	72.57	68.31
8000	116.87	105.13	96.05	88.82	82.94	78.07
9000	131.48	118.27	108.05	99.92	93.30	87.83
10000	146.09	131.41	120.06	111.02	103.67	97.59
11000	160.69	144.56	132.06	122.12	114.04	107.34
12000	175.30	157.70	144.07	133.22	124.40	117.10
13000	189.91	170.84	156.07	144.33	134.77	126.86
14000	204.52	183.98	168.08	155.43	145.14	136.62
15000	219.13	197.12	180.09	166.53	155.51	146.38
16000	233.74	210.26	192.09	177.63	165.87	156.14
17000	248.35	223.40	204.10	188.73	176.24	165.89
18000	262.95	236.55	216.10	199.84	186.61	175.65
19000	277.56	249.69	228.11	210.94	196.97	185.41
20000	292.17	262.83	240.11	222.04	207.34	195.17
21000	306.78	275.97	252.12	233.14	217.71	204.93
22000	321.39	289.11	264.13	244.25	228.07	214.69
23000	336.00	302.25	276.13	255.35	238.44	224.45
24000	350.61	315.39	288.14	266.45	248.81	234.20
25000	365.21	328.54	300.14	277.55	259.18	243.96
30000	438.26	394.24	360.17	333.06	311.01	292.76
35000	511.30	459.95	420.20	388.57	362.85	341.55
40000	584.34	525.66	480.23	444.08	414.68	390.34
45000	657.38	591.36	540.26	499.59	466.52	439.13
50000	730.43	657.07	600.29	555.10	518.35	487.93
55000	803.47	722.78	660.32	610.61	570.19	536.72
60000	876.51	788.49	720.34	666.12	622.02	585.51
65000	949.56	854.19	780.37	721.63	673.86	634.30
70000	1022.60	919.90	840.40	777.14	725.69	683.10
75000	1095.64	985.61	900.43	832.65	777.53	731.89
80000	1168.68	1051.31	960.46	888.16	829.36	780.68
85000	1241.73	1117.02	1020.49	943.67	881.20	829.47
90000	1314.77	1182.73	1080.52	999.18	933.03	878.27
95000	1387.81	1248.44	1140.55	1054.69	984.87	927.06
100000	1460.86	1314.14	1200.57	1110.21	1036.70	975.85
200000	2921.71	2628.29	2401.15	2220.41	2073.41	1951.70
300000	4382.57	3942.43	3601.72	3330.62	3110.11	2927.55
400000	5843.42	5256.57	4802.30	4440.82	4146.81	3903.40
500000	7304.28	6570.72	6002.87	5551.03	5183.52	4879.25

6%

MONTHLY PAYMENT

Necessary to amortize a loan

TERM / AMOUNT	15 YEARS	20 YEARS	25 YEARS	30 YEARS	35 YEARS	40 YEARS
500	4.22	3.58	3.22	3.00	2.85	2.75
600	5.06	4.30	3.87	3.60	3.42	3.30
700	5.91	5.02	4.51	4.20	3.99	3.85
800	6.75	5.73	5.15	4.80	4.56	4.40
900	7.59	6.45	5.80	5.40	5.13	4.95
1000	8.44	7.16	6.44	6.00	5.70	5.50
2000	16.88	14.33	12.89	11.99	11.40	11.00
3000	25.32	21.49	19.33	17.99	17.11	16.51
4000	33.75	28.66	25.77	23.98	22.81	22.01
5000	42.19	35.82	32.22	29.98	28.51	27.51
6000	50.63	42.99	38.66	35.97	34.21	33.01
7000	59.07	50.15	45.10	41.97	39.91	38.51
8000	67.51	57.31	51.54	47.96	45.62	44.02
9000	75.95	64.48	57.99	53.96	51.32	49.52
10000	84.39	71.64	64.43	59.96	57.02	55.02
11000	92.82	78.81	70.87	65.95	62.72	60.52
12000	101.26	85.97	77.32	71.95	68.42	66.03
13000	109.70	93.14	83.76	77.94	74.12	71.53
14000	118.14	100.30	90.20	83.94	79.83	77.03
15000	126.58	107.46	96.65	89.93	85.53	82.53
16000	135.02	114.63	103.09	95.93	91.23	88.03
17000	143.46	121.79	109.53	101.92	96.93	93.54
18000	151.89	128.96	115.97	107.92	102.63	99.04
19000	160.33	136.12	122.42	113.91	108.34	104.54
20000	168.77	143.29	128.86	119.91	114.04	110.04
21000	177.21	150.45	135.30	125.91	119.74	115.54
22000	185.65	157.61	141.75	131.90	125.44	121.05
23000	194.09	164.78	148.19	137.90	131.14	126.55
24000	202.53	171.94	154.63	143.89	136.85	132.05
25000	210.96	179.11	161.08	149.89	142.55	137.55
30000	253.16	214.93	193.29	179.87	171.06	165.06
35000	295.35	250.75	225.51	209.84	199.57	192.57
40000	337.54	286.57	257.72	239.82	228.08	220.09
45000	379.74	322.39	289.94	269.80	256.59	247.60
50000	421.93	358.22	322.15	299.78	285.09	275.11
55000	464.12	394.04	354.37	329.75	313.60	302.62
60000	506.31	429.86	386.58	359.73	342.11	330.13
65000	548.51	465.68	418.80	389.71	370.62	357.64
70000	590.70	501.50	451.01	419.69	399.13	385.15
75000	632.89	537.32	483.23	449.66	427.64	412.66
80000	675.09	573.14	515.44	479.64	456.15	440.17
85000	717.28	608.97	547.66	509.62	484.66	467.68
90000	759.47	644.79	579.87	539.60	513.17	495.19
95000	801.66	680.61	612.09	569.57	541.68	522.70
100000	843.86	716.43	644.30	599.55	570.19	550.21
200000	1687.71	1432.86	1288.60	1199.10	1140.38	1100.43
300000	2531.57	2149.29	1932.90	1798.65	1710.57	1650.64
400000	3375.43	2865.72	2577.21	2398.20	2280.76	2200.85
500000	4219.28	3582.16	3221.51	2997.75	2850.95	2751.07

MONTHLY PAYMENT

Necessary to amortize a loan

6.5%

TERM AMOUNT	1 YEARS	2 YEARS	3 YEARS	4 YEARS	5 YEARS	6 YEARS
500	43.15	22.27	15.32	11.86	9.78	8.40
600	51.78	26.73	18.39	14.23	11.74	10.09
700	60.41	31.18	21.45	16.60	13.70	11.77
800	69.04	35.64	24.52	18.97	15.65	13.45
900	77.67	40.09	27.58	21.34	17.61	15.13
1000	86.30	44.55	30.65	23.71	19.57	16.81
2000	172.59	89.09	61.30	47.43	39.13	33.62
3000	258.89	133.64	91.95	71.14	58.70	50.43
4000	345.19	178.19	122.60	94.86	78.26	67.24
5000	431.48	222.73	153.25	118.57	97.83	84.05
6000	517.78	267.28	183.89	142.29	117.40	100.86
7000	604.07	311.82	214.54	166.00	136.96	117.67
8000	690.37	356.37	245.19	189.72	156.53	134.48
9000	776.67	400.92	275.84	213.43	176.10	151.29
10000	862.96	445.46	306.49	237.15	195.66	168.10
11000	949.26	490.01	337.14	260.86	215.23	184.91
12000	1035.56	534.56	367.79	284.58	234.79	201.72
13000	1121.85	579.10	398.44	308.29	254.36	218.53
14000	1208.15	623.65	429.09	332.01	273.93	235.34
15000	1294.45	668.19	459.74	355.72	293.49	252.15
16000	1380.74	712.74	490.38	379.44	313.06	268.96
17000	1467.04	757.29	521.03	403.15	332.62	285.77
18000	1553.34	801.83	551.68	426.87	352.19	302.58
19000	1639.63	846.38	582.33	450.58	371.76	319.39
20000	1725.93	890.93	612.98	474.30	391.32	336.20
21000	1812.22	935.47	643.63	498.01	410.89	353.01
22000	1898.52	980.02	674.28	521.73	430.46	369.82
23000	1984.82	1024.56	704.93	545.44	450.02	386.63
24000	2071.11	1069.11	735.58	569.16	469.59	403.44
25000	2157.41	1113.66	766.23	592.87	489.15	420.25
30000	2588.89	1336.39	919.47	711.45	586.98	504.30
35000	3020.37	1559.12	1072.72	830.02	684.82	588.35
40000	3451.86	1781.85	1225.96	948.60	782.65	672.40
45000	3883.34	2004.58	1379.21	1067.17	880.48	756.45
50000	4314.82	2227.31	1532.45	1185.75	978.31	840.50
55000	4746.30	2450.04	1685.70	1304.32	1076.14	924.55
60000	5177.79	2672.78	1838.94	1422.90	1173.97	1008.60
65000	5609.27	2895.51	1992.19	1541.47	1271.80	1092.65
70000	6040.75	3118.24	2145.43	1660.05	1369.63	1176.70
75000	6472.23	3340.97	2298.68	1778.62	1467.46	1260.74
80000	6903.71	3563.70	2451.92	1897.20	1565.29	1344.79
85000	7335.20	3786.43	2605.17	2015.77	1663.12	1428.84
90000	7766.68	4009.16	2758.41	2134.35	1760.95	1512.89
95000	8198.16	4231.89	2911.66	2252.92	1858.78	1596.94
100000	8629.64	4454.63	3064.90	2371.50	1956.61	1680.99
200000	17259.28	8909.25	6129.80	4742.99	3913.23	3361.99
300000	25888.93	13363.88	9194.70	7114.49	5869.84	5042.98
400000	34518.57	17818.50	12259.60	9485.98	7826.46	6723.97
500000	43148.21	22273.13	15324.50	11857.48	9783.07	8404.96

6.5%

MONTHLY PAYMENT

Necessary to amortize a loan

TERM / AMOUNT	7 YEARS	8 YEARS	9 YEARS	10 YEARS	11 YEARS	12 YEARS
500	7.42	6.69	6.13	5.68	5.31	5.01
600	8.91	8.03	7.35	6.81	6.37	6.01
700	10.39	9.37	8.58	7.95	7.44	7.01
800	11.88	10.71	9.80	9.08	8.50	8.02
900	13.36	12.05	11.03	10.22	9.56	9.02
1000	14.85	13.39	12.25	11.35	10.62	10.02
2000	29.70	26.77	24.51	22.71	21.25	20.04
3000	44.55	40.16	36.76	34.06	31.87	30.06
4000	59.40	53.54	49.02	45.42	42.50	40.08
5000	74.25	66.93	61.27	56.77	53.12	50.10
6000	89.10	80.32	73.53	68.13	63.74	60.12
7000	103.95	93.70	85.78	79.48	74.37	70.13
8000	118.80	107.09	98.04	90.84	84.99	80.15
9000	133.64	120.48	110.29	102.19	95.61	90.17
10000	148.49	133.86	122.55	113.55	106.24	100.19
11000	163.34	147.25	134.80	124.90	116.86	110.21
12000	178.19	160.63	147.05	136.26	127.49	120.23
13000	193.04	174.02	159.31	147.61	138.11	130.25
14000	207.89	187.41	171.56	158.97	148.73	140.27
15000	222.74	200.79	183.82	170.32	159.36	150.29
16000	237.59	214.18	196.07	181.68	169.98	160.31
17000	252.44	227.57	208.33	193.03	180.60	170.33
18000	267.29	240.95	220.58	204.39	191.23	180.35
19000	282.14	254.34	232.84	215.74	201.85	190.37
20000	296.99	267.72	245.09	227.10	212.48	200.38
21000	311.84	281.11	257.34	238.45	223.10	210.40
22000	326.69	294.50	269.60	249.81	233.72	220.42
23000	341.54	307.88	281.85	261.16	244.35	230.44
24000	356.39	321.27	294.11	272.52	254.97	240.46
25000	371.24	334.66	306.36	283.87	265.59	250.48
30000	445.48	401.59	367.64	340.64	318.71	300.58
35000	519.73	468.52	428.91	397.42	371.83	350.67
40000	593.98	535.45	490.18	454.19	424.95	400.77
45000	668.22	602.38	551.45	510.97	478.07	450.86
50000	742.47	669.31	612.73	567.74	531.19	500.96
55000	816.72	736.24	674.00	624.51	584.31	551.06
60000	890.97	803.17	735.27	681.29	637.43	601.15
65000	965.21	870.11	796.54	738.06	690.54	651.25
70000	1039.46	937.04	857.82	794.84	743.66	701.34
75000	1113.71	1003.97	919.09	851.61	796.78	751.44
80000	1187.95	1070.90	980.36	908.38	849.90	801.54
85000	1262.20	1137.83	1041.63	965.16	903.02	851.63
90000	1336.45	1204.76	1102.91	1021.93	956.14	901.73
95000	1410.70	1271.69	1164.18	1078.71	1009.26	951.83
100000	1484.94	1338.62	1225.45	1135.48	1062.38	1001.92
200000	2969.89	2677.25	2450.90	2270.96	2124.75	2003.84
300000	4454.83	4015.87	3676.35	3406.44	3187.13	3005.76
400000	5939.77	5354.49	4901.81	4541.92	4249.51	4007.68
500000	7424.72	6693.12	6127.26	5677.40	5311.88	5009.61

MONTHLY PAYMENT

Necessary to amortize a loan

6.5%

TERM / AMOUNT	15 YEARS	20 YEARS	25 YEARS	30 YEARS	35 YEARS	40 YEARS
500	4.36	3.73	3.38	3.16	3.02	2.93
600	5.23	4.47	4.05	3.79	3.62	3.51
700	6.10	5.22	4.73	4.42	4.23	4.10
800	6.97	5.96	5.40	5.06	4.83	4.68
900	7.84	6.71	6.08	5.69	5.44	5.27
1000	8.71	7.46	6.75	6.32	6.04	5.85
2000	17.42	14.91	13.50	12.64	12.08	11.71
3000	26.13	22.37	20.26	18.96	18.12	17.56
4000	34.84	29.82	27.01	25.28	24.17	23.42
5000	43.56	37.28	33.76	31.60	30.21	29.27
6000	52.27	44.73	40.51	37.92	36.25	35.13
7000	60.98	52.19	47.26	44.24	42.29	40.98
8000	69.69	59.65	54.02	50.57	48.33	46.84
9000	78.40	67.10	60.77	56.89	54.37	52.69
10000	87.11	74.56	67.52	63.21	60.42	58.55
11000	95.82	82.01	74.27	69.53	66.46	64.40
12000	104.53	89.47	81.02	75.85	72.50	70.25
13000	113.24	96.92	87.78	82.17	78.54	76.11
14000	121.96	104.38	94.53	88.49	84.58	81.96
15000	130.67	111.84	101.28	94.81	90.62	87.82
16000	139.38	119.29	108.03	101.13	96.66	93.67
17000	148.09	126.75	114.79	107.45	102.71	99.53
18000	156.80	134.20	121.54	113.77	108.75	105.38
19000	165.51	141.66	128.29	120.09	114.79	111.24
20000	174.22	149.11	135.04	126.41	120.83	117.09
21000	182.93	156.57	141.79	132.73	126.87	122.95
22000	191.64	164.03	148.55	139.05	132.91	128.80
23000	200.35	171.48	155.30	145.38	138.96	134.66
24000	209.07	178.94	162.05	151.70	145.00	140.51
25000	217.78	186.39	168.80	158.02	151.04	146.36
30000	261.33	223.67	202.56	189.62	181.25	175.64
35000	304.89	260.95	236.32	221.22	211.45	204.91
40000	348.44	298.23	270.08	252.83	241.66	234.18
45000	392.00	335.51	303.84	284.43	271.87	263.46
50000	435.55	372.79	337.60	316.03	302.08	292.73
55000	479.11	410.07	371.36	347.64	332.28	322.00
60000	522.66	447.34	405.12	379.24	362.49	351.27
65000	566.22	484.62	438.88	410.84	392.70	380.55
70000	609.78	521.90	472.65	442.45	422.91	409.82
75000	653.33	559.18	506.41	474.05	453.12	439.09
80000	696.89	596.46	540.17	505.65	483.32	468.37
85000	740.44	633.74	573.93	537.26	513.53	497.64
90000	784.00	671.02	607.69	568.86	543.74	526.91
95000	827.55	708.29	641.45	600.46	573.95	556.18
100000	871.11	745.57	675.21	632.07	604.15	585.46
200000	1742.21	1491.15	1350.41	1264.14	1208.31	1170.91
300000	2613.32	2236.72	2025.62	1896.20	1812.46	1756.37
400000	3484.43	2982.29	2700.83	2528.27	2416.62	2341.83
500000	4355.54	3727.87	3376.04	3160.34	3020.77	2927.28

7%

MONTHLY PAYMENT

Necessary to amortize a loan

TERM / AMOUNT	1 YEARS	2 YEARS	3 YEARS	4 YEARS	5 YEARS	6 YEARS
500	43.26	22.39	15.44	11.97	9.90	8.52
600	51.92	26.86	18.53	14.37	11.88	10.23
700	60.57	31.34	21.61	16.76	13.86	11.93
800	69.22	35.82	24.70	19.16	15.84	13.64
900	77.87	40.30	27.79	21.55	17.82	15.34
1000	86.53	44.77	30.88	23.95	19.80	17.05
2000	173.05	89.55	61.75	47.89	39.60	34.10
3000	259.58	134.32	92.63	71.84	59.40	51.15
4000	346.11	179.09	123.51	95.78	79.20	68.20
5000	432.63	223.86	154.39	119.73	99.01	85.25
6000	519.16	268.64	185.26	143.68	118.81	102.29
7000	605.69	313.41	216.14	167.62	138.61	119.34
8000	692.21	358.18	247.02	191.57	158.41	136.39
9000	778.74	402.95	277.89	215.52	178.21	153.44
10000	865.27	447.73	308.77	239.46	198.01	170.49
11000	951.79	492.50	339.65	263.41	217.81	187.54
12000	1038.32	537.27	370.53	287.35	237.61	204.59
13000	1124.85	582.04	401.40	311.30	257.42	221.64
14000	1211.37	626.82	432.28	335.25	277.22	238.69
15000	1297.90	671.59	463.16	359.19	297.02	255.74
16000	1384.43	716.36	494.03	383.14	316.82	272.78
17000	1470.95	761.13	524.91	407.09	336.62	289.83
18000	1557.48	805.91	555.79	431.03	356.42	306.88
19000	1644.01	850.68	586.66	454.98	376.22	323.93
20000	1730.53	895.45	617.54	478.92	396.02	340.98
21000	1817.06	940.22	648.42	502.87	415.83	358.03
22000	1903.59	985.00	679.30	526.82	435.63	375.08
23000	1990.12	1029.77	710.17	550.76	455.43	392.13
24000	2076.64	1074.54	741.05	574.71	475.23	409.18
25000	2163.17	1119.31	771.93	598.66	495.03	426.23
30000	2595.80	1343.18	926.31	718.39	594.04	511.47
35000	3028.44	1567.04	1080.70	838.12	693.04	596.72
40000	3461.07	1790.90	1235.08	957.85	792.05	681.96
45000	3893.70	2014.77	1389.47	1077.58	891.05	767.21
50000	4326.34	2238.63	1543.85	1197.31	990.06	852.45
55000	4758.97	2462.49	1698.24	1317.04	1089.07	937.70
60000	5191.60	2686.35	1852.63	1436.77	1188.07	1022.94
65000	5624.24	2910.22	2007.01	1556.51	1287.08	1108.19
70000	6056.87	3134.08	2161.40	1676.24	1386.08	1193.43
75000	6489.51	3357.94	2315.78	1795.97	1485.09	1278.68
80000	6922.14	3581.81	2470.17	1915.70	1584.10	1363.92
85000	7354.77	3805.67	2624.55	2035.43	1683.10	1449.17
90000	7787.41	4029.53	2778.94	2155.16	1782.11	1534.41
95000	8220.04	4253.40	2933.32	2274.89	1881.11	1619.66
100000	8652.67	4477.26	3087.71	2394.62	1980.12	1704.90
200000	17305.35	8954.52	6175.42	4789.25	3960.24	3409.80
300000	25958.02	13431.77	9263.13	7183.87	5940.36	5114.70
400000	34610.70	17909.03	12350.84	9578.50	7920.48	6819.60
500000	43263.37	22386.29	15438.55	11973.12	9900.60	8524.50

MONTHLY PAYMENT

Necessary to amortize a loan

7%

TERM / AMOUNT	7 YEARS	8 YEARS	9 YEARS	10 YEARS	11 YEARS	12 YEARS
500	7.55	6.82	6.25	5.81	5.44	5.14
600	9.06	8.18	7.50	6.97	6.53	6.17
700	10.56	9.54	8.75	8.13	7.62	7.20
800	12.07	10.91	10.01	9.29	8.71	8.23
900	13.58	12.27	11.26	10.45	9.80	9.26
1000	15.09	13.63	12.51	11.61	10.88	10.28
2000	30.19	27.27	25.01	23.22	21.77	20.57
3000	45.28	40.90	37.52	34.83	32.65	30.85
4000	60.37	54.53	50.03	46.44	43.54	41.14
5000	75.46	68.17	62.53	58.05	54.42	51.42
6000	90.56	81.80	75.04	69.67	65.30	61.70
7000	105.65	95.44	87.54	81.28	76.19	71.99
8000	120.74	109.07	100.05	92.89	87.07	82.27
9000	135.83	122.70	112.56	104.50	97.96	92.55
10000	150.93	136.34	125.06	116.11	108.84	102.84
11000	166.02	149.97	137.57	127.72	119.73	113.12
12000	181.11	163.60	150.08	139.33	130.61	123.41
13000	196.20	177.24	162.58	150.94	141.49	133.69
14000	211.30	190.87	175.09	162.55	152.38	143.97
15000	226.39	204.51	187.59	174.16	163.26	154.26
16000	241.48	218.14	200.10	185.77	174.15	164.54
17000	256.58	231.77	212.61	197.38	185.03	174.82
18000	271.67	245.41	225.11	209.00	195.91	185.11
19000	286.76	259.04	237.62	220.61	206.80	195.39
20000	301.85	272.67	250.13	232.22	217.68	205.68
21000	316.95	286.31	262.63	243.83	228.57	215.96
22000	332.04	299.94	275.14	255.44	239.45	226.24
23000	347.13	313.58	287.64	267.05	250.33	236.53
24000	362.22	327.21	300.15	278.66	261.22	246.81
25000	377.32	340.84	312.66	290.27	272.10	257.10
30000	452.78	409.01	375.19	348.33	326.52	308.51
35000	528.24	477.18	437.72	406.38	380.94	359.93
40000	603.71	545.35	500.25	464.43	435.36	411.35
45000	679.17	613.52	562.78	522.49	489.78	462.77
50000	754.63	681.69	625.31	580.54	544.21	514.19
55000	830.10	749.85	687.85	638.60	598.63	565.61
60000	905.56	818.02	750.38	696.65	653.05	617.03
65000	981.02	886.19	812.91	754.71	707.47	668.45
70000	1056.49	954.36	875.44	812.76	761.89	719.87
75000	1131.95	1022.53	937.97	870.81	816.31	771.29
80000	1207.41	1090.70	1000.50	928.87	870.73	822.70
85000	1282.88	1158.87	1063.03	986.92	925.15	874.12
90000	1358.34	1227.03	1125.56	1044.98	979.57	925.54
95000	1433.80	1295.20	1188.10	1103.03	1033.99	976.96
100000	1509.27	1363.37	1250.63	1161.08	1088.41	1028.38
200000	3018.54	2726.74	2501.26	2322.17	2176.82	2056.76
300000	4527.80	4090.12	3751.88	3483.25	3265.23	3085.14
400000	6037.07	5453.49	5002.51	4644.34	4353.64	4113.52
500000	7546.34	6816.86	6253.14	5805.42	5442.05	5141.91

7%

MONTHLY PAYMENT

Necessary to amortize a loan

TERM / AMOUNT	15 YEARS	20 YEARS	25 YEARS	30 YEARS	35 YEARS	40 YEARS
500	4.49	3.88	3.53	3.33	3.19	3.11
600	5.39	4.65	4.24	3.99	3.83	3.73
700	6.29	5.43	4.95	4.66	4.47	4.35
800	7.19	6.20	5.65	5.32	5.11	4.97
900	8.09	6.98	6.36	5.99	5.75	5.59
1000	8.99	7.75	7.07	6.65	6.39	6.21
2000	17.98	15.51	14.14	13.31	12.78	12.43
3000	26.96	23.26	21.20	19.96	19.17	18.64
4000	35.95	31.01	28.27	26.61	25.55	24.86
5000	44.94	38.76	35.34	33.27	31.94	31.07
6000	53.93	46.52	42.41	39.92	38.33	37.29
7000	62.92	54.27	49.47	46.57	44.72	43.50
8000	71.91	62.02	56.54	53.22	51.11	49.71
9000	80.89	69.78	63.61	59.88	57.50	55.93
10000	89.88	77.53	70.68	66.53	63.89	62.14
11000	98.87	85.28	77.75	73.18	70.27	68.36
12000	107.86	93.04	84.81	79.84	76.66	74.57
13000	116.85	100.79	91.88	86.49	83.05	80.79
14000	125.84	108.54	98.95	93.14	89.44	87.00
15000	134.82	116.29	106.02	99.80	95.83	93.21
16000	143.81	124.05	113.08	106.45	102.22	99.43
17000	152.80	131.80	120.15	113.10	108.61	105.64
18000	161.79	139.55	127.22	119.75	114.99	111.86
19000	170.78	147.31	134.29	126.41	121.38	118.07
20000	179.77	155.06	141.36	133.06	127.77	124.29
21000	188.75	162.81	148.42	139.71	134.16	130.50
22000	197.74	170.57	155.49	146.37	140.55	136.71
23000	206.73	178.32	162.56	153.02	146.94	142.93
24000	215.72	186.07	169.63	159.67	153.33	149.14
25000	224.71	193.82	176.69	166.33	159.71	155.36
30000	269.65	232.59	212.03	199.59	191.66	186.43
35000	314.59	271.35	247.37	232.86	223.60	217.50
40000	359.53	310.12	282.71	266.12	255.54	248.57
45000	404.47	348.88	318.05	299.39	287.49	279.64
50000	449.41	387.65	353.39	332.65	319.43	310.72
55000	494.36	426.41	388.73	365.92	351.37	341.79
60000	539.30	465.18	424.07	399.18	383.31	372.86
65000	584.24	503.94	459.41	432.45	415.26	403.93
70000	629.18	542.71	494.75	465.71	447.20	435.00
75000	674.12	581.47	530.08	498.98	479.14	466.07
80000	719.06	620.24	565.42	532.24	511.09	497.15
85000	764.00	659.00	600.76	565.51	543.03	528.22
90000	808.95	697.77	636.10	598.77	574.97	559.29
95000	853.89	736.53	671.44	632.04	606.91	590.36
100000	898.83	775.30	706.78	665.30	638.86	621.43
200000	1797.66	1550.60	1413.56	1330.60	1277.71	1242.86
300000	2696.48	2325.90	2120.34	1995.91	1916.57	1864.29
400000	3595.31	3101.20	2827.12	2661.21	2555.43	2485.73
500000	4494.14	3876.49	3533.90	3326.51	3194.28	3107.16

MONTHLY PAYMENT

Necessary to amortize a loan

7.25%

TERM AMOUNT	1 YEARS	2 YEARS	3 YEARS	4 YEARS	5 YEARS	6 YEARS
500	43.32	22.44	15.50	12.03	9.96	8.58
600	51.99	26.93	18.59	14.44	11.95	10.30
700	60.65	31.42	21.69	16.84	13.94	12.02
800	69.31	35.91	24.79	19.25	15.94	13.74
900	77.98	40.40	27.89	21.66	17.93	15.45
1000	86.64	44.89	30.99	24.06	19.92	17.17
2000	173.28	89.77	61.98	48.12	39.84	34.34
3000	259.93	134.66	92.97	72.19	59.76	51.51
4000	346.57	179.54	123.97	96.25	79.68	68.68
5000	433.21	224.43	154.96	120.31	99.60	85.85
6000	519.85	269.32	185.95	144.37	119.52	103.02
7000	606.49	314.20	216.94	168.44	139.44	120.19
8000	693.14	359.09	247.93	192.50	159.35	137.35
9000	779.78	403.97	278.92	216.56	179.27	154.52
10000	866.42	448.86	309.92	240.62	199.19	171.69
11000	953.06	493.75	340.91	264.69	219.11	188.86
12000	1039.70	538.63	371.90	288.75	239.03	206.03
13000	1126.35	583.52	402.89	312.81	258.95	223.20
14000	1212.99	628.40	433.88	336.87	278.87	240.37
15000	1299.63	673.29	464.87	360.94	298.79	257.54
16000	1386.27	718.18	495.86	385.00	318.71	274.71
17000	1472.91	763.06	526.86	409.06	338.63	291.88
18000	1559.56	807.95	557.85	433.12	358.55	309.05
19000	1646.20	852.83	588.84	457.19	378.47	326.22
20000	1732.84	897.72	619.83	481.25	398.39	343.39
21000	1819.48	942.61	650.82	505.31	418.31	360.56
22000	1906.12	987.49	681.81	529.37	438.23	377.72
23000	1992.77	1032.38	712.81	553.44	458.15	394.89
24000	2079.41	1077.26	743.80	577.50	478.06	412.06
25000	2166.05	1122.15	774.79	601.56	497.98	429.23
30000	2599.26	1346.58	929.75	721.87	597.58	515.08
35000	3032.47	1571.01	1084.70	842.18	697.18	600.93
40000	3465.68	1795.44	1239.66	962.50	796.77	686.77
45000	3898.89	2019.87	1394.62	1082.81	896.37	772.62
50000	4332.10	2244.30	1549.58	1203.12	995.97	858.47
55000	4765.31	2468.73	1704.53	1323.43	1095.56	944.31
60000	5198.52	2693.16	1859.49	1443.74	1195.16	1030.16
65000	5631.73	2917.59	2014.45	1564.06	1294.76	1116.00
70000	6064.94	3142.02	2169.41	1684.37	1394.36	1201.85
75000	6498.15	3366.45	2324.36	1804.68	1493.95	1287.70
80000	6931.36	3590.88	2479.32	1924.99	1593.55	1373.54
85000	7364.57	3815.31	2634.28	2045.30	1693.15	1459.39
90000	7797.78	4039.74	2789.24	2165.62	1792.74	1545.24
95000	8230.99	4264.17	2944.20	2285.93	1892.34	1631.08
100000	8664.20	4488.60	3099.15	2406.24	1991.94	1716.93
200000	17328.41	8977.20	6198.31	4812.48	3983.87	3433.86
300000	25992.61	13465.80	9297.46	7218.72	5975.81	5150.79
400000	34656.82	17954.40	12396.61	9624.96	7967.74	6867.72
500000	43321.02	22443.00	15495.76	12031.20	9959.68	8584.65

7.25% MONTHLY PAYMENT

Necessary to amortize a loan

TERM / AMOUNT	7 YEARS	8 YEARS	9 YEARS	10 YEARS	11 YEARS	12 YEARS
500	7.61	6.88	6.32	5.87	5.51	5.21
600	9.13	8.26	7.58	7.04	6.61	6.25
700	10.65	9.63	8.84	8.22	7.71	7.29
800	12.17	11.01	10.11	9.39	8.81	8.33
900	13.69	12.38	11.37	10.57	9.91	9.38
1000	15.22	13.76	12.63	11.74	11.02	10.42
2000	30.43	27.52	25.27	23.48	22.03	20.84
3000	45.65	41.28	37.90	35.22	33.05	31.25
4000	60.86	55.03	50.53	46.96	44.06	41.67
5000	76.08	68.79	63.17	58.70	55.08	52.09
6000	91.29	82.55	75.80	70.44	66.09	62.51
7000	106.51	96.31	88.43	82.18	77.11	72.92
8000	121.72	110.07	101.07	93.92	88.12	83.34
9000	136.94	123.83	113.70	105.66	99.14	93.76
10000	152.15	137.58	126.33	117.40	110.16	104.18
11000	167.37	151.34	138.97	129.14	121.17	114.59
12000	182.58	165.10	151.60	140.88	132.19	125.01
13000	197.80	178.86	164.23	152.62	143.20	135.43
14000	213.01	192.62	176.87	164.36	154.22	145.85
15000	228.23	206.38	189.50	176.10	165.23	156.26
16000	243.44	220.14	202.13	187.84	176.25	166.68
17000	258.66	233.89	214.77	199.58	187.27	177.10
18000	273.87	247.65	227.40	211.32	198.28	187.52
19000	289.09	261.41	240.03	223.06	209.30	197.93
20000	304.30	275.17	252.67	234.80	220.31	208.35
21000	319.52	288.93	265.30	246.54	231.33	218.77
22000	334.73	302.69	277.93	258.28	242.34	229.19
23000	349.95	316.44	290.57	270.02	253.36	239.60
24000	365.16	330.20	303.20	281.76	264.37	250.02
25000	380.38	343.96	315.83	293.50	275.39	260.44
30000	456.46	412.75	379.00	352.20	330.47	312.53
35000	532.53	481.55	442.16	410.90	385.55	364.61
40000	608.61	550.34	505.33	469.60	440.62	416.70
45000	684.68	619.13	568.50	528.30	495.70	468.79
50000	760.76	687.92	631.66	587.01	550.78	520.88
55000	836.84	756.72	694.83	645.71	605.86	572.97
60000	912.91	825.51	758.00	704.41	660.94	625.05
65000	988.99	894.30	821.16	763.11	716.01	677.14
70000	1065.06	963.09	884.33	821.81	771.09	729.23
75000	1141.14	1031.88	947.50	880.51	826.17	781.32
80000	1217.21	1100.68	1010.66	939.21	881.25	833.40
85000	1293.29	1169.47	1073.83	997.91	936.33	885.49
90000	1369.37	1238.26	1136.99	1056.61	991.40	937.58
95000	1445.44	1307.05	1200.16	1115.31	1046.48	989.67
100000	1521.52	1375.85	1263.33	1174.01	1101.56	1041.76
200000	3043.04	2751.69	2526.66	2348.02	2203.12	2083.51
300000	4564.56	4127.54	3789.98	3522.03	3304.68	3125.27
400000	6086.07	5503.38	5053.31	4696.04	4406.24	4167.02
500000	7607.59	6879.23	6316.64	5870.05	5507.80	5208.78

MONTHLY PAYMENT

Necessary to amortize a loan

7.25%

TERM / AMOUNT	15 YEARS	20 YEARS	25 YEARS	30 YEARS	35 YEARS	40 YEARS
500	4.56	3.95	3.61	3.41	3.28	3.20
600	5.48	4.74	4.34	4.09	3.94	3.84
700	6.39	5.53	5.06	4.78	4.60	4.48
800	7.30	6.32	5.78	5.46	5.25	5.12
900	8.22	7.11	6.51	6.14	5.91	5.76
1000	9.13	7.90	7.23	6.82	6.56	6.40
2000	18.26	15.81	14.46	13.64	13.13	12.79
3000	27.39	23.71	21.68	20.47	19.69	19.19
4000	36.51	31.62	28.91	27.29	26.26	25.59
5000	45.64	39.52	36.14	34.11	32.82	31.98
6000	54.77	47.42	43.37	40.93	39.39	38.38
7000	63.90	55.33	50.60	47.75	45.95	44.78
8000	73.03	63.23	57.82	54.57	52.52	51.17
9000	82.16	71.13	65.05	61.40	59.08	57.57
10000	91.29	79.04	72.28	68.22	65.65	63.97
11000	100.41	86.94	79.51	75.04	72.21	70.36
12000	109.54	94.85	86.74	81.86	78.78	76.76
13000	118.67	102.75	93.96	88.68	85.34	83.16
14000	127.80	110.65	101.19	95.50	91.91	89.55
15000	136.93	118.56	108.42	102.33	98.47	95.95
16000	146.06	126.46	115.65	109.15	105.03	102.35
17000	155.19	134.36	122.88	115.97	111.60	108.74
18000	164.32	142.27	130.11	122.79	118.16	115.14
19000	173.44	150.17	137.33	129.61	124.73	121.54
20000	182.57	158.08	144.56	136.44	131.29	127.93
21000	191.70	165.98	151.79	143.26	137.86	134.33
22000	200.83	173.88	159.02	150.08	144.42	140.73
23000	209.96	181.79	166.25	156.90	150.99	147.12
24000	219.09	189.69	173.47	163.72	157.55	153.52
25000	228.22	197.59	180.70	170.54	164.12	159.92
30000	273.86	237.11	216.84	204.65	196.94	191.90
35000	319.50	276.63	252.98	238.76	229.76	223.89
40000	365.15	316.15	289.12	272.87	262.59	255.87
45000	410.79	355.67	325.26	306.98	295.41	287.85
50000	456.43	395.19	361.40	341.09	328.23	319.84
55000	502.07	434.71	397.54	375.20	361.06	351.82
60000	547.72	474.23	433.68	409.31	393.88	383.80
65000	593.36	513.74	469.82	443.41	426.70	415.79
70000	639.00	553.26	505.96	477.52	459.53	447.77
75000	684.65	592.78	542.11	511.63	492.35	479.75
80000	730.29	632.30	578.25	545.74	525.17	511.74
85000	775.93	671.82	614.39	579.85	558.00	543.72
90000	821.58	711.34	650.53	613.96	590.82	575.70
95000	867.22	750.86	686.67	648.07	623.64	607.69
100000	912.86	790.38	722.81	682.18	656.47	639.67
200000	1825.73	1580.75	1445.61	1364.35	1312.93	1279.34
300000	2738.59	2371.13	2168.42	2046.53	1969.40	1919.02
400000	3651.45	3161.50	2891.23	2728.71	2625.87	2558.69
500000	4564.31	3951.88	3614.03	3410.88	3282.34	3198.36

7.5% MONTHLY PAYMENT

Necessary to amortize a loan

TERM / AMOUNT	1 YEARS	2 YEARS	3 YEARS	4 YEARS	5 YEARS	6 YEARS
500	43.38	22.50	15.55	12.09	10.02	8.65
600	52.05	27.00	18.66	14.51	12.02	10.37
700	60.73	31.50	21.77	16.93	14.03	12.10
800	69.41	36.00	24.88	19.34	16.03	13.83
900	78.08	40.50	28.00	21.76	18.03	15.56
1000	86.76	45.00	31.11	24.18	20.04	17.29
2000	173.51	90.00	62.21	48.36	40.08	34.58
3000	260.27	135.00	93.32	72.54	60.11	51.87
4000	347.03	180.00	124.42	96.72	80.15	69.16
5000	433.79	225.00	155.53	120.89	100.19	86.45
6000	520.54	270.00	186.64	145.07	120.23	103.74
7000	607.30	315.00	217.74	169.25	140.27	121.03
8000	694.06	360.00	248.85	193.43	160.30	138.32
9000	780.82	405.00	279.96	217.61	180.34	155.61
10000	867.57	450.00	311.06	241.79	200.38	172.90
11000	954.33	495.00	342.17	265.97	220.42	190.19
12000	1041.09	540.00	373.27	290.15	240.46	207.48
13000	1127.85	584.99	404.38	314.33	260.49	224.77
14000	1214.60	629.99	435.49	338.50	280.53	242.06
15000	1301.36	674.99	466.59	362.68	300.57	259.35
16000	1388.12	719.99	497.70	386.86	320.61	276.64
17000	1474.88	764.99	528.81	411.04	340.65	293.93
18000	1561.63	809.99	559.91	435.22	360.68	311.22
19000	1648.39	854.99	591.02	459.40	380.72	328.51
20000	1735.15	899.99	622.12	483.58	400.76	345.80
21000	1821.91	944.99	653.23	507.76	420.80	363.09
22000	1908.66	989.99	684.34	531.94	440.83	380.38
23000	1995.42	1034.99	715.44	556.11	460.87	397.67
24000	2082.18	1079.99	746.55	580.29	480.91	414.96
25000	2168.94	1124.99	777.66	604.47	500.95	432.25
30000	2602.72	1349.99	933.19	725.37	601.14	518.70
35000	3036.51	1574.99	1088.72	846.26	701.33	605.15
40000	3470.30	1799.98	1244.25	967.16	801.52	691.60
45000	3904.08	2024.98	1399.78	1088.05	901.71	778.06
50000	4337.87	2249.98	1555.31	1208.95	1001.90	864.51
55000	4771.66	2474.98	1710.84	1329.84	1102.09	950.96
60000	5205.45	2699.98	1866.37	1450.73	1202.28	1037.41
65000	5639.23	2924.97	2021.90	1571.63	1302.47	1123.86
70000	6073.02	3149.97	2177.44	1692.52	1402.66	1210.31
75000	6506.81	3374.97	2332.97	1813.42	1502.85	1296.76
80000	6940.59	3599.97	2488.50	1934.31	1603.04	1383.21
85000	7374.38	3824.97	2644.03	2055.21	1703.23	1469.66
90000	7808.17	4049.96	2799.56	2176.10	1803.42	1556.11
95000	8241.95	4274.96	2955.09	2297.00	1903.61	1642.56
100000	8675.74	4499.96	3110.62	2417.89	2003.79	1729.01
200000	17351.48	8999.92	6221.24	4835.78	4007.59	3458.02
300000	26027.23	13499.88	9331.87	7253.67	6011.38	5187.03
400000	34702.97	17999.84	12442.49	9671.56	8015.18	6916.04
500000	43378.71	22499.80	15553.11	12089.45	10018.97	8645.06

MONTHLY PAYMENT

Necessary to amortize a loan

7.5%

TERM / AMOUNT	7 YEARS	8 YEARS	9 YEARS	10 YEARS	11 YEARS	12 YEARS
500	7.67	6.94	6.38	5.94	5.57	5.28
600	9.20	8.33	7.66	7.12	6.69	6.33
700	10.74	9.72	8.93	8.31	7.80	7.39
800	12.27	11.11	10.21	9.50	8.92	8.44
900	13.80	12.50	11.48	10.68	10.03	9.50
1000	15.34	13.88	12.76	11.87	11.15	10.55
2000	30.68	27.77	25.52	23.74	22.30	21.10
3000	46.01	41.65	38.28	35.61	33.44	31.66
4000	61.35	55.54	51.04	47.48	44.59	42.21
5000	76.69	69.42	63.81	59.35	55.74	52.76
6000	92.03	83.30	76.57	71.22	66.89	63.31
7000	107.37	97.19	89.33	83.09	78.04	73.87
8000	122.71	111.07	102.09	94.96	89.18	84.42
9000	138.04	124.95	114.85	106.83	100.33	94.97
10000	153.38	138.84	127.61	118.70	111.48	105.52
11000	168.72	152.72	140.37	130.57	122.63	116.07
12000	184.06	166.61	153.13	142.44	133.78	126.63
13000	199.40	180.49	165.89	154.31	144.92	137.18
14000	214.74	194.37	178.65	166.18	156.07	147.73
15000	230.07	208.26	191.42	178.05	167.22	158.28
16000	245.41	222.14	204.18	189.92	178.37	168.84
17000	260.75	236.03	216.94	201.79	189.52	179.39
18000	276.09	249.91	229.70	213.66	200.66	189.94
19000	291.43	263.79	242.46	225.53	211.81	200.49
20000	306.77	277.68	255.22	237.40	222.96	211.05
21000	322.10	291.56	267.98	249.27	234.11	221.60
22000	337.44	305.45	280.74	261.14	245.26	232.15
23000	352.78	319.33	293.50	273.01	256.40	242.70
24000	368.12	333.21	306.26	284.88	267.55	253.25
25000	383.46	347.10	319.03	296.75	278.70	263.81
30000	460.15	416.52	382.83	356.11	334.44	316.57
35000	536.84	485.94	446.64	415.46	390.18	369.33
40000	613.53	555.35	510.44	474.81	445.92	422.09
45000	690.22	624.77	574.25	534.16	501.66	474.85
50000	766.91	694.19	638.05	593.51	557.40	527.61
55000	843.61	763.61	701.86	652.86	613.14	580.37
60000	920.30	833.03	765.66	712.21	668.88	633.14
65000	996.99	902.45	829.47	771.56	724.62	685.90
70000	1073.68	971.87	893.27	830.91	780.36	738.66
75000	1150.37	1041.29	957.08	890.26	836.10	791.42
80000	1227.06	1110.71	1020.88	949.61	891.84	844.18
85000	1303.75	1180.13	1084.69	1008.97	947.58	896.94
90000	1380.44	1249.55	1148.49	1068.32	1003.32	949.70
95000	1457.14	1318.97	1212.30	1127.67	1059.06	1002.46
100000	1533.83	1388.39	1276.10	1187.02	1114.80	1055.23
200000	3067.66	2776.77	2552.20	2374.04	2229.60	2110.45
300000	4601.48	4165.16	3828.30	3561.05	3344.40	3165.68
400000	6135.31	5553.55	5104.41	4748.07	4459.20	4220.91
500000	7669.14	6941.94	6380.51	5935.09	5574.00	5276.13

7.5%

MONTHLY PAYMENT

Necessary to amortize a loan

TERM / AMOUNT	15 YEARS	20 YEARS	25 YEARS	30 YEARS	35 YEARS	40 YEARS
500	4.64	4.03	3.69	3.50	3.37	3.29
600	5.56	4.83	4.43	4.20	4.05	3.95
700	6.49	5.64	5.17	4.89	4.72	4.61
800	7.42	6.44	5.91	5.59	5.39	5.26
900	8.34	7.25	6.65	6.29	6.07	5.92
1000	9.27	8.06	7.39	6.99	6.74	6.58
2000	18.54	16.11	14.78	13.98	13.48	13.16
3000	27.81	24.17	22.17	20.98	20.23	19.74
4000	37.08	32.22	29.56	27.97	26.97	26.32
5000	46.35	40.28	36.95	34.96	33.71	32.90
6000	55.62	48.34	44.34	41.95	40.45	39.48
7000	64.89	56.39	51.73	48.95	47.20	46.06
8000	74.16	64.45	59.12	55.94	53.94	52.65
9000	83.43	72.50	66.51	62.93	60.68	59.23
10000	92.70	80.56	73.90	69.92	67.42	65.81
11000	101.97	88.62	81.29	76.91	74.17	72.39
12000	111.24	96.67	88.68	83.91	80.91	78.97
13000	120.51	104.73	96.07	90.90	87.65	85.55
14000	129.78	112.78	103.46	97.89	94.39	92.13
15000	139.05	120.84	110.85	104.88	101.14	98.71
16000	148.32	128.89	118.24	111.87	107.88	105.29
17000	157.59	136.95	125.63	118.87	114.62	111.87
18000	166.86	145.01	133.02	125.86	121.36	118.45
19000	176.13	153.06	140.41	132.85	128.11	125.03
20000	185.40	161.12	147.80	139.84	134.85	131.61
21000	194.67	169.17	155.19	146.84	141.59	138.19
22000	203.94	177.23	162.58	153.83	148.33	144.78
23000	213.21	185.29	169.97	160.82	155.08	151.36
24000	222.48	193.34	177.36	167.81	161.82	157.94
25000	231.75	201.40	184.75	174.80	168.56	164.52
30000	278.10	241.68	221.70	209.76	202.27	197.42
35000	324.45	281.96	258.65	244.73	235.98	230.32
40000	370.80	322.24	295.60	279.69	269.70	263.23
45000	417.16	362.52	332.55	314.65	303.41	296.13
50000	463.51	402.80	369.50	349.61	337.12	329.04
55000	509.86	443.08	406.45	384.57	370.83	361.94
60000	556.21	483.36	443.39	419.53	404.55	394.84
65000	602.56	523.64	480.34	454.49	438.26	427.75
70000	648.91	563.92	517.29	489.45	471.97	460.65
75000	695.26	604.19	554.24	524.41	505.68	493.55
80000	741.61	644.47	591.19	559.37	539.39	526.46
85000	787.96	684.75	628.14	594.33	573.11	559.36
90000	834.31	725.03	665.09	629.29	606.82	592.26
95000	880.66	765.31	702.04	664.25	640.53	625.17
100000	927.01	805.59	738.99	699.21	674.24	658.07
200000	1854.02	1611.19	1477.98	1398.43	1348.49	1316.14
300000	2781.04	2416.78	2216.97	2097.64	2022.73	1974.21
400000	3708.05	3222.37	2955.96	2796.86	2696.97	2632.28
500000	4635.06	4027.97	3694.96	3496.07	3371.21	3290.35

MONTHLY PAYMENT

Necessary to amortize a loan

7.75%

TERM / AMOUNT	1 YEARS	2 YEARS	3 YEARS	4 YEARS	5 YEARS	6 YEARS
500	43.44	22.56	15.61	12.15	10.08	8.71
600	52.12	27.07	18.73	14.58	12.09	10.45
700	60.81	31.58	21.85	17.01	14.11	12.19
800	69.50	36.09	24.98	19.44	16.13	13.93
900	78.19	40.60	28.10	21.87	18.14	15.67
1000	86.87	45.11	31.22	24.30	20.16	17.41
2000	173.75	90.23	62.44	48.59	40.31	34.82
3000	260.62	135.34	93.66	72.89	60.47	52.23
4000	347.49	180.45	124.88	97.18	80.63	69.65
5000	434.36	225.57	156.11	121.48	100.78	87.06
6000	521.24	270.68	187.33	145.77	120.94	104.47
7000	608.11	315.79	218.55	170.07	141.10	121.88
8000	694.98	360.91	249.77	194.37	161.26	139.29
9000	781.86	406.02	280.99	218.66	181.41	156.70
10000	868.73	451.13	312.21	242.96	201.57	174.11
11000	955.60	496.25	343.43	267.25	221.73	191.53
12000	1042.47	541.36	374.65	291.55	241.88	208.94
13000	1129.35	586.47	405.88	315.84	262.04	226.35
14000	1216.22	631.59	437.10	340.14	282.20	243.76
15000	1303.09	676.70	468.32	364.44	302.35	261.17
16000	1389.97	721.81	499.54	388.73	322.51	278.58
17000	1476.84	766.93	530.76	413.03	342.67	295.99
18000	1563.71	812.04	561.98	437.32	362.83	313.41
19000	1650.58	857.15	593.20	461.62	382.98	330.82
20000	1737.46	902.27	624.42	485.91	403.14	348.23
21000	1824.33	947.38	655.64	510.21	423.30	365.64
22000	1911.20	992.49	686.87	534.51	443.45	383.05
23000	1998.08	1037.61	718.09	558.80	463.61	400.46
24000	2084.95	1082.72	749.31	583.10	483.77	417.87
25000	2171.82	1127.83	780.53	607.39	503.92	435.29
30000	2606.19	1353.40	936.63	728.87	604.71	522.34
35000	3040.55	1578.97	1092.74	850.35	705.49	609.40
40000	3474.92	1804.53	1248.85	971.83	806.28	696.46
45000	3909.28	2030.10	1404.95	1093.31	907.06	783.51
50000	4343.64	2255.67	1561.06	1214.79	1007.85	870.57
55000	4778.01	2481.23	1717.16	1336.27	1108.63	957.63
60000	5212.37	2706.80	1873.27	1457.74	1209.42	1044.69
65000	5646.74	2932.37	2029.38	1579.22	1310.20	1131.74
70000	6081.10	3157.93	2185.48	1700.70	1410.99	1218.80
75000	6515.47	3383.50	2341.59	1822.18	1511.77	1305.86
80000	6949.83	3609.07	2497.69	1943.66	1612.56	1392.91
85000	7384.19	3834.64	2653.80	2065.14	1713.34	1479.97
90000	7818.56	4060.20	2809.90	2186.62	1814.13	1567.03
95000	8252.92	4285.77	2966.01	2308.10	1914.91	1654.09
100000	8687.29	4511.34	3122.12	2429.57	2015.70	1741.14
200000	17374.58	9022.67	6244.23	4859.15	4031.39	3482.28
300000	26061.86	13534.01	9366.35	7288.72	6047.09	5223.43
400000	34749.15	18045.34	12488.47	9718.30	8062.78	6964.57
500000	43436.44	22556.68	15610.58	12147.87	10078.48	8705.71

7.75%

MONTHLY PAYMENT

Necessary to amortize a loan

TERM / AMOUNT	7 YEARS	8 YEARS	9 YEARS	10 YEARS	11 YEARS	12 YEARS
500	7.73	7.00	6.44	6.00	5.64	5.34
600	9.28	8.41	7.73	7.20	6.77	6.41
700	10.82	9.81	9.02	8.40	7.90	7.48
800	12.37	11.21	10.31	9.60	9.03	8.55
900	13.92	12.61	11.60	10.80	10.15	9.62
1000	15.46	14.01	12.89	12.00	11.28	10.69
2000	30.92	28.02	25.78	24.00	22.56	21.38
3000	46.39	42.03	38.67	36.00	33.84	32.06
4000	61.85	56.04	51.56	48.00	45.13	42.75
5000	77.31	70.05	64.45	60.01	56.41	53.44
6000	92.77	84.06	77.34	72.01	67.69	64.13
7000	108.23	98.07	90.23	84.01	78.97	74.82
8000	123.70	112.08	103.12	96.01	90.25	85.50
9000	139.16	126.09	116.01	108.01	101.53	96.19
10000	154.62	140.10	128.89	120.01	112.81	106.88
11000	170.08	154.11	141.78	132.01	124.09	117.57
12000	185.54	168.12	154.67	144.01	135.38	128.26
13000	201.01	182.13	167.56	156.01	146.66	138.94
14000	216.47	196.14	180.45	168.01	157.94	149.63
15000	231.93	210.15	193.34	180.02	169.22	160.32
16000	247.39	224.16	206.23	192.02	180.50	171.01
17000	262.85	238.17	219.12	204.02	191.78	181.69
18000	278.32	252.18	232.01	216.02	203.06	192.38
19000	293.78	266.19	244.90	228.02	214.34	203.07
20000	309.24	280.20	257.79	240.02	225.63	213.76
21000	324.70	294.21	270.68	252.02	236.91	224.45
22000	340.16	308.22	283.57	264.02	248.19	235.13
23000	355.62	322.23	296.46	276.02	259.47	245.82
24000	371.09	336.24	309.35	288.03	270.75	256.51
25000	386.55	350.25	322.24	300.03	282.03	267.20
30000	463.86	420.30	386.68	360.03	338.44	320.64
35000	541.17	490.35	451.13	420.04	394.85	374.08
40000	618.48	560.40	515.58	480.04	451.25	427.52
45000	695.79	630.45	580.03	540.05	507.66	480.96
50000	773.10	700.50	644.47	600.05	564.06	534.40
55000	850.41	770.55	708.92	660.06	620.47	587.84
60000	927.72	840.60	773.37	720.06	676.88	641.28
65000	1005.03	910.65	837.82	780.07	733.28	694.71
70000	1082.34	980.70	902.26	840.07	789.69	748.15
75000	1159.65	1050.75	966.71	900.08	846.10	801.59
80000	1236.96	1120.80	1031.16	960.09	902.50	855.03
85000	1314.27	1190.85	1095.61	1020.09	958.91	908.47
90000	1391.58	1260.89	1160.05	1080.10	1015.32	961.91
95000	1468.89	1330.94	1224.50	1140.10	1071.72	1015.35
100000	1546.20	1400.99	1288.95	1200.11	1128.13	1068.79
200000	3092.39	2801.99	2577.90	2400.21	2256.26	2137.58
300000	4638.59	4202.98	3866.85	3600.32	3384.39	3206.38
400000	6184.78	5603.98	5155.80	4800.43	4512.51	4275.17
500000	7730.98	7004.97	6444.75	6000.53	5640.64	5343.96

MONTHLY PAYMENT

Necessary to amortize a loan

7.75%

TERM / AMOUNT	15 YEARS	20 YEARS	25 YEARS	30 YEARS	35 YEARS	40 YEARS
500	4.71	4.10	3.78	3.58	3.46	3.38
600	5.65	4.93	4.53	4.30	4.15	4.06
700	6.59	5.75	5.29	5.01	4.85	4.74
800	7.53	6.57	6.04	5.73	5.54	5.41
900	8.47	7.39	6.80	6.45	6.23	6.09
1000	9.41	8.21	7.55	7.16	6.92	6.77
2000	18.83	16.42	15.11	14.33	13.84	13.53
3000	28.24	24.63	22.66	21.49	20.77	20.30
4000	37.65	32.84	30.21	28.66	27.69	27.06
5000	47.06	41.05	37.77	35.82	34.61	33.83
6000	56.48	49.26	45.32	42.98	41.53	40.60
7000	65.89	57.47	52.87	50.15	48.45	47.36
8000	75.30	65.68	60.43	57.31	55.37	54.13
9000	84.71	73.89	67.98	64.48	62.30	60.90
10000	94.13	82.09	75.53	71.64	69.22	67.66
11000	103.54	90.30	83.09	78.81	76.14	74.43
12000	112.95	98.51	90.64	85.97	83.06	81.19
13000	122.37	106.72	98.19	93.13	89.98	87.96
14000	131.78	114.93	105.75	100.30	96.90	94.73
15000	141.19	123.14	113.30	107.46	103.83	101.49
16000	150.60	131.35	120.85	114.63	110.75	108.26
17000	160.02	139.56	128.41	121.79	117.67	115.03
18000	169.43	147.77	135.96	128.95	124.59	121.79
19000	178.84	155.98	143.51	136.12	131.51	128.56
20000	188.26	164.19	151.07	143.28	138.44	135.32
21000	197.67	172.40	158.62	150.45	145.36	142.09
22000	207.08	180.61	166.17	157.61	152.28	148.86
23000	216.49	188.82	173.73	164.77	159.20	155.62
24000	225.91	197.03	181.28	171.94	166.12	162.39
25000	235.32	205.24	188.83	179.10	173.04	169.15
30000	282.38	246.28	226.60	214.92	207.65	202.99
35000	329.45	287.33	264.37	250.74	242.26	236.82
40000	376.51	328.38	302.13	286.56	276.87	270.65
45000	423.57	369.43	339.90	322.39	311.48	304.48
50000	470.64	410.47	377.66	358.21	346.09	338.31
55000	517.70	451.52	415.43	394.03	380.70	372.14
60000	564.77	492.57	453.20	429.85	415.31	405.97
65000	611.83	533.62	490.96	465.67	449.91	439.80
70000	658.89	574.66	528.73	501.49	484.52	473.63
75000	705.96	615.71	566.50	537.31	519.13	507.46
80000	753.02	656.76	604.26	573.13	553.74	541.30
85000	800.08	697.81	642.03	608.95	588.35	575.13
90000	847.15	738.85	679.80	644.77	622.96	608.96
95000	894.21	779.90	717.56	680.59	657.57	642.79
100000	941.28	820.95	755.33	716.41	692.18	676.62
200000	1882.55	1641.90	1510.66	1432.82	1384.35	1353.24
300000	2823.83	2462.85	2265.99	2149.24	2076.53	2029.86
400000	3765.10	3283.79	3021.32	2865.65	2768.70	2706.48
500000	4706.38	4104.74	3776.64	3582.06	3460.88	3383.10

8%

MONTHLY PAYMENT

Necessary to amortize a loan

TERM / AMOUNT	1 YEARS	2 YEARS	3 YEARS	4 YEARS	5 YEARS	6 YEARS
500	43.49	22.61	15.67	12.21	10.14	8.77
600	52.19	27.14	18.80	14.65	12.17	10.52
700	60.89	31.66	21.94	17.09	14.19	12.27
800	69.59	36.18	25.07	19.53	16.22	14.03
900	78.29	40.70	28.20	21.97	18.25	15.78
1000	86.99	45.23	31.34	24.41	20.28	17.53
2000	173.98	90.45	62.67	48.83	40.55	35.07
3000	260.97	135.68	94.01	73.24	60.83	52.60
4000	347.95	180.91	125.35	97.65	81.11	70.13
5000	434.94	226.14	156.68	122.06	101.38	87.67
6000	521.93	271.36	188.02	146.48	121.66	105.20
7000	608.92	316.59	219.35	170.89	141.93	122.73
8000	695.91	361.82	250.69	195.30	162.21	140.27
9000	782.90	407.05	282.03	219.72	182.49	157.80
10000	869.88	452.27	313.36	244.13	202.76	175.33
11000	956.87	497.50	344.70	268.54	223.04	192.87
12000	1043.86	542.73	376.04	292.96	243.32	210.40
13000	1130.85	587.95	407.37	317.37	263.59	227.93
14000	1217.84	633.18	438.71	341.78	283.87	245.47
15000	1304.83	678.41	470.05	366.19	304.15	263.00
16000	1391.81	723.64	501.38	390.61	324.42	280.53
17000	1478.80	768.86	532.72	415.02	344.70	298.07
18000	1565.79	814.09	564.05	439.43	364.98	315.60
19000	1652.78	859.32	595.39	463.85	385.25	333.13
20000	1739.77	904.55	626.73	488.26	405.53	350.66
21000	1826.76	949.77	658.06	512.67	425.80	368.20
22000	1913.75	995.00	689.40	537.08	446.08	385.73
23000	2000.73	1040.23	720.74	561.50	466.36	403.26
24000	2087.72	1085.45	752.07	585.91	486.63	420.80
25000	2174.71	1130.68	783.41	610.32	506.91	438.33
30000	2609.65	1356.82	940.09	732.39	608.29	526.00
35000	3044.60	1582.96	1096.77	854.45	709.67	613.66
40000	3479.54	1809.09	1253.45	976.52	811.06	701.33
45000	3914.48	2035.23	1410.14	1098.58	912.44	789.00
50000	4349.42	2261.36	1566.82	1220.65	1013.82	876.66
55000	4784.36	2487.50	1723.50	1342.71	1115.20	964.33
60000	5219.31	2713.64	1880.18	1464.78	1216.58	1051.99
65000	5654.25	2939.77	2036.86	1586.84	1317.97	1139.66
70000	6089.19	3165.91	2193.55	1708.90	1419.35	1227.33
75000	6524.13	3392.05	2350.23	1830.97	1520.73	1314.99
80000	6959.07	3618.18	2506.91	1953.03	1622.11	1402.66
85000	7394.02	3844.32	2663.59	2075.10	1723.49	1490.33
90000	7828.96	4070.46	2820.27	2197.16	1824.88	1577.99
95000	8263.90	4296.59	2976.95	2319.23	1926.26	1665.66
100000	8698.84	4522.73	3133.64	2441.29	2027.64	1753.32
200000	17397.69	9045.46	6267.27	4882.58	4055.28	3506.65
300000	26096.53	13568.19	9400.91	7323.88	6082.92	5259.97
400000	34795.37	18090.92	12534.55	9765.17	8110.56	7013.30
500000	43494.21	22613.65	15668.18	12206.46	10138.20	8766.62

MONTHLY PAYMENT

Necessary to amortize a loan

8%

TERM / AMOUNT	7 YEARS	8 YEARS	9 YEARS	10 YEARS	11 YEARS	12 YEARS
500	7.79	7.07	6.51	6.07	5.71	5.41
600	9.35	8.48	7.81	7.28	6.85	6.49
700	10.91	9.90	9.11	8.49	7.99	7.58
800	12.47	11.31	10.41	9.71	9.13	8.66
900	14.03	12.72	11.72	10.92	10.27	9.74
1000	15.59	14.14	13.02	12.13	11.42	10.82
2000	31.17	28.27	26.04	24.27	22.83	21.65
3000	46.76	42.41	39.06	36.40	34.25	32.47
4000	62.34	56.55	52.07	48.53	45.66	43.30
5000	77.93	70.68	65.09	60.66	57.08	54.12
6000	93.52	84.82	78.11	72.80	68.49	64.95
7000	109.10	98.96	91.13	84.93	79.91	75.77
8000	124.69	113.09	104.15	97.06	91.32	86.60
9000	140.28	127.23	117.17	109.19	102.74	97.42
10000	155.86	141.37	130.19	121.33	114.15	108.25
11000	171.45	155.50	143.21	133.46	125.57	119.07
12000	187.03	169.64	156.22	145.59	136.99	129.89
13000	202.62	183.78	169.24	157.73	148.40	140.72
14000	218.21	197.91	182.26	169.86	159.82	151.54
15000	233.79	212.05	195.28	181.99	171.23	162.37
16000	249.38	226.19	208.30	194.12	182.65	173.19
17000	264.97	240.32	221.32	206.26	194.06	184.02
18000	280.55	254.46	234.34	218.39	205.48	194.84
19000	296.14	268.60	247.36	230.52	216.89	205.67
20000	311.72	282.73	260.37	242.66	228.31	216.49
21000	327.31	296.87	273.39	254.79	239.72	227.32
22000	342.90	311.01	286.41	266.92	251.14	238.14
23000	358.48	325.14	299.43	279.05	262.56	248.96
24000	374.07	339.28	312.45	291.19	273.97	259.79
25000	389.66	353.42	325.47	303.32	285.39	270.61
30000	467.59	424.10	390.56	363.98	342.46	324.74
35000	545.52	494.78	455.66	424.65	399.54	378.86
40000	623.45	565.47	520.75	485.31	456.62	432.98
45000	701.38	636.15	585.84	545.97	513.70	487.10
50000	779.31	706.83	650.94	606.64	570.77	541.23
55000	857.24	777.52	716.03	667.30	627.85	595.35
60000	935.17	848.20	781.12	727.97	684.93	649.47
65000	1013.10	918.88	846.22	788.63	742.00	703.59
70000	1091.04	989.57	911.31	849.29	799.08	757.72
75000	1168.97	1060.25	976.40	909.96	856.16	811.84
80000	1246.90	1130.93	1041.50	970.62	913.24	865.96
85000	1324.83	1201.62	1106.59	1031.28	970.31	920.08
90000	1402.76	1272.30	1171.68	1091.95	1027.39	974.21
95000	1480.69	1342.98	1236.78	1152.61	1084.47	1028.33
100000	1558.62	1413.67	1301.87	1213.28	1141.54	1082.45
200000	3117.24	2827.34	2603.74	2426.55	2283.09	2164.91
300000	4675.86	4241.00	3905.61	3639.83	3424.63	3247.36
400000	6234.49	5654.67	5207.49	4853.10	4566.18	4329.81
500000	7793.11	7068.34	6509.36	6066.38	5707.72	5412.26

8%

MONTHLY PAYMENT

Necessary to amortize a loan

TERM / AMOUNT	15 YEARS	20 YEARS	25 YEARS	30 YEARS	35 YEARS	40 YEARS
500	4.78	4.18	3.86	3.67	3.55	3.48
600	5.73	5.02	4.63	4.40	4.26	4.17
700	6.69	5.86	5.40	5.14	4.97	4.87
800	7.65	6.69	6.17	5.87	5.68	5.56
900	8.60	7.53	6.95	6.60	6.39	6.26
1000	9.56	8.36	7.72	7.34	7.10	6.95
2000	19.11	16.73	15.44	14.68	14.21	13.91
3000	28.67	25.09	23.15	22.01	21.31	20.86
4000	38.23	33.46	30.87	29.35	28.41	27.81
5000	47.78	41.82	38.59	36.69	35.51	34.77
6000	57.34	50.19	46.31	44.03	42.62	41.72
7000	66.90	58.55	54.03	51.36	49.72	48.67
8000	76.45	66.92	61.75	58.70	56.82	55.62
9000	86.01	75.28	69.46	66.04	63.92	62.58
10000	95.57	83.64	77.18	73.38	71.03	69.53
11000	105.12	92.01	84.90	80.71	78.13	76.48
12000	114.68	100.37	92.62	88.05	85.23	83.44
13000	124.23	108.74	100.34	95.39	92.33	90.39
14000	133.79	117.10	108.05	102.73	99.44	97.34
15000	143.35	125.47	115.77	110.06	106.54	104.30
16000	152.90	133.83	123.49	117.40	113.64	111.25
17000	162.46	142.19	131.21	124.74	120.74	118.20
18000	172.02	150.56	138.93	132.08	127.85	125.16
19000	181.57	158.92	146.65	139.42	134.95	132.11
20000	191.13	167.29	154.36	146.75	142.05	139.06
21000	200.69	175.65	162.08	154.09	149.15	146.02
22000	210.24	184.02	169.80	161.43	156.26	152.97
23000	219.80	192.38	177.52	168.77	163.36	159.92
24000	229.36	200.75	185.24	176.10	170.46	166.87
25000	238.91	209.11	192.95	183.44	177.57	173.83
30000	286.70	250.93	231.54	220.13	213.08	208.59
35000	334.48	292.75	270.14	256.82	248.59	243.36
40000	382.26	334.58	308.73	293.51	284.10	278.12
45000	430.04	376.40	347.32	330.19	319.62	312.89
50000	477.83	418.22	385.91	366.88	355.13	347.66
55000	525.61	460.04	424.50	403.57	390.64	382.42
60000	573.39	501.86	463.09	440.26	426.16	417.19
65000	621.17	543.69	501.68	476.95	461.67	451.95
70000	668.96	585.51	540.27	513.64	497.18	486.72
75000	716.74	627.33	578.86	550.32	532.70	521.48
80000	764.52	669.15	617.45	587.01	568.21	556.25
85000	812.30	710.97	656.04	623.70	603.72	591.01
90000	860.09	752.80	694.63	660.39	639.23	625.78
95000	907.87	794.62	733.23	697.08	674.75	660.55
100000	955.65	836.44	771.82	733.76	710.26	695.31
200000	1911.30	1672.88	1543.63	1467.53	1420.52	1390.62
300000	2866.96	2509.32	2315.45	2201.29	2130.78	2085.94
400000	3822.61	3345.76	3087.26	2935.06	2841.04	2781.25
500000	4778.26	4182.20	3859.08	3668.82	3551.30	3476.56

MONTHLY PAYMENT

Necessary to amortize a loan

8.25%

TERM / AMOUNT	1 YEARS	2 YEARS	3 YEARS	4 YEARS	5 YEARS	6 YEARS
500	43.55	22.67	15.73	12.27	10.20	8.83
600	52.26	27.20	18.87	14.72	12.24	10.59
700	60.97	31.74	22.02	17.17	14.28	12.36
800	69.68	36.27	25.16	19.62	16.32	14.12
900	78.39	40.81	28.31	22.08	18.36	15.89
1000	87.10	45.34	31.45	24.53	20.40	17.66
2000	174.21	90.68	62.90	49.06	40.79	35.31
3000	261.31	136.02	94.36	73.59	61.19	52.97
4000	348.42	181.37	125.81	98.12	81.59	70.62
5000	435.52	226.71	157.26	122.65	101.98	88.28
6000	522.62	272.05	188.71	147.18	122.38	105.93
7000	609.73	317.39	220.16	171.71	142.77	123.59
8000	696.83	362.73	251.61	196.24	163.17	141.24
9000	783.94	408.07	283.07	220.77	183.57	158.90
10000	871.04	453.41	314.52	245.30	203.96	176.56
11000	958.14	498.76	345.97	269.83	224.36	194.21
12000	1045.25	544.10	377.42	294.37	244.76	211.87
13000	1132.35	589.44	408.87	318.90	265.15	229.52
14000	1219.46	634.78	440.33	343.43	285.55	247.18
15000	1306.56	680.12	471.78	367.96	305.94	264.83
16000	1393.67	725.46	503.23	392.49	326.34	282.49
17000	1480.77	770.80	534.68	417.02	346.74	300.14
18000	1567.87	816.15	566.13	441.55	367.13	317.80
19000	1654.98	861.49	597.58	466.08	387.53	335.46
20000	1742.08	906.83	629.04	490.61	407.93	353.11
21000	1829.19	952.17	660.49	515.14	428.32	370.77
22000	1916.29	997.51	691.94	539.67	448.72	388.42
23000	2003.39	1042.85	723.39	564.20	469.11	406.08
24000	2090.50	1088.19	754.84	588.73	489.51	423.73
25000	2177.60	1133.53	786.30	613.26	509.91	441.39
30000	2613.12	1360.24	943.55	735.91	611.89	529.67
35000	3048.64	1586.95	1100.81	858.57	713.87	617.94
40000	3484.16	1813.66	1258.07	981.22	815.85	706.22
45000	3919.68	2040.36	1415.33	1103.87	917.83	794.50
50000	4355.20	2267.07	1572.59	1226.52	1019.81	882.78
55000	4790.72	2493.78	1729.85	1349.17	1121.79	971.06
60000	5226.24	2720.48	1887.11	1471.83	1223.78	1059.33
65000	5661.76	2947.19	2044.37	1594.48	1325.76	1147.61
70000	6097.28	3173.90	2201.63	1717.13	1427.74	1235.89
75000	6532.80	3400.60	2358.89	1839.78	1529.72	1324.17
80000	6968.33	3627.31	2516.15	1962.44	1631.70	1412.44
85000	7403.85	3854.02	2673.40	2085.09	1733.68	1500.72
90000	7839.37	4080.73	2830.66	2207.74	1835.66	1589.00
95000	8274.89	4307.43	2987.92	2330.39	1937.64	1677.28
100000	8710.41	4534.14	3145.18	2453.04	2039.63	1765.56
200000	17420.81	9068.28	6290.36	4906.09	4079.25	3531.11
300000	26131.22	13602.42	9435.55	7359.13	6118.88	5296.67
400000	34841.63	18136.56	12580.73	9812.18	8158.50	7062.22
500000	43552.03	22670.70	15725.91	12265.22	10198.13	8827.78

8.25%

MONTHLY PAYMENT

Necessary to amortize a loan

TERM / AMOUNT	7 YEARS	8 YEARS	9 YEARS	10 YEARS	11 YEARS	12 YEARS
500	7.86	7.13	6.57	6.13	5.78	5.48
600	9.43	8.56	7.89	7.36	6.93	6.58
700	11.00	9.98	9.20	8.59	8.09	7.67
800	12.57	11.41	10.52	9.81	9.24	8.77
900	14.14	12.84	11.83	11.04	10.40	9.87
1000	15.71	14.26	13.15	12.27	11.55	10.96
2000	31.42	28.53	26.30	24.53	23.10	21.92
3000	47.13	42.79	39.45	36.80	34.65	32.89
4000	62.84	57.06	52.59	49.06	46.20	43.85
5000	78.56	71.32	65.74	61.33	57.75	54.81
6000	94.27	85.58	78.89	73.59	69.30	65.77
7000	109.98	99.85	92.04	85.86	80.85	76.73
8000	125.69	114.11	105.19	98.12	92.40	87.70
9000	141.40	128.38	118.34	110.39	103.95	98.66
10000	157.11	142.64	131.49	122.65	115.50	109.62
11000	172.82	156.90	144.64	134.92	127.06	120.58
12000	188.53	171.17	157.78	147.18	138.61	131.54
13000	204.24	185.43	170.93	159.45	150.16	142.51
14000	219.95	199.70	184.08	171.71	161.71	153.47
15000	235.67	213.96	197.23	183.98	173.26	164.43
16000	251.38	228.23	210.38	196.24	184.81	175.39
17000	267.09	242.49	223.53	208.51	196.36	186.36
18000	282.80	256.75	236.68	220.77	207.91	197.32
19000	298.51	271.02	249.82	233.04	219.46	208.28
20000	314.22	285.28	262.97	245.31	231.01	219.24
21000	329.93	299.55	276.12	257.57	242.56	230.20
22000	345.64	313.81	289.27	269.84	254.11	241.17
23000	361.35	328.07	302.42	282.10	265.66	252.13
24000	377.07	342.34	315.57	294.37	277.21	263.09
25000	392.78	356.60	328.72	306.63	288.76	274.05
30000	471.33	427.92	394.46	367.96	346.51	328.86
35000	549.89	499.24	460.20	429.28	404.27	383.67
40000	628.44	570.56	525.95	490.61	462.02	438.48
45000	707.00	641.88	591.69	551.94	519.77	493.29
50000	785.55	713.20	657.43	613.26	577.52	548.10
55000	864.11	784.52	723.18	674.59	635.28	602.91
60000	942.66	855.84	788.92	735.92	693.03	657.72
65000	1021.22	927.16	854.66	797.24	750.78	712.53
70000	1099.77	998.49	920.41	858.57	808.53	767.35
75000	1178.33	1069.81	986.15	919.89	866.29	822.16
80000	1256.88	1141.13	1051.89	981.22	924.04	876.97
85000	1335.44	1212.45	1117.64	1042.55	981.79	931.78
90000	1414.00	1283.77	1183.38	1103.87	1039.54	986.59
95000	1492.55	1355.09	1249.12	1165.20	1097.30	1041.40
100000	1571.11	1426.41	1314.87	1226.53	1155.05	1096.21
200000	3142.21	2852.81	2629.73	2453.05	2310.10	2192.41
300000	4713.32	4279.22	3944.60	3679.58	3465.15	3288.62
400000	6284.42	5705.63	5259.47	4906.11	4620.19	4384.83
500000	7855.53	7132.04	6574.33	6132.63	5775.24	5481.04

MONTHLY PAYMENT

Necessary to amortize a loan

8.25%

TERM AMOUNT	15 YEARS	20 YEARS	25 YEARS	30 YEARS	35 YEARS	40 YEARS
500	4.85	4.26	3.94	3.76	3.64	3.57
600	5.82	5.11	4.73	4.51	4.37	4.28
700	6.79	5.96	5.52	5.26	5.10	5.00
800	7.76	6.82	6.31	6.01	5.83	5.71
900	8.73	7.67	7.10	6.76	6.56	6.43
1000	9.70	8.52	7.88	7.51	7.28	7.14
2000	19.40	17.04	15.77	15.03	14.57	14.28
3000	29.10	25.56	23.65	22.54	21.85	21.42
4000	38.81	34.08	31.54	30.05	29.14	28.57
5000	48.51	42.60	39.42	37.56	36.42	35.71
6000	58.21	51.12	47.31	45.08	43.71	42.85
7000	67.91	59.64	55.19	52.59	50.99	49.99
8000	77.61	68.17	63.08	60.10	58.28	57.13
9000	87.31	76.69	70.96	67.61	65.56	64.27
10000	97.01	85.21	78.85	75.13	72.85	71.41
11000	106.72	93.73	86.73	82.64	80.13	78.56
12000	116.42	102.25	94.61	90.15	87.42	85.70
13000	126.12	110.77	102.50	97.66	94.70	92.84
14000	135.82	119.29	110.38	105.18	101.99	99.98
15000	145.52	127.81	118.27	112.69	109.27	107.12
16000	155.22	136.33	126.15	120.20	116.56	114.26
17000	164.92	144.85	134.04	127.72	123.84	121.40
18000	174.63	153.37	141.92	135.23	131.13	128.54
19000	184.33	161.89	149.81	142.74	138.41	135.69
20000	194.03	170.41	157.69	150.25	145.70	142.83
21000	203.73	178.93	165.57	157.77	152.98	149.97
22000	213.43	187.45	173.46	165.28	160.27	157.11
23000	223.13	195.98	181.34	172.79	167.55	164.25
24000	232.83	204.50	189.23	180.30	174.84	171.39
25000	242.54	213.02	197.11	187.82	182.12	178.53
30000	291.04	255.62	236.54	225.38	218.55	214.24
35000	339.55	298.22	275.96	262.94	254.97	249.95
40000	388.06	340.83	315.38	300.51	291.40	285.66
45000	436.56	383.43	354.80	338.07	327.82	321.36
50000	485.07	426.03	394.23	375.63	364.25	357.07
55000	533.58	468.64	433.65	413.20	400.67	392.78
60000	582.08	511.24	473.07	450.76	437.09	428.48
65000	630.59	553.84	512.49	488.32	473.52	464.19
70000	679.10	596.45	551.92	525.89	509.94	499.90
75000	727.61	639.05	591.34	563.45	546.37	535.60
80000	776.11	681.65	630.76	601.01	582.79	571.31
85000	824.62	724.26	670.18	638.58	619.22	607.02
90000	873.13	766.86	709.61	676.14	655.64	642.72
95000	921.63	809.46	749.03	713.70	692.07	678.43
100000	970.14	852.07	788.45	751.27	728.49	714.14
200000	1940.28	1704.13	1576.90	1502.53	1456.98	1428.28
300000	2910.42	2556.20	2365.35	2253.80	2185.47	2142.42
400000	3880.56	3408.26	3153.80	3005.07	2913.96	2856.56
500000	4850.70	4260.33	3942.25	3756.33	3642.46	3570.69

8.5%

MONTHLY PAYMENT

Necessary to amortize a loan

TERM / AMOUNT	1 YEARS	2 YEARS	3 YEARS	4 YEARS	5 YEARS	6 YEARS
500	43.61	22.73	15.78	12.32	10.26	8.89
600	52.33	27.27	18.94	14.79	12.31	10.67
700	61.05	31.82	22.10	17.25	14.36	12.44
800	69.78	36.36	25.25	19.72	16.41	14.22
900	78.50	40.91	28.41	22.18	18.46	16.00
1000	87.22	45.46	31.57	24.65	20.52	17.78
2000	174.44	90.91	63.14	49.30	41.03	35.56
3000	261.66	136.37	94.70	73.94	61.55	53.34
4000	348.88	181.82	126.27	98.59	82.07	71.11
5000	436.10	227.28	157.84	123.24	102.58	88.89
6000	523.32	272.73	189.41	147.89	123.10	106.67
7000	610.54	318.19	220.97	172.54	143.62	124.45
8000	697.76	363.65	252.54	197.19	164.13	142.23
9000	784.98	409.10	284.11	221.83	184.65	160.01
10000	872.20	454.56	315.68	246.48	205.17	177.78
11000	959.42	500.01	347.24	271.13	225.68	195.56
12000	1046.64	545.47	378.81	295.78	246.20	213.34
13000	1133.86	590.92	410.38	320.43	266.71	231.12
14000	1221.08	636.38	441.95	345.08	287.23	248.90
15000	1308.30	681.84	473.51	369.72	307.75	266.68
16000	1395.52	727.29	505.08	394.37	328.26	284.45
17000	1482.74	772.75	536.65	419.02	348.78	302.23
18000	1569.96	818.20	568.22	443.67	369.30	320.01
19000	1657.18	863.66	599.78	468.32	389.81	337.79
20000	1744.40	909.11	631.35	492.97	410.33	355.57
21000	1831.62	954.57	662.92	517.61	430.85	373.35
22000	1918.84	1000.02	694.49	542.26	451.36	391.12
23000	2006.05	1045.48	726.05	566.91	471.88	408.90
24000	2093.27	1090.94	757.62	591.56	492.40	426.68
25000	2180.49	1136.39	789.19	616.21	512.91	444.46
30000	2616.59	1363.67	947.03	739.45	615.50	533.35
35000	3052.69	1590.95	1104.86	862.69	718.08	622.24
40000	3488.79	1818.23	1262.70	985.93	820.66	711.14
45000	3924.89	2045.51	1420.54	1109.17	923.24	800.03
50000	4360.99	2272.78	1578.38	1232.42	1025.83	888.92
55000	4797.09	2500.06	1736.21	1355.66	1128.41	977.81
60000	5233.19	2727.34	1894.05	1478.90	1230.99	1066.70
65000	5669.29	2954.62	2051.89	1602.14	1333.57	1155.59
70000	6105.38	3181.90	2209.73	1725.38	1436.16	1244.49
75000	6541.48	3409.18	2367.57	1848.62	1538.74	1333.38
80000	6977.58	3636.45	2525.40	1971.86	1641.32	1422.27
85000	7413.68	3863.73	2683.24	2095.11	1743.91	1511.16
90000	7849.78	4091.01	2841.08	2218.35	1846.49	1600.05
95000	8285.88	4318.29	2998.92	2341.59	1949.07	1688.95
100000	8721.98	4545.57	3156.75	2464.83	2051.65	1777.84
200000	17443.96	9091.13	6313.51	4929.66	4103.31	3555.68
300000	26165.93	13636.70	9470.26	7394.49	6154.96	5333.52
400000	34887.91	18182.27	12627.01	9859.32	8206.61	7111.35
500000	43609.89	22727.84	15783.77	12324.15	10258.27	8889.19

MONTHLY PAYMENT

Necessary to amortize a loan

8.5%

TERM / AMOUNT	7 YEARS	8 YEARS	9 YEARS	10 YEARS	11 YEARS	12 YEARS
500	7.92	7.20	6.64	6.20	5.84	5.55
600	9.50	8.64	7.97	7.44	7.01	6.66
700	11.09	10.07	9.30	8.68	8.18	7.77
800	12.67	11.51	10.62	9.92	9.35	8.88
900	14.25	12.95	11.95	11.16	10.52	9.99
1000	15.84	14.39	13.28	12.40	11.69	11.10
2000	31.67	28.78	26.56	24.80	23.37	22.20
3000	47.51	43.18	39.84	37.20	35.06	33.30
4000	63.35	57.57	53.12	49.59	46.75	44.40
5000	79.18	71.96	66.40	61.99	58.43	55.50
6000	95.02	86.35	79.68	74.39	70.12	66.60
7000	110.86	100.74	92.96	86.79	81.80	77.70
8000	126.69	115.14	106.23	99.19	93.49	88.80
9000	142.53	129.53	119.51	111.59	105.18	99.91
10000	158.36	143.92	132.79	123.99	116.86	111.01
11000	174.20	158.31	146.07	136.38	128.55	122.11
12000	190.04	172.71	159.35	148.78	140.24	133.21
13000	205.87	187.10	172.63	161.18	151.92	144.31
14000	221.71	201.49	185.91	173.58	163.61	155.41
15000	237.55	215.88	199.19	185.98	175.30	166.51
16000	253.38	230.27	212.47	198.38	186.98	177.61
17000	269.22	244.67	225.75	210.78	198.67	188.71
18000	285.06	259.06	239.03	223.17	210.36	199.81
19000	300.89	273.45	252.31	235.57	222.04	210.91
20000	316.73	287.84	265.59	247.97	233.73	222.01
21000	332.57	302.23	278.87	260.37	245.41	233.11
22000	348.40	316.63	292.15	272.77	257.10	244.21
23000	364.24	331.02	305.43	285.17	268.79	255.31
24000	380.08	345.41	318.70	297.57	280.47	266.41
25000	395.91	359.80	331.98	309.96	292.16	277.51
30000	475.09	431.76	398.38	371.96	350.59	333.02
35000	554.28	503.72	464.78	433.95	409.02	388.52
40000	633.46	575.69	531.17	495.94	467.46	444.02
45000	712.64	647.65	597.57	557.94	525.89	499.53
50000	791.82	719.61	663.97	619.93	584.32	555.03
55000	871.01	791.57	730.36	681.92	642.75	610.53
60000	950.19	863.53	796.76	743.91	701.18	666.03
65000	1029.37	935.49	863.16	805.91	759.62	721.54
70000	1108.55	1007.45	929.55	867.90	818.05	777.04
75000	1187.74	1079.41	995.95	929.89	876.48	832.54
80000	1266.92	1151.37	1062.35	991.89	934.91	888.04
85000	1346.10	1223.33	1128.74	1053.88	993.34	943.55
90000	1425.28	1295.29	1195.14	1115.87	1051.78	999.05
95000	1504.47	1367.25	1261.54	1177.86	1110.21	1054.55
100000	1583.65	1439.21	1327.94	1239.86	1168.64	1110.06
200000	3167.30	2878.43	2655.87	2479.71	2337.28	2220.11
300000	4750.95	4317.64	3983.81	3719.57	3505.92	3330.17
400000	6334.59	5756.85	5311.74	4959.43	4674.56	4440.22
500000	7918.24	7196.06	6639.68	6199.28	5843.20	5550.28

8.5%

MONTHLY PAYMENT

Necessary to amortize a loan

TERM / AMOUNT	15 YEARS	20 YEARS	25 YEARS	30 YEARS	35 YEARS	40 YEARS
500	4.92	4.34	4.03	3.84	3.73	3.67
600	5.91	5.21	4.83	4.61	4.48	4.40
700	6.89	6.07	5.64	5.38	5.23	5.13
800	7.88	6.94	6.44	6.15	5.97	5.86
900	8.86	7.81	7.25	6.92	6.72	6.60
1000	9.85	8.68	8.05	7.69	7.47	7.33
2000	19.69	17.36	16.10	15.38	14.94	14.66
3000	29.54	26.03	24.16	23.07	22.41	21.99
4000	39.39	34.71	32.21	30.76	29.87	29.32
5000	49.24	43.39	40.26	38.45	37.34	36.65
6000	59.08	52.07	48.31	46.13	44.81	43.99
7000	68.93	60.75	56.37	53.82	52.28	51.32
8000	78.78	69.43	64.42	61.51	59.75	58.65
9000	88.63	78.10	72.47	69.20	67.22	65.98
10000	98.47	86.78	80.52	76.89	74.69	73.31
11000	108.32	95.46	88.57	84.58	82.15	80.64
12000	118.17	104.14	96.63	92.27	89.62	87.97
13000	128.02	112.82	104.68	99.96	97.09	95.30
14000	137.86	121.50	112.73	107.65	104.56	102.63
15000	147.71	130.17	120.78	115.34	112.03	109.96
16000	157.56	138.85	128.84	123.03	119.50	117.30
17000	167.41	147.53	136.89	130.72	126.97	124.63
18000	177.25	156.21	144.94	138.40	134.43	131.96
19000	187.10	164.89	152.99	146.09	141.90	139.29
20000	196.95	173.56	161.05	153.78	149.37	146.62
21000	206.80	182.24	169.10	161.47	156.84	153.95
22000	216.64	190.92	177.15	169.16	164.31	161.28
23000	226.49	199.60	185.20	176.85	171.78	168.61
24000	236.34	208.28	193.25	184.54	179.25	175.94
25000	246.18	216.96	201.31	192.23	186.72	183.27
30000	295.42	260.35	241.57	230.67	224.06	219.93
35000	344.66	303.74	281.83	269.12	261.40	256.58
40000	393.90	347.13	322.09	307.57	298.74	293.24
45000	443.13	390.52	362.35	346.01	336.09	329.89
50000	492.37	433.91	402.61	384.46	373.43	366.55
55000	541.61	477.30	442.87	422.90	410.77	403.20
60000	590.84	520.69	483.14	461.35	448.12	439.86
65000	640.08	564.09	523.40	499.79	485.46	476.51
70000	689.32	607.48	563.66	538.24	522.80	513.17
75000	738.55	650.87	603.92	576.69	560.15	549.82
80000	787.79	694.26	644.18	615.13	597.49	586.48
85000	837.03	737.65	684.44	653.58	634.83	623.13
90000	886.27	781.04	724.70	692.02	672.17	659.78
95000	935.50	824.43	764.97	730.47	709.52	696.44
100000	984.74	867.82	805.23	768.91	746.86	733.09
200000	1969.48	1735.65	1610.45	1537.83	1493.72	1466.19
300000	2954.22	2603.47	2415.68	2306.74	2240.58	2199.28
400000	3938.96	3471.29	3220.91	3075.65	2987.44	2932.38
500000	4923.70	4339.12	4026.14	3844.57	3734.30	3665.47

MONTHLY PAYMENT

Necessary to amortize a loan

8.75%

TERM / AMOUNT	1 YEARS	2 YEARS	3 YEARS	4 YEARS	5 YEARS	6 YEARS
500	43.67	22.79	15.84	12.38	10.32	8.95
600	52.40	27.34	19.01	14.86	12.38	10.74
700	61.13	31.90	22.18	17.34	14.45	12.53
800	69.87	36.46	25.35	19.81	16.51	14.32
900	78.60	41.01	28.52	22.29	18.57	16.11
1000	87.34	45.57	31.68	24.77	20.64	17.90
2000	174.67	91.14	63.37	49.53	41.27	35.80
3000	262.01	136.71	95.05	74.30	61.91	53.71
4000	349.34	182.28	126.73	99.07	82.55	71.61
5000	436.68	227.85	158.42	123.83	103.19	89.51
6000	524.01	273.42	190.10	148.60	123.82	107.41
7000	611.35	318.99	221.78	173.37	144.46	125.31
8000	698.68	364.56	253.47	198.13	165.10	143.21
9000	786.02	410.13	285.15	222.90	185.74	161.12
10000	873.36	455.70	316.84	247.67	206.37	179.02
11000	960.69	501.27	348.52	272.43	227.01	196.92
12000	1048.03	546.84	380.20	297.20	247.65	214.82
13000	1135.36	592.41	411.89	321.96	268.28	232.72
14000	1222.70	637.98	443.57	346.73	288.92	250.62
15000	1310.03	683.55	475.25	371.50	309.56	268.53
16000	1397.37	729.12	506.94	396.26	330.20	286.43
17000	1484.70	774.69	538.62	421.03	350.83	304.33
18000	1572.04	820.26	570.30	445.80	371.47	322.23
19000	1659.38	865.83	601.99	470.56	392.11	340.13
20000	1746.71	911.40	633.67	495.33	412.74	358.03
21000	1834.05	956.97	665.35	520.10	433.38	375.94
22000	1921.38	1002.54	697.04	544.86	454.02	393.84
23000	2008.72	1048.11	728.72	569.63	474.66	411.74
24000	2096.05	1093.68	760.40	594.40	495.29	429.64
25000	2183.39	1139.25	792.09	619.16	515.93	447.54
30000	2620.07	1367.10	950.51	743.00	619.12	537.05
35000	3056.75	1594.95	1108.92	866.83	722.30	626.56
40000	3493.42	1822.80	1267.34	990.66	825.49	716.07
45000	3930.10	2050.66	1425.76	1114.49	928.68	805.58
50000	4366.78	2278.51	1584.18	1238.33	1031.86	895.09
55000	4803.46	2506.36	1742.59	1362.16	1135.05	984.59
60000	5240.14	2734.21	1901.01	1485.99	1238.23	1074.10
65000	5676.81	2962.06	2059.43	1609.82	1341.42	1163.61
70000	6113.49	3189.91	2217.85	1733.66	1444.61	1253.12
75000	6550.17	3417.76	2376.26	1857.49	1547.79	1342.63
80000	6986.85	3645.61	2534.68	1981.32	1650.98	1432.14
85000	7423.52	3873.46	2693.10	2105.15	1754.16	1521.65
90000	7860.20	4101.31	2851.52	2228.99	1857.35	1611.15
95000	8296.88	4329.16	3009.93	2352.82	1960.54	1700.66
100000	8733.56	4557.01	3168.35	2476.65	2063.72	1790.17
200000	17467.12	9114.02	6336.70	4953.30	4127.45	3580.34
300000	26200.68	13671.04	9505.05	7429.95	6191.17	5370.51
400000	34934.23	18228.05	12673.40	9906.60	8254.89	7160.68
500000	43667.79	22785.06	15841.75	12383.25	10318.62	8950.86

8.75%

MONTHLY PAYMENT

Necessary to amortize a loan

TERM AMOUNT	7 YEARS	8 YEARS	9 YEARS	10 YEARS	11 YEARS	12 YEARS
500	7.98	7.26	6.71	6.27	5.91	5.62
600	9.58	8.71	8.05	7.52	7.09	6.74
700	11.17	10.16	9.39	8.77	8.28	7.87
800	12.77	11.62	10.73	10.03	9.46	8.99
900	14.37	13.07	12.07	11.28	10.64	10.12
1000	15.96	14.52	13.41	12.53	11.82	11.24
2000	31.92	29.04	26.82	25.07	23.65	22.48
3000	47.89	43.56	40.23	37.60	35.47	33.72
4000	63.85	58.08	53.64	50.13	47.29	44.96
5000	79.81	72.60	67.05	62.66	59.12	56.20
6000	95.77	87.13	80.46	75.20	70.94	67.44
7000	111.74	101.65	93.88	87.73	82.76	78.68
8000	127.70	116.17	107.29	100.26	94.59	89.92
9000	143.66	130.69	120.70	112.79	106.41	101.16
10000	159.62	145.21	134.11	125.33	118.23	112.40
11000	175.59	159.73	147.52	137.86	130.05	123.64
12000	191.55	174.25	160.93	150.39	141.88	134.88
13000	207.51	188.77	174.34	162.92	153.70	146.12
14000	223.47	203.29	187.75	175.46	165.52	157.36
15000	239.44	217.81	201.16	187.99	177.35	168.60
16000	255.40	232.33	214.57	200.52	189.17	179.84
17000	271.36	246.85	227.98	213.06	200.99	191.08
18000	287.32	261.38	241.39	225.59	212.82	202.32
19000	303.29	275.90	254.80	238.12	224.64	213.56
20000	319.25	290.42	268.22	250.65	236.46	224.80
21000	335.21	304.94	281.63	263.19	248.29	236.04
22000	351.17	319.46	295.04	275.72	260.11	247.28
23000	367.14	333.98	308.45	288.25	271.93	258.52
24000	383.10	348.50	321.86	300.78	283.76	269.76
25000	399.06	363.02	335.27	313.32	295.58	281.00
30000	478.87	435.63	402.32	375.98	354.70	337.20
35000	558.69	508.23	469.38	438.64	413.81	393.40
40000	638.50	580.83	536.43	501.31	472.93	449.60
45000	718.31	653.44	603.48	563.97	532.04	505.80
50000	798.12	726.04	670.54	626.63	591.16	562.00
55000	877.94	798.65	737.59	689.30	650.27	618.20
60000	957.75	871.25	804.65	751.96	709.39	674.40
65000	1037.56	943.85	871.70	814.62	768.51	730.60
70000	1117.37	1016.46	938.75	877.29	827.62	786.80
75000	1197.19	1089.06	1005.81	939.95	886.74	843.00
80000	1277.00	1161.67	1072.86	1002.61	945.85	899.20
85000	1356.81	1234.27	1139.92	1065.28	1004.97	955.40
90000	1436.62	1306.88	1206.97	1127.94	1064.09	1011.60
95000	1516.44	1379.48	1274.02	1190.60	1123.20	1067.80
100000	1596.25	1452.08	1341.08	1253.27	1182.32	1124.00
200000	3192.50	2904.17	2682.15	2506.54	2364.63	2247.99
300000	4788.75	4356.25	4023.23	3759.80	3546.95	3371.99
400000	6385.00	5808.34	5364.31	5013.07	4729.27	4495.99
500000	7981.25	7260.42	6705.38	6266.34	5911.58	5619.98

MONTHLY PAYMENT

Necessary to amortize a loan

8.75%

TERM / AMOUNT	15 YEARS	20 YEARS	25 YEARS	30 YEARS	35 YEARS	40 YEARS
500	5.00	4.42	4.11	3.93	3.83	3.76
600	6.00	5.30	4.93	4.72	4.59	4.51
700	7.00	6.19	5.76	5.51	5.36	5.27
800	8.00	7.07	6.58	6.29	6.12	6.02
900	9.00	7.95	7.40	7.08	6.89	6.77
1000	9.99	8.84	8.22	7.87	7.65	7.52
2000	19.99	17.67	16.44	15.73	15.31	15.04
3000	29.98	26.51	24.66	23.60	22.96	22.57
4000	39.98	35.35	32.89	31.47	30.61	30.09
5000	49.97	44.19	41.11	39.34	38.27	37.61
6000	59.97	53.02	49.33	47.20	45.92	45.13
7000	69.96	61.86	57.55	55.07	53.58	52.65
8000	79.96	70.70	65.77	62.94	61.23	60.17
9000	89.95	79.53	73.99	70.80	68.88	67.70
10000	99.94	88.37	82.21	78.67	76.54	75.22
11000	109.94	97.21	90.44	86.54	84.19	82.74
12000	119.93	106.05	98.66	94.40	91.84	90.26
13000	129.93	114.88	106.88	102.27	99.50	97.78
14000	139.92	123.72	115.10	110.14	107.15	105.30
15000	149.92	132.56	123.32	118.01	114.80	112.83
16000	159.91	141.39	131.54	125.87	122.46	120.35
17000	169.91	150.23	139.76	133.74	130.11	127.87
18000	179.90	159.07	147.99	141.61	137.77	135.39
19000	189.90	167.91	156.21	149.47	145.42	142.91
20000	199.89	176.74	164.43	157.34	153.07	150.43
21000	209.88	185.58	172.65	165.21	160.73	157.96
22000	219.88	194.42	180.87	173.07	168.38	165.48
23000	229.87	203.25	189.09	180.94	176.03	173.00
24000	239.87	212.09	197.31	188.81	183.69	180.52
25000	249.86	220.93	205.54	196.68	191.34	188.04
30000	299.83	265.11	246.64	236.01	229.61	225.65
35000	349.81	309.30	287.75	275.35	267.88	263.26
40000	399.78	353.48	328.86	314.68	306.15	300.87
45000	449.75	397.67	369.96	354.02	344.41	338.48
50000	499.72	441.86	411.07	393.35	382.68	376.09
55000	549.70	486.04	452.18	432.69	420.95	413.69
60000	599.67	530.23	493.29	472.02	459.22	451.30
65000	649.64	574.41	534.39	511.36	497.49	488.91
70000	699.61	618.60	575.50	550.69	535.75	526.52
75000	749.59	662.78	616.61	590.03	574.02	564.13
80000	799.56	706.97	657.71	629.36	612.29	601.74
85000	849.53	751.15	698.82	668.70	650.56	639.34
90000	899.50	795.34	739.93	708.03	688.83	676.95
95000	949.48	839.53	781.04	747.37	727.09	714.56
100000	999.45	883.71	822.14	786.70	765.36	752.17
200000	1998.90	1767.42	1644.29	1573.40	1530.73	1504.34
300000	2998.35	2651.13	2466.43	2360.10	2296.09	2256.51
400000	3997.79	3534.84	3288.57	3146.80	3061.45	3008.68
500000	4997.24	4418.55	4110.72	3933.50	3826.82	3760.85

9%

MONTHLY PAYMENT

Necessary to amortize a loan

TERM / AMOUNT	1 YEARS	2 YEARS	3 YEARS	4 YEARS	5 YEARS	6 YEARS
500	43.73	22.84	15.90	12.44	10.38	9.01
600	52.47	27.41	19.08	14.93	12.46	10.82
700	61.22	31.98	22.26	17.42	14.53	12.62
800	69.96	36.55	25.44	19.91	16.61	14.42
900	78.71	41.12	28.62	22.40	18.68	16.22
1000	87.45	45.68	31.80	24.89	20.76	18.03
2000	174.90	91.37	63.60	49.77	41.52	36.05
3000	262.35	137.05	95.40	74.66	62.28	54.08
4000	349.81	182.74	127.20	99.54	83.03	72.10
5000	437.26	228.42	159.00	124.43	103.79	90.13
6000	524.71	274.11	190.80	149.31	124.55	108.15
7000	612.16	319.79	222.60	174.20	145.31	126.18
8000	699.61	365.48	254.40	199.08	166.07	144.20
9000	787.06	411.16	286.20	223.97	186.83	162.23
10000	874.51	456.85	318.00	248.85	207.58	180.26
11000	961.97	502.53	349.80	273.74	228.34	198.28
12000	1049.42	548.22	381.60	298.62	249.10	216.31
13000	1136.87	593.90	413.40	323.51	269.86	234.33
14000	1224.32	639.59	445.20	348.39	290.62	252.36
15000	1311.77	685.27	477.00	373.28	311.38	270.38
16000	1399.22	730.96	508.80	398.16	332.13	288.41
17000	1486.68	776.64	540.60	423.05	352.89	306.43
18000	1574.13	822.33	572.40	447.93	373.65	324.46
19000	1661.58	868.01	604.19	472.82	394.41	342.49
20000	1749.03	913.69	635.99	497.70	415.17	360.51
21000	1836.48	959.38	667.79	522.59	435.93	378.54
22000	1923.93	1005.06	699.59	547.47	456.68	396.56
23000	2011.38	1050.75	731.39	572.36	477.44	414.59
24000	2098.84	1096.43	763.19	597.24	498.20	432.61
25000	2186.29	1142.12	794.99	622.13	518.96	450.64
30000	2623.54	1370.54	953.99	746.55	622.75	540.77
35000	3060.80	1598.97	1112.99	870.98	726.54	630.89
40000	3498.06	1827.39	1271.99	995.40	830.33	721.02
45000	3935.32	2055.81	1430.99	1119.83	934.13	811.15
50000	4372.57	2284.24	1589.99	1244.25	1037.92	901.28
55000	4809.83	2512.66	1748.99	1368.68	1141.71	991.40
60000	5247.09	2741.08	1907.98	1493.10	1245.50	1081.53
65000	5684.35	2969.51	2066.98	1617.53	1349.29	1171.66
70000	6121.60	3197.93	2225.98	1741.95	1453.08	1261.79
75000	6558.86	3426.36	2384.98	1866.38	1556.88	1351.92
80000	6996.12	3654.78	2543.98	1990.80	1660.67	1442.04
85000	7433.38	3883.20	2702.98	2115.23	1764.46	1532.17
90000	7870.63	4111.63	2861.98	2239.65	1868.25	1622.30
95000	8307.89	4340.05	3020.97	2364.08	1972.04	1712.43
100000	8745.15	4568.47	3179.97	2488.50	2075.84	1802.55
200000	17490.30	9136.95	6359.95	4977.01	4151.67	3605.11
300000	26235.44	13705.42	9539.92	7465.51	6227.51	5407.66
400000	34980.59	18273.90	12719.89	9954.02	8303.34	7210.21
500000	43725.74	22842.37	15899.87	12442.52	10379.18	9012.77

MONTHLY PAYMENT

Necessary to amortize a loan

9%

TERM AMOUNT	7 YEARS	8 YEARS	9 YEARS	10 YEARS	11 YEARS	12 YEARS
500	8.04	7.33	6.77	6.33	5.98	5.69
600	9.65	8.79	8.13	7.60	7.18	6.83
700	11.26	10.26	9.48	8.87	8.37	7.97
800	12.87	11.72	10.83	10.13	9.57	9.10
900	14.48	13.19	12.19	11.40	10.76	10.24
1000	16.09	14.65	13.54	12.67	11.96	11.38
2000	32.18	29.30	27.09	25.34	23.92	22.76
3000	48.27	43.95	40.63	38.00	35.88	34.14
4000	64.36	58.60	54.17	50.67	47.84	45.52
5000	80.45	73.25	67.71	63.34	59.80	56.90
6000	96.53	87.90	81.26	76.01	71.76	68.28
7000	112.62	102.55	94.80	88.67	83.73	79.66
8000	128.71	117.20	108.34	101.34	95.69	91.04
9000	144.80	131.85	121.89	114.01	107.65	102.42
10000	160.89	146.50	135.43	126.68	119.61	113.80
11000	176.98	161.15	148.97	139.34	131.57	125.18
12000	193.07	175.80	162.51	152.01	143.53	136.56
13000	209.16	190.45	176.06	164.68	155.49	147.94
14000	225.25	205.10	189.60	177.35	167.45	159.32
15000	241.34	219.75	203.14	190.01	179.41	170.70
16000	257.43	234.40	216.69	202.68	191.37	182.08
17000	273.51	249.05	230.23	215.35	203.33	193.47
18000	289.60	263.70	243.77	228.02	215.29	204.85
19000	305.69	278.35	257.32	240.68	227.26	216.23
20000	321.78	293.00	270.86	253.35	239.22	227.61
21000	337.87	307.65	284.40	266.02	251.18	238.99
22000	353.96	322.30	297.94	278.69	263.14	250.37
23000	370.05	336.95	311.49	291.35	275.10	261.75
24000	386.14	351.60	325.03	304.02	287.06	273.13
25000	402.23	366.26	338.57	316.69	299.02	284.51
30000	482.67	439.51	406.29	380.03	358.82	341.41
35000	563.12	512.76	474.00	443.37	418.63	398.31
40000	643.56	586.01	541.72	506.70	478.43	455.21
45000	724.01	659.26	609.43	570.04	538.24	512.11
50000	804.45	732.51	677.15	633.38	598.04	569.02
55000	884.90	805.76	744.86	696.72	657.84	625.92
60000	965.34	879.01	812.57	760.05	717.65	682.82
65000	1045.79	952.26	880.29	823.39	777.45	739.72
70000	1126.24	1025.51	948.00	886.73	837.26	796.62
75000	1206.68	1098.77	1015.72	950.07	897.06	853.52
80000	1287.13	1172.02	1083.43	1013.41	956.86	910.42
85000	1367.57	1245.27	1151.15	1076.74	1016.67	967.33
90000	1448.02	1318.52	1218.86	1140.08	1076.47	1024.23
95000	1528.46	1391.77	1286.58	1203.42	1136.28	1081.13
100000	1608.91	1465.02	1354.29	1266.76	1196.08	1138.03
200000	3217.82	2930.04	2708.58	2533.52	2392.16	2276.06
300000	4826.72	4395.06	4062.87	3800.27	3588.24	3414.09
400000	6435.63	5860.08	5417.16	5067.03	4784.32	4552.12
500000	8044.54	7325.10	6771.45	6333.79	5980.40	5690.15

9%

MONTHLY PAYMENT

Necessary to amortize a loan

TERM / AMOUNT	15 YEARS	20 YEARS	25 YEARS	30 YEARS	35 YEARS	40 YEARS
500	5.07	4.50	4.20	4.02	3.92	3.86
600	6.09	5.40	5.04	4.83	4.70	4.63
700	7.10	6.30	5.87	5.63	5.49	5.40
800	8.11	7.20	6.71	6.44	6.27	6.17
900	9.13	8.10	7.55	7.24	7.06	6.94
1000	10.14	9.00	8.39	8.05	7.84	7.71
2000	20.29	17.99	16.78	16.09	15.68	15.43
3000	30.43	26.99	25.18	24.14	23.52	23.14
4000	40.57	35.99	33.57	32.18	31.36	30.85
5000	50.71	44.99	41.96	40.23	39.20	38.57
6000	60.86	53.98	50.35	48.28	47.04	46.28
7000	71.00	62.98	58.74	56.32	54.88	54.00
8000	81.14	71.98	67.14	64.37	62.72	61.71
9000	91.28	80.98	75.53	72.42	70.56	69.42
10000	101.43	89.97	83.92	80.46	78.40	77.14
11000	111.57	98.97	92.31	88.51	86.24	84.85
12000	121.71	107.97	100.70	96.55	94.08	92.56
13000	131.85	116.96	109.10	104.60	101.92	100.28
14000	142.00	125.96	117.49	112.65	109.76	107.99
15000	152.14	134.96	125.88	120.69	117.60	115.70
16000	162.28	143.96	134.27	128.74	125.44	123.42
17000	172.43	152.95	142.66	136.79	133.28	131.13
18000	182.57	161.95	151.06	144.83	141.12	138.85
19000	192.71	170.95	159.45	152.88	148.96	146.56
20000	202.85	179.95	167.84	160.92	156.80	154.27
21000	213.00	188.94	176.23	168.97	164.64	161.99
22000	223.14	197.94	184.62	177.02	172.48	169.70
23000	233.28	206.94	193.02	185.06	180.32	177.41
24000	243.42	215.93	201.41	193.11	188.16	185.13
25000	253.57	224.93	209.80	201.16	196.00	192.84
30000	304.28	269.92	251.76	241.39	235.20	231.41
35000	354.99	314.90	293.72	281.62	274.40	269.98
40000	405.71	359.89	335.68	321.85	313.60	308.54
45000	456.42	404.88	377.64	362.08	352.80	347.11
50000	507.13	449.86	419.60	402.31	392.00	385.68
55000	557.85	494.85	461.56	442.54	431.20	424.25
60000	608.56	539.84	503.52	482.77	470.40	462.82
65000	659.27	584.82	545.48	523.00	509.60	501.38
70000	709.99	629.81	587.44	563.24	548.80	539.95
75000	760.70	674.79	629.40	603.47	587.99	578.52
80000	811.41	719.78	671.36	643.70	627.19	617.09
85000	862.13	764.77	713.32	683.93	666.39	655.66
90000	912.84	809.75	755.28	724.16	705.59	694.23
95000	963.55	854.74	797.24	764.39	744.79	732.79
100000	1014.27	899.73	839.20	804.62	783.99	771.36
200000	2028.53	1799.45	1678.39	1609.25	1567.99	1542.72
300000	3042.80	2699.18	2517.59	2413.87	2351.98	2314.08
400000	4057.07	3598.90	3356.79	3218.49	3135.97	3085.45
500000	5071.33	4498.63	4195.98	4023.11	3919.96	3856.81

MONTHLY PAYMENT

Necessary to amortize a loan

9.25%

TERM / AMOUNT	1 YEARS	2 YEARS	3 YEARS	4 YEARS	5 YEARS	6 YEARS
500	43.78	22.90	15.96	12.50	10.44	9.07
600	52.54	27.48	19.15	15.00	12.53	10.89
700	61.30	32.06	22.34	17.50	14.62	12.70
800	70.05	36.64	25.53	20.00	16.70	14.52
900	78.81	41.22	28.72	22.50	18.79	16.33
1000	87.57	45.80	31.92	25.00	20.88	18.15
2000	175.13	91.60	63.83	50.01	41.76	36.30
3000	262.70	137.40	95.75	75.01	62.64	54.45
4000	350.27	183.20	127.66	100.02	83.52	72.60
5000	437.84	229.00	159.58	125.02	104.40	90.75
6000	525.40	274.80	191.50	150.02	125.28	108.90
7000	612.97	320.60	223.41	175.03	146.16	127.05
8000	700.54	366.40	255.33	200.03	167.04	145.20
9000	788.11	412.20	287.25	225.04	187.92	163.35
10000	875.67	458.00	319.16	250.04	208.80	181.50
11000	963.24	503.79	351.08	275.04	229.68	199.65
12000	1050.81	549.59	382.99	300.05	250.56	217.80
13000	1138.38	595.39	414.91	325.05	271.44	235.95
14000	1225.94	641.19	446.83	350.05	292.32	254.10
15000	1313.51	686.99	478.74	375.06	313.20	272.25
16000	1401.08	732.79	510.66	400.06	334.08	290.40
17000	1488.65	778.59	542.58	425.07	354.96	308.55
18000	1576.21	824.39	574.49	450.07	375.84	326.70
19000	1663.78	870.19	606.41	475.07	396.72	344.85
20000	1751.35	915.99	638.32	500.08	417.60	363.00
21000	1838.92	961.79	670.24	525.08	438.48	381.15
22000	1926.48	1007.59	702.16	550.09	459.36	399.30
23000	2014.05	1053.39	734.07	575.09	480.24	417.45
24000	2101.62	1099.19	765.99	600.09	501.12	435.60
25000	2189.19	1144.99	797.91	625.10	522.00	453.75
30000	2627.02	1373.99	957.49	750.12	626.40	544.50
35000	3064.86	1602.98	1117.07	875.14	730.80	635.25
40000	3502.70	1831.98	1276.65	1000.16	835.20	725.99
45000	3940.54	2060.98	1436.23	1125.18	939.60	816.74
50000	4378.37	2289.98	1595.81	1250.20	1043.99	907.49
55000	4816.21	2518.97	1755.39	1375.22	1148.39	998.24
60000	5254.05	2747.97	1914.97	1500.24	1252.79	1088.99
65000	5691.88	2976.97	2074.55	1625.25	1357.19	1179.74
70000	6129.72	3205.97	2234.13	1750.27	1461.59	1270.49
75000	6567.56	3434.96	2393.72	1875.29	1565.99	1361.24
80000	7005.40	3663.96	2553.30	2000.31	1670.39	1451.99
85000	7443.23	3892.96	2712.88	2125.33	1774.79	1542.74
90000	7881.07	4121.96	2872.46	2250.35	1879.19	1633.49
95000	8318.91	4350.96	3032.04	2375.37	1983.59	1724.24
100000	8756.75	4579.95	3191.62	2500.39	2087.99	1814.99
200000	17513.49	9159.91	6383.24	5000.78	4175.98	3629.97
300000	26270.24	13739.86	9574.86	7501.18	6263.97	5444.96
400000	35026.98	18319.81	12766.49	10001.57	8351.96	7259.95
500000	43783.73	22899.77	15958.11	12501.96	10439.95	9074.93

9.25%

MONTHLY PAYMENT

Necessary to amortize a loan

TERM / AMOUNT	7 YEARS	8 YEARS	9 YEARS	10 YEARS	11 YEARS	12 YEARS
500	8.11	7.39	6.84	6.40	6.05	5.76
600	9.73	8.87	8.21	7.68	7.26	6.91
700	11.35	10.35	9.57	8.96	8.47	8.07
800	12.97	11.82	10.94	10.24	9.68	9.22
900	14.59	13.30	12.31	11.52	10.89	10.37
1000	16.22	14.78	13.68	12.80	12.10	11.52
2000	32.43	29.56	27.35	25.61	24.20	23.04
3000	48.65	44.34	41.03	38.41	36.30	34.56
4000	64.86	59.12	54.70	51.21	48.40	46.09
5000	81.08	73.90	68.38	64.02	60.50	57.61
6000	97.30	88.68	82.05	76.82	72.60	69.13
7000	113.51	103.46	95.73	89.62	84.70	80.65
8000	129.73	118.24	109.41	102.43	96.79	92.17
9000	145.95	133.02	123.08	115.23	108.89	103.69
10000	162.16	147.80	136.76	128.03	120.99	115.22
11000	178.38	162.58	150.43	140.84	133.09	126.74
12000	194.59	177.36	164.11	153.64	145.19	138.26
13000	210.81	192.14	177.79	166.44	157.29	149.78
14000	227.03	206.92	191.46	179.25	169.39	161.30
15000	243.24	221.70	205.14	192.05	181.49	172.82
16000	259.46	236.48	218.81	204.85	193.59	184.35
17000	275.68	251.26	232.49	217.66	205.69	195.87
18000	291.89	266.04	246.16	230.46	217.79	207.39
19000	308.11	280.82	259.84	243.26	229.89	218.91
20000	324.32	295.60	273.52	256.07	241.99	230.43
21000	340.54	310.38	287.19	268.87	254.09	241.95
22000	356.76	325.16	300.87	281.67	266.18	253.47
23000	372.97	339.95	314.54	294.48	278.28	265.00
24000	389.19	354.73	328.22	307.28	290.38	276.52
25000	405.41	369.51	341.89	320.08	302.48	288.04
30000	486.49	443.41	410.27	384.10	362.98	345.65
35000	567.57	517.31	478.65	448.11	423.48	403.25
40000	648.65	591.21	547.03	512.13	483.97	460.86
45000	729.73	665.11	615.41	576.15	544.47	518.47
50000	810.81	739.01	683.79	640.16	604.96	576.08
55000	891.89	812.91	752.17	704.18	665.46	633.69
60000	972.97	886.81	820.55	768.20	725.96	691.29
65000	1054.06	960.71	888.93	832.21	786.45	748.90
70000	1135.14	1034.62	957.30	896.23	846.95	806.51
75000	1216.22	1108.52	1025.68	960.25	907.45	864.12
80000	1297.30	1182.42	1094.06	1024.26	967.94	921.73
85000	1378.38	1256.32	1162.44	1088.28	1028.44	979.33
90000	1459.46	1330.22	1230.82	1152.29	1088.94	1036.94
95000	1540.54	1404.12	1299.20	1216.31	1149.43	1094.55
100000	1621.62	1478.02	1367.58	1280.33	1209.93	1152.16
200000	3243.25	2956.04	2735.15	2560.65	2419.86	2304.31
300000	4864.87	4434.07	4102.73	3840.98	3629.79	3456.47
400000	6486.50	5912.09	5470.31	5121.31	4839.72	4608.63
500000	8108.12	7390.11	6837.89	6401.64	6049.65	5760.78

MONTHLY PAYMENT

Necessary to amortize a loan

9.25%

TERM / AMOUNT	15 YEARS	20 YEARS	25 YEARS	30 YEARS	35 YEARS	40 YEARS
500	5.15	4.58	4.28	4.11	4.01	3.95
600	6.18	5.50	5.14	4.94	4.82	4.74
700	7.20	6.41	5.99	5.76	5.62	5.53
800	8.23	7.33	6.85	6.58	6.42	6.33
900	9.26	8.24	7.71	7.40	7.22	7.12
1000	10.29	9.16	8.56	8.23	8.03	7.91
2000	20.58	18.32	17.13	16.45	16.05	15.81
3000	30.88	27.48	25.69	24.68	24.08	23.72
4000	41.17	36.63	34.26	32.91	32.11	31.63
5000	51.46	45.79	42.82	41.13	40.14	39.53
6000	61.75	54.95	51.38	49.36	48.16	47.44
7000	72.04	64.11	59.95	57.59	56.19	55.35
8000	82.34	73.27	68.51	65.81	64.22	63.25
9000	92.63	82.43	77.07	74.04	72.25	71.16
10000	102.92	91.59	85.64	82.27	80.27	79.07
11000	113.21	100.75	94.20	90.49	88.30	86.97
12000	123.50	109.90	102.77	98.72	96.33	94.88
13000	133.79	119.06	111.33	106.95	104.36	102.79
14000	144.09	128.22	119.89	115.17	112.38	110.69
15000	154.38	137.38	128.46	123.40	120.41	118.60
16000	164.67	146.54	137.02	131.63	128.44	126.51
17000	174.96	155.70	145.58	139.85	136.47	134.41
18000	185.25	164.86	154.15	148.08	144.49	142.32
19000	195.55	174.01	162.71	156.31	152.52	150.23
20000	205.84	183.17	171.28	164.54	160.55	158.13
21000	216.13	192.33	179.84	172.76	168.58	166.04
22000	226.42	201.49	188.40	180.99	176.60	173.95
23000	236.71	210.65	196.97	189.22	184.63	181.85
24000	247.01	219.81	205.53	197.44	192.66	189.76
25000	257.30	228.97	214.10	205.67	200.69	197.67
30000	308.76	274.76	256.91	246.80	240.82	237.20
35000	360.22	320.55	299.73	287.94	280.96	276.73
40000	411.68	366.35	342.55	329.07	321.10	316.26
45000	463.14	412.14	385.37	370.20	361.23	355.80
50000	514.60	457.93	428.19	411.34	401.37	395.33
55000	566.06	503.73	471.01	452.47	441.51	434.86
60000	617.52	549.52	513.83	493.61	481.65	474.40
65000	668.97	595.31	556.65	534.74	521.78	513.93
70000	720.43	641.11	599.47	575.87	561.92	553.46
75000	771.89	686.90	642.29	617.01	602.06	593.00
80000	823.35	732.69	685.11	658.14	642.20	632.53
85000	874.81	778.49	727.92	699.27	682.33	672.06
90000	926.27	824.28	770.74	740.41	722.47	711.59
95000	977.73	870.07	813.56	781.54	762.61	751.13
100000	1029.19	915.87	856.38	822.68	802.74	790.66
200000	2058.38	1831.73	1712.76	1645.35	1605.49	1581.32
300000	3087.58	2747.60	2569.15	2468.03	2408.23	2371.98
400000	4116.77	3663.47	3425.53	3290.70	3210.98	3162.64
500000	5145.96	4579.33	4281.91	4113.38	4013.72	3953.30

9.5%

MONTHLY PAYMENT

Necessary to amortize a loan

TERM AMOUNT	1 YEARS	2 YEARS	3 YEARS	4 YEARS	5 YEARS	6 YEARS
500	43.84	22.96	16.02	12.56	10.50	9.14
600	52.61	27.55	19.22	15.07	12.60	10.96
700	61.38	32.14	22.42	17.59	14.70	12.79
800	70.15	36.73	25.63	20.10	16.80	14.62
900	78.92	41.32	28.83	22.61	18.90	16.45
1000	87.68	45.91	32.03	25.12	21.00	18.27
2000	175.37	91.83	64.07	50.25	42.00	36.55
3000	263.05	137.74	96.10	75.37	63.01	54.82
4000	350.73	183.66	128.13	100.49	84.01	73.10
5000	438.42	229.57	160.16	125.62	105.01	91.37
6000	526.10	275.49	192.20	150.74	126.01	109.65
7000	613.78	321.40	224.23	175.86	147.01	127.92
8000	701.47	367.32	256.26	200.99	168.01	146.20
9000	789.15	413.23	288.30	226.11	189.02	164.47
10000	876.84	459.14	320.33	251.23	210.02	182.75
11000	964.52	505.06	352.36	276.35	231.02	201.02
12000	1052.20	550.97	384.40	301.48	252.02	219.30
13000	1139.89	596.89	416.43	326.60	273.02	237.57
14000	1227.57	642.80	448.46	351.72	294.03	255.85
15000	1315.25	688.72	480.49	376.85	315.03	274.12
16000	1402.94	734.63	512.53	401.97	336.03	292.40
17000	1490.62	780.55	544.56	427.09	357.03	310.67
18000	1578.30	826.46	576.59	452.22	378.03	328.94
19000	1665.99	872.38	608.63	477.34	399.04	347.22
20000	1753.67	918.29	640.66	502.46	420.04	365.49
21000	1841.35	964.20	672.69	527.59	441.04	383.77
22000	1929.04	1010.12	704.72	552.71	462.04	402.04
23000	2016.72	1056.03	736.76	577.83	483.04	420.32
24000	2104.40	1101.95	768.79	602.96	504.04	438.59
25000	2192.09	1147.86	800.82	628.08	525.05	456.87
30000	2630.51	1377.43	960.99	753.69	630.06	548.24
35000	3068.92	1607.01	1121.15	879.31	735.07	639.61
40000	3507.34	1836.58	1281.32	1004.93	840.07	730.99
45000	3945.76	2066.15	1441.48	1130.54	945.08	822.36
50000	4384.18	2295.72	1601.65	1256.16	1050.09	913.73
55000	4822.59	2525.30	1761.81	1381.77	1155.10	1005.11
60000	5261.01	2754.87	1921.98	1507.39	1260.11	1096.48
65000	5699.43	2984.44	2082.14	1633.00	1365.12	1187.85
70000	6137.85	3214.01	2242.31	1758.62	1470.13	1279.23
75000	6576.26	3443.59	2402.47	1884.24	1575.14	1370.60
80000	7014.68	3673.16	2562.64	2009.85	1680.15	1461.98
85000	7453.10	3902.73	2722.80	2135.47	1785.16	1553.35
90000	7891.52	4132.30	2882.97	2261.08	1890.17	1644.72
95000	8329.93	4361.88	3043.13	2386.70	1995.18	1736.10
100000	8768.35	4591.45	3203.29	2512.31	2100.19	1827.47
200000	17536.70	9182.90	6406.59	5024.63	4200.37	3654.94
300000	26305.05	13774.35	9609.88	7536.94	6300.56	5482.41
400000	35073.40	18365.80	12813.18	10049.25	8400.74	7309.88
500000	43841.76	22957.25	16016.47	12561.57	10500.93	9137.35

MONTHLY PAYMENT

Necessary to amortize a loan

9.5%

TERM / AMOUNT	7 YEARS	8 YEARS	9 YEARS	10 YEARS	11 YEARS	12 YEARS
500	8.17	7.46	6.90	6.47	6.12	5.83
600	9.81	8.95	8.29	7.76	7.34	7.00
700	11.44	10.44	9.67	9.06	8.57	8.16
800	13.08	11.93	11.05	10.35	9.79	9.33
900	14.71	13.42	12.43	11.65	11.01	10.50
1000	16.34	14.91	13.81	12.94	12.24	11.66
2000	32.69	29.82	27.62	25.88	24.48	23.33
3000	49.03	44.73	41.43	38.82	36.72	34.99
4000	65.38	59.64	55.24	51.76	48.95	46.65
5000	81.72	74.55	69.05	64.70	61.19	58.32
6000	98.06	89.47	82.86	77.64	73.43	69.98
7000	114.41	104.38	96.67	90.58	85.67	81.65
8000	130.75	119.29	110.47	103.52	97.91	93.31
9000	147.10	134.20	124.28	116.46	110.15	104.97
10000	163.44	149.11	138.09	129.40	122.39	116.64
11000	179.78	164.02	151.90	142.34	134.63	128.30
12000	196.13	178.93	165.71	155.28	146.86	139.96
13000	212.47	193.84	179.52	168.22	159.10	151.63
14000	228.82	208.75	193.33	181.16	171.34	163.29
15000	245.16	223.66	207.14	194.10	183.58	174.96
16000	261.50	238.57	220.95	207.04	195.82	186.62
17000	277.85	253.49	234.76	219.98	208.06	198.28
18000	294.19	268.40	248.57	232.92	220.30	209.95
19000	310.54	283.31	262.38	245.86	232.53	221.61
20000	326.88	298.22	276.19	258.80	244.77	233.27
21000	343.22	313.13	290.00	271.73	257.01	244.94
22000	359.57	328.04	303.81	284.67	269.25	256.60
23000	375.91	342.95	317.62	297.61	281.49	268.27
24000	392.26	357.86	331.42	310.55	293.73	279.93
25000	408.60	372.77	345.23	323.49	305.97	291.59
30000	490.32	447.33	414.28	388.19	367.16	349.91
35000	572.04	521.88	483.33	452.89	428.35	408.23
40000	653.76	596.44	552.37	517.59	489.55	466.55
45000	735.48	670.99	621.42	582.29	550.74	524.87
50000	817.20	745.54	690.47	646.99	611.93	583.19
55000	898.92	820.10	759.51	711.69	673.13	641.51
60000	980.64	894.65	828.56	776.39	734.32	699.82
65000	1062.36	969.21	897.61	841.08	795.51	758.14
70000	1144.08	1043.76	966.66	905.78	856.71	816.46
75000	1225.80	1118.32	1035.70	970.48	917.90	874.78
80000	1307.52	1192.87	1104.75	1035.18	979.09	933.10
85000	1389.24	1267.43	1173.80	1099.88	1040.28	991.42
90000	1470.96	1341.98	1242.84	1164.58	1101.48	1049.74
95000	1552.68	1416.53	1311.89	1229.28	1162.67	1108.05
100000	1634.40	1491.09	1380.94	1293.98	1223.86	1166.37
200000	3268.80	2982.18	2761.87	2587.95	2447.73	2332.75
300000	4903.19	4473.27	4142.81	3881.93	3671.59	3499.12
400000	6537.59	5964.35	5523.74	5175.90	4895.46	4665.49
500000	8171.99	7455.44	6904.68	6469.88	6119.32	5831.87

9.5%

MONTHLY PAYMENT

Necessary to amortize a loan

TERM / AMOUNT	15 YEARS	20 YEARS	25 YEARS	30 YEARS	35 YEARS	40 YEARS
500	5.22	4.66	4.37	4.20	4.11	4.05
600	6.27	5.59	5.24	5.05	4.93	4.86
700	7.31	6.52	6.12	5.89	5.75	5.67
800	8.35	7.46	6.99	6.73	6.57	6.48
900	9.40	8.39	7.86	7.57	7.39	7.29
1000	10.44	9.32	8.74	8.41	8.22	8.10
2000	20.88	18.64	17.47	16.82	16.43	16.20
3000	31.33	27.96	26.21	25.23	24.65	24.30
4000	41.77	37.29	34.95	33.63	32.86	32.40
5000	52.21	46.61	43.68	42.04	41.08	40.50
6000	62.65	55.93	52.42	50.45	49.30	48.60
7000	73.10	65.25	61.16	58.86	57.51	56.70
8000	83.54	74.57	69.90	67.27	65.73	64.80
9000	93.98	83.89	78.63	75.68	73.95	72.91
10000	104.42	93.21	87.37	84.09	82.16	81.01
11000	114.86	102.53	96.11	92.49	90.38	89.11
12000	125.31	111.86	104.84	100.90	98.59	97.21
13000	135.75	121.18	113.58	109.31	106.81	105.31
14000	146.19	130.50	122.32	117.72	115.03	113.41
15000	156.63	139.82	131.05	126.13	123.24	121.51
16000	167.08	149.14	139.79	134.54	131.46	129.61
17000	177.52	158.46	148.53	142.95	139.67	137.71
18000	187.96	167.78	157.27	151.35	147.89	145.81
19000	198.40	177.10	166.00	159.76	156.11	153.91
20000	208.84	186.43	174.74	168.17	164.32	162.01
21000	219.29	195.75	183.48	176.58	172.54	170.11
22000	229.73	205.07	192.21	184.99	180.75	178.21
23000	240.17	214.39	200.95	193.40	188.97	186.31
24000	250.61	223.71	209.69	201.81	197.19	194.41
25000	261.06	233.03	218.42	210.21	205.40	202.52
30000	313.27	279.64	262.11	252.26	246.48	243.02
35000	365.48	326.25	305.79	294.30	287.56	283.52
40000	417.69	372.85	349.48	336.34	328.64	324.02
45000	469.90	419.46	393.16	378.38	369.73	364.53
50000	522.11	466.07	436.85	420.43	410.81	405.03
55000	574.32	512.67	480.53	462.47	451.89	445.53
60000	626.53	559.28	524.22	504.51	492.97	486.04
65000	678.75	605.89	567.90	546.56	534.05	526.54
70000	730.96	652.49	611.59	588.60	575.13	567.04
75000	783.17	699.10	655.27	630.64	616.21	607.55
80000	835.38	745.70	698.96	672.68	657.29	648.05
85000	887.59	792.31	742.64	714.73	698.37	688.55
90000	939.80	838.92	786.33	756.77	739.45	729.06
95000	992.01	885.52	830.01	798.81	780.53	769.56
100000	1044.22	932.13	873.70	840.85	821.61	810.06
200000	2088.45	1864.26	1747.39	1681.71	1643.22	1620.12
300000	3132.67	2796.39	2621.09	2522.56	2464.83	2430.18
400000	4176.90	3728.52	3494.79	3363.42	3286.45	3240.25
500000	5221.12	4660.66	4368.48	4204.27	4108.06	4050.31

MONTHLY PAYMENT

Necessary to amortize a loan

9.75%

TERM / AMOUNT	1 YEARS	2 YEARS	3 YEARS	4 YEARS	5 YEARS	6 YEARS
500	43.90	23.01	16.07	12.62	10.56	9.20
600	52.68	27.62	19.29	15.15	12.67	11.04
700	61.46	32.22	22.50	17.67	14.79	12.88
800	70.24	36.82	25.72	20.19	16.90	14.72
900	79.02	41.43	28.93	22.72	19.01	16.56
1000	87.80	46.03	32.15	25.24	21.12	18.40
2000	175.60	92.06	64.30	50.49	42.25	36.80
3000	263.40	138.09	96.45	75.73	63.37	55.20
4000	351.20	184.12	128.60	100.97	84.50	73.60
5000	439.00	230.15	160.75	126.21	105.62	92.00
6000	526.80	276.18	192.90	151.46	126.75	110.40
7000	614.60	322.21	225.05	176.70	147.87	128.80
8000	702.40	368.24	257.20	201.94	168.99	147.20
9000	790.20	414.27	289.35	227.18	190.12	165.60
10000	878.00	460.30	321.50	252.43	211.24	184.00
11000	965.80	506.33	353.65	277.67	232.37	202.40
12000	1053.60	552.36	385.80	302.91	253.49	220.80
13000	1141.40	598.39	417.95	328.15	274.62	239.20
14000	1229.20	644.41	450.10	353.40	295.74	257.60
15000	1316.99	690.44	482.25	378.64	316.86	276.00
16000	1404.79	736.47	514.40	403.88	337.99	294.40
17000	1492.59	782.50	546.55	429.13	359.11	312.80
18000	1580.39	828.53	578.70	454.37	380.24	331.20
19000	1668.19	874.56	610.85	479.61	401.36	349.60
20000	1755.99	920.59	643.00	504.85	422.48	368.00
21000	1843.79	966.62	675.15	530.10	443.61	386.40
22000	1931.59	1012.65	707.30	555.34	464.73	404.80
23000	2019.39	1058.68	739.45	580.58	485.86	423.20
24000	2107.19	1104.71	771.60	605.82	506.98	441.60
25000	2194.99	1150.74	803.75	631.07	528.11	460.00
30000	2633.99	1380.89	964.50	757.28	633.73	552.00
35000	3072.99	1611.04	1125.25	883.49	739.35	644.00
40000	3511.99	1841.18	1286.00	1009.71	844.97	736.00
45000	3950.98	2071.33	1446.75	1135.92	950.59	828.00
50000	4389.98	2301.48	1607.50	1262.13	1056.21	920.00
55000	4828.98	2531.63	1768.25	1388.35	1161.83	1012.00
60000	5267.98	2761.78	1929.00	1514.56	1267.45	1104.00
65000	5706.98	2991.93	2089.75	1640.77	1373.08	1196.00
70000	6145.98	3222.07	2250.50	1766.99	1478.70	1288.00
75000	6584.97	3452.22	2411.25	1893.20	1584.32	1380.00
80000	7023.97	3682.37	2572.00	2019.42	1689.94	1472.00
85000	7462.97	3912.52	2732.74	2145.63	1795.56	1564.00
90000	7901.97	4142.67	2893.49	2271.84	1901.18	1656.00
95000	8340.97	4372.81	3054.24	2398.06	2006.80	1748.00
100000	8779.97	4602.96	3214.99	2524.27	2112.42	1840.00
200000	17559.93	9205.92	6429.99	5048.54	4224.85	3680.00
300000	26339.90	13808.89	9644.98	7572.81	6337.27	5520.00
400000	35119.86	18411.85	12859.98	10097.08	8449.70	7360.01
500000	43899.83	23014.81	16074.97	12621.35	10562.12	9200.01

9.75% MONTHLY PAYMENT

Necessary to amortize a loan

TERM / AMOUNT	7 YEARS	8 YEARS	9 YEARS	10 YEARS	11 YEARS	12 YEARS
500	8.24	7.52	6.97	6.54	6.19	5.90
600	9.88	9.03	8.37	7.85	7.43	7.08
700	11.53	10.53	9.76	9.15	8.67	8.26
800	13.18	12.03	11.15	10.46	9.90	9.45
900	14.83	13.54	12.55	11.77	11.14	10.63
1000	16.47	15.04	13.94	13.08	12.38	11.81
2000	32.94	30.08	27.89	26.15	24.76	23.61
3000	49.42	45.13	41.83	39.23	37.14	35.42
4000	65.89	60.17	55.77	52.31	49.52	47.23
5000	82.36	75.21	69.72	65.39	61.89	59.03
6000	98.83	90.25	83.66	78.46	74.27	70.84
7000	115.31	105.30	97.61	91.54	86.65	82.65
8000	131.78	120.34	111.55	104.62	99.03	94.45
9000	148.25	135.38	125.49	117.69	111.41	106.26
10000	164.72	150.42	139.44	130.77	123.79	118.07
11000	181.20	165.46	153.38	143.85	136.17	129.87
12000	197.67	180.51	167.32	156.92	148.55	141.68
13000	214.14	195.55	181.27	170.00	160.92	153.49
14000	230.61	210.59	195.21	183.08	173.30	165.30
15000	247.08	225.63	209.15	196.16	185.68	177.10
16000	263.56	240.68	223.10	209.23	198.06	188.91
17000	280.03	255.72	237.04	222.31	210.44	200.72
18000	296.50	270.76	250.99	235.39	222.82	212.52
19000	312.97	285.80	264.93	248.46	235.20	224.33
20000	329.45	300.84	278.87	261.54	247.58	236.14
21000	345.92	315.89	292.82	274.62	259.96	247.94
22000	362.39	330.93	306.76	287.69	272.33	259.75
23000	378.86	345.97	320.70	300.77	284.71	271.56
24000	395.34	361.01	334.65	313.85	297.09	283.36
25000	411.81	376.06	348.59	326.93	309.47	295.17
30000	494.17	451.27	418.31	392.31	371.37	354.20
35000	576.53	526.48	488.03	457.70	433.26	413.24
40000	658.89	601.69	557.75	523.08	495.15	472.27
45000	741.25	676.90	627.46	588.47	557.05	531.31
50000	823.61	752.11	697.18	653.85	618.94	590.34
55000	905.98	827.32	766.90	719.24	680.84	649.37
60000	988.34	902.53	836.62	784.62	742.73	708.41
65000	1070.70	977.74	906.34	850.01	804.62	767.44
70000	1153.06	1052.95	976.06	915.39	866.52	826.48
75000	1235.42	1128.17	1045.77	980.78	928.41	885.51
80000	1317.78	1203.38	1115.49	1046.16	990.31	944.54
85000	1400.15	1278.59	1185.21	1111.55	1052.20	1003.58
90000	1482.51	1353.80	1254.93	1176.93	1114.10	1062.61
95000	1564.87	1429.01	1324.65	1242.32	1175.99	1121.65
100000	1647.23	1504.22	1394.37	1307.70	1237.88	1180.68
200000	3294.46	3008.44	2788.73	2615.40	2475.77	2361.36
300000	4941.69	4512.66	4183.10	3923.11	3713.65	3542.04
400000	6588.92	6016.88	5577.47	5230.81	4951.54	4722.72
500000	8236.15	7521.10	6971.83	6538.51	6189.42	5903.40

MONTHLY PAYMENT

Necessary to amortize a loan

9.75%

TERM / AMOUNT	15 YEARS	20 YEARS	25 YEARS	30 YEARS	35 YEARS	40 YEARS
500	5.30	4.74	4.46	4.30	4.20	4.15
600	6.36	5.69	5.35	5.15	5.04	4.98
700	7.42	6.64	6.24	6.01	5.88	5.81
800	8.47	7.59	7.13	6.87	6.72	6.64
900	9.53	8.54	8.02	7.73	7.57	7.47
1000	10.59	9.49	8.91	8.59	8.41	8.30
2000	21.19	18.97	17.82	17.18	16.81	16.59
3000	31.78	28.46	26.73	25.77	25.22	24.89
4000	42.37	37.94	35.65	34.37	33.62	33.18
5000	52.97	47.43	44.56	42.96	42.03	41.48
6000	63.56	56.91	53.47	51.55	50.44	49.77
7000	74.16	66.40	62.38	60.14	58.84	58.07
8000	84.75	75.88	71.29	68.73	67.25	66.36
9000	95.34	85.37	80.20	77.32	75.65	74.66
10000	105.94	94.85	89.11	85.92	84.06	82.96
11000	116.53	104.34	98.03	94.51	92.46	91.25
12000	127.12	113.82	106.94	103.10	100.87	99.55
13000	137.72	123.31	115.85	111.69	109.28	107.84
14000	148.31	132.79	124.76	120.28	117.68	116.14
15000	158.90	142.28	133.67	128.87	126.09	124.43
16000	169.50	151.76	142.58	137.46	134.49	132.73
17000	180.09	161.25	151.49	146.06	142.90	141.02
18000	190.69	170.73	160.40	154.65	151.31	149.32
19000	201.28	180.22	169.32	163.24	159.71	157.62
20000	211.87	189.70	178.23	171.83	168.12	165.91
21000	222.47	199.19	187.14	180.42	176.52	174.21
22000	233.06	208.67	196.05	189.01	184.93	182.50
23000	243.65	218.16	204.96	197.61	193.34	190.80
24000	254.25	227.64	213.87	206.20	201.74	199.09
25000	264.84	237.13	222.78	214.79	210.15	207.39
30000	317.81	284.56	267.34	257.75	252.18	248.87
35000	370.78	331.98	311.90	300.70	294.21	290.35
40000	423.75	379.41	356.45	343.66	336.24	331.82
45000	476.71	426.83	401.01	386.62	378.27	373.30
50000	529.68	474.26	445.57	429.58	420.29	414.78
55000	582.65	521.68	490.13	472.53	462.32	456.26
60000	635.62	569.11	534.68	515.49	504.35	497.74
65000	688.59	616.54	579.24	558.45	546.38	539.21
70000	741.55	663.96	623.80	601.41	588.41	580.69
75000	794.52	711.39	668.35	644.37	630.44	622.17
80000	847.49	758.81	712.91	687.32	672.47	663.65
85000	900.46	806.24	757.47	730.28	714.50	705.12
90000	953.43	853.67	802.02	773.24	756.53	746.60
95000	1006.39	901.09	846.58	816.20	798.56	788.08
100000	1059.36	948.52	891.14	859.15	840.59	829.56
200000	2118.73	1897.03	1782.27	1718.31	1681.18	1659.12
300000	3178.09	2845.55	2673.41	2577.46	2521.77	2488.68
400000	4237.45	3794.07	3564.55	3436.62	3362.36	3318.23
500000	5296.81	4742.58	4455.69	4295.77	4202.95	4147.79

10%

MONTHLY PAYMENT

Necessary to amortize a loan

TERM / AMOUNT	1 YEARS	2 YEARS	3 YEARS	4 YEARS	5 YEARS	6 YEARS
500	43.96	23.07	16.13	12.68	10.62	9.26
600	52.75	27.69	19.36	15.22	12.75	11.12
700	61.54	32.30	22.59	17.75	14.87	12.97
800	70.33	36.92	25.81	20.29	17.00	14.82
900	79.12	41.53	29.04	22.83	19.12	16.67
1000	87.92	46.14	32.27	25.36	21.25	18.53
2000	175.83	92.29	64.53	50.73	42.49	37.05
3000	263.75	138.43	96.80	76.09	63.74	55.58
4000	351.66	184.58	129.07	101.45	84.99	74.10
5000	439.58	230.72	161.34	126.81	106.24	92.63
6000	527.50	276.87	193.60	152.18	127.48	111.16
7000	615.41	323.01	225.87	177.54	148.73	129.68
8000	703.33	369.16	258.14	202.90	169.98	148.21
9000	791.24	415.30	290.40	228.26	191.22	166.73
10000	879.16	461.45	322.67	253.63	212.47	185.26
11000	967.07	507.59	354.94	278.99	233.72	203.78
12000	1054.99	553.74	387.21	304.35	254.96	222.31
13000	1142.91	599.88	419.47	329.71	276.21	240.84
14000	1230.82	646.03	451.74	355.08	297.46	259.36
15000	1318.74	692.17	484.01	380.44	318.71	277.89
16000	1406.65	738.32	516.27	405.80	339.95	296.41
17000	1494.57	784.46	548.54	431.16	361.20	314.94
18000	1582.49	830.61	580.81	456.53	382.45	333.47
19000	1670.40	876.75	613.08	481.89	403.69	351.99
20000	1758.32	922.90	645.34	507.25	424.94	370.52
21000	1846.23	969.04	677.61	532.61	446.19	389.04
22000	1934.15	1015.19	709.88	557.98	467.43	407.57
23000	2022.07	1061.33	742.15	583.34	488.68	426.09
24000	2109.98	1107.48	774.41	608.70	509.93	444.62
25000	2197.90	1153.62	806.68	634.06	531.18	463.15
30000	2637.48	1384.35	968.02	760.88	637.41	555.78
35000	3077.06	1615.07	1129.35	887.69	743.65	648.40
40000	3516.64	1845.80	1290.69	1014.50	849.88	741.03
45000	3956.21	2076.52	1452.02	1141.32	956.12	833.66
50000	4395.79	2307.25	1613.36	1268.13	1062.35	926.29
55000	4835.37	2537.97	1774.70	1394.94	1168.59	1018.92
60000	5274.95	2768.70	1936.03	1521.76	1274.82	1111.55
65000	5714.53	2999.42	2097.37	1648.57	1381.06	1204.18
70000	6154.11	3230.14	2258.70	1775.38	1487.29	1296.81
75000	6593.69	3460.87	2420.04	1902.19	1593.53	1389.44
80000	7033.27	3691.59	2581.37	2029.01	1699.76	1482.07
85000	7472.85	3922.32	2742.71	2155.82	1806.00	1574.70
90000	7912.43	4153.04	2904.05	2282.63	1912.23	1667.33
95000	8352.01	4383.77	3065.38	2409.45	2018.47	1759.95
100000	8791.59	4614.49	3226.72	2536.26	2124.70	1852.58
200000	17583.18	9228.99	6453.44	5072.52	4249.41	3705.17
300000	26374.77	13843.48	9680.16	7608.78	6374.11	5557.75
400000	35166.35	18457.97	12906.87	10145.03	8498.82	7410.34
500000	43957.94	23072.46	16133.59	12681.29	10623.52	9262.92

MONTHLY PAYMENT

Necessary to amortize a loan

10%

TERM AMOUNT	7 YEARS	8 YEARS	9 YEARS	10 YEARS	11 YEARS	12 YEARS
500	8.30	7.59	7.04	6.61	6.26	5.98
600	9.96	9.10	8.45	7.93	7.51	7.17
700	11.62	10.62	9.86	9.25	8.76	8.37
800	13.28	12.14	11.26	10.57	10.02	9.56
900	14.94	13.66	12.67	11.89	11.27	10.76
1000	16.60	15.17	14.08	13.22	12.52	11.95
2000	33.20	30.35	28.16	26.43	25.04	23.90
3000	49.80	45.52	42.24	39.65	37.56	35.85
4000	66.40	60.70	56.31	52.86	50.08	47.80
5000	83.01	75.87	70.39	66.08	62.60	59.75
6000	99.61	91.04	84.47	79.29	75.12	71.70
7000	116.21	106.22	98.55	92.51	87.64	83.66
8000	132.81	121.39	112.63	105.72	100.16	95.61
9000	149.41	136.57	126.71	118.94	112.68	107.56
10000	166.01	151.74	140.79	132.15	125.20	119.51
11000	182.61	166.92	154.87	145.37	137.72	131.46
12000	199.21	182.09	168.94	158.58	150.24	143.41
13000	215.82	197.26	183.02	171.80	162.76	155.36
14000	232.42	212.44	197.10	185.01	175.28	167.31
15000	249.02	227.61	211.18	198.23	187.80	179.26
16000	265.62	242.79	225.26	211.44	200.32	191.21
17000	282.22	257.96	239.34	224.66	212.84	203.16
18000	298.82	273.13	253.42	237.87	225.36	215.11
19000	315.42	288.31	267.50	251.09	237.88	227.06
20000	332.02	303.48	281.57	264.30	250.40	239.02
21000	348.62	318.66	295.65	277.52	262.92	250.97
22000	365.23	333.83	309.73	290.73	275.44	262.92
23000	381.83	349.01	323.81	303.95	287.96	274.87
24000	398.43	364.18	337.89	317.16	300.48	286.82
25000	415.03	379.35	351.97	330.38	313.00	298.77
30000	498.04	455.22	422.36	396.45	375.60	358.52
35000	581.04	531.10	492.75	462.53	438.20	418.28
40000	664.05	606.97	563.15	528.60	500.80	478.03
45000	747.05	682.84	633.54	594.68	563.39	537.79
50000	830.06	758.71	703.93	660.75	625.99	597.54
55000	913.07	834.58	774.33	726.83	688.59	657.29
60000	996.07	910.45	844.72	792.90	751.19	717.05
65000	1079.08	986.32	915.11	858.98	813.79	776.80
70000	1162.08	1062.19	985.51	925.06	876.39	836.55
75000	1245.09	1138.06	1055.90	991.13	938.99	896.31
80000	1328.09	1213.93	1126.29	1057.21	1001.59	956.06
85000	1411.10	1289.80	1196.69	1123.28	1064.19	1015.82
90000	1494.11	1365.67	1267.08	1189.36	1126.79	1075.57
95000	1577.11	1441.55	1337.48	1255.43	1189.39	1135.32
100000	1660.12	1517.42	1407.87	1321.51	1251.99	1195.08
200000	3320.24	3034.83	2815.74	2643.01	2503.98	2390.16
300000	4980.36	4552.25	4223.61	3964.52	3755.96	3585.23
400000	6640.47	6069.67	5631.47	5286.03	5007.95	4780.31
500000	8300.59	7587.08	7039.34	6607.54	6259.94	5975.39

10%

MONTHLY PAYMENT

Necessary to amortize a loan

TERM / AMOUNT	15 YEARS	20 YEARS	25 YEARS	30 YEARS	35 YEARS	40 YEARS
500	5.37	4.83	4.54	4.39	4.30	4.25
600	6.45	5.79	5.45	5.27	5.16	5.09
700	7.52	6.76	6.36	6.14	6.02	5.94
800	8.60	7.72	7.27	7.02	6.88	6.79
900	9.67	8.69	8.18	7.90	7.74	7.64
1000	10.75	9.65	9.09	8.78	8.60	8.49
2000	21.49	19.30	18.17	17.55	17.19	16.98
3000	32.24	28.95	27.26	26.33	25.79	25.47
4000	42.98	38.60	36.35	35.10	34.39	33.97
5000	53.73	48.25	45.44	43.88	42.98	42.46
6000	64.48	57.90	54.52	52.65	51.58	50.95
7000	75.22	67.55	63.61	61.43	60.18	59.44
8000	85.97	77.20	72.70	70.21	68.77	67.93
9000	96.71	86.85	81.78	78.98	77.37	76.42
10000	107.46	96.50	90.87	87.76	85.97	84.91
11000	118.21	106.15	99.96	96.53	94.56	93.41
12000	128.95	115.80	109.04	105.31	103.16	101.90
13000	139.70	125.45	118.13	114.08	111.76	110.39
14000	150.44	135.10	127.22	122.86	120.35	118.88
15000	161.19	144.75	136.31	131.64	128.95	127.37
16000	171.94	154.40	145.39	140.41	137.55	135.86
17000	182.68	164.05	154.48	149.19	146.14	144.35
18000	193.43	173.70	163.57	157.96	154.74	152.85
19000	204.17	183.35	172.65	166.74	163.34	161.34
20000	214.92	193.00	181.74	175.51	171.93	169.83
21000	225.67	202.65	190.83	184.29	180.53	178.32
22000	236.41	212.30	199.91	193.07	189.13	186.81
23000	247.16	221.95	209.00	201.84	197.72	195.30
24000	257.91	231.61	218.09	210.62	206.32	203.80
25000	268.65	241.26	227.18	219.39	214.92	212.29
30000	322.38	289.51	272.61	263.27	257.90	254.74
35000	376.11	337.76	318.05	307.15	300.89	297.20
40000	429.84	386.01	363.48	351.03	343.87	339.66
45000	483.57	434.26	408.92	394.91	386.85	382.12
50000	537.30	482.51	454.35	438.79	429.84	424.57
55000	591.03	530.76	499.79	482.66	472.82	467.03
60000	644.76	579.01	545.22	526.54	515.80	509.49
65000	698.49	627.26	590.66	570.42	558.79	551.94
70000	752.22	675.52	636.09	614.30	601.77	594.40
75000	805.95	723.77	681.53	658.18	644.75	636.86
80000	859.68	772.02	726.96	702.06	687.74	679.32
85000	913.41	820.27	772.40	745.94	730.72	721.77
90000	967.14	868.52	817.83	789.81	773.71	764.23
95000	1020.87	916.77	863.27	833.69	816.69	806.69
100000	1074.61	965.02	908.70	877.57	859.67	849.15
200000	2149.21	1930.04	1817.40	1755.14	1719.34	1698.29
300000	3223.82	2895.06	2726.10	2632.71	2579.02	2547.44
400000	4298.42	3860.09	3634.80	3510.29	3438.69	3396.58
500000	5373.03	4825.11	4543.50	4387.86	4298.36	4245.73

MONTHLY PAYMENT

Necessary to amortize a loan

10.25%

TERM / AMOUNT	1 YEARS	2 YEARS	3 YEARS	4 YEARS	5 YEARS	6 YEARS
500	44.02	23.13	16.19	12.74	10.69	9.33
600	52.82	27.76	19.43	15.29	12.82	11.19
700	61.62	32.38	22.67	17.84	14.96	13.06
800	70.43	37.01	25.91	20.39	17.10	14.92
900	79.23	41.63	29.15	22.93	19.23	16.79
1000	88.03	46.26	32.38	25.48	21.37	18.65
2000	176.06	92.52	64.77	50.97	42.74	37.30
3000	264.10	138.78	97.15	76.45	64.11	55.96
4000	352.13	185.04	129.54	101.93	85.48	74.61
5000	440.16	231.30	161.92	127.41	106.85	93.26
6000	528.19	277.56	194.31	152.90	128.22	111.91
7000	616.23	323.82	226.69	178.38	149.59	130.57
8000	704.26	370.08	259.08	203.86	170.96	149.22
9000	792.29	416.34	291.46	229.35	192.33	167.87
10000	880.32	462.60	323.85	254.83	213.70	186.52
11000	968.35	508.86	356.23	280.31	235.07	205.17
12000	1056.39	555.12	388.62	305.79	256.44	223.83
13000	1144.42	601.39	421.00	331.28	277.81	242.48
14000	1232.45	647.65	453.39	356.76	299.18	261.13
15000	1320.48	693.91	485.77	382.24	320.55	279.78
16000	1408.52	740.17	518.16	407.73	341.92	298.43
17000	1496.55	786.43	550.54	433.21	363.29	317.09
18000	1584.58	832.69	582.92	458.69	384.66	335.74
19000	1672.61	878.95	615.31	484.17	406.04	354.39
20000	1760.64	925.21	647.69	509.66	427.41	373.04
21000	1848.68	971.47	680.08	535.14	448.78	391.70
22000	1936.71	1017.73	712.46	560.62	470.15	410.35
23000	2024.74	1063.99	744.85	586.10	491.52	429.00
24000	2112.77	1110.25	777.23	611.59	512.89	447.65
25000	2200.81	1156.51	809.62	637.07	534.26	466.30
30000	2640.97	1387.81	971.54	764.48	641.11	559.56
35000	3081.13	1619.11	1133.46	891.90	747.96	652.83
40000	3521.29	1850.42	1295.39	1019.31	854.81	746.09
45000	3961.45	2081.72	1457.31	1146.73	961.66	839.35
50000	4401.61	2313.02	1619.23	1274.14	1068.51	932.61
55000	4841.77	2544.32	1781.16	1401.55	1175.36	1025.87
60000	5281.93	2775.62	1943.08	1528.97	1282.22	1119.13
65000	5722.09	3006.93	2105.00	1656.38	1389.07	1212.39
70000	6162.25	3238.23	2266.93	1783.80	1495.92	1305.65
75000	6602.42	3469.53	2428.85	1911.21	1602.77	1398.91
80000	7042.58	3700.83	2590.78	2038.63	1709.62	1492.17
85000	7482.74	3932.13	2752.70	2166.04	1816.47	1585.43
90000	7922.90	4163.44	2914.62	2293.45	1923.32	1678.69
95000	8363.06	4394.74	3076.55	2420.87	2030.18	1771.95
100000	8803.22	4626.04	3238.47	2548.28	2137.03	1865.22
200000	17606.44	9252.08	6476.94	5096.56	4274.05	3730.43
300000	26409.66	13878.12	9715.41	7644.84	6411.08	5595.65
400000	35212.88	18504.16	12953.88	10193.13	8548.11	7460.86
500000	44016.10	23130.20	16192.34	12741.41	10685.13	9326.08

10.25% MONTHLY PAYMENT

Necessary to amortize a loan

TERM / AMOUNT	7 YEARS	8 YEARS	9 YEARS	10 YEARS	11 YEARS	12 YEARS
500	8.37	7.65	7.11	6.68	6.33	6.05
600	10.04	9.18	8.53	8.01	7.60	7.26
700	11.71	10.71	9.95	9.35	8.86	8.47
800	13.38	12.25	11.37	10.68	10.13	9.68
900	15.06	13.78	12.79	12.02	11.40	10.89
1000	16.73	15.31	14.21	13.35	12.66	12.10
2000	33.46	30.61	28.43	26.71	25.32	24.19
3000	50.19	45.92	42.64	40.06	37.99	36.29
4000	66.92	61.23	56.86	53.42	50.65	48.38
5000	83.65	76.53	71.07	66.77	63.31	60.48
6000	100.38	91.84	85.29	80.12	75.97	72.57
7000	117.11	107.15	99.50	93.48	88.63	84.67
8000	133.85	122.45	113.72	106.83	101.29	96.77
9000	150.58	137.76	127.93	120.19	113.96	108.86
10000	167.31	153.07	142.14	133.54	126.62	120.96
11000	184.04	168.37	156.36	146.89	139.28	133.05
12000	200.77	183.68	170.57	160.25	151.94	145.15
13000	217.50	198.99	184.79	173.60	164.60	157.24
14000	234.23	214.29	199.00	186.95	177.26	169.34
15000	250.96	229.60	213.22	200.31	189.93	181.43
16000	267.69	244.91	227.43	213.66	202.59	193.53
17000	284.42	260.22	241.65	227.02	215.25	205.63
18000	301.15	275.52	255.86	240.37	227.91	217.72
19000	317.88	290.83	270.07	253.72	240.57	229.82
20000	334.61	306.14	284.29	267.08	253.24	241.91
21000	351.34	321.44	298.50	280.43	265.90	254.01
22000	368.07	336.75	312.72	293.79	278.56	266.10
23000	384.80	352.06	326.93	307.14	291.22	278.20
24000	401.54	367.36	341.15	320.49	303.88	290.30
25000	418.27	382.67	355.36	333.85	316.54	302.39
30000	501.92	459.20	426.43	400.62	379.85	362.87
35000	585.57	535.74	497.50	467.39	443.16	423.35
40000	669.23	612.27	568.58	534.16	506.47	483.83
45000	752.88	688.80	639.65	600.93	569.78	544.30
50000	836.53	765.34	710.72	667.70	633.09	604.78
55000	920.19	841.87	781.79	734.46	696.40	665.26
60000	1003.84	918.41	852.87	801.23	759.71	725.74
65000	1087.49	994.94	923.94	868.00	823.01	786.22
70000	1171.15	1071.47	995.01	934.77	886.32	846.70
75000	1254.80	1148.01	1066.08	1001.54	949.63	907.17
80000	1338.45	1224.54	1137.15	1068.31	1012.94	967.65
85000	1422.10	1301.08	1208.23	1135.08	1076.25	1028.13
90000	1505.76	1377.61	1279.30	1201.85	1139.56	1088.61
95000	1589.41	1454.14	1350.37	1268.62	1202.87	1149.09
100000	1673.06	1530.68	1421.44	1335.39	1266.18	1209.57
200000	3346.13	3061.35	2842.88	2670.78	2532.35	2419.13
300000	5019.19	4592.03	4264.33	4006.17	3798.53	3628.70
400000	6692.26	6122.71	5685.77	5341.56	5064.70	4838.26
500000	8365.32	7653.38	7107.21	6676.95	6330.88	6047.83

MONTHLY PAYMENT

Necessary to amortize a loan

10.25%

TERM / AMOUNT	15 YEARS	20 YEARS	25 YEARS	30 YEARS	35 YEARS	40 YEARS
500	5.45	4.91	4.63	4.48	4.39	4.34
600	6.54	5.89	5.56	5.38	5.27	5.21
700	7.63	6.87	6.48	6.27	6.15	6.08
800	8.72	7.85	7.41	7.17	7.03	6.95
900	9.81	8.83	8.34	8.06	7.91	7.82
1000	10.90	9.82	9.26	8.96	8.79	8.69
2000	21.80	19.63	18.53	17.92	17.58	17.38
3000	32.70	29.45	27.79	26.88	26.37	26.06
4000	43.60	39.27	37.06	35.84	35.15	34.75
5000	54.50	49.08	46.32	44.81	43.94	43.44
6000	65.40	58.90	55.58	53.77	52.73	52.13
7000	76.30	68.72	64.85	62.73	61.52	60.82
8000	87.20	78.53	74.11	71.69	70.31	69.51
9000	98.10	88.35	83.37	80.65	79.10	78.19
10000	109.00	98.16	92.64	89.61	87.89	86.88
11000	119.89	107.98	101.90	98.57	96.67	95.57
12000	130.79	117.80	111.17	107.53	105.46	104.26
13000	141.69	127.61	120.43	116.49	114.25	112.95
14000	152.59	137.43	129.69	125.45	123.04	121.63
15000	163.49	147.25	138.96	134.42	131.83	130.32
16000	174.39	157.06	148.22	143.38	140.62	139.01
17000	185.29	166.88	157.49	152.34	149.41	147.70
18000	196.19	176.70	166.75	161.30	158.19	156.39
19000	207.09	186.51	176.01	170.26	166.98	165.08
20000	217.99	196.33	185.28	179.22	175.77	173.76
21000	228.89	206.15	194.54	188.18	184.56	182.45
22000	239.79	215.96	203.80	197.14	193.35	191.14
23000	250.69	225.78	213.07	206.10	202.14	199.83
24000	261.59	235.59	222.33	215.06	210.93	208.52
25000	272.49	245.41	231.60	224.03	219.71	217.20
30000	326.99	294.49	277.91	268.83	263.66	260.65
35000	381.48	343.58	324.23	313.64	307.60	304.09
40000	435.98	392.66	370.55	358.44	351.54	347.53
45000	490.48	441.74	416.87	403.25	395.49	390.97
50000	544.98	490.82	463.19	448.05	439.43	434.41
55000	599.47	539.90	509.51	492.86	483.37	477.85
60000	653.97	588.99	555.83	537.66	527.31	521.29
65000	708.47	638.07	602.15	582.47	571.26	564.73
70000	762.97	687.15	648.47	627.27	615.20	608.17
75000	817.46	736.23	694.79	672.08	659.14	651.61
80000	871.96	785.31	741.11	716.88	703.08	695.05
85000	926.46	834.40	787.43	761.69	747.03	738.50
90000	980.96	883.48	833.74	806.49	790.97	781.94
95000	1035.45	932.56	880.06	851.30	834.91	825.38
100000	1089.95	981.64	926.38	896.10	878.86	868.82
200000	2179.90	1963.29	1852.77	1792.20	1757.71	1737.64
300000	3269.85	2944.93	2779.15	2688.30	2636.57	2606.45
400000	4359.80	3926.57	3705.53	3584.41	3515.42	3475.27
500000	5449.75	4908.22	4631.92	4480.51	4394.28	4344.09

10.5%

MONTHLY PAYMENT

Necessary to amortize a loan

TERM AMOUNT	1 YEARS	2 YEARS	3 YEARS	4 YEARS	5 YEARS	6 YEARS
500	44.07	23.19	16.25	12.80	10.75	9.39
600	52.89	27.83	19.50	15.36	12.90	11.27
700	61.70	32.46	22.75	17.92	15.05	13.15
800	70.52	37.10	26.00	20.48	17.20	15.02
900	79.33	41.74	29.25	23.04	19.34	16.90
1000	88.15	46.38	32.50	25.60	21.49	18.78
2000	176.30	92.75	65.00	51.21	42.99	37.56
3000	264.45	139.13	97.51	76.81	64.48	56.34
4000	352.59	185.50	130.01	102.41	85.98	75.12
5000	440.74	231.88	162.51	128.02	107.47	93.89
6000	528.89	278.26	195.01	153.62	128.96	112.67
7000	617.04	324.63	227.52	179.22	150.46	131.45
8000	705.19	371.01	260.02	204.83	171.95	150.23
9000	793.34	417.38	292.52	230.43	193.45	169.01
10000	881.49	463.76	325.02	256.03	214.94	187.79
11000	969.63	510.14	357.53	281.64	236.43	206.57
12000	1057.78	556.51	390.03	307.24	257.93	225.35
13000	1145.93	602.89	422.53	332.84	279.42	244.13
14000	1234.08	649.26	455.03	358.45	300.91	262.91
15000	1322.23	695.64	487.54	384.05	322.41	281.68
16000	1410.38	742.02	520.04	409.65	343.90	300.46
17000	1498.53	788.39	552.54	435.26	365.40	319.24
18000	1586.67	834.77	585.04	460.86	386.89	338.02
19000	1674.82	881.14	617.55	486.46	408.38	356.80
20000	1762.97	927.52	650.05	512.07	429.88	375.58
21000	1851.12	973.90	682.55	537.67	451.37	394.36
22000	1939.27	1020.27	715.05	563.27	472.87	413.14
23000	2027.42	1066.65	747.56	588.88	494.36	431.92
24000	2115.57	1113.02	780.06	614.48	515.85	450.70
25000	2203.72	1159.40	812.56	640.08	537.35	469.47
30000	2644.46	1391.28	975.07	768.10	644.82	563.37
35000	3085.20	1623.16	1137.59	896.12	752.29	657.26
40000	3525.94	1855.04	1300.10	1024.14	859.76	751.16
45000	3966.69	2086.92	1462.61	1152.15	967.23	845.05
50000	4407.43	2318.80	1625.12	1280.17	1074.70	938.95
55000	4848.17	2550.68	1787.63	1408.19	1182.16	1032.84
60000	5288.92	2782.56	1950.15	1536.20	1289.63	1126.74
65000	5729.66	3014.44	2112.66	1664.22	1397.10	1220.63
70000	6170.40	3246.32	2275.17	1792.24	1504.57	1314.53
75000	6611.15	3478.20	2437.68	1920.25	1612.04	1408.42
80000	7051.89	3710.08	2600.20	2048.27	1719.51	1502.32
85000	7492.63	3941.96	2762.71	2176.29	1826.98	1596.21
90000	7933.37	4173.84	2925.22	2304.30	1934.45	1690.11
95000	8374.12	4405.72	3087.73	2432.32	2041.92	1784.00
100000	8814.86	4637.60	3250.24	2560.34	2149.39	1877.90
200000	17629.72	9275.21	6500.49	5120.68	4298.78	3755.79
300000	26444.58	13912.81	9750.73	7681.01	6448.17	5633.69
400000	35259.44	18550.42	13000.98	10241.35	8597.56	7511.59
500000	44074.30	23188.02	16251.22	12801.69	10746.95	9389.48

MONTHLY PAYMENT

Necessary to amortize a loan

10.5%

TERM / AMOUNT	7 YEARS	8 YEARS	9 YEARS	10 YEARS	11 YEARS	12 YEARS
500	8.43	7.72	7.18	6.75	6.40	6.12
600	10.12	9.26	8.61	8.10	7.68	7.34
700	11.80	10.81	10.05	9.45	8.96	8.57
800	13.49	12.35	11.48	10.79	10.24	9.79
900	15.17	13.90	12.92	12.14	11.52	11.02
1000	16.86	15.44	14.35	13.49	12.80	12.24
2000	33.72	30.88	28.70	26.99	25.61	24.48
3000	50.58	46.32	43.05	40.48	38.41	36.72
4000	67.44	61.76	57.40	53.97	51.22	48.97
5000	84.30	77.20	71.75	67.47	64.02	61.21
6000	101.16	92.64	86.11	80.96	76.83	73.45
7000	118.02	108.08	100.46	94.45	89.63	85.69
8000	134.89	123.52	114.81	107.95	102.44	97.93
9000	151.75	138.96	129.16	121.44	115.24	110.17
10000	168.61	154.40	143.51	134.93	128.04	122.41
11000	185.47	169.84	157.86	148.43	140.85	134.66
12000	202.33	185.28	172.21	161.92	153.65	146.90
13000	219.19	200.72	186.56	175.42	166.46	159.14
14000	236.05	216.16	200.91	188.91	179.26	171.38
15000	252.91	231.60	215.26	202.40	192.07	183.62
16000	269.77	247.04	229.61	215.90	204.87	195.86
17000	286.63	262.48	243.96	229.39	217.68	208.10
18000	303.49	277.92	258.32	242.88	230.48	220.35
19000	320.35	293.36	272.67	256.38	243.28	232.59
20000	337.21	308.80	287.02	269.87	256.09	244.83
21000	354.07	324.24	301.37	283.36	268.89	257.07
22000	370.93	339.68	315.72	296.86	281.70	269.31
23000	387.80	355.12	330.07	310.35	294.50	281.55
24000	404.66	370.56	344.42	323.84	307.31	293.79
25000	421.52	386.00	358.77	337.34	320.11	306.04
30000	505.82	463.20	430.53	404.80	384.13	367.24
35000	590.12	540.40	502.28	472.27	448.16	428.45
40000	674.43	617.60	574.03	539.74	512.18	489.66
45000	758.73	694.80	645.79	607.21	576.20	550.86
50000	843.03	772.00	717.54	674.67	640.22	612.07
55000	927.34	849.20	789.30	742.14	704.25	673.28
60000	1011.64	926.40	861.05	809.61	768.27	734.48
65000	1095.94	1003.60	932.81	877.08	832.29	795.69
70000	1180.25	1080.80	1004.56	944.54	896.31	856.90
75000	1264.55	1158.00	1076.31	1012.01	960.33	918.11
80000	1348.85	1235.20	1148.07	1079.48	1024.36	979.31
85000	1433.16	1312.40	1219.82	1146.95	1088.38	1040.52
90000	1517.46	1389.60	1291.58	1214.41	1152.40	1101.73
95000	1601.76	1466.80	1363.33	1281.88	1216.42	1162.93
100000	1686.07	1544.00	1435.09	1349.35	1280.45	1224.14
200000	3372.13	3088.00	2870.17	2698.70	2560.89	2448.28
300000	5058.20	4632.00	4305.26	4048.05	3841.34	3672.42
400000	6744.27	6176.01	5740.34	5397.40	5121.78	4896.56
500000	8430.34	7720.01	7175.43	6746.75	6402.23	6120.70

10.5% MONTHLY PAYMENT

Necessary to amortize a loan

TERM / AMOUNT	15 YEARS	20 YEARS	25 YEARS	30 YEARS	35 YEARS	40 YEARS
500	5.53	4.99	4.72	4.57	4.49	4.44
600	6.63	5.99	5.67	5.49	5.39	5.33
700	7.74	6.99	6.61	6.40	6.29	6.22
800	8.84	7.99	7.55	7.32	7.19	7.11
900	9.95	8.99	8.50	8.23	8.08	8.00
1000	11.05	9.98	9.44	9.15	8.98	8.89
2000	22.11	19.97	18.88	18.29	17.96	17.77
3000	33.16	29.95	28.33	27.44	26.94	26.66
4000	44.22	39.94	37.77	36.59	35.93	35.54
5000	55.27	49.92	47.21	45.74	44.91	44.43
6000	66.32	59.90	56.65	54.88	53.89	53.31
7000	77.38	69.89	66.09	64.03	62.87	62.20
8000	88.43	79.87	75.53	73.18	71.85	71.09
9000	99.49	89.85	84.98	82.33	80.83	79.97
10000	110.54	99.84	94.42	91.47	89.81	88.86
11000	121.59	109.82	103.86	100.62	98.79	97.74
12000	132.65	119.81	113.30	109.77	107.78	106.63
13000	143.70	129.79	122.74	118.92	116.76	115.51
14000	154.76	139.77	132.19	128.06	125.74	124.40
15000	165.81	149.76	141.63	137.21	134.72	133.29
16000	176.86	159.74	151.07	146.36	143.70	142.17
17000	187.92	169.72	160.51	155.51	152.68	151.06
18000	198.97	179.71	169.95	164.65	161.66	159.94
19000	210.03	189.69	179.39	173.80	170.65	168.83
20000	221.08	199.68	188.84	182.95	179.63	177.71
21000	232.13	209.66	198.28	192.10	188.61	186.60
22000	243.19	219.64	207.72	201.24	197.59	195.49
23000	254.24	229.63	217.16	210.39	206.57	204.37
24000	265.30	239.61	226.60	219.54	215.55	213.26
25000	276.35	249.59	236.05	228.68	224.53	222.14
30000	331.62	299.51	283.25	274.42	269.44	266.57
35000	386.89	349.43	330.46	320.16	314.35	311.00
40000	442.16	399.35	377.67	365.90	359.25	355.43
45000	497.43	449.27	424.88	411.63	404.16	399.86
50000	552.70	499.19	472.09	457.37	449.07	444.29
55000	607.97	549.11	519.30	503.11	493.97	488.71
60000	663.24	599.03	566.51	548.84	538.88	533.14
65000	718.51	648.95	613.72	594.58	583.79	577.57
70000	773.78	698.87	660.93	640.32	628.69	622.00
75000	829.05	748.78	708.14	686.05	673.60	666.43
80000	884.32	798.70	755.35	731.79	718.51	710.86
85000	939.59	848.62	802.55	777.53	763.41	755.28
90000	994.86	898.54	849.76	823.27	808.32	799.71
95000	1050.13	948.46	896.97	869.00	853.23	844.14
100000	1105.40	998.38	944.18	914.74	898.13	888.57
200000	2210.80	1996.76	1888.36	1829.48	1796.27	1777.14
300000	3316.20	2995.14	2832.55	2744.22	2694.40	2665.71
400000	4421.60	3993.52	3776.73	3658.96	3592.54	3554.28
500000	5526.99	4991.90	4720.91	4573.70	4490.67	4442.85

MONTHLY PAYMENT

Necessary to amortize a loan

10.75%

TERM AMOUNT	1 YEARS	2 YEARS	3 YEARS	4 YEARS	5 YEARS	6 YEARS
500	44.13	23.25	16.31	12.86	10.81	9.45
600	52.96	27.90	19.57	15.43	12.97	11.34
700	61.79	32.54	22.83	18.01	15.13	13.23
800	70.61	37.19	26.10	20.58	17.29	15.13
900	79.44	41.84	29.36	23.15	19.46	17.02
1000	88.27	46.49	32.62	25.72	21.62	18.91
2000	176.53	92.98	65.24	51.45	43.24	37.81
3000	264.80	139.48	97.86	77.17	64.85	56.72
4000	353.06	185.97	130.48	102.90	86.47	75.63
5000	441.33	232.46	163.10	128.62	108.09	94.53
6000	529.59	278.95	195.72	154.35	129.71	113.44
7000	617.86	325.44	228.34	180.07	151.33	132.34
8000	706.12	371.93	260.96	205.79	172.94	151.25
9000	794.39	418.43	293.58	231.52	194.56	170.16
10000	882.65	464.92	326.20	257.24	216.18	189.06
11000	970.92	511.41	358.82	282.97	237.80	207.97
12000	1059.18	557.90	391.45	308.69	259.42	226.88
13000	1147.45	604.39	424.07	334.42	281.03	245.78
14000	1235.71	650.89	456.69	360.14	302.65	264.69
15000	1323.98	697.38	489.31	385.86	324.27	283.59
16000	1412.24	743.87	521.93	411.59	345.89	302.50
17000	1500.51	790.36	554.55	437.31	367.51	321.41
18000	1588.77	836.85	587.17	463.04	389.12	340.31
19000	1677.04	883.35	619.79	488.76	410.74	359.22
20000	1765.30	929.84	652.41	514.49	432.36	378.13
21000	1853.57	976.33	685.03	540.21	453.98	397.03
22000	1941.83	1022.82	717.65	565.93	475.59	415.94
23000	2030.10	1069.31	750.27	591.66	497.21	434.84
24000	2118.36	1115.80	782.89	617.38	518.83	453.75
25000	2206.63	1162.30	815.51	643.11	540.45	472.66
30000	2647.95	1394.76	978.61	771.73	648.54	567.19
35000	3089.28	1627.21	1141.72	900.35	756.63	661.72
40000	3530.60	1859.67	1304.82	1028.97	864.72	756.25
45000	3971.93	2092.13	1467.92	1157.59	972.81	850.78
50000	4413.25	2324.59	1631.02	1286.21	1080.90	945.31
55000	4854.58	2557.05	1794.12	1414.84	1188.99	1039.85
60000	5295.91	2789.51	1957.23	1543.46	1297.08	1134.38
65000	5737.23	3021.97	2120.33	1672.08	1405.17	1228.91
70000	6178.56	3254.43	2283.43	1800.70	1513.26	1323.44
75000	6619.88	3486.89	2446.53	1929.32	1621.35	1417.97
80000	7061.21	3719.35	2609.64	2057.94	1729.44	1512.50
85000	7502.53	3951.81	2772.74	2186.56	1837.53	1607.03
90000	7943.86	4184.27	2935.84	2315.19	1945.62	1701.57
95000	8385.18	4416.73	3098.94	2443.81	2053.71	1796.10
100000	8826.51	4649.19	3262.05	2572.43	2161.80	1890.63
200000	17653.02	9298.37	6524.09	5144.86	4323.59	3781.26
300000	26479.53	13947.56	9786.14	7717.28	6485.39	5671.88
400000	35306.04	18596.74	13048.18	10289.71	8647.18	7562.51
500000	44132.54	23245.93	16310.23	12862.14	10808.98	9453.14

10.75% MONTHLY PAYMENT

Necessary to amortize a loan

TERM / AMOUNT	7 YEARS	8 YEARS	9 YEARS	10 YEARS	11 YEARS	12 YEARS
500	8.50	7.79	7.24	6.82	6.47	6.19
600	10.19	9.34	8.69	8.18	7.77	7.43
700	11.89	10.90	10.14	9.54	9.06	8.67
800	13.59	12.46	11.59	10.91	10.36	9.91
900	15.29	14.02	13.04	12.27	11.65	11.15
1000	16.99	15.57	14.49	13.63	12.95	12.39
2000	33.98	31.15	28.98	27.27	25.90	24.78
3000	50.97	46.72	43.46	40.90	38.84	37.16
4000	67.97	62.30	57.95	54.54	51.79	49.55
5000	84.96	77.87	72.44	68.17	64.74	61.94
6000	101.95	93.44	86.93	81.80	77.69	74.33
7000	118.94	109.02	101.42	95.44	90.64	86.72
8000	135.93	124.59	115.90	109.07	103.58	99.10
9000	152.92	140.17	130.39	122.70	116.53	111.49
10000	169.91	155.74	144.88	136.34	129.48	123.88
11000	186.90	171.31	159.37	149.97	142.43	136.27
12000	203.90	186.89	173.86	163.61	155.38	148.66
13000	220.89	202.46	188.34	177.24	168.32	161.04
14000	237.88	218.03	202.83	190.87	181.27	173.43
15000	254.87	233.61	217.32	204.51	194.22	185.82
16000	271.86	249.18	231.81	218.14	207.17	198.21
17000	288.85	264.76	246.30	231.78	220.12	210.60
18000	305.84	280.33	260.78	245.41	233.06	222.98
19000	322.83	295.90	275.27	259.04	246.01	235.37
20000	339.83	311.48	289.76	272.68	258.96	247.76
21000	356.82	327.05	304.25	286.31	271.91	260.15
22000	373.81	342.63	318.74	299.95	284.86	272.54
23000	390.80	358.20	333.22	313.58	297.80	284.92
24000	407.79	373.77	347.71	327.21	310.75	297.31
25000	424.78	389.35	362.20	340.85	323.70	309.70
30000	509.74	467.22	434.64	409.02	388.44	371.64
35000	594.69	545.09	507.08	477.19	453.18	433.58
40000	679.65	622.96	579.52	545.35	517.92	495.52
45000	764.61	700.83	651.96	613.52	582.66	557.46
50000	849.56	778.70	724.40	681.69	647.40	619.40
55000	934.52	856.56	796.84	749.86	712.14	681.34
60000	1019.48	934.43	869.28	818.03	776.88	743.28
65000	1104.43	1012.30	941.72	886.20	841.62	805.22
70000	1189.39	1090.17	1014.16	954.37	906.36	867.16
75000	1274.35	1168.04	1086.60	1022.54	971.10	929.10
80000	1359.30	1245.91	1159.04	1090.71	1035.84	991.04
85000	1444.26	1323.78	1231.48	1158.88	1100.58	1052.98
90000	1529.21	1401.65	1303.92	1227.05	1165.32	1114.92
95000	1614.17	1479.52	1376.36	1295.22	1230.06	1176.86
100000	1699.13	1557.39	1448.80	1363.39	1294.80	1238.80
200000	3398.25	3114.78	2897.60	2726.77	2589.60	2477.61
300000	5097.38	4672.17	4346.40	4090.16	3884.40	3716.41
400000	6796.51	6229.56	5795.20	5453.55	5179.20	4955.22
500000	8495.64	7786.95	7244.00	6816.93	6474.00	6194.02

MONTHLY PAYMENT

Necessary to amortize a loan

10.75%

TERM AMOUNT	15 YEARS	20 YEARS	25 YEARS	30 YEARS	35 YEARS	40 YEARS
500	5.60	5.08	4.81	4.67	4.59	4.54
600	6.73	6.09	5.77	5.60	5.51	5.45
700	7.85	7.11	6.73	6.53	6.42	6.36
800	8.97	8.12	7.70	7.47	7.34	7.27
900	10.09	9.14	8.66	8.40	8.26	8.18
1000	11.21	10.15	9.62	9.33	9.18	9.08
2000	22.42	20.30	19.24	18.67	18.35	18.17
3000	33.63	30.46	28.86	28.00	27.53	27.25
4000	44.84	40.61	38.48	37.34	36.70	36.34
5000	56.05	50.76	48.10	46.67	45.88	45.42
6000	67.26	60.91	57.73	56.01	55.05	54.50
7000	78.47	71.07	67.35	65.34	64.23	63.59
8000	89.68	81.22	76.97	74.68	73.40	72.67
9000	100.89	91.37	86.59	84.01	82.58	81.76
10000	112.09	101.52	96.21	93.35	91.75	90.84
11000	123.30	111.68	105.83	102.68	100.93	99.92
12000	134.51	121.83	115.45	112.02	110.10	109.01
13000	145.72	131.98	125.07	121.35	119.28	118.09
14000	156.93	142.13	134.69	130.69	128.45	127.18
15000	168.14	152.28	144.31	140.02	137.63	136.26
16000	179.35	162.44	153.93	149.36	146.80	145.34
17000	190.56	172.59	163.56	158.69	155.98	154.43
18000	201.77	182.74	173.18	168.03	165.15	163.51
19000	212.98	192.89	182.80	177.36	174.33	172.60
20000	224.19	203.05	192.42	186.70	183.50	181.68
21000	235.40	213.20	202.04	196.03	192.68	190.76
22000	246.61	223.35	211.66	205.37	201.85	199.85
23000	257.82	233.50	221.28	214.70	211.03	208.93
24000	269.03	243.65	230.90	224.04	220.20	218.02
25000	280.24	253.81	240.52	233.37	229.38	227.10
30000	336.28	304.57	288.63	280.04	275.25	272.52
35000	392.33	355.33	336.73	326.72	321.13	317.94
40000	448.38	406.09	384.84	373.39	367.00	363.36
45000	504.43	456.85	432.94	420.07	412.88	408.78
50000	560.47	507.61	481.05	466.74	458.75	454.20
55000	616.52	558.38	529.15	513.41	504.63	499.62
60000	672.57	609.14	577.26	560.09	550.50	545.04
65000	728.62	659.90	625.36	606.76	596.38	590.46
70000	784.66	710.66	673.46	653.44	642.25	635.88
75000	840.71	761.42	721.57	700.11	688.13	681.30
80000	896.76	812.18	769.67	746.79	734.00	726.72
85000	952.81	862.94	817.78	793.46	779.88	772.14
90000	1008.85	913.71	865.88	840.13	825.75	817.56
95000	1064.90	964.47	913.99	886.81	871.63	862.98
100000	1120.95	1015.23	962.09	933.48	917.50	908.40
200000	2241.90	2030.46	1924.19	1866.96	1835.01	1816.79
300000	3362.84	3045.69	2886.28	2800.44	2752.51	2725.19
400000	4483.79	4060.92	3848.37	3733.93	3670.01	3633.59
500000	5604.74	5076.14	4810.46	4667.41	4587.51	4541.99

11%

MONTHLY PAYMENT

Necessary to amortize a loan

TERM / AMOUNT	1 YEARS	2 YEARS	3 YEARS	4 YEARS	5 YEARS	6 YEARS
500	44.19	23.30	16.37	12.92	10.87	9.52
600	53.03	27.96	19.64	15.51	13.05	11.42
700	61.87	32.63	22.92	18.09	15.22	13.32
800	70.71	37.29	26.19	20.68	17.39	15.23
900	79.54	41.95	29.46	23.26	19.57	17.13
1000	88.38	46.61	32.74	25.85	21.74	19.03
2000	176.76	93.22	65.48	51.69	43.48	38.07
3000	265.14	139.82	98.22	77.54	65.23	57.10
4000	353.53	186.43	130.95	103.38	86.97	76.14
5000	441.91	233.04	163.69	129.23	108.71	95.17
6000	530.29	279.65	196.43	155.07	130.45	114.20
7000	618.67	326.25	229.17	180.92	152.20	133.24
8000	707.05	372.86	261.91	206.76	173.94	152.27
9000	795.43	419.47	294.65	232.61	195.68	171.31
10000	883.82	466.08	327.39	258.46	217.42	190.34
11000	972.20	512.69	360.13	284.30	239.17	209.37
12000	1060.58	559.29	392.86	310.15	260.91	228.41
13000	1148.96	605.90	425.60	335.99	282.65	247.44
14000	1237.34	652.51	458.34	361.84	304.39	266.48
15000	1325.72	699.12	491.08	387.68	326.14	285.51
16000	1414.11	745.73	523.82	413.53	347.88	304.55
17000	1502.49	792.33	556.56	439.37	369.62	323.58
18000	1590.87	838.94	589.30	465.22	391.36	342.61
19000	1679.25	885.55	622.04	491.06	413.11	361.65
20000	1767.63	932.16	654.77	516.91	434.85	380.68
21000	1856.01	978.76	687.51	542.76	456.59	399.72
22000	1944.40	1025.37	720.25	568.60	478.33	418.75
23000	2032.78	1071.98	752.99	594.45	500.08	437.78
24000	2121.16	1118.59	785.73	620.29	521.82	456.82
25000	2209.54	1165.20	818.47	646.14	543.56	475.85
30000	2651.45	1398.24	982.16	775.37	652.27	571.02
35000	3093.36	1631.27	1145.86	904.59	760.98	666.19
40000	3535.27	1864.31	1309.55	1033.82	869.70	761.36
45000	3977.17	2097.35	1473.24	1163.05	978.41	856.53
50000	4419.08	2330.39	1636.94	1292.28	1087.12	951.70
55000	4860.99	2563.43	1800.63	1421.50	1195.83	1046.87
60000	5302.90	2796.47	1964.32	1550.73	1304.55	1142.04
65000	5744.81	3029.51	2128.02	1679.96	1413.26	1237.22
70000	6186.72	3262.55	2291.71	1809.19	1521.97	1332.39
75000	6628.62	3495.59	2455.40	1938.41	1630.68	1427.56
80000	7070.53	3728.63	2619.10	2067.64	1739.39	1522.73
85000	7512.44	3961.67	2782.79	2196.87	1848.11	1617.90
90000	7954.35	4194.71	2946.48	2326.10	1956.82	1713.07
95000	8396.26	4427.74	3110.18	2455.32	2065.53	1808.24
100000	8838.17	4660.78	3273.87	2584.55	2174.24	1903.41
200000	17676.33	9321.57	6547.74	5169.10	4348.48	3806.82
300000	26514.50	13982.35	9821.62	7753.66	6522.73	5710.22
400000	35352.66	18643.14	13095.49	10338.21	8696.97	7613.63
500000	44190.83	23303.92	16369.36	12922.76	10871.21	9517.04

MONTHLY PAYMENT

Necessary to amortize a loan

11%

TERM AMOUNT	7 YEARS	8 YEARS	9 YEARS	10 YEARS	11 YEARS	12 YEARS
500	8.56	7.85	7.31	6.89	6.55	6.27
600	10.27	9.43	8.78	8.27	7.86	7.52
700	11.99	11.00	10.24	9.64	9.16	8.77
800	13.70	12.57	11.70	11.02	10.47	10.03
900	15.41	14.14	13.16	12.40	11.78	11.28
1000	17.12	15.71	14.63	13.78	13.09	12.54
2000	34.24	31.42	29.25	27.55	26.18	25.07
3000	51.37	47.13	43.88	41.33	39.28	37.61
4000	68.49	62.83	58.50	55.10	52.37	50.14
5000	85.61	78.54	73.13	68.88	65.46	62.68
6000	102.73	94.25	87.76	82.65	78.55	75.21
7000	119.86	109.96	102.38	96.43	91.65	87.75
8000	136.98	125.67	117.01	110.20	104.74	100.28
9000	154.10	141.38	131.63	123.98	117.83	112.82
10000	171.22	157.08	146.26	137.75	130.92	125.36
11000	188.35	172.79	160.88	151.53	144.02	137.89
12000	205.47	188.50	175.51	165.30	157.11	150.43
13000	222.59	204.21	190.14	179.08	170.20	162.96
14000	239.71	219.92	204.76	192.85	183.29	175.50
15000	256.84	235.63	219.39	206.63	196.39	188.03
16000	273.96	251.33	234.01	220.40	209.48	200.57
17000	291.08	267.04	248.64	234.18	222.57	213.10
18000	308.20	282.75	263.27	247.95	235.66	225.64
19000	325.33	298.46	277.89	261.73	248.75	238.18
20000	342.45	314.17	292.52	275.50	261.85	250.71
21000	359.57	329.88	307.14	289.28	274.94	263.25
22000	376.69	345.59	321.77	303.05	288.03	275.78
23000	393.82	361.29	336.39	316.83	301.12	288.32
24000	410.94	377.00	351.02	330.60	314.22	300.85
25000	428.06	392.71	365.65	344.38	327.31	313.39
30000	513.67	471.25	438.78	413.25	392.77	376.07
35000	599.29	549.79	511.91	482.13	458.23	438.74
40000	684.90	628.34	585.03	551.00	523.69	501.42
45000	770.51	706.88	658.16	619.88	589.16	564.10
50000	856.12	785.42	731.29	688.75	654.62	626.78
55000	941.73	863.96	804.42	757.63	720.08	689.46
60000	1027.35	942.51	877.55	826.50	785.54	752.13
65000	1112.96	1021.05	950.68	895.38	851.00	814.81
70000	1198.57	1099.59	1023.81	964.25	916.46	877.49
75000	1284.18	1178.13	1096.94	1033.13	981.93	940.17
80000	1369.79	1256.67	1170.07	1102.00	1047.39	1002.84
85000	1455.41	1335.22	1243.20	1170.88	1112.85	1065.52
90000	1541.02	1413.76	1316.33	1239.75	1178.31	1128.20
95000	1626.63	1492.30	1389.46	1308.63	1243.77	1190.88
100000	1712.24	1570.84	1462.59	1377.50	1309.23	1253.56
200000	3424.49	3141.69	2925.17	2755.00	2618.47	2507.11
300000	5136.73	4712.53	4387.76	4132.50	3927.70	3760.67
400000	6848.97	6283.37	5850.34	5510.00	5236.94	5014.22
500000	8561.22	7854.21	7312.93	6887.50	6546.17	6267.78

11%

MONTHLY PAYMENT

Necessary to amortize a loan

TERM / AMOUNT	15 YEARS	20 YEARS	25 YEARS	30 YEARS	35 YEARS	40 YEARS
500	5.68	5.16	4.90	4.76	4.68	4.64
600	6.82	6.19	5.88	5.71	5.62	5.57
700	7.96	7.23	6.86	6.67	6.56	6.50
800	9.09	8.26	7.84	7.62	7.50	7.43
900	10.23	9.29	8.82	8.57	8.43	8.35
1000	11.37	10.32	9.80	9.52	9.37	9.28
2000	22.73	20.64	19.60	19.05	18.74	18.57
3000	34.10	30.97	29.40	28.57	28.11	27.85
4000	45.46	41.29	39.20	38.09	37.48	37.13
5000	56.83	51.61	49.01	47.62	46.85	46.41
6000	68.20	61.93	58.81	57.14	56.22	55.70
7000	79.56	72.25	68.61	66.66	65.59	64.98
8000	90.93	82.58	78.41	76.19	74.96	74.26
9000	102.29	92.90	88.21	85.71	84.33	83.55
10000	113.66	103.22	98.01	95.23	93.70	92.83
11000	125.03	113.54	107.81	104.76	103.07	102.11
12000	136.39	123.86	117.61	114.28	112.43	111.40
13000	147.76	134.18	127.41	123.80	121.80	120.68
14000	159.12	144.51	137.22	133.33	131.17	129.96
15000	170.49	154.83	147.02	142.85	140.54	139.24
16000	181.86	165.15	156.82	152.37	149.91	148.53
17000	193.22	175.47	166.62	161.89	159.28	157.81
18000	204.59	185.79	176.42	171.42	168.65	167.09
19000	215.95	196.12	186.22	180.94	178.02	176.38
20000	227.32	206.44	196.02	190.46	187.39	185.66
21000	238.69	216.76	205.82	199.99	196.76	194.94
22000	250.05	227.08	215.62	209.51	206.13	204.22
23000	261.42	237.40	225.43	219.03	215.50	213.51
24000	272.78	247.73	235.23	228.56	224.87	222.79
25000	284.15	258.05	245.03	238.08	234.24	232.07
30000	340.98	309.66	294.03	285.70	281.09	278.49
35000	397.81	361.27	343.04	333.31	327.94	324.90
40000	454.64	412.88	392.05	380.93	374.78	371.32
45000	511.47	464.48	441.05	428.55	421.63	417.73
50000	568.30	516.09	490.06	476.16	468.48	464.15
55000	625.13	567.70	539.06	523.78	515.33	510.56
60000	681.96	619.31	588.07	571.39	562.17	556.98
65000	738.79	670.92	637.07	619.01	609.02	603.39
70000	795.62	722.53	686.08	666.63	655.87	649.81
75000	852.45	774.14	735.08	714.24	702.72	696.22
80000	909.28	825.75	784.09	761.86	749.57	742.64
85000	966.11	877.36	833.10	809.47	796.41	789.05
90000	1022.94	928.97	882.10	857.09	843.26	835.46
95000	1079.77	980.58	931.11	904.71	890.11	881.88
100000	1136.60	1032.19	980.11	952.32	936.96	928.29
200000	2273.19	2064.38	1960.23	1904.65	1873.92	1856.59
300000	3409.79	3096.57	2940.34	2856.97	2810.87	2784.88
400000	4546.39	4128.75	3920.45	3809.29	3747.83	3713.18
500000	5682.98	5160.94	4900.57	4761.62	4684.79	4641.47

MONTHLY PAYMENT

Necessary to amortize a loan

11.25%

TERM / AMOUNT	1 YEARS	2 YEARS	3 YEARS	4 YEARS	5 YEARS	6 YEARS
500	44.25	23.36	16.43	12.98	10.93	9.58
600	53.10	28.03	19.71	15.58	13.12	11.50
700	61.95	32.71	23.00	18.18	15.31	13.41
800	70.80	37.38	26.29	20.77	17.49	15.33
900	79.65	42.05	29.57	23.37	19.68	17.25
1000	88.50	46.72	32.86	25.97	21.87	19.16
2000	177.00	93.45	65.71	51.93	43.73	38.32
3000	265.49	140.17	98.57	77.90	65.60	57.49
4000	353.99	186.90	131.43	103.87	87.47	76.65
5000	442.49	233.62	164.29	129.84	109.34	95.81
6000	530.99	280.34	197.14	155.80	131.20	114.97
7000	619.49	327.07	230.00	181.77	153.07	134.14
8000	707.99	373.79	262.86	207.74	174.94	153.30
9000	796.48	420.52	295.72	233.70	196.81	172.46
10000	884.98	467.24	328.57	259.67	218.67	191.62
11000	973.48	513.96	361.43	285.64	240.54	210.79
12000	1061.98	560.69	394.29	311.61	262.41	229.95
13000	1150.48	607.41	427.14	337.57	284.28	249.11
14000	1238.98	654.14	460.00	363.54	306.14	268.27
15000	1327.47	700.86	492.86	389.51	328.01	287.44
16000	1415.97	747.58	525.72	415.47	349.88	306.60
17000	1504.47	794.31	558.57	441.44	371.74	325.76
18000	1592.97	841.03	591.43	467.41	393.61	344.92
19000	1681.47	887.76	624.29	493.37	415.48	364.09
20000	1769.97	934.48	657.14	519.34	437.35	383.25
21000	1858.46	981.20	690.00	545.31	459.21	402.41
22000	1946.96	1027.93	722.86	571.28	481.08	421.57
23000	2035.46	1074.65	755.72	597.24	502.95	440.73
24000	2123.96	1121.38	788.57	623.21	524.82	459.90
25000	2212.46	1168.10	821.43	649.18	546.68	479.06
30000	2654.95	1401.72	985.72	779.01	656.02	574.87
35000	3097.44	1635.34	1150.00	908.85	765.36	670.68
40000	3539.93	1868.96	1314.29	1038.68	874.69	766.49
45000	3982.42	2102.58	1478.58	1168.52	984.03	862.31
50000	4424.92	2336.20	1642.86	1298.35	1093.37	958.12
55000	4867.41	2569.82	1807.15	1428.19	1202.70	1053.93
60000	5309.90	2803.44	1971.43	1558.03	1312.04	1149.74
65000	5752.39	3037.06	2135.72	1687.86	1421.38	1245.55
70000	6194.88	3270.68	2300.01	1817.70	1530.71	1341.37
75000	6637.37	3504.30	2464.29	1947.53	1640.05	1437.18
80000	7079.87	3737.92	2628.58	2077.37	1749.38	1532.99
85000	7522.36	3971.54	2792.86	2207.20	1858.72	1628.80
90000	7964.85	4205.16	2957.15	2337.04	1968.06	1724.61
95000	8407.34	4438.78	3121.44	2466.87	2077.39	1820.43
100000	8849.83	4672.40	3285.72	2596.71	2186.73	1916.24
200000	17699.66	9344.80	6571.45	5193.42	4373.46	3832.47
300000	26549.49	14017.20	9857.17	7790.13	6560.19	5748.71
400000	35399.33	18689.60	13142.89	10386.84	8746.92	7664.95
500000	44249.16	23362.00	16428.62	12983.55	10933.65	9581.19

11.25% MONTHLY PAYMENT

Necessary to amortize a loan

TERM / AMOUNT	7 YEARS	8 YEARS	9 YEARS	10 YEARS	11 YEARS	12 YEARS
500	8.63	7.92	7.38	6.96	6.62	6.34
600	10.35	9.51	8.86	8.35	7.94	7.61
700	12.08	11.09	10.34	9.74	9.27	8.88
800	13.80	12.67	11.81	11.13	10.59	10.15
900	15.53	14.26	13.29	12.53	11.91	11.42
1000	17.25	15.84	14.76	13.92	13.24	12.68
2000	34.51	31.69	29.53	27.83	26.48	25.37
3000	51.76	47.53	44.29	41.75	39.71	38.05
4000	69.02	63.37	59.06	55.67	52.95	50.74
5000	86.27	79.22	73.82	69.58	66.19	63.42
6000	103.53	95.06	88.59	83.50	79.43	76.10
7000	120.78	110.91	103.35	97.42	92.66	88.79
8000	138.03	126.75	118.12	111.34	105.90	101.47
9000	155.29	142.59	132.88	125.25	119.14	114.16
10000	172.54	158.44	147.64	139.17	132.38	126.84
11000	189.80	174.28	162.41	153.09	145.61	139.52
12000	207.05	190.12	177.17	167.00	158.85	152.21
13000	224.30	205.97	191.94	180.92	172.09	164.89
14000	241.56	221.81	206.70	194.84	185.33	177.58
15000	258.81	237.65	221.47	208.75	198.56	190.26
16000	276.07	253.50	236.23	222.67	211.80	202.94
17000	293.32	269.34	251.00	236.59	225.04	215.63
18000	310.58	285.18	265.76	250.50	238.28	228.31
19000	327.83	301.03	280.52	264.42	251.51	240.99
20000	345.08	316.87	295.29	278.34	264.75	253.68
21000	362.34	332.72	310.05	292.25	277.99	266.36
22000	379.59	348.56	324.82	306.17	291.23	279.05
23000	396.85	364.40	339.58	320.09	304.46	291.73
24000	414.10	380.25	354.35	334.01	317.70	304.41
25000	431.35	396.09	369.11	347.92	330.94	317.10
30000	517.63	475.31	442.93	417.51	397.13	380.52
35000	603.90	554.53	516.75	487.09	463.31	443.94
40000	690.17	633.74	590.58	556.68	529.50	507.36
45000	776.44	712.96	664.40	626.26	595.69	570.78
50000	862.71	792.18	738.22	695.84	661.88	634.20
55000	948.98	871.40	812.04	765.43	728.06	697.62
60000	1035.25	950.62	885.86	835.01	794.25	761.04
65000	1121.52	1029.83	959.69	904.60	860.44	824.46
70000	1207.79	1109.05	1033.51	974.18	926.63	887.88
75000	1294.06	1188.27	1107.33	1043.77	992.81	951.29
80000	1380.33	1267.49	1181.15	1113.35	1059.00	1014.71
85000	1466.60	1346.70	1254.98	1182.94	1125.19	1078.13
90000	1552.88	1425.92	1328.80	1252.52	1191.38	1141.55
95000	1639.15	1505.14	1402.62	1322.10	1257.56	1204.97
100000	1725.42	1584.36	1476.44	1391.69	1323.75	1268.39
200000	3450.83	3168.72	2952.88	2783.38	2647.50	2536.79
300000	5176.25	4753.08	4429.32	4175.07	3971.26	3805.18
400000	6901.67	6337.43	5905.76	5566.76	5295.01	5073.57
500000	8627.08	7921.79	7382.21	6958.45	6618.76	6341.96

MONTHLY PAYMENT

Necessary to amortize a loan

11.25%

TERM / AMOUNT	15 YEARS	20 YEARS	25 YEARS	30 YEARS	35 YEARS	40 YEARS
500	5.76	5.25	4.99	4.86	4.78	4.74
600	6.91	6.30	5.99	5.83	5.74	5.69
700	8.07	7.34	6.99	6.80	6.70	6.64
800	9.22	8.39	7.99	7.77	7.65	7.59
900	10.37	9.44	8.98	8.74	8.61	8.53
1000	11.52	10.49	9.98	9.71	9.56	9.48
2000	23.05	20.99	19.96	19.43	19.13	18.97
3000	34.57	31.48	29.95	29.14	28.69	28.45
4000	46.09	41.97	39.93	38.85	38.26	37.93
5000	57.62	52.46	49.91	48.56	47.82	47.41
6000	69.14	62.96	59.89	58.28	57.39	56.90
7000	80.66	73.45	69.88	67.99	66.95	66.38
8000	92.19	83.94	79.86	77.70	76.52	75.86
9000	103.71	94.43	89.84	87.41	86.08	85.34
10000	115.23	104.93	99.82	97.13	95.65	94.83
11000	126.76	115.42	109.81	106.84	105.21	104.31
12000	138.28	125.91	119.79	116.55	114.78	113.79
13000	149.80	136.40	129.77	126.26	124.34	123.27
14000	161.33	146.90	139.75	135.98	133.91	132.76
15000	172.85	157.39	149.74	145.69	143.47	142.24
16000	184.38	167.88	159.72	155.40	153.04	151.72
17000	195.90	178.37	169.70	165.11	162.60	161.20
18000	207.42	188.87	179.68	174.83	172.17	170.69
19000	218.95	199.36	189.67	184.54	181.73	180.17
20000	230.47	209.85	199.65	194.25	191.30	189.65
21000	241.99	220.34	209.63	203.96	200.86	199.13
22000	253.52	230.84	219.61	213.68	210.43	208.62
23000	265.04	241.33	229.60	223.39	219.99	218.10
24000	276.56	251.82	239.58	233.10	229.56	227.58
25000	288.09	262.31	249.56	242.82	239.12	237.06
30000	345.70	314.78	299.47	291.38	286.95	284.48
35000	403.32	367.24	349.38	339.94	334.77	331.89
40000	460.94	419.70	399.30	388.50	382.60	379.30
45000	518.56	472.17	449.21	437.07	430.42	426.72
50000	576.17	524.63	499.12	485.63	478.25	474.13
55000	633.79	577.09	549.03	534.19	526.07	521.54
60000	691.41	629.55	598.94	582.76	573.90	568.95
65000	749.02	682.02	648.86	631.32	621.72	616.37
70000	806.64	734.48	698.77	679.88	669.55	663.78
75000	864.26	786.94	748.68	728.45	717.37	711.19
80000	921.88	839.40	798.59	777.01	765.20	758.61
85000	979.49	891.87	848.50	825.57	813.02	806.02
90000	1037.11	944.33	898.42	874.14	860.84	853.43
95000	1094.73	996.79	948.33	922.70	908.67	900.84
100000	1152.34	1049.26	998.24	971.26	956.49	948.26
200000	2304.69	2098.51	1996.48	1942.52	1912.99	1896.51
300000	3457.03	3147.77	2994.72	2913.78	2869.48	2844.77
400000	4609.38	4197.02	3992.96	3885.05	3825.98	3793.03
500000	5761.72	5246.28	4991.20	4856.31	4782.47	4741.29

11.5%

MONTHLY PAYMENT

Necessary to amortize a loan

TERM / AMOUNT	1 YEARS	2 YEARS	3 YEARS	4 YEARS	5 YEARS	6 YEARS
500	44.31	23.42	16.49	13.04	11.00	9.65
600	53.17	28.10	19.79	15.65	13.20	11.57
700	62.03	32.79	23.08	18.26	15.39	13.50
800	70.89	37.47	26.38	20.87	17.59	15.43
900	79.75	42.16	29.68	23.48	19.79	17.36
1000	88.62	46.84	32.98	26.09	21.99	19.29
2000	177.23	93.68	65.95	52.18	43.99	38.58
3000	265.85	140.52	98.93	78.27	65.98	57.87
4000	354.46	187.36	131.90	104.36	87.97	77.16
5000	443.08	234.20	164.88	130.45	109.96	96.46
6000	531.69	281.04	197.86	156.53	131.96	115.75
7000	620.31	327.88	230.83	182.62	153.95	135.04
8000	708.92	374.72	263.81	208.71	175.94	154.33
9000	797.54	421.56	296.78	234.80	197.93	173.62
10000	886.15	468.40	329.76	260.89	219.93	192.91
11000	974.77	515.24	362.74	286.98	241.92	212.20
12000	1063.38	562.08	395.71	313.07	263.91	231.49
13000	1152.00	608.92	428.69	339.16	285.90	250.79
14000	1240.61	655.76	461.66	365.25	307.90	270.08
15000	1329.23	702.60	494.64	391.34	329.89	289.37
16000	1417.84	749.45	527.62	417.42	351.88	308.66
17000	1506.46	796.29	560.59	443.51	373.87	327.95
18000	1595.07	843.13	593.57	469.60	395.87	347.24
19000	1683.69	889.97	626.54	495.69	417.86	366.53
20000	1772.30	936.81	659.52	521.78	439.85	385.82
21000	1860.92	983.65	692.50	547.87	461.84	405.11
22000	1949.53	1030.49	725.47	573.96	483.84	424.41
23000	2038.15	1077.33	758.45	600.05	505.83	443.70
24000	2126.76	1124.17	791.42	626.14	527.82	462.99
25000	2215.38	1171.01	824.40	652.23	549.82	482.28
30000	2658.45	1405.21	989.28	782.67	659.78	578.73
35000	3101.53	1639.41	1154.16	913.12	769.74	675.19
40000	3544.60	1873.61	1319.04	1043.56	879.70	771.65
45000	3987.68	2107.81	1483.92	1174.01	989.67	868.10
50000	4430.75	2342.02	1648.80	1304.45	1099.63	964.56
55000	4873.83	2576.22	1813.68	1434.90	1209.59	1061.01
60000	5316.90	2810.42	1978.56	1565.34	1319.56	1157.47
65000	5759.98	3044.62	2143.44	1695.79	1429.52	1253.93
70000	6203.05	3278.82	2308.32	1826.23	1539.48	1350.38
75000	6646.13	3513.02	2473.20	1956.68	1649.45	1446.84
80000	7089.20	3747.23	2638.08	2087.12	1759.41	1543.29
85000	7532.28	3981.43	2802.96	2217.57	1869.37	1639.75
90000	7975.35	4215.63	2967.84	2348.01	1979.33	1736.20
95000	8418.43	4449.83	3132.72	2478.46	2089.30	1832.66
100000	8861.51	4684.03	3297.60	2608.90	2199.26	1929.12
200000	17723.01	9368.06	6595.20	5217.80	4398.52	3858.23
300000	26584.52	14052.09	9892.80	7826.70	6597.78	5787.35
400000	35446.02	18736.13	13190.40	10435.60	8797.04	7716.46
500000	44307.53	23420.16	16488.00	13044.50	10996.30	9645.58

MONTHLY PAYMENT

Necessary to amortize a loan

11.5%

TERM / AMOUNT	7 YEARS	8 YEARS	9 YEARS	10 YEARS	11 YEARS	12 YEARS
500	8.69	7.99	7.45	7.03	6.69	6.42
600	10.43	9.59	8.94	8.44	8.03	7.70
700	12.17	11.19	10.43	9.84	9.37	8.98
800	13.91	12.78	11.92	11.25	10.71	10.27
900	15.65	14.38	13.41	12.65	12.05	11.55
1000	17.39	15.98	14.90	14.06	13.38	12.83
2000	34.77	31.96	29.81	28.12	26.77	25.67
3000	52.16	47.94	44.71	42.18	40.15	38.50
4000	69.55	63.92	59.61	56.24	53.53	51.33
5000	86.93	79.90	74.52	70.30	66.92	64.17
6000	104.32	95.88	89.42	84.36	80.30	77.00
7000	121.71	111.86	104.33	98.42	93.68	89.83
8000	139.09	127.83	119.23	112.48	107.07	102.67
9000	156.48	143.81	134.13	126.54	120.45	115.50
10000	173.86	159.79	149.04	140.60	133.84	128.33
11000	191.25	175.77	163.94	154.65	147.22	141.16
12000	208.64	191.75	178.84	168.71	160.60	154.00
13000	226.02	207.73	193.75	182.77	173.99	166.83
14000	243.41	223.71	208.65	196.83	187.37	179.66
15000	260.80	239.69	223.55	210.89	200.75	192.50
16000	278.18	255.67	238.46	224.95	214.14	205.33
17000	295.57	271.65	253.36	239.01	227.52	218.16
18000	312.96	287.63	268.27	253.07	240.90	231.00
19000	330.34	303.61	283.17	267.13	254.29	243.83
20000	347.73	319.59	298.07	281.19	267.67	256.66
21000	365.12	335.57	312.98	295.25	281.05	269.50
22000	382.50	351.55	327.88	309.31	294.44	282.33
23000	399.89	367.53	342.78	323.37	307.82	295.16
24000	417.28	383.50	357.69	337.43	321.20	308.00
25000	434.66	399.48	372.59	351.49	334.59	320.83
30000	521.59	479.38	447.11	421.79	401.51	384.99
35000	608.53	559.28	521.63	492.08	468.42	449.16
40000	695.46	639.17	596.15	562.38	535.34	513.33
45000	782.39	719.07	670.66	632.68	602.26	577.49
50000	869.32	798.97	745.18	702.98	669.18	641.66
55000	956.26	878.87	819.70	773.27	736.09	705.82
60000	1043.19	958.76	894.22	843.57	803.01	769.99
65000	1130.12	1038.66	968.74	913.87	869.93	834.16
70000	1217.05	1118.56	1043.26	984.17	936.85	898.32
75000	1303.98	1198.45	1117.77	1054.47	1003.76	962.49
80000	1390.92	1278.35	1192.29	1124.76	1070.68	1026.65
85000	1477.85	1358.25	1266.81	1195.06	1137.60	1090.82
90000	1564.78	1438.14	1341.33	1265.36	1204.52	1154.98
95000	1651.71	1518.04	1415.85	1335.66	1271.43	1219.15
100000	1738.65	1597.94	1490.37	1405.95	1338.35	1283.32
200000	3477.29	3195.87	2980.73	2811.91	2676.70	2566.63
300000	5215.94	4793.81	4471.10	4217.86	4015.05	3849.95
400000	6954.58	6391.75	5961.46	5623.82	5353.40	5133.27
500000	8693.23	7989.69	7451.83	7029.77	6691.75	6416.58

11.5%

MONTHLY PAYMENT

Necessary to amortize a loan

TERM / AMOUNT	15 YEARS	20 YEARS	25 YEARS	30 YEARS	35 YEARS	40 YEARS
500	5.84	5.33	5.08	4.95	4.88	4.84
600	7.01	6.40	6.10	5.94	5.86	5.81
700	8.18	7.47	7.12	6.93	6.83	6.78
800	9.35	8.53	8.13	7.92	7.81	7.75
900	10.51	9.60	9.15	8.91	8.78	8.71
1000	11.68	10.66	10.16	9.90	9.76	9.68
2000	23.36	21.33	20.33	19.81	19.52	19.37
3000	35.05	31.99	30.49	29.71	29.28	29.05
4000	46.73	42.66	40.66	39.61	39.04	38.73
5000	58.41	53.32	50.82	49.51	48.81	48.41
6000	70.09	63.99	60.99	59.42	58.57	58.10
7000	81.77	74.65	71.15	69.32	68.33	67.78
8000	93.46	85.31	81.32	79.22	78.09	77.46
9000	105.14	95.98	91.48	89.13	87.85	87.15
10000	116.82	106.64	101.65	99.03	97.61	96.83
11000	128.50	117.31	111.81	108.93	107.37	106.51
12000	140.18	127.97	121.98	118.83	117.13	116.19
13000	151.86	138.64	132.14	128.74	126.89	125.88
14000	163.55	149.30	142.31	138.64	136.66	135.56
15000	175.23	159.96	152.47	148.54	146.42	145.24
16000	186.91	170.63	162.64	158.45	156.18	154.93
17000	198.59	181.29	172.80	168.35	165.94	164.61
18000	210.27	191.96	182.96	178.25	175.70	174.29
19000	221.96	202.62	193.13	188.16	185.46	183.97
20000	233.64	213.29	203.29	198.06	195.22	193.66
21000	245.32	223.95	213.46	207.96	204.98	203.34
22000	257.00	234.61	223.62	217.86	214.74	213.02
23000	268.68	245.28	233.79	227.77	224.50	222.70
24000	280.37	255.94	243.95	237.67	234.27	232.39
25000	292.05	266.61	254.12	247.57	244.03	242.07
30000	350.46	319.93	304.94	297.09	292.83	290.48
35000	408.87	373.25	355.76	346.60	341.64	338.90
40000	467.28	426.57	406.59	396.12	390.44	387.31
45000	525.69	479.89	457.41	445.63	439.25	435.73
50000	584.09	533.21	508.23	495.15	488.05	484.14
55000	642.50	586.54	559.06	544.66	536.86	532.56
60000	700.91	639.86	609.88	594.17	585.66	580.97
65000	759.32	693.18	660.70	643.69	634.47	629.38
70000	817.73	746.50	711.53	693.20	683.28	677.80
75000	876.14	799.82	762.35	742.72	732.08	726.21
80000	934.55	853.14	813.18	792.23	780.89	774.63
85000	992.96	906.47	864.00	841.75	829.69	823.04
90000	1051.37	959.79	914.82	891.26	878.50	871.45
95000	1109.78	1013.11	965.65	940.78	927.30	919.87
100000	1168.19	1066.43	1016.47	990.29	976.11	968.28
200000	2336.38	2132.86	2032.94	1980.58	1952.21	1936.56
300000	3504.57	3199.29	3049.41	2970.87	2928.32	2904.85
400000	4672.76	4265.72	4065.88	3961.17	3904.43	3873.13
500000	5840.95	5332.15	5082.34	4951.46	4880.54	4841.41

MONTHLY PAYMENT

Necessary to amortize a loan

11.75%

TERM / AMOUNT	1 YEARS	2 YEARS	3 YEARS	4 YEARS	5 YEARS	6 YEARS
500	44.37	23.48	16.55	13.11	11.06	9.71
600	53.24	28.17	19.86	15.73	13.27	11.65
700	62.11	32.87	23.17	18.35	15.48	13.59
800	70.99	37.57	26.48	20.97	17.69	15.54
900	79.86	42.26	29.79	23.59	19.91	17.48
1000	88.73	46.96	33.10	26.21	22.12	19.42
2000	177.46	93.91	66.19	52.42	44.24	38.84
3000	266.20	140.87	99.29	78.63	66.35	58.26
4000	354.93	187.83	132.38	104.85	88.47	77.68
5000	443.66	234.78	165.48	131.06	110.59	97.10
6000	532.39	281.74	198.57	157.27	132.71	116.52
7000	621.12	328.70	231.67	183.48	154.83	135.94
8000	709.86	375.65	264.76	209.69	176.95	155.36
9000	798.59	422.61	297.86	235.90	199.06	174.78
10000	887.32	469.57	330.95	262.11	221.18	194.20
11000	976.05	516.52	364.05	288.32	243.30	213.62
12000	1064.78	563.48	397.14	314.54	265.42	233.05
13000	1153.51	610.44	430.24	340.75	287.54	252.47
14000	1242.25	657.40	463.33	366.96	309.66	271.89
15000	1330.98	704.35	496.43	393.17	331.77	291.31
16000	1419.71	751.31	529.52	419.38	353.89	310.73
17000	1508.44	798.27	562.62	445.59	376.01	330.15
18000	1597.17	845.22	595.71	471.80	398.13	349.57
19000	1685.91	892.18	628.81	498.01	420.25	368.99
20000	1774.64	939.14	661.90	524.23	442.37	388.41
21000	1863.37	986.09	695.00	550.44	464.48	407.83
22000	1952.10	1033.05	728.09	576.65	486.60	427.25
23000	2040.83	1080.01	761.19	602.86	508.72	446.67
24000	2129.57	1126.96	794.28	629.07	530.84	466.09
25000	2218.30	1173.92	827.38	655.28	552.96	485.51
30000	2661.96	1408.70	992.85	786.34	663.55	582.61
35000	3105.62	1643.49	1158.33	917.39	774.14	679.72
40000	3549.28	1878.27	1323.80	1048.45	884.73	776.82
45000	3992.93	2113.06	1489.28	1179.51	995.32	873.92
50000	4436.59	2347.84	1654.75	1310.56	1105.92	971.02
55000	4880.25	2582.62	1820.23	1441.62	1216.51	1068.12
60000	5323.91	2817.41	1985.70	1572.68	1327.10	1165.23
65000	5767.57	3052.19	2151.18	1703.73	1437.69	1262.33
70000	6211.23	3286.98	2316.65	1834.79	1548.28	1359.43
75000	6654.89	3521.76	2482.13	1965.84	1658.87	1456.53
80000	7098.55	3756.54	2647.60	2096.90	1769.47	1553.63
85000	7542.21	3991.33	2813.08	2227.96	1880.06	1650.74
90000	7985.87	4226.11	2978.55	2359.01	1990.65	1747.84
95000	8429.53	4460.90	3144.03	2490.07	2101.24	1844.94
100000	8873.19	4695.68	3309.50	2621.13	2211.83	1942.04
200000	17746.38	9391.36	6619.01	5242.25	4423.66	3884.09
300000	26619.56	14087.04	9928.51	7863.38	6635.50	5826.13
400000	35492.75	18782.72	13238.01	10484.50	8847.33	7768.17
500000	44365.94	23478.40	16547.52	13105.63	11059.16	9710.22

11.75%

MONTHLY PAYMENT

Necessary to amortize a loan

TERM / AMOUNT	7 YEARS	8 YEARS	9 YEARS	10 YEARS	11 YEARS	12 YEARS
500	8.76	8.06	7.52	7.10	6.77	6.49
600	10.51	9.67	9.03	8.52	8.12	7.79
700	12.26	11.28	10.53	9.94	9.47	9.09
800	14.02	12.89	12.03	11.36	10.82	10.39
900	15.77	14.50	13.54	12.78	12.18	11.68
1000	17.52	16.12	15.04	14.20	13.53	12.98
2000	35.04	32.23	30.09	28.41	27.06	25.97
3000	52.56	48.35	45.13	42.61	40.59	38.95
4000	70.08	64.46	60.17	56.81	54.12	51.93
5000	87.60	80.58	75.22	71.01	67.65	64.92
6000	105.12	96.69	90.26	85.22	81.18	77.90
7000	122.64	112.81	105.31	99.42	94.71	90.88
8000	140.15	128.93	120.35	113.62	108.24	103.87
9000	157.67	145.04	135.39	127.83	121.77	116.85
10000	175.19	161.16	150.44	142.03	135.30	129.83
11000	192.71	177.27	165.48	156.23	148.83	142.82
12000	210.23	193.39	180.52	170.44	162.36	155.80
13000	227.75	209.51	195.57	184.64	175.89	168.78
14000	245.27	225.62	210.61	198.84	189.42	181.77
15000	262.79	241.74	225.65	213.04	202.95	194.75
16000	280.31	257.85	240.70	227.25	216.48	207.73
17000	297.83	273.97	255.74	241.45	230.01	220.72
18000	315.35	290.08	270.78	255.65	243.55	233.70
19000	332.87	306.20	285.83	269.86	257.08	246.68
20000	350.39	322.32	300.87	284.06	270.61	259.67
21000	367.91	338.43	315.92	298.26	284.14	272.65
22000	385.42	354.55	330.96	312.46	297.67	285.63
23000	402.94	370.66	346.00	326.67	311.20	298.61
24000	420.46	386.78	361.05	340.87	324.73	311.60
25000	437.98	402.89	376.09	355.07	338.26	324.58
30000	525.58	483.47	451.31	426.09	405.91	389.50
35000	613.18	564.05	526.53	497.10	473.56	454.41
40000	700.77	644.63	601.74	568.12	541.21	519.33
45000	788.37	725.21	676.96	639.13	608.86	584.25
50000	875.97	805.79	752.18	710.15	676.51	649.16
55000	963.56	886.37	827.40	781.16	744.17	714.08
60000	1051.16	966.95	902.62	852.18	811.82	779.00
65000	1138.76	1047.53	977.83	923.19	879.47	843.91
70000	1226.35	1128.11	1053.05	994.21	947.12	908.83
75000	1313.95	1208.68	1128.27	1065.22	1014.77	973.74
80000	1401.55	1289.26	1203.49	1136.24	1082.42	1038.66
85000	1489.14	1369.84	1278.71	1207.25	1150.07	1103.58
90000	1576.74	1450.42	1353.92	1278.27	1217.73	1168.49
95000	1664.34	1531.00	1429.14	1349.28	1285.38	1233.41
100000	1751.93	1611.58	1504.36	1420.29	1353.03	1298.33
200000	3503.86	3223.16	3008.72	2840.59	2706.06	2596.65
300000	5255.80	4834.74	4513.08	4260.88	4059.09	3894.98
400000	7007.73	6446.32	6017.44	5681.18	5412.12	5193.30
500000	8759.66	8057.90	7521.80	7101.47	6765.15	6491.63

MONTHLY PAYMENT

Necessary to amortize a loan

11.75%

TERM / AMOUNT	15 YEARS	20 YEARS	25 YEARS	30 YEARS	35 YEARS	40 YEARS
500	5.92	5.42	5.17	5.05	4.98	4.94
600	7.10	6.50	6.21	6.06	5.97	5.93
700	8.29	7.59	7.24	7.07	6.97	6.92
800	9.47	8.67	8.28	8.08	7.97	7.91
900	10.66	9.75	9.31	9.08	8.96	8.90
1000	11.84	10.84	10.35	10.09	9.96	9.88
2000	23.68	21.67	20.70	20.19	19.92	19.77
3000	35.52	32.51	31.04	30.28	29.87	29.65
4000	47.37	43.35	41.39	40.38	39.83	39.53
5000	59.21	54.19	51.74	50.47	49.79	49.42
6000	71.05	65.02	62.09	60.56	59.75	59.30
7000	82.89	75.86	72.44	70.66	69.71	69.19
8000	94.73	86.70	82.78	80.75	79.66	79.07
9000	106.57	97.53	93.13	90.85	89.62	88.95
10000	118.41	108.37	103.48	100.94	99.58	98.84
11000	130.25	119.21	113.83	111.04	109.54	108.72
12000	142.10	130.04	124.18	121.13	119.50	118.60
13000	153.94	140.88	134.52	131.22	129.45	128.49
14000	165.78	151.72	144.87	141.32	139.41	138.37
15000	177.62	162.56	155.22	151.41	149.37	148.25
16000	189.46	173.39	165.57	161.51	159.33	158.14
17000	201.30	184.23	175.92	171.60	169.28	168.02
18000	213.14	195.07	186.26	181.69	179.24	177.91
19000	224.98	205.90	196.61	191.79	189.20	187.79
20000	236.83	216.74	206.96	201.88	199.16	197.67
21000	248.67	227.58	217.31	211.98	209.12	207.56
22000	260.51	238.42	227.66	222.07	219.07	217.44
23000	272.35	249.25	238.00	232.16	229.03	227.32
24000	284.19	260.09	248.35	242.26	238.99	237.21
25000	296.03	270.93	258.70	252.35	248.95	247.09
30000	355.24	325.11	310.44	302.82	298.74	296.51
35000	414.45	379.30	362.18	353.29	348.53	345.93
40000	473.65	433.48	413.92	403.76	398.32	395.35
45000	532.86	487.67	465.66	454.23	448.11	444.76
50000	592.07	541.85	517.40	504.70	497.90	494.18
55000	651.27	596.04	569.14	555.18	547.69	543.60
60000	710.48	650.22	620.88	605.65	597.48	593.02
65000	769.69	704.41	672.62	656.12	647.27	642.44
70000	828.89	758.59	724.36	706.59	697.06	691.85
75000	888.10	812.78	776.10	757.06	746.85	741.27
80000	947.31	866.97	827.84	807.53	796.64	790.69
85000	1006.51	921.15	879.58	858.00	846.42	840.11
90000	1065.72	975.34	931.32	908.47	896.21	889.53
95000	1124.92	1029.52	983.06	958.94	946.00	938.95
100000	1184.13	1083.71	1034.80	1009.41	995.79	988.36
200000	2368.26	2167.41	2069.60	2018.82	1991.59	1976.73
300000	3552.39	3251.12	3104.39	3028.23	2987.38	2965.09
400000	4736.53	4334.83	4139.19	4037.64	3983.18	3953.46
500000	5920.66	5418.54	5173.99	5047.05	4978.97	4941.82

12%

MONTHLY PAYMENT

Necessary to amortize a loan

TERM / AMOUNT	1 YEARS	2 YEARS	3 YEARS	4 YEARS	5 YEARS	6 YEARS
500	44.42	23.54	16.61	13.17	11.12	9.78
600	53.31	28.24	19.93	15.80	13.35	11.73
700	62.19	32.95	23.25	18.43	15.57	13.69
800	71.08	37.66	26.57	21.07	17.80	15.64
900	79.96	42.37	29.89	23.70	20.02	17.60
1000	88.85	47.07	33.21	26.33	22.24	19.55
2000	177.70	94.15	66.43	52.67	44.49	39.10
3000	266.55	141.22	99.64	79.00	66.73	58.65
4000	355.40	188.29	132.86	105.34	88.98	78.20
5000	444.24	235.37	166.07	131.67	111.22	97.75
6000	533.09	282.44	199.29	158.00	133.47	117.30
7000	621.94	329.51	232.50	184.34	155.71	136.85
8000	710.79	376.59	265.71	210.67	177.96	156.40
9000	799.64	423.66	298.93	237.00	200.20	175.95
10000	888.49	470.73	332.14	263.34	222.44	195.50
11000	977.34	517.81	365.36	289.67	244.69	215.05
12000	1066.19	564.88	398.57	316.01	266.93	234.60
13000	1155.03	611.96	431.79	342.34	289.18	254.15
14000	1243.88	659.03	465.00	368.67	311.42	273.70
15000	1332.73	706.10	498.21	395.01	333.67	293.25
16000	1421.58	753.18	531.43	421.34	355.91	312.80
17000	1510.43	800.25	564.64	447.68	378.16	332.35
18000	1599.28	847.32	597.86	474.01	400.40	351.90
19000	1688.13	894.40	631.07	500.34	422.64	371.45
20000	1776.98	941.47	664.29	526.68	444.89	391.00
21000	1865.82	988.54	697.50	553.01	467.13	410.55
22000	1954.67	1035.62	730.71	579.34	489.38	430.10
23000	2043.52	1082.69	763.93	605.68	511.62	449.65
24000	2132.37	1129.76	797.14	632.01	533.87	469.20
25000	2221.22	1176.84	830.36	658.35	556.11	488.75
30000	2665.46	1412.20	996.43	790.02	667.33	586.51
35000	3109.71	1647.57	1162.50	921.68	778.56	684.26
40000	3553.95	1882.94	1328.57	1053.35	889.78	782.01
45000	3998.20	2118.31	1494.64	1185.02	1001.00	879.76
50000	4442.44	2353.67	1660.72	1316.69	1112.22	977.51
55000	4886.68	2589.04	1826.79	1448.36	1223.44	1075.26
60000	5330.93	2824.41	1992.86	1580.03	1334.67	1173.01
65000	5775.17	3059.78	2158.93	1711.70	1445.89	1270.76
70000	6219.42	3295.14	2325.00	1843.37	1557.11	1368.51
75000	6663.66	3530.51	2491.07	1975.04	1668.33	1466.26
80000	7107.90	3765.88	2657.14	2106.71	1779.56	1564.02
85000	7552.15	4001.25	2823.22	2238.38	1890.78	1661.77
90000	7996.39	4236.61	2989.29	2370.05	2002.00	1759.52
95000	8440.63	4471.98	3155.36	2501.71	2113.22	1857.27
100000	8884.88	4707.35	3321.43	2633.38	2224.44	1955.02
200000	17769.76	9414.69	6642.86	5266.77	4448.89	3910.04
300000	26654.64	14122.04	9964.29	7900.15	6673.33	5865.06
400000	35539.52	18829.39	13285.72	10533.53	8897.78	7820.08
500000	44424.39	23536.74	16607.15	13166.92	11122.22	9775.10

MONTHLY PAYMENT

Necessary to amortize a loan

12%

TERM / AMOUNT	7 YEARS	8 YEARS	9 YEARS	10 YEARS	11 YEARS	12 YEARS
500	8.83	8.13	7.59	7.17	6.84	6.57
600	10.59	9.75	9.11	8.61	8.21	7.88
700	12.36	11.38	10.63	10.04	9.57	9.19
800	14.12	13.00	12.15	11.48	10.94	10.51
900	15.89	14.63	13.67	12.91	12.31	11.82
1000	17.65	16.25	15.18	14.35	13.68	13.13
2000	35.31	32.51	30.37	28.69	27.36	26.27
3000	52.96	48.76	45.55	43.04	41.03	39.40
4000	70.61	65.01	60.74	57.39	54.71	52.54
5000	88.26	81.26	75.92	71.74	68.39	65.67
6000	105.92	97.52	91.11	86.08	82.07	78.81
7000	123.57	113.77	106.29	100.43	95.75	91.94
8000	141.22	130.02	121.47	114.78	109.42	105.07
9000	158.87	146.28	136.66	129.12	123.10	118.21
10000	176.53	162.53	151.84	143.47	136.78	131.34
11000	194.18	178.78	167.03	157.82	150.46	144.48
12000	211.83	195.03	182.21	172.17	164.13	157.61
13000	229.49	211.29	197.40	186.51	177.81	170.74
14000	247.14	227.54	212.58	200.86	191.49	183.88
15000	264.79	243.79	227.76	215.21	205.17	197.01
16000	282.44	260.05	242.95	229.55	218.85	210.15
17000	300.10	276.30	258.13	243.90	232.52	223.28
18000	317.75	292.55	273.32	258.25	246.20	236.42
19000	335.40	308.80	288.50	272.59	259.88	249.55
20000	353.05	325.06	303.68	286.94	273.56	262.68
21000	370.71	341.31	318.87	301.29	287.24	275.82
22000	388.36	357.56	334.05	315.64	300.91	288.95
23000	406.01	373.82	349.24	329.98	314.59	302.09
24000	423.67	390.07	364.42	344.33	328.27	315.22
25000	441.32	406.32	379.61	358.68	341.95	328.35
30000	529.58	487.59	455.53	430.41	410.34	394.03
35000	617.85	568.85	531.45	502.15	478.73	459.70
40000	706.11	650.11	607.37	573.88	547.12	525.37
45000	794.37	731.38	683.29	645.62	615.50	591.04
50000	882.64	812.64	759.21	717.35	683.89	656.71
55000	970.90	893.91	835.13	789.09	752.28	722.38
60000	1059.16	975.17	911.05	860.83	820.67	788.05
65000	1147.43	1056.43	986.98	932.56	889.06	853.72
70000	1235.69	1137.70	1062.90	1004.30	957.45	919.39
75000	1323.95	1218.96	1138.82	1076.03	1025.84	985.06
80000	1412.22	1300.23	1214.74	1147.77	1094.23	1050.74
85000	1500.48	1381.49	1290.66	1219.50	1162.62	1116.41
90000	1588.75	1462.76	1366.58	1291.24	1231.01	1182.08
95000	1677.01	1544.02	1442.50	1362.97	1299.40	1247.75
100000	1765.27	1625.28	1518.42	1434.71	1367.79	1313.42
200000	3530.55	3250.57	3036.85	2869.42	2735.58	2626.84
300000	5295.82	4875.85	4555.27	4304.13	4103.36	3940.26
400000	7061.09	6501.14	6073.69	5738.84	5471.15	5253.68
500000	8826.37	8126.42	7592.12	7173.55	6838.94	6567.10

12%

MONTHLY PAYMENT

Necessary to amortize a loan

TERM / AMOUNT	15 YEARS	20 YEARS	25 YEARS	30 YEARS	35 YEARS	40 YEARS
500	6.00	5.51	5.27	5.14	5.08	5.04
600	7.20	6.61	6.32	6.17	6.09	6.05
700	8.40	7.71	7.37	7.20	7.11	7.06
800	9.60	8.81	8.43	8.23	8.12	8.07
900	10.80	9.91	9.48	9.26	9.14	9.08
1000	12.00	11.01	10.53	10.29	10.16	10.08
2000	24.00	22.02	21.06	20.57	20.31	20.17
3000	36.01	33.03	31.60	30.86	30.47	30.25
4000	48.01	44.04	42.13	41.14	40.62	40.34
5000	60.01	55.05	52.66	51.43	50.78	50.42
6000	72.01	66.07	63.19	61.72	60.93	60.51
7000	84.01	77.08	73.73	72.00	71.09	70.59
8000	96.01	88.09	84.26	82.29	81.24	80.68
9000	108.02	99.10	94.79	92.58	91.40	90.76
10000	120.02	110.11	105.32	102.86	101.55	100.85
11000	132.02	121.12	115.85	113.15	111.71	110.93
12000	144.02	132.13	126.39	123.43	121.87	121.02
13000	156.02	143.14	136.92	133.72	132.02	131.10
14000	168.02	154.15	147.45	144.01	142.18	141.19
15000	180.03	165.16	157.98	154.29	152.33	151.27
16000	192.03	176.17	168.52	164.58	162.49	161.36
17000	204.03	187.18	179.05	174.86	172.64	171.44
18000	216.03	198.20	189.58	185.15	182.80	181.53
19000	228.03	209.21	200.11	195.44	192.95	191.61
20000	240.03	220.22	210.64	205.72	203.11	201.70
21000	252.04	231.23	221.18	216.01	213.27	211.78
22000	264.04	242.24	231.71	226.29	223.42	221.87
23000	276.04	253.25	242.24	236.58	233.58	231.95
24000	288.04	264.26	252.77	246.87	243.73	242.04
25000	300.04	275.27	263.31	257.15	253.89	252.12
30000	360.05	330.33	315.97	308.58	304.66	302.55
35000	420.06	385.38	368.63	360.01	355.44	352.97
40000	480.07	440.43	421.29	411.45	406.22	403.40
45000	540.08	495.49	473.95	462.88	457.00	453.82
50000	600.08	550.54	526.61	514.31	507.77	504.25
55000	660.09	605.60	579.27	565.74	558.55	554.67
60000	720.10	660.65	631.93	617.17	609.33	605.10
65000	780.11	715.71	684.60	668.60	660.11	655.52
70000	840.12	770.76	737.26	720.03	710.88	705.95
75000	900.13	825.81	789.92	771.46	761.66	756.37
80000	960.13	880.87	842.58	822.89	812.44	806.80
85000	1020.14	935.92	895.24	874.32	863.22	857.22
90000	1080.15	990.98	947.90	925.75	913.99	907.65
95000	1140.16	1046.03	1000.56	977.18	964.77	958.07
100000	1200.17	1101.09	1053.22	1028.61	1015.55	1008.50
200000	2400.34	2202.17	2106.45	2057.23	2031.10	2017.00
300000	3600.50	3303.26	3159.67	3085.84	3046.65	3025.50
400000	4800.67	4404.34	4212.90	4114.45	4062.20	4034.00
500000	6000.84	5505.43	5266.12	5143.06	5077.75	5042.50

MONTHLY PAYMENT

Necessary to amortize a loan

12.25%

TERM / AMOUNT	1 YEARS	2 YEARS	3 YEARS	4 YEARS	5 YEARS	6 YEARS
500	44.48	23.60	16.67	13.23	11.19	9.84
600	53.38	28.31	20.00	15.87	13.42	11.81
700	62.28	33.03	23.33	18.52	15.66	13.78
800	71.17	37.75	26.67	21.17	17.90	15.74
900	80.07	42.47	30.00	23.81	20.13	17.71
1000	88.97	47.19	33.33	26.46	22.37	19.68
2000	177.93	94.38	66.67	52.91	44.74	39.36
3000	266.90	141.57	100.00	79.37	67.11	59.04
4000	355.86	188.76	133.34	105.83	89.48	78.72
5000	444.83	235.95	166.67	132.28	111.85	98.40
6000	533.79	283.14	200.00	158.74	134.23	118.08
7000	622.76	330.33	233.34	185.20	156.60	137.76
8000	711.73	377.52	266.67	211.65	178.97	157.44
9000	800.69	424.71	300.00	238.11	201.34	177.12
10000	889.66	471.90	333.34	264.57	223.71	196.80
11000	978.62	519.09	366.67	291.02	246.08	216.48
12000	1067.59	566.28	400.01	317.48	268.45	236.17
13000	1156.56	613.47	433.34	343.94	290.82	255.85
14000	1245.52	660.66	466.67	370.39	313.19	275.53
15000	1334.49	707.85	500.01	396.85	335.56	295.21
16000	1423.45	755.04	533.34	423.31	357.94	314.89
17000	1512.42	802.24	566.68	449.76	380.31	334.57
18000	1601.38	849.43	600.01	476.22	402.68	354.25
19000	1690.35	896.62	633.34	502.68	425.05	373.93
20000	1779.32	943.81	666.68	529.14	447.42	393.61
21000	1868.28	991.00	700.01	555.59	469.79	413.29
22000	1957.25	1038.19	733.34	582.05	492.16	432.97
23000	2046.21	1085.38	766.68	608.51	514.53	452.65
24000	2135.18	1132.57	800.01	634.96	536.90	472.33
25000	2224.14	1179.76	833.35	661.42	559.27	492.01
30000	2668.97	1415.71	1000.02	793.70	671.13	590.41
35000	3113.80	1651.66	1166.68	925.99	782.98	688.82
40000	3558.63	1887.61	1333.35	1058.27	894.84	787.22
45000	4003.46	2123.56	1500.02	1190.55	1006.69	885.62
50000	4448.29	2359.52	1666.69	1322.84	1118.55	984.02
55000	4893.12	2595.47	1833.36	1455.12	1230.40	1082.42
60000	5337.95	2831.42	2000.03	1587.41	1342.26	1180.83
65000	5782.78	3067.37	2166.70	1719.69	1454.11	1279.23
70000	6227.60	3303.32	2333.37	1851.97	1565.97	1377.63
75000	6672.43	3539.27	2500.04	1984.26	1677.82	1476.03
80000	7117.26	3775.22	2666.71	2116.54	1789.68	1574.44
85000	7562.09	4011.18	2833.38	2248.82	1901.53	1672.84
90000	8006.92	4247.13	3000.05	2381.11	2013.39	1771.24
95000	8451.75	4483.08	3166.71	2513.39	2125.24	1869.64
100000	8896.58	4719.03	3333.38	2645.68	2237.10	1968.04
200000	17793.16	9438.06	6666.77	5291.35	4474.20	3936.09
300000	26689.73	14157.09	10000.15	7937.03	6711.30	5904.13
400000	35586.31	18876.12	13333.54	10582.70	8948.39	7872.18
500000	44482.89	23595.15	16666.92	13228.38	11185.49	9840.22

12.25% MONTHLY PAYMENT

Necessary to amortize a loan

TERM / AMOUNT	7 YEARS	8 YEARS	9 YEARS	10 YEARS	11 YEARS	12 YEARS
500	8.89	8.20	7.66	7.25	6.91	6.64
600	10.67	9.83	9.20	8.70	8.30	7.97
700	12.45	11.47	10.73	10.14	9.68	9.30
800	14.23	13.11	12.26	11.59	11.06	10.63
900	16.01	14.75	13.79	13.04	12.44	11.96
1000	17.79	16.39	15.33	14.49	13.83	13.29
2000	35.57	32.78	30.65	28.98	27.65	26.57
3000	53.36	49.17	45.98	43.48	41.48	39.86
4000	71.15	65.56	61.30	57.97	55.31	53.14
5000	88.93	81.95	76.63	72.46	69.13	66.43
6000	106.72	98.34	91.95	86.95	82.96	79.72
7000	124.51	114.73	107.28	101.44	96.78	93.00
8000	142.29	131.12	122.60	115.94	110.61	106.29
9000	160.08	147.51	137.93	130.43	124.44	119.57
10000	177.87	163.91	153.26	144.92	138.26	132.86
11000	195.65	180.30	168.58	159.41	152.09	146.15
12000	213.44	196.69	183.91	173.90	165.92	159.43
13000	231.23	213.08	199.23	188.40	179.74	172.72
14000	249.01	229.47	214.56	202.89	193.57	186.00
15000	266.80	245.86	229.88	217.38	207.39	199.29
16000	284.59	262.25	245.21	231.87	221.22	212.58
17000	302.37	278.64	260.53	246.36	235.05	225.86
18000	320.16	295.03	275.86	260.86	248.87	239.15
19000	337.95	311.42	291.19	275.35	262.70	252.43
20000	355.73	327.81	306.51	289.84	276.53	265.72
21000	373.52	344.20	321.84	304.33	290.35	279.01
22000	391.31	360.59	337.16	318.82	304.18	292.29
23000	409.09	376.98	352.49	333.32	318.00	305.58
24000	426.88	393.37	367.81	347.81	331.83	318.86
25000	444.67	409.76	383.14	362.30	345.66	332.15
30000	533.60	491.72	459.77	434.76	414.79	398.58
35000	622.53	573.67	536.39	507.22	483.92	465.01
40000	711.47	655.62	613.02	579.68	553.05	531.44
45000	800.40	737.57	689.65	652.14	622.18	597.87
50000	889.34	819.53	766.28	724.60	691.31	664.30
55000	978.27	901.48	842.91	797.06	760.44	730.73
60000	1067.20	983.43	919.53	869.52	829.58	797.16
65000	1156.14	1065.38	996.16	941.98	898.71	863.59
70000	1245.07	1147.34	1072.79	1014.44	967.84	930.02
75000	1334.00	1229.29	1149.42	1086.90	1036.97	996.45
80000	1422.94	1311.24	1226.04	1159.36	1106.10	1062.88
85000	1511.87	1393.19	1302.67	1231.82	1175.23	1129.31
90000	1600.80	1475.15	1379.30	1304.28	1244.36	1195.74
95000	1689.74	1557.10	1455.93	1376.74	1313.49	1262.17
100000	1778.67	1639.05	1532.56	1449.20	1382.63	1328.60
200000	3557.34	3278.10	3065.11	2898.40	2765.25	2657.19
300000	5336.01	4917.15	4597.67	4347.60	4147.88	3985.79
400000	7114.68	6556.21	6130.22	5796.79	5530.50	5314.39
500000	8893.35	8195.26	7662.78	7245.99	6913.13	6642.98

MONTHLY PAYMENT
Necessary to amortize a loan

12.25%

TERM / AMOUNT	15 YEARS	20 YEARS	25 YEARS	30 YEARS	35 YEARS	40 YEARS
500	6.08	5.59	5.36	5.24	5.18	5.14
600	7.30	6.71	6.43	6.29	6.21	6.17
700	8.51	7.83	7.50	7.34	7.25	7.20
800	9.73	8.95	8.57	8.38	8.28	8.23
900	10.95	10.07	9.65	9.43	9.32	9.26
1000	12.16	11.19	10.72	10.48	10.35	10.29
2000	24.33	22.37	21.43	20.96	20.71	20.57
3000	36.49	33.56	32.15	31.44	31.06	30.86
4000	48.65	44.74	42.87	41.92	41.41	41.15
5000	60.81	55.93	53.59	52.39	51.77	51.43
6000	72.98	67.11	64.30	62.87	62.12	61.72
7000	85.14	78.30	75.02	73.35	72.48	72.01
8000	97.30	89.49	85.74	83.83	82.83	82.29
9000	109.47	100.67	96.46	94.31	93.18	92.58
10000	121.63	111.86	107.17	104.79	103.54	102.87
11000	133.79	123.04	117.89	115.27	113.89	113.16
12000	145.96	134.23	128.61	125.75	124.24	123.44
13000	158.12	145.41	139.33	136.23	134.60	133.73
14000	170.28	156.60	150.04	146.71	144.95	144.02
15000	182.44	167.78	160.76	157.18	155.31	154.30
16000	194.61	178.97	171.48	167.66	165.66	164.59
17000	206.77	190.16	182.20	178.14	176.01	174.88
18000	218.93	201.34	192.91	188.62	186.37	185.16
19000	231.10	212.53	203.63	199.10	196.72	195.45
20000	243.26	223.71	214.35	209.58	207.07	205.74
21000	255.42	234.90	225.07	220.06	217.43	216.02
22000	267.59	246.08	235.78	230.54	227.78	226.31
23000	279.75	257.27	246.50	241.02	238.14	236.60
24000	291.91	268.46	257.22	251.50	248.49	246.88
25000	304.07	279.64	267.94	261.97	258.84	257.17
30000	364.89	335.57	321.52	314.37	310.61	308.61
35000	425.70	391.50	375.11	366.76	362.38	360.04
40000	486.52	447.43	428.70	419.16	414.15	411.47
45000	547.33	503.35	482.28	471.55	465.92	462.91
50000	608.15	559.28	535.87	523.95	517.69	514.34
55000	668.96	615.21	589.46	576.34	569.45	565.78
60000	729.78	671.14	643.05	628.74	621.22	617.21
65000	790.59	727.07	696.63	681.13	672.99	668.65
70000	851.41	783.00	750.22	733.53	724.76	720.08
75000	912.22	838.92	803.81	785.92	776.53	771.51
80000	973.04	894.85	857.40	838.32	828.30	822.95
85000	1033.85	950.78	910.98	890.71	880.07	874.38
90000	1094.67	1006.71	964.57	943.11	931.83	925.82
95000	1155.48	1062.64	1018.16	995.50	983.60	977.25
100000	1216.30	1118.56	1071.74	1047.90	1035.37	1028.69
200000	2432.60	2237.13	2143.49	2095.79	2070.74	2057.37
300000	3648.90	3355.69	3215.23	3143.69	3106.11	3086.06
400000	4865.19	4474.26	4286.98	4191.59	4141.48	4114.74
500000	6081.49	5592.82	5358.72	5239.48	5176.86	5143.43

12.5%

MONTHLY PAYMENT

Necessary to amortize a loan

TERM / AMOUNT	1 YEARS	2 YEARS	3 YEARS	4 YEARS	5 YEARS	6 YEARS
500	44.54	23.65	16.73	13.29	11.25	9.91
600	53.45	28.38	20.07	15.95	13.50	11.89
700	62.36	33.12	23.42	18.61	15.75	13.87
800	71.27	37.85	26.76	21.26	18.00	15.85
900	80.17	42.58	30.11	23.92	20.25	17.83
1000	89.08	47.31	33.45	26.58	22.50	19.81
2000	178.17	94.61	66.91	53.16	45.00	39.62
3000	267.25	141.92	100.36	79.74	67.49	59.43
4000	356.33	189.23	133.81	106.32	89.99	79.24
5000	445.41	236.54	167.27	132.90	112.49	99.06
6000	534.50	283.84	200.72	159.48	134.99	118.87
7000	623.58	331.15	234.18	186.06	157.49	138.68
8000	712.66	378.46	267.63	212.64	179.98	158.49
9000	801.75	425.77	301.08	239.22	202.48	178.30
10000	890.83	473.07	334.54	265.80	224.98	198.11
11000	979.91	520.38	367.99	292.38	247.48	217.92
12000	1068.99	567.69	401.44	318.96	269.98	237.73
13000	1158.08	615.00	434.90	345.54	292.47	257.55
14000	1247.16	662.30	468.35	372.12	314.97	277.36
15000	1336.24	709.61	501.80	398.70	337.47	297.17
16000	1425.33	756.92	535.26	425.28	359.97	316.98
17000	1514.41	804.22	568.71	451.86	382.46	336.79
18000	1603.49	851.53	602.17	478.44	404.96	356.60
19000	1692.57	898.84	635.62	505.02	427.46	376.41
20000	1781.66	946.15	669.07	531.60	449.96	396.22
21000	1870.74	993.45	702.53	558.18	472.46	416.03
22000	1959.82	1040.76	735.98	584.76	494.95	435.85
23000	2048.91	1088.07	769.43	611.34	517.45	455.66
24000	2137.99	1135.38	802.89	637.92	539.95	475.47
25000	2227.07	1182.68	836.34	664.50	562.45	495.28
30000	2672.49	1419.22	1003.61	797.40	674.94	594.34
35000	3117.90	1655.76	1170.88	930.30	787.43	693.39
40000	3563.31	1892.29	1338.15	1063.20	899.92	792.45
45000	4008.73	2128.83	1505.41	1196.10	1012.41	891.50
50000	4454.14	2365.37	1672.68	1329.00	1124.90	990.56
55000	4899.56	2601.90	1839.95	1461.90	1237.39	1089.61
60000	5344.97	2838.44	2007.22	1594.80	1349.88	1188.67
65000	5790.39	3074.98	2174.49	1727.70	1462.37	1287.73
70000	6235.80	3311.51	2341.75	1860.60	1574.86	1386.78
75000	6681.21	3548.05	2509.02	1993.50	1687.35	1485.84
80000	7126.63	3784.58	2676.29	2126.40	1799.84	1584.89
85000	7572.04	4021.12	2843.56	2259.30	1912.32	1683.95
90000	8017.46	4257.66	3010.83	2392.20	2024.81	1783.01
95000	8462.87	4494.19	3178.09	2525.10	2137.30	1882.06
100000	8908.29	4730.73	3345.36	2658.00	2249.79	1981.12
200000	17816.57	9461.46	6690.73	5316.00	4499.59	3962.24
300000	26724.86	14192.19	10036.09	7974.00	6749.38	5943.35
400000	35633.15	18922.92	13381.45	10632.00	8999.18	7924.47
500000	44541.43	23653.65	16726.81	13290.00	11248.97	9905.59

MONTHLY PAYMENT
Necessary to amortize a loan

12.5%

TERM / AMOUNT	7 YEARS	8 YEARS	9 YEARS	10 YEARS	11 YEARS	12 YEARS
500	8.96	8.26	7.73	7.32	6.99	6.72
600	10.75	9.92	9.28	8.78	8.39	8.06
700	12.54	11.57	10.83	10.25	9.78	9.41
800	14.34	13.22	12.37	11.71	11.18	10.75
900	16.13	14.88	13.92	13.17	12.58	12.09
1000	17.92	16.53	15.47	14.64	13.98	13.44
2000	35.84	33.06	30.94	29.28	27.95	26.88
3000	53.76	49.59	46.40	43.91	41.93	40.32
4000	71.68	66.12	61.87	58.55	55.90	53.75
5000	89.61	82.64	77.34	73.19	69.88	67.19
6000	107.53	99.17	92.81	87.83	83.85	80.63
7000	125.45	115.70	108.27	102.46	97.83	94.07
8000	143.37	132.23	123.74	117.10	111.80	107.51
9000	161.29	148.76	139.21	131.74	125.78	120.95
10000	179.21	165.29	154.68	146.38	139.75	134.39
11000	197.13	181.82	170.14	161.01	153.73	147.82
12000	215.05	198.35	185.61	175.65	167.71	161.26
13000	232.98	214.87	201.08	190.29	181.68	174.70
14000	250.90	231.40	216.55	204.93	195.66	188.14
15000	268.82	247.93	232.01	219.56	209.63	201.58
16000	286.74	264.46	247.48	234.20	223.61	215.02
17000	304.66	280.99	262.95	248.84	237.58	228.46
18000	322.58	297.52	278.42	263.48	251.56	241.89
19000	340.50	314.05	293.88	278.11	265.53	255.33
20000	358.42	330.58	309.35	292.75	279.51	268.77
21000	376.35	347.10	324.82	307.39	293.48	282.21
22000	394.27	363.63	340.29	322.03	307.46	295.65
23000	412.19	380.16	355.75	336.67	321.43	309.09
24000	430.11	396.69	371.22	351.30	335.41	322.53
25000	448.03	413.22	386.69	365.94	349.39	335.96
30000	537.64	495.86	464.03	439.13	419.26	403.16
35000	627.24	578.51	541.36	512.32	489.14	470.35
40000	716.85	661.15	618.70	585.50	559.02	537.54
45000	806.46	743.80	696.04	658.69	628.89	604.74
50000	896.06	826.44	773.38	731.88	698.77	671.93
55000	985.67	909.08	850.72	805.07	768.65	739.12
60000	1075.27	991.73	928.05	878.26	838.53	806.31
65000	1164.88	1074.37	1005.39	951.45	908.40	873.51
70000	1254.49	1157.02	1082.73	1024.63	978.28	940.70
75000	1344.09	1239.66	1160.07	1097.82	1048.16	1007.89
80000	1433.70	1322.30	1237.40	1171.01	1118.03	1075.09
85000	1523.31	1404.95	1314.74	1244.20	1187.91	1142.28
90000	1612.91	1487.59	1392.08	1317.39	1257.79	1209.47
95000	1702.52	1570.24	1469.42	1390.57	1327.67	1276.66
100000	1792.12	1652.88	1546.76	1463.76	1397.54	1343.86
200000	3584.25	3305.76	3093.51	2927.52	2795.09	2687.71
300000	5376.37	4958.64	4640.27	4391.29	4192.63	4031.57
400000	7168.50	6611.52	6187.02	5855.05	5590.17	5375.43
500000	8960.62	8264.40	7733.78	7318.81	6987.71	6719.29

12.5%

MONTHLY PAYMENT

Necessary to amortize a loan

TERM / AMOUNT	15 YEARS	20 YEARS	25 YEARS	30 YEARS	35 YEARS	40 YEARS
500	6.16	5.68	5.45	5.34	5.28	5.24
600	7.40	6.82	6.54	6.40	6.33	6.29
700	8.63	7.95	7.63	7.47	7.39	7.34
800	9.86	9.09	8.72	8.54	8.44	8.39
900	11.09	10.23	9.81	9.61	9.50	9.44
1000	12.33	11.36	10.90	10.67	10.55	10.49
2000	24.65	22.72	21.81	21.35	21.11	20.98
3000	36.98	34.08	32.71	32.02	31.66	31.47
4000	49.30	45.45	43.61	42.69	42.21	41.96
5000	61.63	56.81	54.52	53.36	52.76	52.45
6000	73.95	68.17	65.42	64.04	63.32	62.94
7000	86.28	79.53	76.32	74.71	73.87	73.42
8000	98.60	90.89	87.23	85.38	84.42	83.91
9000	110.93	102.25	98.13	96.05	94.97	94.40
10000	123.25	113.61	109.04	106.73	105.53	104.89
11000	135.58	124.98	119.94	117.40	116.08	115.38
12000	147.90	136.34	130.84	128.07	126.63	125.87
13000	160.23	147.70	141.75	138.74	137.18	136.36
14000	172.55	159.06	152.65	149.42	147.74	146.85
15000	184.88	170.42	163.55	160.09	158.29	157.34
16000	197.20	181.78	174.46	170.76	168.84	167.83
17000	209.53	193.14	185.36	181.43	179.39	178.32
18000	221.85	204.51	196.26	192.11	189.95	188.81
19000	234.18	215.87	207.17	202.78	200.50	199.29
20000	246.50	227.23	218.07	213.45	211.05	209.78
21000	258.83	238.59	228.97	224.12	221.60	220.27
22000	271.15	249.95	239.88	234.80	232.16	230.76
23000	283.48	261.31	250.78	245.47	242.71	241.25
24000	295.81	272.67	261.68	256.14	253.26	251.74
25000	308.13	284.04	272.59	266.81	263.81	262.23
30000	369.76	340.84	327.11	320.18	316.58	314.68
35000	431.38	397.65	381.62	373.54	369.34	367.12
40000	493.01	454.46	436.14	426.90	422.10	419.57
45000	554.63	511.26	490.66	480.27	474.86	472.01
50000	616.26	568.07	545.18	533.63	527.63	524.46
55000	677.89	624.88	599.69	586.99	580.39	576.91
60000	739.51	681.68	654.21	640.35	633.15	629.35
65000	801.14	738.49	708.73	693.72	685.92	681.80
70000	862.77	795.30	763.25	747.08	738.68	734.24
75000	924.39	852.11	817.77	800.44	791.44	786.69
80000	986.02	908.91	872.28	853.81	844.20	839.14
85000	1047.64	965.72	926.80	907.17	896.97	891.58
90000	1109.27	1022.53	981.32	960.53	949.73	944.03
95000	1170.90	1079.33	1035.84	1013.89	1002.49	996.47
100000	1232.52	1136.14	1090.35	1067.26	1055.25	1048.92
200000	2465.04	2272.28	2180.71	2134.52	2110.51	2097.84
300000	3697.57	3408.42	3271.06	3201.77	3165.76	3146.76
400000	4930.09	4544.56	4361.42	4269.03	4221.02	4195.68
500000	6162.61	5680.70	5451.77	5336.29	5276.27	5244.60

MONTHLY PAYMENT

Necessary to amortize a loan

12.75%

TERM / AMOUNT	1 YEARS	2 YEARS	3 YEARS	4 YEARS	5 YEARS	6 YEARS
500	44.60	23.71	16.79	13.35	11.31	9.97
600	53.52	28.45	20.14	16.02	13.58	11.97
700	62.44	33.20	23.50	18.69	15.84	13.96
800	71.36	37.94	26.86	21.36	18.10	15.95
900	80.28	42.68	30.22	24.03	20.36	17.95
1000	89.20	47.42	33.57	26.70	22.63	19.94
2000	178.40	94.85	67.15	53.41	45.25	39.88
3000	267.60	142.27	100.72	80.11	67.88	59.83
4000	356.80	189.70	134.29	106.81	90.50	79.77
5000	446.00	237.12	167.87	133.52	113.13	99.71
6000	535.20	284.55	201.44	160.22	135.75	119.65
7000	624.40	331.97	235.02	186.93	158.38	139.60
8000	713.60	379.40	268.59	213.63	181.00	159.54
9000	802.80	426.82	302.16	240.33	203.63	179.48
10000	892.00	474.24	335.74	267.04	226.25	199.42
11000	981.20	521.67	369.31	293.74	248.88	219.37
12000	1070.40	569.09	402.88	320.44	271.50	239.31
13000	1159.60	616.52	436.46	347.15	294.13	259.25
14000	1248.80	663.94	470.03	373.85	316.75	279.19
15000	1338.00	711.37	503.60	400.55	339.38	299.14
16000	1427.20	758.79	537.18	427.26	362.00	319.08
17000	1516.40	806.22	570.75	453.96	384.63	339.02
18000	1605.60	853.64	604.33	480.66	407.26	358.96
19000	1694.80	901.07	637.90	507.37	429.88	378.91
20000	1784.00	948.49	671.47	534.07	452.51	398.85
21000	1873.20	995.91	705.05	560.78	475.13	418.79
22000	1962.40	1043.34	738.62	587.48	497.76	438.73
23000	2051.60	1090.76	772.19	614.18	520.38	458.68
24000	2140.80	1138.19	805.77	640.89	543.01	478.62
25000	2230.00	1185.61	839.34	667.59	565.63	498.56
30000	2676.00	1422.73	1007.21	801.11	678.76	598.27
35000	3122.00	1659.86	1175.08	934.63	791.89	697.98
40000	3568.00	1896.98	1342.95	1068.14	905.01	797.70
45000	4014.00	2134.10	1510.81	1201.66	1018.14	897.41
50000	4460.00	2371.22	1678.68	1335.18	1131.27	997.12
55000	4906.00	2608.35	1846.55	1468.70	1244.39	1096.83
60000	5352.00	2845.47	2014.42	1602.21	1357.52	1196.54
65000	5798.00	3082.59	2182.29	1735.73	1470.64	1296.26
70000	6244.00	3319.71	2350.16	1869.25	1583.77	1395.97
75000	6690.00	3556.84	2518.02	2002.77	1696.90	1495.68
80000	7136.00	3793.96	2685.89	2136.29	1810.02	1595.39
85000	7582.00	4031.08	2853.76	2269.80	1923.15	1695.10
90000	8028.00	4268.20	3021.63	2403.32	2036.28	1794.82
95000	8474.00	4505.33	3189.50	2536.84	2149.40	1894.53
100000	8920.00	4742.45	3357.37	2670.36	2262.53	1994.24
200000	17840.01	9484.90	6714.73	5340.72	4525.06	3988.48
300000	26760.01	14227.34	10072.10	8011.07	6787.59	5982.72
400000	35680.01	18969.79	13429.47	10681.43	9050.12	7976.96
500000	44600.01	23712.24	16786.83	13351.79	11312.65	9971.20

12.75% MONTHLY PAYMENT

Necessary to amortize a loan

TERM / AMOUNT	7 YEARS	8 YEARS	9 YEARS	10 YEARS	11 YEARS	12 YEARS
500	9.03	8.33	7.81	7.39	7.06	6.80
600	10.83	10.00	9.37	8.87	8.48	8.16
700	12.64	11.67	10.93	10.35	9.89	9.51
800	14.45	13.33	12.49	11.83	11.30	10.87
900	16.25	15.00	14.05	13.31	12.71	12.23
1000	18.06	16.67	15.61	14.78	14.13	13.59
2000	36.11	33.34	31.22	29.57	28.25	27.18
3000	54.17	50.00	46.83	44.35	42.38	40.78
4000	72.23	66.67	62.44	59.14	56.50	54.37
5000	90.28	83.34	78.05	73.92	70.63	67.96
6000	108.34	100.01	93.66	88.70	84.75	81.55
7000	126.39	116.67	109.27	103.49	98.88	95.14
8000	144.45	133.34	124.88	118.27	113.00	108.74
9000	162.51	150.01	140.49	133.06	127.13	122.33
10000	180.56	166.68	156.10	147.84	141.25	135.92
11000	198.62	183.34	171.71	162.62	155.38	149.51
12000	216.68	200.01	187.32	177.41	169.50	163.10
13000	234.73	216.68	202.93	192.19	183.63	176.70
14000	252.79	233.35	218.54	206.98	197.76	190.29
15000	270.84	250.02	234.15	221.76	211.88	203.88
16000	288.90	266.68	249.76	236.54	226.01	217.47
17000	306.96	283.35	265.37	251.33	240.13	231.06
18000	325.01	300.02	280.98	266.11	254.26	244.66
19000	343.07	316.69	296.59	280.90	268.38	258.25
20000	361.13	333.35	312.20	295.68	282.51	271.84
21000	379.18	350.02	327.81	310.46	296.63	285.43
22000	397.24	366.69	343.43	325.25	310.76	299.02
23000	415.30	383.36	359.04	340.03	324.88	312.62
24000	433.35	400.03	374.65	354.82	339.01	326.21
25000	451.41	416.69	390.26	369.60	353.13	339.80
30000	541.69	500.03	468.31	443.52	423.76	407.76
35000	631.97	583.37	546.36	517.44	494.39	475.72
40000	722.25	666.71	624.41	591.36	565.02	543.68
45000	812.53	750.05	702.46	665.28	635.64	611.64
50000	902.82	833.39	780.51	739.20	706.27	679.60
55000	993.10	916.72	858.56	813.12	776.90	747.56
60000	1083.38	1000.06	936.61	887.04	847.52	815.52
65000	1173.66	1083.40	1014.67	960.96	918.15	883.48
70000	1263.94	1166.74	1092.72	1034.88	988.78	951.44
75000	1354.22	1250.08	1170.77	1108.80	1059.40	1019.40
80000	1444.51	1333.42	1248.82	1182.72	1130.03	1087.36
85000	1534.79	1416.76	1326.87	1256.64	1200.66	1155.32
90000	1625.07	1500.10	1404.92	1330.56	1271.28	1223.28
95000	1715.35	1583.43	1482.97	1404.48	1341.91	1291.24
100000	1805.63	1666.77	1561.02	1478.40	1412.54	1359.20
200000	3611.26	3333.54	3122.05	2956.80	2825.08	2718.40
300000	5416.90	5000.32	4683.07	4435.19	4237.61	4077.60
400000	7222.53	6667.09	6244.09	5913.59	5650.15	5436.80
500000	9028.16	8333.86	7805.12	7391.99	7062.69	6796.00

MONTHLY PAYMENT

Necessary to amortize a loan

12.75%

TERM / AMOUNT	15 YEARS	20 YEARS	25 YEARS	30 YEARS	35 YEARS	40 YEARS
500	6.24	5.77	5.55	5.43	5.38	5.35
600	7.49	6.92	6.65	6.52	6.45	6.42
700	8.74	8.08	7.76	7.61	7.53	7.48
800	9.99	9.23	8.87	8.69	8.60	8.55
900	11.24	10.38	9.98	9.78	9.68	9.62
1000	12.49	11.54	11.09	10.87	10.75	10.69
2000	24.98	23.08	22.18	21.73	21.50	21.38
3000	37.47	34.61	33.27	32.60	32.26	32.08
4000	49.95	46.15	44.36	43.47	43.01	42.77
5000	62.44	57.69	55.45	54.33	53.76	53.46
6000	74.93	69.23	66.54	65.20	64.51	64.15
7000	87.42	80.77	77.63	76.07	75.26	74.84
8000	99.91	92.30	88.72	86.94	86.02	85.54
9000	112.40	103.84	99.81	97.80	96.77	96.23
10000	124.88	115.38	110.91	108.67	107.52	106.92
11000	137.37	126.92	122.00	119.54	118.27	117.61
12000	149.86	138.46	133.09	130.40	129.02	128.30
13000	162.35	150.00	144.18	141.27	139.78	139.00
14000	174.84	161.53	155.27	152.14	150.53	149.69
15000	187.33	173.07	166.36	163.00	161.28	160.38
16000	199.81	184.61	177.45	173.87	172.03	171.07
17000	212.30	196.15	188.54	184.74	182.78	181.76
18000	224.79	207.69	199.63	195.60	193.54	192.46
19000	237.28	219.22	210.72	206.47	204.29	203.15
20000	249.77	230.76	221.81	217.34	215.04	213.84
21000	262.26	242.30	232.90	228.21	225.79	224.53
22000	274.74	253.84	243.99	239.07	236.54	235.22
23000	287.23	265.38	255.08	249.94	247.30	245.92
24000	299.72	276.91	266.17	260.81	258.05	256.61
25000	312.21	288.45	277.26	271.67	268.80	267.30
30000	374.65	346.14	332.72	326.01	322.56	320.76
35000	437.09	403.83	388.17	380.34	376.32	374.22
40000	499.53	461.52	443.62	434.68	430.08	427.68
45000	561.98	519.22	499.07	489.01	483.84	481.14
50000	624.42	576.91	554.53	543.35	537.60	534.60
55000	686.86	634.60	609.98	597.68	591.36	588.06
60000	749.30	692.29	665.43	652.02	645.12	641.52
65000	811.74	749.98	720.88	706.35	698.88	694.98
70000	874.19	807.67	776.34	760.69	752.64	748.44
75000	936.63	865.36	831.79	815.02	806.40	801.90
80000	999.07	923.05	887.24	869.35	860.16	855.36
85000	1061.51	980.74	942.69	923.69	913.92	908.82
90000	1123.95	1038.43	998.15	978.02	967.68	962.28
95000	1186.40	1096.12	1053.60	1032.36	1021.44	1015.74
100000	1248.84	1153.81	1109.05	1086.69	1075.20	1069.20
200000	2497.67	2307.62	2218.10	2173.39	2150.39	2138.39
300000	3746.51	3461.43	3327.16	3260.08	3225.59	3207.59
400000	4995.35	4615.25	4436.21	4346.77	4300.78	4276.79
500000	6244.18	5769.06	5545.26	5433.47	5375.98	5345.98

13% MONTHLY PAYMENT

Necessary to amortize a loan

TERM / AMOUNT	1 YEARS	2 YEARS	3 YEARS	4 YEARS	5 YEARS	6 YEARS
500	44.66	23.77	16.85	13.41	11.38	10.04
600	53.59	28.53	20.22	16.10	13.65	12.04
700	62.52	33.28	23.59	18.78	15.93	14.05
800	71.45	38.03	26.96	21.46	18.20	16.06
900	80.39	42.79	30.32	24.14	20.48	18.07
1000	89.32	47.54	33.69	26.83	22.75	20.07
2000	178.63	95.08	67.39	53.65	45.51	40.15
3000	267.95	142.63	101.08	80.48	68.26	60.22
4000	357.27	190.17	134.78	107.31	91.01	80.30
5000	446.59	237.71	168.47	134.14	113.77	100.37
6000	535.90	285.25	202.16	160.96	136.52	120.44
7000	625.22	332.79	235.86	187.79	159.27	140.52
8000	714.54	380.33	269.55	214.62	182.02	160.59
9000	803.86	427.88	303.25	241.45	204.78	180.67
10000	893.17	475.42	336.94	268.27	227.53	200.74
11000	982.49	522.96	370.63	295.10	250.28	220.82
12000	1071.81	570.50	404.33	321.93	273.04	240.89
13000	1161.12	618.04	438.02	348.76	295.79	260.96
14000	1250.44	665.59	471.72	375.58	318.54	281.04
15000	1339.76	713.13	505.41	402.41	341.30	301.11
16000	1429.08	760.67	539.10	429.24	364.05	321.19
17000	1518.39	808.21	572.80	456.07	386.80	341.26
18000	1607.71	855.75	606.49	482.89	409.56	361.33
19000	1697.03	903.29	640.19	509.72	432.31	381.41
20000	1786.35	950.84	673.88	536.55	455.06	401.48
21000	1875.66	998.38	707.57	563.38	477.81	421.56
22000	1964.98	1045.92	741.27	590.20	500.57	441.63
23000	2054.30	1093.46	774.96	617.03	523.32	461.70
24000	2143.61	1141.00	808.65	643.86	546.07	481.78
25000	2232.93	1188.55	842.35	670.69	568.83	501.85
30000	2679.52	1426.25	1010.82	804.82	682.59	602.22
35000	3126.10	1663.96	1179.29	938.96	796.36	702.59
40000	3572.69	1901.67	1347.76	1073.10	910.12	802.96
45000	4019.28	2139.38	1516.23	1207.24	1023.89	903.33
50000	4465.86	2377.09	1684.70	1341.37	1137.65	1003.71
55000	4912.45	2614.80	1853.17	1475.51	1251.42	1104.08
60000	5359.04	2852.51	2021.64	1609.65	1365.18	1204.45
65000	5805.62	3090.22	2190.11	1743.79	1478.95	1304.82
70000	6252.21	3327.93	2358.58	1877.92	1592.72	1405.19
75000	6698.80	3565.64	2527.05	2012.06	1706.48	1505.56
80000	7145.38	3803.35	2695.52	2146.20	1820.25	1605.93
85000	7591.97	4041.05	2863.99	2280.34	1934.01	1706.30
90000	8038.55	4278.76	3032.46	2414.47	2047.78	1806.67
95000	8485.14	4516.47	3200.93	2548.61	2161.54	1907.04
100000	8931.73	4754.18	3369.40	2682.75	2275.31	2007.41
200000	17863.46	9508.36	6738.79	5365.50	4550.61	4014.82
300000	26795.18	14262.55	10108.19	8048.25	6825.92	6022.23
400000	35726.91	19016.73	13477.58	10731.00	9101.23	8029.64
500000	44658.64	23770.91	16846.98	13413.75	11376.54	10037.05

MONTHLY PAYMENT

Necessary to amortize a loan

13%

TERM / AMOUNT	7 YEARS	8 YEARS	9 YEARS	10 YEARS	11 YEARS	12 YEARS
500	9.10	8.40	7.88	7.47	7.14	6.87
600	10.92	10.08	9.45	8.96	8.57	8.25
700	12.73	11.77	11.03	10.45	9.99	9.62
800	14.55	13.45	12.60	11.94	11.42	11.00
900	16.37	15.13	14.18	13.44	12.85	12.37
1000	18.19	16.81	15.75	14.93	14.28	13.75
2000	36.38	33.61	31.51	29.86	28.55	27.49
3000	54.58	50.42	47.26	44.79	42.83	41.24
4000	72.77	67.23	63.01	59.72	57.10	54.99
5000	90.96	84.04	78.77	74.66	71.38	68.73
6000	109.15	100.84	94.52	89.59	85.66	82.48
7000	127.34	117.65	110.28	104.52	99.93	96.22
8000	145.54	134.46	126.03	119.45	114.21	109.97
9000	163.73	151.27	141.78	134.38	128.48	123.72
10000	181.92	168.07	157.54	149.31	142.76	137.46
11000	200.11	184.88	173.29	164.24	157.04	151.21
12000	218.30	201.69	189.04	179.17	171.31	164.96
13000	236.50	218.49	204.80	194.10	185.59	178.70
14000	254.69	235.30	220.55	209.04	199.87	192.45
15000	272.88	252.11	236.30	223.97	214.14	206.19
16000	291.07	268.92	252.06	238.90	228.42	219.94
17000	309.26	285.72	267.81	253.83	242.69	233.69
18000	327.46	302.53	283.56	268.76	256.97	247.43
19000	345.65	319.34	299.32	283.69	271.25	261.18
20000	363.84	336.15	315.07	298.62	285.52	274.93
21000	382.03	352.95	330.83	313.55	299.80	288.67
22000	400.22	369.76	346.58	328.48	314.07	302.42
23000	418.42	386.57	362.33	343.41	328.35	316.16
24000	436.61	403.37	378.09	358.35	342.63	329.91
25000	454.80	420.18	393.84	373.28	356.90	343.66
30000	545.76	504.22	472.61	447.93	428.28	412.39
35000	636.72	588.25	551.38	522.59	499.66	481.12
40000	727.68	672.29	630.14	597.24	571.04	549.85
45000	818.64	756.33	708.91	671.90	642.42	618.58
50000	909.60	840.36	787.68	746.55	713.81	687.31
55000	1000.56	924.40	866.45	821.21	785.19	756.04
60000	1091.52	1008.44	945.22	895.86	856.57	824.78
65000	1182.48	1092.47	1023.98	970.52	927.95	893.51
70000	1273.44	1176.51	1102.75	1045.18	999.33	962.24
75000	1364.40	1260.54	1181.52	1119.83	1070.71	1030.97
80000	1455.36	1344.58	1260.29	1194.49	1142.09	1099.70
85000	1546.32	1428.62	1339.05	1269.14	1213.47	1168.43
90000	1637.28	1512.65	1417.82	1343.80	1284.85	1237.16
95000	1728.24	1596.69	1496.59	1418.45	1356.23	1305.89
100000	1819.20	1680.73	1575.36	1493.11	1427.61	1374.63
200000	3638.39	3361.45	3150.72	2986.21	2855.22	2749.25
300000	5457.59	5042.18	4726.08	4479.32	4282.83	4123.88
400000	7276.79	6722.90	6301.44	5972.43	5710.44	5498.50
500000	9095.98	8403.63	7876.79	7465.54	7138.05	6873.13

13%

MONTHLY PAYMENT

Necessary to amortize a loan

TERM / AMOUNT	15 YEARS	20 YEARS	25 YEARS	30 YEARS	35 YEARS	40 YEARS
500	6.33	5.86	5.64	5.53	5.48	5.45
600	7.59	7.03	6.77	6.64	6.57	6.54
700	8.86	8.20	7.89	7.74	7.67	7.63
800	10.12	9.37	9.02	8.85	8.76	8.72
900	11.39	10.54	10.15	9.96	9.86	9.81
1000	12.65	11.72	11.28	11.06	10.95	10.90
2000	25.30	23.43	22.56	22.12	21.90	21.79
3000	37.96	35.15	33.84	33.19	32.86	32.69
4000	50.61	46.86	45.11	44.25	43.81	43.58
5000	63.26	58.58	56.39	55.31	54.76	54.48
6000	75.91	70.29	67.67	66.37	65.71	65.37
7000	88.57	82.01	78.95	77.43	76.66	76.27
8000	101.22	93.73	90.23	88.50	87.62	87.16
9000	113.87	105.44	101.51	99.56	98.57	98.06
10000	126.52	117.16	112.78	110.62	109.52	108.95
11000	139.18	128.87	124.06	121.68	120.47	119.85
12000	151.83	140.59	135.34	132.74	131.42	130.74
13000	164.48	152.30	146.62	143.81	142.38	141.64
14000	177.13	164.02	157.90	154.87	153.33	152.53
15000	189.79	175.74	169.18	165.93	164.28	163.43
16000	202.44	187.45	180.45	176.99	175.23	174.32
17000	215.09	199.17	191.73	188.05	186.18	185.22
18000	227.74	210.88	203.01	199.12	197.13	196.11
19000	240.40	222.60	214.29	210.18	208.09	207.01
20000	253.05	234.32	225.57	221.24	219.04	217.90
21000	265.70	246.03	236.85	232.30	229.99	228.80
22000	278.35	257.75	248.12	243.36	240.94	239.69
23000	291.01	269.46	259.40	254.43	251.89	250.59
24000	303.66	281.18	270.68	265.49	262.85	261.48
25000	316.31	292.89	281.96	276.55	273.80	272.38
30000	379.57	351.47	338.35	331.86	328.56	326.85
35000	442.83	410.05	394.74	387.17	383.32	381.33
40000	506.10	468.63	451.13	442.48	438.08	435.81
45000	569.36	527.21	507.53	497.79	492.84	490.28
50000	632.62	585.79	563.92	553.10	547.60	544.76
55000	695.88	644.37	620.31	608.41	602.36	599.23
60000	759.15	702.95	676.70	663.72	657.12	653.71
65000	822.41	761.52	733.09	719.03	711.88	708.18
70000	885.67	820.10	789.48	774.34	766.64	762.66
75000	948.93	878.68	845.88	829.65	821.39	817.14
80000	1012.19	937.26	902.27	884.96	876.15	871.61
85000	1075.46	995.84	958.66	940.27	930.91	926.09
90000	1138.72	1054.42	1015.05	995.58	985.67	980.56
95000	1201.98	1113.00	1071.44	1050.89	1040.43	1035.04
100000	1265.24	1171.58	1127.84	1106.20	1095.19	1089.51
200000	2530.48	2343.15	2255.67	2212.40	2190.39	2179.03
300000	3795.73	3514.73	3383.51	3318.60	3285.58	3268.54
400000	5060.97	4686.30	4511.34	4424.80	4380.77	4358.06
500000	6326.21	5857.88	5639.18	5531.00	5475.97	5447.57

MONTHLY PAYMENT

Necessary to amortize a loan

13.5%

TERM / AMOUNT	1 YEARS	2 YEARS	3 YEARS	4 YEARS	5 YEARS	6 YEARS
500	44.78	23.89	16.97	13.54	11.50	10.17
600	53.73	28.67	20.36	16.25	13.81	12.20
700	62.69	33.44	23.75	18.95	16.11	14.24
800	71.64	38.22	27.15	21.66	18.41	16.27
900	80.60	43.00	30.54	24.37	20.71	18.31
1000	89.55	47.78	33.94	27.08	23.01	20.34
2000	179.10	95.55	67.87	54.15	46.02	40.68
3000	268.66	143.33	101.81	81.23	69.03	61.02
4000	358.21	191.11	135.74	108.31	92.04	81.36
5000	447.76	238.89	169.68	135.38	115.05	101.69
6000	537.31	286.66	203.61	162.46	138.06	122.03
7000	626.86	334.44	237.55	189.53	161.07	142.37
8000	716.42	382.22	271.48	216.61	184.08	162.71
9000	805.97	429.99	305.42	243.69	207.09	183.05
10000	895.52	477.77	339.35	270.76	230.10	203.39
11000	985.07	525.55	373.29	297.84	253.11	223.73
12000	1074.62	573.32	407.22	324.92	276.12	244.07
13000	1164.18	621.10	441.16	351.99	299.13	264.41
14000	1253.73	668.88	475.09	379.07	322.14	284.75
15000	1343.28	716.66	509.03	406.14	345.15	305.08
16000	1432.83	764.43	542.96	433.22	368.16	325.42
17000	1522.38	812.21	576.90	460.30	391.17	345.76
18000	1611.94	859.99	610.84	487.37	414.18	366.10
19000	1701.49	907.76	644.77	514.45	437.19	386.44
20000	1791.04	955.54	678.71	541.53	460.20	406.78
21000	1880.59	1003.32	712.64	568.60	483.21	427.12
22000	1970.14	1051.09	746.58	595.68	506.22	447.46
23000	2059.70	1098.87	780.51	622.76	529.23	467.80
24000	2149.25	1146.65	814.45	649.83	552.24	488.14
25000	2238.80	1194.43	848.38	676.91	575.25	508.47
30000	2686.56	1433.31	1018.06	812.29	690.30	610.17
35000	3134.32	1672.20	1187.74	947.67	805.34	711.86
40000	3582.08	1911.08	1357.41	1083.05	920.39	813.56
45000	4029.84	2149.97	1527.09	1218.43	1035.44	915.25
50000	4477.60	2388.85	1696.76	1353.82	1150.49	1016.95
55000	4925.36	2627.74	1866.44	1489.20	1265.54	1118.64
60000	5373.12	2866.62	2036.12	1624.58	1380.59	1220.34
65000	5820.88	3105.51	2205.79	1759.96	1495.64	1322.03
70000	6268.64	3344.39	2375.47	1895.34	1610.69	1423.73
75000	6716.40	3583.28	2545.15	2030.72	1725.74	1525.42
80000	7164.16	3822.16	2714.82	2166.11	1840.79	1627.12
85000	7611.92	4061.05	2884.50	2301.49	1955.84	1728.81
90000	8059.68	4299.93	3054.18	2436.87	2070.89	1830.51
95000	8507.44	4538.82	3223.85	2572.25	2185.94	1932.20
100000	8955.20	4777.70	3393.53	2707.63	2300.98	2033.90
200000	17910.41	9555.40	6787.06	5415.26	4601.97	4067.79
300000	26865.61	14333.10	10180.59	8122.90	6902.95	6101.69
400000	35820.81	19110.81	13574.11	10830.53	9203.94	8135.58
500000	44776.01	23888.51	16967.64	13538.16	11504.92	10169.48

13.5%

MONTHLY PAYMENT

Necessary to amortize a loan

TERM / AMOUNT	7 YEARS	8 YEARS	9 YEARS	10 YEARS	11 YEARS	12 YEARS
500	9.23	8.54	8.02	7.61	7.29	7.03
600	11.08	10.25	9.63	9.14	8.75	8.43
700	12.93	11.96	11.23	10.66	10.21	9.84
800	14.77	13.67	12.83	12.18	11.66	11.25
900	16.62	15.38	14.44	13.70	13.12	12.65
1000	18.46	17.09	16.04	15.23	14.58	14.06
2000	36.93	34.18	32.08	30.45	29.16	28.11
3000	55.39	51.26	48.13	45.68	43.74	42.17
4000	73.86	68.35	64.17	60.91	58.32	56.23
5000	92.32	85.44	80.21	76.14	72.90	70.29
6000	110.79	102.53	96.25	91.36	87.48	84.34
7000	129.25	119.62	112.30	106.59	102.06	98.40
8000	147.72	136.71	128.34	121.82	116.64	112.46
9000	166.18	153.79	144.38	137.05	131.22	126.51
10000	184.65	170.88	160.42	152.27	145.80	140.57
11000	203.11	187.97	176.47	167.50	160.38	154.63
12000	221.58	205.06	192.51	182.73	174.96	168.69
13000	240.04	222.15	208.55	197.96	189.54	182.74
14000	258.51	239.23	224.59	213.18	204.12	196.80
15000	276.97	256.32	240.63	228.41	218.70	210.86
16000	295.44	273.41	256.68	243.64	233.28	224.91
17000	313.90	290.50	272.72	258.87	247.86	238.97
18000	332.37	307.59	288.76	274.09	262.44	253.03
19000	350.83	324.68	304.80	289.32	277.02	267.09
20000	369.30	341.76	320.85	304.55	291.60	281.14
21000	387.76	358.85	336.89	319.78	306.18	295.20
22000	406.23	375.94	352.93	335.00	320.76	309.26
23000	424.69	393.03	368.97	350.23	335.34	323.31
24000	443.16	410.12	385.02	365.46	349.92	337.37
25000	461.62	427.20	401.06	380.69	364.50	351.43
30000	553.95	512.64	481.27	456.82	437.40	421.72
35000	646.27	598.09	561.48	532.96	510.30	492.00
40000	738.60	683.53	641.69	609.10	583.19	562.29
45000	830.92	768.97	721.90	685.23	656.09	632.57
50000	923.24	854.41	802.12	761.37	728.99	702.86
55000	1015.57	939.85	882.33	837.51	801.89	773.14
60000	1107.89	1025.29	962.54	913.65	874.79	843.43
65000	1200.22	1110.73	1042.75	989.78	947.69	913.72
70000	1292.54	1196.17	1122.96	1065.92	1020.59	984.00
75000	1384.87	1281.61	1203.17	1142.06	1093.49	1054.29
80000	1477.19	1367.05	1283.39	1218.19	1166.39	1124.57
85000	1569.52	1452.49	1363.60	1294.33	1239.29	1194.86
90000	1661.84	1537.93	1443.81	1370.47	1312.19	1265.15
95000	1754.16	1623.38	1524.02	1446.61	1385.09	1335.43
100000	1846.49	1708.82	1604.23	1522.74	1457.99	1405.72
200000	3692.98	3417.63	3208.46	3045.49	2915.97	2811.43
300000	5539.47	5126.45	4812.69	4568.23	4373.96	4217.15
400000	7385.96	6835.26	6416.93	6090.97	5831.95	5622.87
500000	9232.45	8544.08	8021.16	7613.71	7289.93	7028.59

MONTHLY PAYMENT

Necessary to amortize a loan

13.5%

TERM / AMOUNT	15 YEARS	20 YEARS	25 YEARS	30 YEARS	35 YEARS	40 YEARS
500	6.49	6.04	5.83	5.73	5.68	5.65
600	7.79	7.24	6.99	6.87	6.81	6.78
700	9.09	8.45	8.16	8.02	7.95	7.91
800	10.39	9.66	9.33	9.16	9.08	9.04
900	11.68	10.87	10.49	10.31	10.22	10.17
1000	12.98	12.07	11.66	11.45	11.35	11.30
2000	25.97	24.15	23.31	22.91	22.71	22.61
3000	38.95	36.22	34.97	34.36	34.06	33.91
4000	51.93	48.29	46.63	45.82	45.41	45.21
5000	64.92	60.37	58.28	57.27	56.77	56.51
6000	77.90	72.44	69.94	68.72	68.12	67.82
7000	90.88	84.52	81.60	80.18	79.47	79.12
8000	103.87	96.59	93.25	91.63	90.83	90.42
9000	116.85	108.66	104.91	103.09	102.18	101.72
10000	129.83	120.74	116.56	114.54	113.53	113.03
11000	142.82	132.81	128.22	126.00	124.89	124.33
12000	155.80	144.88	139.88	137.45	136.24	135.63
13000	168.78	156.96	151.53	148.90	147.59	146.93
14000	181.76	169.03	163.19	160.36	158.95	158.24
15000	194.75	181.11	174.85	171.81	170.30	169.54
16000	207.73	193.18	186.50	183.27	181.65	180.84
17000	220.71	205.25	198.16	194.72	193.01	192.14
18000	233.70	217.33	209.82	206.17	204.36	203.45
19000	246.68	229.40	221.47	217.63	215.71	214.75
20000	259.66	241.47	233.13	229.08	227.07	226.05
21000	272.65	253.55	244.79	240.54	238.42	237.35
22000	285.63	265.62	256.44	251.99	249.77	248.66
23000	298.61	277.70	268.10	263.44	261.13	259.96
24000	311.60	289.77	279.75	274.90	272.48	271.26
25000	324.58	301.84	291.41	286.35	283.84	282.57
30000	389.50	362.21	349.69	343.62	340.60	339.08
35000	454.41	422.58	407.98	400.89	397.37	395.59
40000	519.33	482.95	466.26	458.16	454.14	452.10
45000	584.24	543.32	524.54	515.44	510.90	508.62
50000	649.16	603.69	582.82	572.71	567.67	565.13
55000	714.08	664.06	641.10	629.98	624.44	621.64
60000	778.99	724.42	699.39	687.25	681.20	678.16
65000	843.91	784.79	757.67	744.52	737.97	734.67
70000	908.82	845.16	815.95	801.79	794.74	791.18
75000	973.74	905.53	874.23	859.06	851.51	847.70
80000	1038.65	965.90	932.52	916.33	908.27	904.21
85000	1103.57	1026.27	990.80	973.60	965.04	960.72
90000	1168.49	1086.64	1049.08	1030.87	1021.81	1017.24
95000	1233.40	1147.01	1107.36	1088.14	1078.57	1073.75
100000	1298.32	1207.37	1165.64	1145.41	1135.34	1130.26
200000	2596.64	2414.75	2331.29	2290.82	2270.68	2260.52
300000	3894.96	3622.12	3496.93	3436.24	3406.02	3390.78
400000	5193.27	4829.50	4662.58	4581.65	4541.36	4521.04
500000	6491.59	6036.87	5828.22	5727.06	5676.70	5651.31

14%

MONTHLY PAYMENT

Necessary to amortize a loan

TERM / AMOUNT	1 YEARS	2 YEARS	3 YEARS	4 YEARS	5 YEARS	6 YEARS
500	44.89	24.01	17.09	13.66	11.63	10.30
600	53.87	28.81	20.51	16.40	13.96	12.36
700	62.85	33.61	23.92	19.13	16.29	14.42
800	71.83	38.41	27.34	21.86	18.61	16.48
900	80.81	43.21	30.76	24.59	20.94	18.55
1000	89.79	48.01	34.18	27.33	23.27	20.61
2000	179.57	96.03	68.36	54.65	46.54	41.21
3000	269.36	144.04	102.53	81.98	69.80	61.82
4000	359.15	192.05	136.71	109.31	93.07	82.42
5000	448.94	240.06	170.89	136.63	116.34	103.03
6000	538.72	288.08	205.07	163.96	139.61	123.63
7000	628.51	336.09	239.24	191.29	162.88	144.24
8000	718.30	384.10	273.42	218.61	186.15	164.85
9000	808.08	432.12	307.60	245.94	209.41	185.45
10000	897.87	480.13	341.78	273.26	232.68	206.06
11000	987.66	528.14	375.95	300.59	255.95	226.66
12000	1077.45	576.15	410.13	327.92	279.22	247.27
13000	1167.23	624.17	444.31	355.24	302.49	267.87
14000	1257.02	672.18	478.49	382.57	325.76	288.48
15000	1346.81	720.19	512.66	409.90	349.02	309.09
16000	1436.59	768.21	546.84	437.22	372.29	329.69
17000	1526.38	816.22	581.02	464.55	395.56	350.30
18000	1616.17	864.23	615.20	491.88	418.83	370.90
19000	1705.96	912.24	649.37	519.20	442.10	391.51
20000	1795.74	960.26	683.55	546.53	465.37	412.11
21000	1885.53	1008.27	717.73	573.86	488.63	432.72
22000	1975.32	1056.28	751.91	601.18	511.90	453.33
23000	2065.10	1104.30	786.09	628.51	535.17	473.93
24000	2154.89	1152.31	820.26	655.84	558.44	494.54
25000	2244.68	1200.32	854.44	683.16	581.71	515.14
30000	2693.61	1440.39	1025.33	819.79	698.05	618.17
35000	3142.55	1680.45	1196.22	956.43	814.39	721.20
40000	3591.48	1920.52	1367.11	1093.06	930.73	824.23
45000	4040.42	2160.58	1537.99	1229.69	1047.07	927.26
50000	4489.36	2400.64	1708.88	1366.32	1163.41	1030.29
55000	4938.29	2640.71	1879.77	1502.96	1279.75	1133.32
60000	5387.23	2880.77	2050.66	1639.59	1396.10	1236.34
65000	5836.16	3120.84	2221.55	1776.22	1512.44	1339.37
70000	6285.10	3360.90	2392.43	1912.85	1628.78	1442.40
75000	6734.03	3600.97	2563.32	2049.49	1745.12	1545.43
80000	7182.97	3841.03	2734.21	2186.12	1861.46	1648.46
85000	7631.90	4081.10	2905.10	2322.75	1977.80	1751.49
90000	8080.84	4321.16	3075.99	2459.38	2094.14	1854.52
95000	8529.78	4561.22	3246.87	2596.02	2210.48	1957.55
100000	8978.71	4801.29	3417.76	2732.65	2326.83	2060.57
200000	17957.42	9602.58	6835.53	5465.30	4653.65	4121.15
300000	26936.14	14403.86	10253.29	8197.94	6980.48	6181.72
400000	35914.85	19205.15	13671.05	10930.59	9307.30	8242.30
500000	44893.56	24006.44	17088.81	13663.24	11634.13	10302.87

MONTHLY PAYMENT

Necessary to amortize a loan

14%

TERM / AMOUNT	7 YEARS	8 YEARS	9 YEARS	10 YEARS	11 YEARS	12 YEARS
500	9.37	8.69	8.17	7.76	7.44	7.19
600	11.24	10.42	9.80	9.32	8.93	8.62
700	13.12	12.16	11.43	10.87	10.42	10.06
800	14.99	13.90	13.07	12.42	11.91	11.50
900	16.87	15.63	14.70	13.97	13.40	12.93
1000	18.74	17.37	16.33	15.53	14.89	14.37
2000	37.48	34.74	32.67	31.05	29.77	28.74
3000	56.22	52.11	49.00	46.58	44.66	43.11
4000	74.96	69.49	65.33	62.11	59.55	57.49
5000	93.70	86.86	81.67	77.63	74.43	71.86
6000	112.44	104.23	98.00	93.16	89.32	86.23
7000	131.18	121.60	114.34	108.69	104.21	100.60
8000	149.92	138.97	130.67	124.21	119.09	114.97
9000	168.66	156.34	147.00	139.74	133.98	129.34
10000	187.40	173.72	163.34	155.27	148.87	143.71
11000	206.14	191.09	179.67	170.79	163.75	158.08
12000	224.88	208.46	196.00	186.32	178.64	172.46
13000	243.62	225.83	212.34	201.85	193.53	186.83
14000	262.36	243.20	228.67	217.37	208.41	201.20
15000	281.10	260.57	245.01	232.90	223.30	215.57
16000	299.84	277.94	261.34	248.43	238.19	229.94
17000	318.58	295.32	277.67	263.95	253.07	244.31
18000	337.32	312.69	294.01	279.48	267.96	258.68
19000	356.06	330.06	310.34	295.01	282.85	273.05
20000	374.80	347.43	326.67	310.53	297.73	287.43
21000	393.54	364.80	343.01	326.06	312.62	301.80
22000	412.28	382.17	359.34	341.59	327.51	316.17
23000	431.02	399.54	375.68	357.11	342.39	330.54
24000	449.76	416.92	392.01	372.64	357.28	344.91
25000	468.50	434.29	408.34	388.17	372.17	359.28
30000	562.20	521.15	490.01	465.80	446.60	431.14
35000	655.90	608.00	571.68	543.43	521.03	502.99
40000	749.60	694.86	653.35	621.07	595.47	574.85
45000	843.30	781.72	735.02	698.70	669.90	646.71
50000	937.00	868.58	816.69	776.33	744.33	718.56
55000	1030.70	955.43	898.35	853.97	818.77	790.42
60000	1124.40	1042.29	980.02	931.60	893.20	862.28
65000	1218.10	1129.15	1061.69	1009.23	967.63	934.13
70000	1311.80	1216.01	1143.36	1086.87	1042.07	1005.99
75000	1405.50	1302.86	1225.03	1164.50	1116.50	1077.85
80000	1499.20	1389.72	1306.70	1242.13	1190.93	1149.70
85000	1592.90	1476.58	1388.36	1319.76	1265.37	1221.56
90000	1686.60	1563.44	1470.03	1397.40	1339.80	1293.41
95000	1780.30	1650.29	1551.70	1475.03	1414.23	1365.27
100000	1874.00	1737.15	1633.37	1552.66	1488.67	1437.13
200000	3748.00	3474.30	3266.74	3105.33	2977.33	2874.25
300000	5622.00	5211.45	4900.11	4657.99	4466.00	4311.38
400000	7496.00	6948.60	6533.48	6210.66	5954.66	5748.51
500000	9370.01	8685.75	8166.85	7763.32	7443.33	7185.64

14%

MONTHLY PAYMENT

Necessary to amortize a loan

TERM / AMOUNT	15 YEARS	20 YEARS	25 YEARS	30 YEARS	35 YEARS	40 YEARS
500	6.66	6.22	6.02	5.92	5.88	5.86
600	7.99	7.46	7.22	7.11	7.05	7.03
700	9.32	8.70	8.43	8.29	8.23	8.20
800	10.65	9.95	9.63	9.48	9.41	9.37
900	11.99	11.19	10.83	10.66	10.58	10.54
1000	13.32	12.44	12.04	11.85	11.76	11.71
2000	26.63	24.87	24.08	23.70	23.51	23.42
3000	39.95	37.31	36.11	35.55	35.27	35.13
4000	53.27	49.74	48.15	47.39	47.03	46.85
5000	66.59	62.18	60.19	59.24	58.78	58.56
6000	79.90	74.61	72.23	71.09	70.54	70.27
7000	93.22	87.05	84.26	82.94	82.30	81.98
8000	106.54	99.48	96.30	94.79	94.05	93.69
9000	119.86	111.92	108.34	106.64	105.81	105.40
10000	133.17	124.35	120.38	118.49	117.57	117.11
11000	146.49	136.79	132.41	130.34	129.32	128.83
12000	159.81	149.22	144.45	142.18	141.08	140.54
13000	173.13	161.66	156.49	154.03	152.84	152.25
14000	186.44	174.09	168.53	165.88	164.59	163.96
15000	199.76	186.53	180.56	177.73	176.35	175.67
16000	213.08	198.96	192.60	189.58	188.11	187.38
17000	226.40	211.40	204.64	201.43	199.86	199.09
18000	239.71	223.83	216.68	213.28	211.62	210.81
19000	253.03	236.27	228.71	225.13	223.38	222.52
20000	266.35	248.70	240.75	236.97	235.13	234.23
21000	279.67	261.14	252.79	248.82	246.89	245.94
22000	292.98	273.57	264.83	260.67	258.65	257.65
23000	306.30	286.01	276.87	272.52	270.40	269.36
24000	319.62	298.44	288.90	284.37	282.16	281.07
25000	332.94	310.88	300.94	296.22	293.92	292.79
30000	399.52	373.06	361.13	355.46	352.70	351.34
35000	466.11	435.23	421.32	414.71	411.49	409.90
40000	532.70	497.41	481.50	473.95	470.27	468.46
45000	599.28	559.58	541.69	533.19	529.05	527.01
50000	665.87	621.76	601.88	592.44	587.84	585.57
55000	732.46	683.94	662.07	651.68	646.62	644.13
60000	799.04	746.11	722.26	710.92	705.40	702.68
65000	865.63	808.29	782.44	770.17	764.19	761.24
70000	932.22	870.46	842.63	829.41	822.97	819.80
75000	998.81	932.64	902.82	888.65	881.75	878.36
80000	1065.39	994.82	963.01	947.90	940.54	936.91
85000	1131.98	1056.99	1023.20	1007.14	999.32	995.47
90000	1198.57	1119.17	1083.38	1066.38	1058.11	1054.03
95000	1265.15	1181.34	1143.57	1125.63	1116.89	1112.58
100000	1331.74	1243.52	1203.76	1184.87	1175.67	1171.14
200000	2663.48	2487.04	2407.52	2369.74	2351.35	2342.28
300000	3995.22	3730.56	3611.28	3554.62	3527.02	3513.42
400000	5326.97	4974.08	4815.04	4739.49	4702.69	4684.56
500000	6658.71	6217.60	6018.81	5924.36	5878.37	5855.70

MONTHLY PAYMENT

Necessary to amortize a loan

14.5%

TERM / AMOUNT	1 YEARS	2 YEARS	3 YEARS	4 YEARS	5 YEARS	6 YEARS
500	45.01	24.12	17.21	13.79	11.76	10.44
600	54.01	28.95	20.65	16.55	14.12	12.52
700	63.02	33.77	24.09	19.30	16.47	14.61
800	72.02	38.60	27.54	22.06	18.82	16.70
900	81.02	43.42	30.98	24.82	21.18	18.79
1000	90.02	48.25	34.42	27.58	23.53	20.87
2000	180.05	96.50	68.84	55.16	47.06	41.75
3000	270.07	144.75	103.26	82.73	70.58	62.62
4000	360.09	193.00	137.68	110.31	94.11	83.50
5000	450.11	241.25	172.10	137.89	117.64	104.37
6000	540.14	289.50	206.53	165.47	141.17	125.25
7000	630.16	337.75	240.95	193.05	164.70	146.12
8000	720.18	386.00	275.37	220.62	188.23	167.00
9000	810.20	434.24	309.79	248.20	211.75	187.87
10000	900.23	482.49	344.21	275.78	235.28	208.74
11000	990.25	530.74	378.63	303.36	258.81	229.62
12000	1080.27	578.99	413.05	330.94	282.34	250.49
13000	1170.29	627.24	447.47	358.51	305.87	271.37
14000	1260.32	675.49	481.89	386.09	329.40	292.24
15000	1350.34	723.74	516.31	413.67	352.92	313.12
16000	1440.36	771.99	550.74	441.25	376.45	333.99
17000	1530.38	820.24	585.16	468.83	399.98	354.87
18000	1620.41	868.49	619.58	496.40	423.51	375.74
19000	1710.43	916.74	654.00	523.98	447.04	396.61
20000	1800.45	964.99	688.42	551.56	470.57	417.49
21000	1890.47	1013.24	722.84	579.14	494.09	438.36
22000	1980.50	1061.49	757.26	606.71	517.62	459.24
23000	2070.52	1109.74	791.68	634.29	541.15	480.11
24000	2160.54	1157.99	826.10	661.87	564.68	500.99
25000	2250.56	1206.24	860.52	689.45	588.21	521.86
30000	2700.68	1447.48	1032.63	827.34	705.85	626.23
35000	3150.79	1688.73	1204.73	965.23	823.49	730.60
40000	3600.90	1929.98	1376.84	1103.12	941.13	834.98
45000	4051.01	2171.22	1548.94	1241.01	1058.77	939.35
50000	4501.13	2412.47	1721.05	1378.90	1176.41	1043.72
55000	4951.24	2653.72	1893.15	1516.79	1294.06	1148.09
60000	5401.35	2894.97	2065.26	1654.68	1411.70	1252.47
65000	5851.47	3136.21	2237.36	1792.57	1529.34	1356.84
70000	6301.58	3377.46	2409.47	1930.46	1646.98	1461.21
75000	6751.69	3618.71	2581.57	2068.35	1764.62	1565.58
80000	7201.80	3859.95	2753.68	2206.24	1882.26	1669.95
85000	7651.92	4101.20	2925.78	2344.13	1999.90	1774.33
90000	8102.03	4342.45	3097.89	2482.02	2117.55	1878.70
95000	8552.14	4583.70	3269.99	2619.91	2235.19	1983.07
100000	9002.25	4824.94	3442.10	2757.80	2352.83	2087.44
200000	18004.51	9649.89	6884.20	5515.59	4705.66	4174.89
300000	27006.76	14474.83	10326.29	8273.39	7058.48	6262.33
400000	36009.02	19299.77	13768.39	11031.18	9411.31	8349.77
500000	45011.27	24124.71	17210.49	13788.98	11764.14	10437.21

14.5%

MONTHLY PAYMENT

Necessary to amortize a loan

TERM / AMOUNT	7 YEARS	8 YEARS	9 YEARS	10 YEARS	11 YEARS	12 YEARS
500	9.51	8.83	8.31	7.91	7.60	7.34
600	11.41	10.59	9.98	9.50	9.12	8.81
700	13.31	12.36	11.64	11.08	10.64	10.28
800	15.21	14.13	13.30	12.66	12.16	11.75
900	17.12	15.89	14.96	14.25	13.68	13.22
1000	19.02	17.66	16.63	15.83	15.20	14.69
2000	38.03	35.31	33.26	31.66	30.39	29.38
3000	57.05	52.97	49.88	47.49	45.59	44.07
4000	76.07	70.63	66.51	63.31	60.79	58.75
5000	95.09	88.29	83.14	79.14	75.98	73.44
6000	114.10	105.94	99.77	94.97	91.18	88.13
7000	133.12	123.60	116.39	110.80	106.38	102.82
8000	152.14	141.26	133.02	126.63	121.57	117.51
9000	171.16	158.92	149.65	142.46	136.77	132.20
10000	190.17	176.57	166.28	158.29	151.96	146.88
11000	209.19	194.23	182.90	174.12	167.16	161.57
12000	228.21	211.89	199.53	189.94	182.36	176.26
13000	247.22	229.54	216.16	205.77	197.55	190.95
14000	266.24	247.20	232.79	221.60	212.75	205.64
15000	285.26	264.86	249.42	237.43	227.95	220.33
16000	304.28	282.52	266.04	253.26	243.14	235.02
17000	323.29	300.17	282.67	269.09	258.34	249.70
18000	342.31	317.83	299.30	284.92	273.54	264.39
19000	361.33	335.49	315.93	300.74	288.73	279.08
20000	380.35	353.15	332.55	316.57	303.93	293.77
21000	399.36	370.80	349.18	332.40	319.13	308.46
22000	418.38	388.46	365.81	348.23	334.32	323.15
23000	437.40	406.12	382.44	364.06	349.52	337.84
24000	456.42	423.77	399.07	379.89	364.71	352.52
25000	475.43	441.43	415.69	395.72	379.91	367.21
30000	570.52	529.72	498.83	474.86	455.89	440.65
35000	665.61	618.00	581.97	554.00	531.88	514.10
40000	760.69	706.29	665.11	633.15	607.86	587.54
45000	855.78	794.58	748.25	712.29	683.84	660.98
50000	950.87	882.86	831.39	791.43	759.82	734.42
55000	1045.95	971.15	914.52	870.58	835.80	807.87
60000	1141.04	1059.44	997.66	949.72	911.79	881.31
65000	1236.12	1147.72	1080.80	1028.86	987.77	954.75
70000	1331.21	1236.01	1163.94	1108.01	1063.75	1028.19
75000	1426.30	1324.29	1247.08	1187.15	1139.73	1101.64
80000	1521.38	1412.58	1330.22	1266.29	1215.72	1175.08
85000	1616.47	1500.87	1413.36	1345.44	1291.70	1248.52
90000	1711.56	1589.15	1496.49	1424.58	1367.68	1321.96
95000	1806.64	1677.44	1579.63	1503.72	1443.66	1395.41
100000	1901.73	1765.73	1662.77	1582.87	1519.64	1468.85
200000	3803.46	3531.45	3325.54	3165.74	3039.29	2937.70
300000	5705.19	5297.18	4988.32	4748.60	4558.93	4406.55
400000	7606.92	7062.90	6651.09	6331.47	6078.58	5875.40
500000	9508.65	8828.63	8313.86	7914.34	7598.22	7344.24

MONTHLY PAYMENT

Necessary to amortize a loan

14.5%

TERM / AMOUNT	15 YEARS	20 YEARS	25 YEARS	30 YEARS	35 YEARS	40 YEARS
500	6.83	6.40	6.21	6.12	6.08	6.06
600	8.19	7.68	7.45	7.35	7.30	7.27
700	9.56	8.96	8.70	8.57	8.51	8.48
800	10.92	10.24	9.94	9.80	9.73	9.70
900	12.29	11.52	11.18	11.02	10.95	10.91
1000	13.66	12.80	12.42	12.25	12.16	12.12
2000	27.31	25.60	24.84	24.49	24.32	24.24
3000	40.97	38.40	37.26	36.74	36.49	36.36
4000	54.62	51.20	49.69	48.98	48.65	48.49
5000	68.28	64.00	62.11	61.23	60.81	60.61
6000	81.93	76.80	74.53	73.47	72.97	72.73
7000	95.59	89.60	86.95	85.72	85.13	84.85
8000	109.24	102.40	99.37	97.96	97.29	96.97
9000	122.90	115.20	111.79	110.21	109.46	109.09
10000	136.55	128.00	124.22	122.46	121.62	121.21
11000	150.21	140.80	136.64	134.70	133.78	133.33
12000	163.86	153.60	149.06	146.95	145.94	145.46
13000	177.52	166.40	161.48	159.19	158.10	157.58
14000	191.17	179.20	173.90	171.44	170.26	169.70
15000	204.83	192.00	186.32	183.68	182.43	181.82
16000	218.48	204.80	198.75	195.93	194.59	193.94
17000	232.14	217.60	211.17	208.17	206.75	206.06
18000	245.79	230.40	223.59	220.42	218.91	218.18
19000	259.45	243.20	236.01	232.67	231.07	230.31
20000	273.10	256.00	248.43	244.91	243.23	242.43
21000	286.76	268.80	260.85	257.16	255.40	254.55
22000	300.41	281.60	273.28	269.40	267.56	266.67
23000	314.07	294.40	285.70	281.65	279.72	278.79
24000	327.72	307.20	298.12	293.89	291.88	290.91
25000	341.38	320.00	310.54	306.14	304.04	303.03
30000	409.65	384.00	372.65	367.37	364.85	363.64
35000	477.93	448.00	434.76	428.59	425.66	424.25
40000	546.20	512.00	496.87	489.82	486.47	484.85
45000	614.48	576.00	558.97	551.05	547.28	545.46
50000	682.75	640.00	621.08	612.28	608.09	606.07
55000	751.03	704.00	683.19	673.51	668.89	666.67
60000	819.30	768.00	745.30	734.73	729.70	727.28
65000	887.58	832.00	807.41	795.96	790.51	787.89
70000	955.85	896.00	869.51	857.19	851.32	848.49
75000	1024.13	960.00	931.62	918.42	912.13	909.10
80000	1092.40	1024.00	993.73	979.64	972.94	969.71
85000	1160.68	1088.00	1055.84	1040.87	1033.74	1030.31
90000	1228.95	1152.00	1117.95	1102.10	1094.55	1090.92
95000	1297.23	1216.00	1180.05	1163.33	1155.36	1151.53
100000	1365.50	1280.00	1242.16	1224.56	1216.17	1212.13
200000	2731.00	2560.00	2484.33	2449.11	2432.34	2424.27
300000	4096.50	3839.99	3726.49	3673.67	3648.51	3636.40
400000	5462.00	5119.99	4968.65	4898.22	4864.68	4848.53
500000	6827.50	6399.99	6210.81	6122.78	6080.85	6060.66

15%

MONTHLY PAYMENT

Necessary to amortize a loan

TERM / AMOUNT	1 YEARS	2 YEARS	3 YEARS	4 YEARS	5 YEARS	6 YEARS
500	45.13	24.24	17.33	13.92	11.89	10.57
600	54.15	29.09	20.80	16.70	14.27	12.69
700	63.18	33.94	24.27	19.48	16.65	14.80
800	72.21	38.79	27.73	22.26	19.03	16.92
900	81.23	43.64	31.20	25.05	21.41	19.03
1000	90.26	48.49	34.67	27.83	23.79	21.15
2000	180.52	96.97	69.33	55.66	47.58	42.29
3000	270.77	145.46	104.00	83.49	71.37	63.44
4000	361.03	193.95	138.66	111.32	95.16	84.58
5000	451.29	242.43	173.33	139.15	118.95	105.73
6000	541.55	290.92	207.99	166.98	142.74	126.87
7000	631.81	339.41	242.66	194.82	166.53	148.02
8000	722.07	387.89	277.32	222.65	190.32	169.16
9000	812.32	436.38	311.99	250.48	214.11	190.31
10000	902.58	484.87	346.65	278.31	237.90	211.45
11000	992.84	533.35	381.32	306.14	261.69	232.60
12000	1083.10	581.84	415.98	333.97	285.48	253.74
13000	1173.36	630.33	450.65	361.80	309.27	274.89
14000	1263.62	678.81	485.31	389.63	333.06	296.03
15000	1353.87	727.30	519.98	417.46	356.85	317.18
16000	1444.13	775.79	554.65	445.29	380.64	338.32
17000	1534.39	824.27	589.31	473.12	404.43	359.47
18000	1624.65	872.76	623.98	500.95	428.22	380.61
19000	1714.91	921.25	658.64	528.78	452.01	401.76
20000	1805.17	969.73	693.31	556.61	475.80	422.90
21000	1895.42	1018.22	727.97	584.45	499.59	444.05
22000	1985.68	1066.71	762.64	612.28	523.38	465.19
23000	2075.94	1115.19	797.30	640.11	547.17	486.34
24000	2166.20	1163.68	831.97	667.94	570.96	507.48
25000	2256.46	1212.17	866.63	695.77	594.75	528.63
30000	2707.75	1454.60	1039.96	834.92	713.70	634.35
35000	3159.04	1697.03	1213.29	974.08	832.65	740.08
40000	3610.33	1939.47	1386.61	1113.23	951.60	845.80
45000	4061.62	2181.90	1559.94	1252.38	1070.55	951.53
50000	4512.92	2424.33	1733.27	1391.54	1189.50	1057.25
55000	4964.21	2666.77	1906.59	1530.69	1308.45	1162.98
60000	5415.50	2909.20	2079.92	1669.84	1427.40	1268.70
65000	5866.79	3151.63	2253.25	1809.00	1546.35	1374.43
70000	6318.08	3394.07	2426.57	1948.15	1665.30	1480.15
75000	6769.37	3636.50	2599.90	2087.31	1784.24	1585.88
80000	7220.66	3878.93	2773.23	2226.46	1903.19	1691.60
85000	7671.96	4121.37	2946.55	2365.61	2022.14	1797.33
90000	8123.25	4363.80	3119.88	2504.77	2141.09	1903.05
95000	8574.54	4606.23	3293.21	2643.92	2260.04	2008.78
100000	9025.83	4848.66	3466.53	2783.07	2378.99	2114.50
200000	18051.66	9697.33	6933.07	5566.15	4757.99	4229.00
300000	27077.49	14545.99	10399.60	8349.22	7136.98	6343.50
400000	36103.32	19394.66	13866.13	11132.30	9515.97	8458.01
500000	45129.16	24243.32	17332.66	13915.37	11894.97	10572.51

MONTHLY PAYMENT

Necessary to amortize a loan

15%

TERM / AMOUNT	7 YEARS	8 YEARS	9 YEARS	10 YEARS	11 YEARS	12 YEARS
500	9.65	8.97	8.46	8.07	7.75	7.50
600	11.58	10.77	10.15	9.68	9.31	9.01
700	13.51	12.56	11.85	11.29	10.86	10.51
800	15.44	14.36	13.54	12.91	12.41	12.01
900	17.37	16.15	15.23	14.52	13.96	13.51
1000	19.30	17.95	16.92	16.13	15.51	15.01
2000	38.59	35.89	33.85	32.27	31.02	30.02
3000	57.89	53.84	50.77	48.40	46.53	45.03
4000	77.19	71.78	67.70	64.53	62.04	60.04
5000	96.48	89.73	84.62	80.67	77.55	75.04
6000	115.78	107.67	101.55	96.80	93.05	90.05
7000	135.08	125.62	118.47	112.93	108.56	105.06
8000	154.37	143.56	135.39	129.07	124.07	120.07
9000	173.67	161.51	152.32	145.20	139.58	135.08
10000	192.97	179.45	169.24	161.33	155.09	150.09
11000	212.26	197.40	186.17	177.47	170.60	165.10
12000	231.56	215.34	203.09	193.60	186.11	180.11
13000	250.86	233.29	220.02	209.74	201.62	195.11
14000	270.15	251.24	236.94	225.87	217.13	210.12
15000	289.45	269.18	253.87	242.00	232.64	225.13
16000	308.75	287.13	270.79	258.14	248.15	240.14
17000	328.04	305.07	287.71	274.27	263.66	255.15
18000	347.34	323.02	304.64	290.40	279.16	270.16
19000	366.64	340.96	321.56	306.54	294.67	285.17
20000	385.94	358.91	338.49	322.67	310.18	300.18
21000	405.23	376.85	355.41	338.80	325.69	315.18
22000	424.53	394.80	372.34	354.94	341.20	330.19
23000	443.83	412.74	389.26	371.07	356.71	345.20
24000	463.12	430.69	406.18	387.20	372.22	360.21
25000	482.42	448.64	423.11	403.34	387.73	375.22
30000	578.90	538.36	507.73	484.00	465.27	450.26
35000	675.39	628.09	592.35	564.67	542.82	525.31
40000	771.87	717.82	676.97	645.34	620.37	600.35
45000	868.35	807.54	761.60	726.01	697.91	675.39
50000	964.84	897.27	846.22	806.67	775.46	750.44
55000	1061.32	987.00	930.84	887.34	853.00	825.48
60000	1157.81	1076.72	1015.46	968.01	930.55	900.53
65000	1254.29	1166.45	1100.08	1048.68	1008.09	975.57
70000	1350.77	1256.18	1184.70	1129.34	1085.64	1050.61
75000	1447.26	1345.91	1269.33	1210.01	1163.19	1125.66
80000	1543.74	1435.63	1353.95	1290.68	1240.73	1200.70
85000	1640.22	1525.36	1438.57	1371.35	1318.28	1275.75
90000	1736.71	1615.09	1523.19	1452.01	1395.82	1350.79
95000	1833.19	1704.81	1607.81	1532.68	1473.37	1425.83
100000	1929.68	1794.54	1692.43	1613.35	1550.91	1500.88
200000	3859.35	3589.08	3384.87	3226.70	3101.83	3001.75
300000	5789.03	5383.62	5077.30	4840.05	4652.74	4502.63
400000	7718.70	7178.16	6769.73	6453.40	6203.66	6003.51
500000	9648.38	8972.70	8462.17	8066.75	7754.57	7504.38

15%

MONTHLY PAYMENT

Necessary to amortize a loan

TERM / AMOUNT	15 YEARS	20 YEARS	25 YEARS	30 YEARS	35 YEARS	40 YEARS
500	7.00	6.58	6.40	6.32	6.28	6.27
600	8.40	7.90	7.68	7.59	7.54	7.52
700	9.80	9.22	8.97	8.85	8.80	8.77
800	11.20	10.53	10.25	10.12	10.05	10.03
900	12.60	11.85	11.53	11.38	11.31	11.28
1000	14.00	13.17	12.81	12.64	12.57	12.53
2000	27.99	26.34	25.62	25.29	25.14	25.06
3000	41.99	39.50	38.42	37.93	37.70	37.60
4000	55.98	52.67	51.23	50.58	50.27	50.13
5000	69.98	65.84	64.04	63.22	62.84	62.66
6000	83.98	79.01	76.85	75.87	75.41	75.19
7000	97.97	92.18	89.66	88.51	87.98	87.73
8000	111.97	105.34	102.47	101.16	100.55	100.26
9000	125.96	118.51	115.27	113.80	113.11	112.79
10000	139.96	131.68	128.08	126.44	125.68	125.32
11000	153.95	144.85	140.89	139.09	138.25	137.85
12000	167.95	158.01	153.70	151.73	150.82	150.39
13000	181.95	171.18	166.51	164.38	163.39	162.92
14000	195.94	184.35	179.32	177.02	175.95	175.45
15000	209.94	197.52	192.12	189.67	188.52	187.98
16000	223.93	210.69	204.93	202.31	201.09	200.52
17000	237.93	223.85	217.74	214.96	213.66	213.05
18000	251.93	237.02	230.55	227.60	226.23	225.58
19000	265.92	250.19	243.36	240.24	238.79	238.11
20000	279.92	263.36	256.17	252.89	251.36	250.64
21000	293.91	276.53	268.97	265.53	263.93	263.18
22000	307.91	289.69	281.78	278.18	276.50	275.71
23000	321.91	302.86	294.59	290.82	289.07	288.24
24000	335.90	316.03	307.40	303.47	301.64	300.77
25000	349.90	329.20	320.21	316.11	314.20	313.31
30000	419.88	395.04	384.25	379.33	377.04	375.97
35000	489.86	460.88	448.29	442.56	439.88	438.63
40000	559.83	526.72	512.33	505.78	502.73	501.29
45000	629.81	592.56	576.37	569.00	565.57	563.95
50000	699.79	658.39	640.42	632.22	628.41	626.61
55000	769.77	724.23	704.46	695.44	691.25	689.27
60000	839.75	790.07	768.50	758.67	754.09	751.93
65000	909.73	855.91	832.54	821.89	816.93	814.60
70000	979.71	921.75	896.58	885.11	879.77	877.26
75000	1049.69	987.59	960.62	948.33	942.61	939.92
80000	1119.67	1053.43	1024.66	1011.56	1005.45	1002.58
85000	1189.65	1119.27	1088.71	1074.78	1068.29	1065.24
90000	1259.63	1185.11	1152.75	1138.00	1131.13	1127.90
95000	1329.61	1250.95	1216.79	1201.22	1193.97	1190.56
100000	1399.59	1316.79	1280.83	1264.44	1256.81	1253.22
200000	2799.17	2633.58	2561.66	2528.89	2513.63	2506.45
300000	4198.76	3950.37	3842.49	3793.33	3770.44	3759.67
400000	5598.35	5267.16	5123.32	5057.78	5027.25	5012.90
500000	6997.94	6583.95	6404.15	6322.22	6284.07	6266.12

MONTHLY PAYMENT

Necessary to amortize a loan

15.5%

TERM / AMOUNT	1 YEARS	2 YEARS	3 YEARS	4 YEARS	5 YEARS	6 YEARS
500	45.25	24.36	17.46	14.04	12.03	10.71
600	54.30	29.23	20.95	16.85	14.43	12.85
700	63.35	34.11	24.44	19.66	16.84	14.99
800	72.40	38.98	27.93	22.47	19.24	17.13
900	81.44	43.85	31.42	25.28	21.65	19.28
1000	90.49	48.72	34.91	28.08	24.05	21.42
2000	180.99	97.45	69.82	56.17	48.11	42.83
3000	271.48	146.17	104.73	84.25	72.16	64.25
4000	361.98	194.90	139.64	112.34	96.21	85.67
5000	452.47	243.62	174.55	140.42	120.27	107.09
6000	542.97	292.35	209.46	168.51	144.32	128.50
7000	633.46	341.07	244.37	196.59	168.37	149.92
8000	723.96	389.80	279.29	224.68	192.43	171.34
9000	814.45	438.52	314.20	252.76	216.48	192.76
10000	904.94	487.25	349.11	280.85	240.53	214.17
11000	995.44	535.97	384.02	308.93	264.59	235.59
12000	1085.93	584.69	418.93	337.02	288.64	257.01
13000	1176.43	633.42	453.84	365.10	312.69	278.43
14000	1266.92	682.14	488.75	393.19	336.74	299.84
15000	1357.42	730.87	523.66	421.27	360.80	321.26
16000	1447.91	779.59	558.57	449.36	384.85	342.68
17000	1538.41	828.32	593.48	477.44	408.90	364.10
18000	1628.90	877.04	628.39	505.53	432.96	385.51
19000	1719.39	925.77	663.30	533.61	457.01	406.93
20000	1809.89	974.49	698.21	561.70	481.06	428.35
21000	1900.38	1023.22	733.12	589.78	505.12	449.77
22000	1990.88	1071.94	768.03	617.87	529.17	471.18
23000	2081.37	1120.66	802.95	645.95	553.22	492.60
24000	2171.87	1169.39	837.86	674.04	577.28	514.02
25000	2262.36	1218.11	872.77	702.12	601.33	535.44
30000	2714.83	1461.74	1047.32	842.55	721.60	642.52
35000	3167.30	1705.36	1221.87	982.97	841.86	749.61
40000	3619.78	1948.98	1396.43	1123.39	962.13	856.70
45000	4072.25	2192.60	1570.98	1263.82	1082.39	963.79
50000	4524.72	2436.23	1745.53	1404.24	1202.66	1070.87
55000	4977.19	2679.85	1920.09	1544.67	1322.93	1177.96
60000	5429.66	2923.47	2094.64	1685.09	1443.19	1285.05
65000	5882.14	3167.10	2269.19	1825.52	1563.46	1392.14
70000	6334.61	3410.72	2443.75	1965.94	1683.72	1499.22
75000	6787.08	3654.34	2618.30	2106.36	1803.99	1606.31
80000	7239.55	3897.96	2792.85	2246.79	1924.26	1713.40
85000	7692.03	4141.59	2967.41	2387.21	2044.52	1820.49
90000	8144.50	4385.21	3141.96	2527.64	2164.79	1927.57
95000	8596.97	4628.83	3316.51	2668.06	2285.05	2034.66
100000	9049.44	4872.45	3491.07	2808.49	2405.32	2141.75
200000	18098.88	9744.91	6982.14	5616.97	4810.64	4283.50
300000	27148.32	14617.36	10473.20	8425.46	7215.96	6425.25
400000	36197.77	19489.82	13964.27	11233.94	9621.28	8567.00
500000	45247.21	24362.27	17455.34	14042.43	12026.60	10708.74

15.5%

MONTHLY PAYMENT

Necessary to amortize a loan

TERM / AMOUNT	7 YEARS	8 YEARS	9 YEARS	10 YEARS	11 YEARS	12 YEARS
500	9.79	9.12	8.61	8.22	7.91	7.67
600	11.75	10.94	10.33	9.86	9.49	9.20
700	13.70	12.77	12.06	11.51	11.08	10.73
800	15.66	14.59	13.78	13.15	12.66	12.27
900	17.62	16.41	15.50	14.80	14.24	13.80
1000	19.58	18.24	17.22	16.44	15.82	15.33
2000	39.16	36.47	34.45	32.88	31.65	30.66
3000	58.74	54.71	51.67	49.32	47.47	46.00
4000	78.31	72.94	68.89	65.76	63.30	61.33
5000	97.89	91.18	86.12	82.21	79.12	76.66
6000	117.47	109.42	103.34	98.65	94.95	91.99
7000	137.05	127.65	120.56	115.09	110.77	107.32
8000	156.63	145.89	137.79	131.53	126.60	122.66
9000	176.21	164.12	155.01	147.97	142.42	137.99
10000	195.78	182.36	172.24	164.41	158.25	153.32
11000	215.36	200.60	189.46	180.85	174.07	168.65
12000	234.94	218.83	206.68	197.29	189.90	183.98
13000	254.52	237.07	223.91	213.73	205.72	199.32
14000	274.10	255.30	241.13	230.17	221.55	214.65
15000	293.68	273.54	258.35	246.62	237.37	229.98
16000	313.25	291.77	275.58	263.06	253.20	245.31
17000	332.83	310.01	292.80	279.50	269.02	260.64
18000	352.41	328.25	310.02	295.94	284.85	275.98
19000	371.99	346.48	327.25	312.38	300.67	291.31
20000	391.57	364.72	344.47	328.82	316.49	306.64
21000	411.15	382.95	361.69	345.26	332.32	321.97
22000	430.72	401.19	378.92	361.70	348.14	337.30
23000	450.30	419.43	396.14	378.14	363.97	352.64
24000	469.88	437.66	413.36	394.59	379.79	367.97
25000	489.46	455.90	430.59	411.03	395.62	383.30
30000	587.35	547.08	516.71	493.23	474.74	459.96
35000	685.24	638.26	602.82	575.44	553.87	536.62
40000	783.13	729.44	688.94	657.64	632.99	613.28
45000	881.03	820.62	775.06	739.85	712.11	689.94
50000	978.92	911.80	861.18	822.05	791.24	766.60
55000	1076.81	1002.98	947.29	904.26	870.36	843.26
60000	1174.70	1094.16	1033.41	986.46	949.48	919.92
65000	1272.59	1185.33	1119.53	1068.67	1028.61	996.58
70000	1370.48	1276.51	1205.65	1150.87	1107.73	1073.24
75000	1468.38	1367.69	1291.76	1233.08	1186.86	1149.90
80000	1566.27	1458.87	1377.88	1315.28	1265.98	1226.56
85000	1664.16	1550.05	1464.00	1397.49	1345.10	1303.22
90000	1762.05	1641.23	1550.12	1479.69	1424.23	1379.88
95000	1859.94	1732.41	1636.23	1561.90	1503.35	1456.54
100000	1957.83	1823.59	1722.35	1644.11	1582.47	1533.20
200000	3915.67	3647.18	3444.71	3288.21	3164.95	3066.41
300000	5873.50	5470.78	5167.06	4932.32	4747.42	4599.61
400000	7831.34	7294.37	6889.41	6576.42	6329.90	6132.82
500000	9789.17	9117.96	8611.76	8220.53	7912.37	7666.02

MONTHLY PAYMENT

Necessary to amortize a loan

15.5%

TERM / AMOUNT	15 YEARS	20 YEARS	25 YEARS	30 YEARS	35 YEARS	40 YEARS
500	7.17	6.77	6.60	6.52	6.49	6.47
600	8.60	8.12	7.92	7.83	7.79	7.77
700	10.04	9.48	9.24	9.13	9.08	9.06
800	11.47	10.83	10.56	10.44	10.38	10.36
900	12.91	12.18	11.88	11.74	11.68	11.65
1000	14.34	13.54	13.20	13.05	12.98	12.94
2000	28.68	27.08	26.39	26.09	25.95	25.89
3000	43.02	40.62	39.59	39.14	38.93	38.83
4000	57.36	54.16	52.79	52.18	51.90	51.78
5000	71.70	67.69	65.99	65.23	64.88	64.72
6000	86.04	81.23	79.18	78.27	77.86	77.66
7000	100.38	94.77	92.38	91.32	90.83	90.61
8000	114.72	108.31	105.58	104.36	103.81	103.55
9000	129.06	121.85	118.78	117.41	116.78	116.50
10000	143.40	135.39	131.97	130.45	129.76	129.44
11000	157.74	148.93	145.17	143.50	142.73	142.38
12000	172.08	162.47	158.37	156.54	155.71	155.33
13000	186.42	176.00	171.57	169.59	168.69	168.27
14000	200.76	189.54	184.76	182.63	181.66	181.22
15000	215.10	203.08	197.96	195.68	194.64	194.16
16000	229.44	216.62	211.16	208.72	207.61	207.10
17000	243.78	230.16	224.36	221.77	220.59	220.05
18000	258.12	243.70	237.55	234.81	233.57	232.99
19000	272.46	257.24	250.75	247.86	246.54	245.94
20000	286.80	270.78	263.95	260.90	259.52	258.88
21000	301.14	284.31	277.15	273.95	272.49	271.82
22000	315.48	297.85	290.34	286.99	285.47	284.77
23000	329.82	311.39	303.54	300.04	298.44	297.71
24000	344.16	324.93	316.74	313.08	311.42	310.66
25000	358.50	338.47	329.94	326.13	324.40	323.60
30000	430.20	406.16	395.92	391.36	389.28	388.32
35000	501.90	473.86	461.91	456.58	454.15	453.04
40000	573.60	541.55	527.90	521.81	519.03	517.76
45000	645.30	609.25	593.89	587.03	583.91	582.48
50000	717.00	676.94	659.87	652.26	648.79	647.20
55000	788.69	744.63	725.86	717.48	713.67	711.92
60000	860.39	812.33	791.85	782.71	778.55	776.64
65000	932.09	880.02	857.83	847.94	843.43	841.36
70000	1003.79	947.72	923.82	913.16	908.31	906.08
75000	1075.49	1015.41	989.81	978.39	973.19	970.80
80000	1147.19	1083.10	1055.80	1043.61	1038.07	1035.52
85000	1218.89	1150.80	1121.78	1108.84	1102.95	1100.24
90000	1290.59	1218.49	1187.77	1174.07	1167.83	1164.96
95000	1362.29	1286.19	1253.76	1239.29	1232.71	1229.68
100000	1433.99	1353.88	1319.75	1304.52	1297.58	1294.40
200000	2867.98	2707.76	2639.49	2609.03	2595.17	2588.80
300000	4301.97	4061.64	3959.24	3913.55	3892.75	3883.20
400000	5735.96	5415.52	5278.98	5218.07	5190.34	5177.60
500000	7169.95	6769.40	6598.73	6522.58	6487.92	6472.00

16%

MONTHLY PAYMENT

Necessary to amortize a loan

TERM AMOUNT	1 YEARS	2 YEARS	3 YEARS	4 YEARS	5 YEARS	6 YEARS
500	45.37	24.48	17.58	14.17	12.16	10.85
600	54.44	29.38	21.09	17.00	14.59	13.02
700	63.51	34.27	24.61	19.84	17.02	15.18
800	72.58	39.17	28.13	22.67	19.45	17.35
900	81.66	44.07	31.64	25.51	21.89	19.52
1000	90.73	48.96	35.16	28.34	24.32	21.69
2000	181.46	97.93	70.31	56.68	48.64	43.38
3000	272.19	146.89	105.47	85.02	72.95	65.08
4000	362.92	195.85	140.63	113.36	97.27	86.77
5000	453.65	244.82	175.79	141.70	121.59	108.46
6000	544.39	293.78	210.94	170.04	145.91	130.15
7000	635.12	342.74	246.10	198.38	170.23	151.84
8000	725.85	391.70	281.26	226.72	194.54	173.53
9000	816.58	440.67	316.41	255.06	218.86	195.23
10000	907.31	489.63	351.57	283.40	243.18	216.92
11000	998.04	538.59	386.73	311.74	267.50	238.61
12000	1088.77	587.56	421.88	340.08	291.82	260.30
13000	1179.50	636.52	457.04	368.42	316.13	281.99
14000	1270.23	685.48	492.20	396.76	340.45	303.69
15000	1360.96	734.45	527.36	425.10	364.77	325.38
16000	1451.69	783.41	562.51	453.44	389.09	347.07
17000	1542.42	832.37	597.67	481.78	413.41	368.76
18000	1633.16	881.34	632.83	510.13	437.73	390.45
19000	1723.89	930.30	667.98	538.47	462.04	412.14
20000	1814.62	979.26	703.14	566.81	486.36	433.84
21000	1905.35	1028.23	738.30	595.15	510.68	455.53
22000	1996.08	1077.19	773.45	623.49	535.00	477.22
23000	2086.81	1126.15	808.61	651.83	559.32	498.91
24000	2177.54	1175.11	843.77	680.17	583.63	520.60
25000	2268.27	1224.08	878.93	708.51	607.95	542.30
30000	2721.93	1468.89	1054.71	850.21	729.54	650.76
35000	3175.58	1713.71	1230.50	991.91	851.13	759.21
40000	3629.23	1958.52	1406.28	1133.61	972.72	867.67
45000	4082.89	2203.34	1582.07	1275.31	1094.31	976.13
50000	4536.54	2448.16	1757.85	1417.01	1215.90	1084.59
55000	4990.20	2692.97	1933.64	1558.72	1337.49	1193.05
60000	5443.85	2937.79	2109.42	1700.42	1459.08	1301.51
65000	5897.51	3182.60	2285.21	1842.12	1580.67	1409.97
70000	6351.16	3427.42	2460.99	1983.82	1702.26	1518.43
75000	6804.81	3672.23	2636.78	2125.52	1823.85	1626.89
80000	7258.47	3917.05	2812.56	2267.22	1945.44	1735.35
85000	7712.12	4161.86	2988.35	2408.92	2067.03	1843.81
90000	8165.78	4406.68	3164.13	2550.63	2188.63	1952.27
95000	8619.43	4651.50	3339.92	2692.33	2310.22	2060.72
100000	9073.09	4896.31	3515.70	2834.03	2431.81	2169.18
200000	18146.17	9792.62	7031.41	5668.06	4863.61	4338.37
300000	27219.26	14688.93	10547.11	8502.08	7295.42	6507.55
400000	36292.34	19585.24	14062.81	11336.11	9727.22	8676.74
500000	45365.43	24481.56	17578.52	14170.14	12159.03	10845.92

MONTHLY PAYMENT

Necessary to amortize a loan

16%

TERM / AMOUNT	7 YEARS	8 YEARS	9 YEARS	10 YEARS	11 YEARS	12 YEARS
500	9.93	9.26	8.76	8.38	8.07	7.83
600	11.92	11.12	10.52	10.05	9.69	9.39
700	13.90	12.97	12.27	11.73	11.30	10.96
800	15.89	14.82	14.02	13.40	12.91	12.53
900	17.88	16.68	15.77	15.08	14.53	14.09
1000	19.86	18.53	17.53	16.75	16.14	15.66
2000	39.72	37.06	35.05	33.50	32.29	31.32
3000	59.59	55.59	52.58	50.25	48.43	46.97
4000	79.45	74.12	70.10	67.01	64.57	62.63
5000	99.31	92.64	87.63	83.76	80.72	78.29
6000	119.17	111.17	105.15	100.51	96.86	93.95
7000	139.03	129.70	122.68	117.26	113.00	109.61
8000	158.90	148.23	140.20	134.01	129.15	125.27
9000	178.76	166.76	157.73	150.76	145.29	140.92
10000	198.62	185.29	175.25	167.51	161.43	156.58
11000	218.48	203.82	192.78	184.26	177.57	172.24
12000	238.34	222.35	210.30	201.02	193.72	187.90
13000	258.21	240.87	227.83	217.77	209.86	203.56
14000	278.07	259.40	245.35	234.52	226.00	219.22
15000	297.93	277.93	262.88	251.27	242.15	234.87
16000	317.79	296.46	280.40	268.02	258.29	250.53
17000	337.66	314.99	297.93	284.77	274.43	266.19
18000	357.52	333.52	315.45	301.52	290.58	281.85
19000	377.38	352.05	332.98	318.27	306.72	297.51
20000	397.24	370.58	350.51	335.03	322.86	313.17
21000	417.10	389.10	368.03	351.78	339.01	328.82
22000	436.97	407.63	385.56	368.53	355.15	344.48
23000	456.83	426.16	403.08	385.28	371.29	360.14
24000	476.69	444.69	420.61	402.03	387.44	375.80
25000	496.55	463.22	438.13	418.78	403.58	391.46
30000	595.86	555.86	525.76	502.54	484.30	469.75
35000	695.17	648.51	613.38	586.30	565.01	548.04
40000	794.48	741.15	701.01	670.05	645.73	626.33
45000	893.79	833.80	788.64	753.81	726.44	704.62
50000	993.10	926.44	876.26	837.57	807.16	782.91
55000	1092.41	1019.08	963.89	921.32	887.87	861.20
60000	1191.72	1111.73	1051.52	1005.08	968.59	939.50
65000	1291.03	1204.37	1139.14	1088.84	1049.31	1017.79
70000	1390.34	1297.02	1226.77	1172.59	1130.02	1096.08
75000	1489.65	1389.66	1314.39	1256.35	1210.74	1174.37
80000	1588.97	1482.30	1402.02	1340.10	1291.45	1252.66
85000	1688.28	1574.95	1489.65	1423.86	1372.17	1330.95
90000	1787.59	1667.59	1577.27	1507.62	1452.89	1409.24
95000	1886.90	1760.23	1664.90	1591.37	1533.60	1487.53
100000	1986.21	1852.88	1752.53	1675.13	1614.32	1565.83
200000	3972.41	3705.76	3505.05	3350.26	3228.63	3131.65
300000	5958.62	5558.64	5257.58	5025.39	4842.95	4697.48
400000	7944.83	7411.51	7010.10	6700.52	6457.27	6263.30
500000	9931.03	9264.39	8762.63	8375.66	8071.59	7829.13

16%

MONTHLY PAYMENT

Necessary to amortize a loan

TERM / AMOUNT	15 YEARS	20 YEARS	25 YEARS	30 YEARS	35 YEARS	40 YEARS
500	7.34	6.96	6.79	6.72	6.69	6.68
600	8.81	8.35	8.15	8.07	8.03	8.01
700	10.28	9.74	9.51	9.41	9.37	9.35
800	11.75	11.13	10.87	10.76	10.71	10.69
900	13.22	12.52	12.23	12.10	12.05	12.02
1000	14.69	13.91	13.59	13.45	13.38	13.36
2000	29.37	27.83	27.18	26.90	26.77	26.71
3000	44.06	41.74	40.77	40.34	40.15	40.07
4000	58.75	55.65	54.36	53.79	53.54	53.43
5000	73.44	69.56	67.94	67.24	66.92	66.78
6000	88.12	83.48	81.53	80.69	80.31	80.14
7000	102.81	97.39	95.12	94.13	93.69	93.50
8000	117.50	111.30	108.71	107.58	107.08	106.85
9000	132.18	125.21	122.30	121.03	120.46	120.21
10000	146.87	139.13	135.89	134.48	133.85	133.56
11000	161.56	153.04	149.48	147.92	147.23	146.92
12000	176.24	166.95	163.07	161.37	160.62	160.28
13000	190.93	180.86	176.66	174.82	174.00	173.63
14000	205.62	194.78	190.24	188.27	187.39	186.99
15000	220.31	208.69	203.83	201.71	200.77	200.35
16000	234.99	222.60	217.42	215.16	214.16	213.70
17000	249.68	236.51	231.01	228.61	227.54	227.06
18000	264.37	250.43	244.60	242.06	240.92	240.42
19000	279.05	264.34	258.19	255.50	254.31	253.77
20000	293.74	278.25	271.78	268.95	267.69	267.13
21000	308.43	292.16	285.37	282.40	281.08	280.49
22000	323.11	306.08	298.96	295.85	294.46	293.84
23000	337.80	319.99	312.54	309.29	307.85	307.20
24000	352.49	333.90	326.13	322.74	321.23	320.56
25000	367.18	347.81	339.72	336.19	334.62	333.91
30000	440.61	417.38	407.67	403.43	401.54	400.69
35000	514.05	486.94	475.61	470.66	468.46	467.48
40000	587.48	556.50	543.56	537.90	535.39	534.26
45000	660.92	626.07	611.50	605.14	602.31	601.04
50000	734.35	695.63	679.44	672.38	669.23	667.82
55000	807.79	765.19	747.39	739.62	736.16	734.61
60000	881.22	834.75	815.33	806.85	803.08	801.39
65000	954.66	904.32	883.28	874.09	870.01	868.17
70000	1028.09	973.88	951.22	941.33	936.93	934.95
75000	1101.53	1043.44	1019.17	1008.57	1003.85	1001.74
80000	1174.96	1113.00	1087.11	1075.81	1070.78	1068.52
85000	1248.40	1182.57	1155.06	1143.04	1137.70	1135.30
90000	1321.83	1252.13	1223.00	1210.28	1204.62	1202.08
95000	1395.27	1321.69	1290.94	1277.52	1271.55	1268.87
100000	1468.70	1391.26	1358.89	1344.76	1338.47	1335.65
200000	2937.40	2782.51	2717.78	2689.51	2676.94	2671.30
300000	4406.10	4173.77	4076.67	4034.27	4015.41	4006.95
400000	5874.80	5565.02	5435.56	5379.03	5353.88	5342.59
500000	7343.50	6956.28	6794.44	6723.78	6692.35	6678.24

MONTHLY PAYMENT

Necessary to amortize a loan

16.5%

TERM / AMOUNT	1 YEARS	2 YEARS	3 YEARS	4 YEARS	5 YEARS	6 YEARS
500	45.48	24.60	17.70	14.30	12.29	10.98
600	54.58	29.52	21.24	17.16	14.75	13.18
700	63.68	34.44	24.78	20.02	17.21	15.38
800	72.77	39.36	28.32	22.88	19.67	17.57
900	81.87	44.28	31.86	25.74	22.13	19.77
1000	90.97	49.20	35.40	28.60	24.58	21.97
2000	181.94	98.40	70.81	57.19	49.17	43.94
3000	272.90	147.61	106.21	85.79	73.75	65.90
4000	363.87	196.81	141.62	114.39	98.34	87.87
5000	454.84	246.01	177.02	142.99	122.92	109.84
6000	545.81	295.21	212.43	171.58	147.51	131.81
7000	636.77	344.42	247.83	200.18	172.09	153.78
8000	727.74	393.62	283.24	228.78	196.68	175.74
9000	818.71	442.82	318.64	257.37	221.26	197.71
10000	909.68	492.02	354.04	285.97	245.85	219.68
11000	1000.64	541.23	389.45	314.57	270.43	241.65
12000	1091.61	590.43	424.85	343.16	295.01	263.62
13000	1182.58	639.63	460.26	371.76	319.60	285.58
14000	1273.55	688.83	495.66	400.36	344.18	307.55
15000	1364.51	738.04	531.07	428.96	368.77	329.52
16000	1455.48	787.24	566.47	457.55	393.35	351.49
17000	1546.45	836.44	601.87	486.15	417.94	373.46
18000	1637.42	885.64	637.28	514.75	442.52	395.43
19000	1728.39	934.84	672.68	543.34	467.11	417.39
20000	1819.35	984.05	708.09	571.94	491.69	439.36
21000	1910.32	1033.25	743.49	600.54	516.27	461.33
22000	2001.29	1082.45	778.90	629.13	540.86	483.30
23000	2092.26	1131.65	814.30	657.73	565.44	505.27
24000	2183.22	1180.86	849.71	686.33	590.03	527.23
25000	2274.19	1230.06	885.11	714.93	614.61	549.20
30000	2729.03	1476.07	1062.13	857.91	737.54	659.04
35000	3183.87	1722.08	1239.15	1000.90	860.46	768.88
40000	3638.71	1968.09	1416.18	1143.88	983.38	878.72
45000	4093.54	2214.11	1593.20	1286.87	1106.30	988.56
50000	4548.38	2460.12	1770.22	1429.85	1229.23	1098.40
55000	5003.22	2706.13	1947.24	1572.84	1352.15	1208.24
60000	5458.06	2952.14	2124.26	1715.82	1475.07	1318.08
65000	5912.90	3198.15	2301.28	1858.81	1597.99	1427.92
70000	6367.73	3444.16	2478.31	2001.79	1720.92	1537.76
75000	6822.57	3690.18	2655.33	2144.78	1843.84	1647.60
80000	7277.41	3936.19	2832.35	2287.76	1966.76	1757.44
85000	7732.25	4182.20	3009.37	2430.75	2089.68	1867.28
90000	8187.09	4428.21	3186.39	2573.73	2212.61	1977.13
95000	8641.93	4674.22	3363.42	2716.72	2335.53	2086.97
100000	9096.76	4920.24	3540.44	2859.70	2458.45	2196.81
200000	18193.53	9840.47	7080.88	5719.40	4916.90	4393.61
300000	27290.29	14760.71	10621.31	8579.10	7375.36	6590.42
400000	36387.05	19680.94	14161.75	11438.80	9833.81	8787.22
500000	45483.82	24601.18	17702.19	14298.50	12292.26	10984.03

16.5%

MONTHLY PAYMENT

Necessary to amortize a loan

TERM / AMOUNT	7 YEARS	8 YEARS	9 YEARS	10 YEARS	11 YEARS	12 YEARS
500	10.07	9.41	8.91	8.53	8.23	7.99
600	12.09	11.29	10.70	10.24	9.88	9.59
700	14.10	13.18	12.48	11.94	11.53	11.19
800	16.12	15.06	14.26	13.65	13.17	12.79
900	18.13	16.94	16.05	15.36	14.82	14.39
1000	20.15	18.82	17.83	17.06	16.46	15.99
2000	40.30	37.65	35.66	34.13	32.93	31.97
3000	60.44	56.47	53.49	51.19	49.39	47.96
4000	80.59	75.30	71.32	68.26	65.86	63.95
5000	100.74	94.12	89.15	85.32	82.32	79.94
6000	120.89	112.94	106.98	102.39	98.79	95.92
7000	141.04	131.77	124.81	119.45	115.25	111.91
8000	161.18	150.59	142.64	136.51	131.72	127.90
9000	181.33	169.42	160.47	153.58	148.18	143.89
10000	201.48	188.24	178.29	170.64	164.64	159.87
11000	221.63	207.06	196.12	187.71	181.11	175.86
12000	241.77	225.89	213.95	204.77	197.57	191.85
13000	261.92	244.71	231.78	221.83	214.04	207.84
14000	282.07	263.54	249.61	238.90	230.50	223.82
15000	302.22	282.36	267.44	255.96	246.97	239.81
16000	322.37	301.18	285.27	273.03	263.43	255.80
17000	342.51	320.01	303.10	290.09	279.89	271.78
18000	362.66	338.83	320.93	307.16	296.36	287.77
19000	382.81	357.66	338.76	324.22	312.82	303.76
20000	402.96	376.48	356.59	341.28	329.29	319.75
21000	423.11	395.30	374.42	358.35	345.75	335.73
22000	443.25	414.13	392.25	375.41	362.22	351.72
23000	463.40	432.95	410.08	392.48	378.68	367.71
24000	483.55	451.78	427.91	409.54	395.15	383.70
25000	503.70	470.60	445.74	426.61	411.61	399.68
30000	604.44	564.72	534.88	511.93	493.93	479.62
35000	705.18	658.84	624.03	597.25	576.25	559.56
40000	805.92	752.96	713.18	682.57	658.58	639.49
45000	906.66	847.08	802.33	767.89	740.90	719.43
50000	1007.39	941.20	891.47	853.21	823.22	799.37
55000	1108.13	1035.32	980.62	938.53	905.54	879.30
60000	1208.87	1129.44	1069.77	1023.85	987.86	959.24
65000	1309.61	1223.56	1158.92	1109.17	1070.18	1039.18
70000	1410.35	1317.68	1248.06	1194.50	1152.51	1119.11
75000	1511.09	1411.80	1337.21	1279.82	1234.83	1199.05
80000	1611.83	1505.92	1426.36	1365.14	1317.15	1278.99
85000	1712.57	1600.04	1515.51	1450.46	1399.47	1358.92
90000	1813.31	1694.16	1604.65	1535.78	1481.79	1438.86
95000	1914.05	1788.28	1693.80	1621.10	1564.12	1518.80
100000	2014.79	1882.40	1782.95	1706.42	1646.44	1598.73
200000	4029.58	3764.79	3565.90	3412.85	3292.88	3197.47
300000	6044.37	5647.19	5348.84	5119.27	4939.31	4796.20
400000	8059.16	7529.59	7131.79	6825.69	6585.75	6394.93
500000	10073.94	9411.99	8914.74	8532.11	8232.19	7993.67

MONTHLY PAYMENT

Necessary to amortize a loan

16.5%

TERM / AMOUNT	15 YEARS	20 YEARS	25 YEARS	30 YEARS	35 YEARS	40 YEARS
500	7.52	7.14	6.99	6.93	6.90	6.88
600	9.02	8.57	8.39	8.31	8.28	8.26
700	10.53	10.00	9.79	9.70	9.66	9.64
800	12.03	11.43	11.19	11.08	11.04	11.02
900	13.53	12.86	12.58	12.47	12.42	12.39
1000	15.04	14.29	13.98	13.85	13.79	13.77
2000	30.07	28.58	27.96	27.70	27.59	27.54
3000	45.11	42.87	41.95	41.55	41.38	41.31
4000	60.15	57.16	55.93	55.41	55.18	55.08
5000	75.19	71.45	69.91	69.26	68.97	68.85
6000	90.22	85.73	83.89	83.11	82.77	82.62
7000	105.26	100.02	97.88	96.96	96.56	96.39
8000	120.30	114.31	111.86	110.81	110.36	110.16
9000	135.33	128.60	125.84	124.66	124.15	123.93
10000	150.37	142.89	139.82	138.51	137.95	137.70
11000	165.41	157.18	153.81	152.37	151.74	151.47
12000	180.45	171.47	167.79	166.22	165.53	165.24
13000	195.48	185.76	181.77	180.07	179.33	179.00
14000	210.52	200.05	195.75	193.92	193.12	192.77
15000	225.56	214.34	209.74	207.77	206.92	206.54
16000	240.59	228.62	223.72	221.62	220.71	220.31
17000	255.63	242.91	237.70	235.48	234.51	234.08
18000	270.67	257.20	251.68	249.33	248.30	247.85
19000	285.70	271.49	265.67	263.18	262.10	261.62
20000	300.74	285.78	279.65	277.03	275.89	275.39
21000	315.78	300.07	293.63	290.88	289.69	289.16
22000	330.82	314.36	307.61	304.73	303.48	302.93
23000	345.85	328.65	321.60	318.58	317.27	316.70
24000	360.89	342.94	335.58	332.44	331.07	330.47
25000	375.93	357.23	349.56	346.29	344.86	344.24
30000	451.11	428.67	419.47	415.54	413.84	413.09
35000	526.30	500.12	489.39	484.80	482.81	481.94
40000	601.48	571.56	559.30	554.06	551.78	550.78
45000	676.67	643.01	629.21	623.32	620.75	619.63
50000	751.85	714.45	699.12	692.57	689.73	688.48
55000	827.04	785.90	769.03	761.83	758.70	757.33
60000	902.23	857.34	838.95	831.09	827.67	826.18
65000	977.41	928.79	908.86	900.35	896.65	895.02
70000	1052.60	1000.23	978.77	969.60	965.62	963.87
75000	1127.78	1071.68	1048.68	1038.86	1034.59	1032.72
80000	1202.97	1143.12	1118.60	1108.12	1103.56	1101.57
85000	1278.15	1214.57	1188.51	1177.38	1172.54	1170.42
90000	1353.34	1286.01	1258.42	1246.63	1241.51	1239.26
95000	1428.52	1357.46	1328.33	1315.89	1310.48	1308.11
100000	1503.71	1428.90	1398.24	1385.15	1379.45	1376.96
200000	3007.42	2857.80	2796.49	2770.30	2758.91	2753.92
300000	4511.13	4286.70	4194.73	4155.44	4138.36	4130.88
400000	6014.83	5715.60	5592.98	5540.59	5517.82	5507.84
500000	7518.54	7144.50	6991.22	6925.74	6897.27	6884.80

17%

MONTHLY PAYMENT

Necessary to amortize a loan

TERM / AMOUNT	1 YEARS	2 YEARS	3 YEARS	4 YEARS	5 YEARS	6 YEARS
500	45.60	24.72	17.83	14.43	12.43	11.12
600	54.72	29.67	21.39	17.31	14.91	13.35
700	63.84	34.61	24.96	20.20	17.40	15.57
800	72.96	39.55	28.52	23.08	19.88	17.80
900	82.08	44.50	32.09	25.97	22.37	20.02
1000	91.20	49.44	35.65	28.86	24.85	22.25
2000	182.41	98.88	71.31	57.71	49.71	44.49
3000	273.61	148.33	106.96	86.57	74.56	66.74
4000	364.82	197.77	142.61	115.42	99.41	88.98
5000	456.02	247.21	178.26	144.28	124.26	111.23
6000	547.23	296.65	213.92	173.13	149.12	133.48
7000	638.43	346.10	249.57	201.99	173.97	155.72
8000	729.64	395.54	285.22	230.84	198.82	177.97
9000	820.84	444.98	320.87	259.70	223.67	200.22
10000	912.05	494.42	356.53	288.55	248.53	222.46
11000	1003.25	543.86	392.18	317.41	273.38	244.71
12000	1094.46	593.31	427.83	346.26	298.23	266.95
13000	1185.66	642.75	463.49	375.12	323.08	289.20
14000	1276.87	692.19	499.14	403.97	347.94	311.45
15000	1368.07	741.63	534.79	432.83	372.79	333.69
16000	1459.28	791.08	570.44	461.68	397.64	355.94
17000	1550.48	840.52	606.10	490.54	422.49	378.18
18000	1641.69	889.96	641.75	519.39	447.35	400.43
19000	1732.89	939.40	677.40	548.25	472.20	422.68
20000	1824.10	988.85	713.05	577.10	497.05	444.92
21000	1915.30	1038.29	748.71	605.96	521.90	467.17
22000	2006.50	1087.73	784.36	634.81	546.76	489.41
23000	2097.71	1137.17	820.01	663.67	571.61	511.66
24000	2188.91	1186.61	855.67	692.52	596.46	533.91
25000	2280.12	1236.06	891.32	721.38	621.31	556.15
30000	2736.14	1483.27	1069.58	865.65	745.58	667.38
35000	3192.17	1730.48	1247.85	1009.93	869.84	778.61
40000	3648.19	1977.69	1426.11	1154.20	994.10	889.85
45000	4104.21	2224.90	1604.37	1298.48	1118.37	1001.08
50000	4560.24	2472.11	1782.64	1442.75	1242.63	1112.31
55000	5016.26	2719.32	1960.90	1587.03	1366.89	1223.54
60000	5472.29	2966.54	2139.16	1731.30	1491.15	1334.77
65000	5928.31	3213.75	2317.43	1875.58	1615.42	1446.00
70000	6384.33	3460.96	2495.69	2019.85	1739.68	1557.23
75000	6840.36	3708.17	2673.95	2164.13	1863.94	1668.46
80000	7296.38	3955.38	2852.22	2308.40	1988.21	1779.69
85000	7752.40	4202.59	3030.48	2452.68	2112.47	1890.92
90000	8208.43	4449.80	3208.75	2596.95	2236.73	2002.15
95000	8664.45	4697.02	3387.01	2741.23	2360.99	2113.38
100000	9120.48	4944.23	3565.27	2885.50	2485.26	2224.61
200000	18240.95	9888.45	7130.55	5771.01	4970.52	4449.23
300000	27361.43	14832.68	10695.82	8656.51	7455.77	6673.84
400000	36481.90	19776.91	14261.09	11542.02	9941.03	8898.45
500000	45602.38	24721.13	17826.36	14427.52	12426.29	11123.07

MONTHLY PAYMENT

Necessary to amortize a loan

17%

TERM / AMOUNT	7 YEARS	8 YEARS	9 YEARS	10 YEARS	11 YEARS	12 YEARS
500	10.22	9.56	9.07	8.69	8.39	8.16
600	12.26	11.47	10.88	10.43	10.07	9.79
700	14.31	13.39	12.70	12.17	11.75	11.42
800	16.35	15.30	14.51	13.90	13.43	13.06
900	18.39	17.21	16.32	15.64	15.11	14.69
1000	20.44	19.12	18.14	17.38	16.79	16.32
2000	40.87	38.24	36.27	34.76	33.58	32.64
3000	61.31	57.36	54.41	52.14	50.36	48.96
4000	81.74	76.49	72.54	69.52	67.15	65.28
5000	102.18	95.61	90.68	86.90	83.94	81.60
6000	122.61	114.73	108.82	104.28	100.73	97.92
7000	143.05	133.85	126.95	121.66	117.52	114.23
8000	163.49	152.97	145.09	139.04	134.31	130.55
9000	183.92	172.09	163.23	156.42	151.09	146.87
10000	204.36	191.21	181.36	173.80	167.88	163.19
11000	224.79	210.34	199.50	191.18	184.67	179.51
12000	245.23	229.46	217.63	208.56	201.46	195.83
13000	265.67	248.58	235.77	225.94	218.25	212.15
14000	286.10	267.70	253.91	243.32	235.04	228.47
15000	306.54	286.82	272.04	260.70	251.82	244.79
16000	326.97	305.94	290.18	278.08	268.61	261.11
17000	347.41	325.06	308.32	295.46	285.40	277.43
18000	367.84	344.19	326.45	312.84	302.19	293.75
19000	388.28	363.31	344.59	330.22	318.98	310.07
20000	408.72	382.43	362.72	347.60	335.77	326.38
21000	429.15	401.55	380.86	364.98	352.55	342.70
22000	449.59	420.67	399.00	382.35	369.34	359.02
23000	470.02	439.79	417.13	399.73	386.13	375.34
24000	490.46	458.91	435.27	417.11	402.92	391.66
25000	510.90	478.04	453.40	434.49	419.71	407.98
30000	613.07	573.64	544.09	521.39	503.65	489.58
35000	715.25	669.25	634.77	608.29	587.59	571.17
40000	817.43	764.86	725.45	695.19	671.53	652.77
45000	919.61	860.47	816.13	782.09	755.47	734.37
50000	1021.79	956.07	906.81	868.99	839.42	815.96
55000	1123.97	1051.68	997.49	955.89	923.36	897.56
60000	1226.15	1147.29	1088.17	1042.79	1007.30	979.15
65000	1328.33	1242.89	1178.85	1129.68	1091.24	1060.75
70000	1430.51	1338.50	1269.53	1216.58	1175.18	1142.35
75000	1532.69	1434.11	1360.21	1303.48	1259.12	1223.94
80000	1634.86	1529.72	1450.90	1390.38	1343.07	1305.54
85000	1737.04	1625.32	1541.58	1477.28	1427.01	1387.13
90000	1839.22	1720.93	1632.26	1564.18	1510.95	1468.73
95000	1941.40	1816.54	1722.94	1651.08	1594.89	1550.33
100000	2043.58	1912.15	1813.62	1737.98	1678.83	1631.92
200000	4087.16	3824.29	3627.24	3475.95	3357.66	3263.85
300000	6130.74	5736.44	5440.86	5213.93	5036.50	4895.77
400000	8174.32	7648.58	7254.48	6951.91	6715.33	6527.69
500000	10217.90	9560.73	9068.09	8689.88	8394.16	8159.61

17%

MONTHLY PAYMENT

Necessary to amortize a loan

TERM / AMOUNT	15 YEARS	20 YEARS	25 YEARS	30 YEARS	35 YEARS	40 YEARS
500	7.70	7.33	7.19	7.13	7.10	7.09
600	9.23	8.80	8.63	8.55	8.52	8.51
700	10.77	10.27	10.06	9.98	9.94	9.93
800	12.31	11.73	11.50	11.41	11.36	11.35
900	13.85	13.20	12.94	12.83	12.78	12.76
1000	15.39	14.67	14.38	14.26	14.21	14.18
2000	30.78	29.34	28.76	28.51	28.41	28.37
3000	46.17	44.00	43.13	42.77	42.62	42.55
4000	61.56	58.67	57.51	57.03	56.82	56.73
5000	76.95	73.34	71.89	71.28	71.03	70.92
6000	92.34	88.01	86.27	85.54	85.23	85.10
7000	107.73	102.68	100.65	99.80	99.44	99.28
8000	123.12	117.34	115.02	114.05	113.64	113.47
9000	138.51	132.01	129.40	128.31	127.85	127.65
10000	153.90	146.68	143.78	142.57	142.05	141.83
11000	169.29	161.35	158.16	156.82	156.26	156.02
12000	184.68	176.02	172.54	171.08	170.46	170.20
13000	200.07	190.68	186.91	185.34	184.67	184.38
14000	215.46	205.35	201.29	199.59	198.87	198.57
15000	230.85	220.02	215.67	213.85	213.08	212.75
16000	246.24	234.69	230.05	228.11	227.28	226.93
17000	261.63	249.36	244.43	242.36	241.49	241.12
18000	277.02	264.02	258.80	256.62	255.69	255.30
19000	292.41	278.69	273.18	270.88	269.90	269.48
20000	307.80	293.36	287.56	285.14	284.11	283.66
21000	323.19	308.03	301.94	299.39	298.31	297.85
22000	338.58	322.70	316.32	313.65	312.52	312.03
23000	353.97	337.36	330.69	327.91	326.72	326.21
24000	369.36	352.03	345.07	342.16	340.93	340.40
25000	384.75	366.70	359.45	356.42	355.13	354.58
30000	461.70	440.04	431.34	427.70	426.16	425.50
35000	538.65	513.38	503.23	498.99	497.18	496.41
40000	615.60	586.72	575.12	570.27	568.21	567.33
45000	692.55	660.06	647.01	641.55	639.24	638.25
50000	769.50	733.40	718.90	712.84	710.26	709.16
55000	846.45	806.74	790.79	784.12	781.29	780.08
60000	923.40	880.08	862.68	855.41	852.32	850.99
65000	1000.35	953.42	934.57	926.69	923.34	921.91
70000	1077.30	1026.76	1006.46	997.97	994.37	992.83
75000	1154.25	1100.10	1078.35	1069.26	1065.39	1063.74
80000	1231.20	1173.44	1150.24	1140.54	1136.42	1134.66
85000	1308.15	1246.78	1222.13	1211.82	1207.45	1205.58
90000	1385.10	1320.12	1294.02	1283.11	1278.47	1276.49
95000	1462.05	1393.46	1365.91	1354.39	1349.50	1347.41
100000	1539.00	1466.80	1437.80	1425.68	1420.53	1418.32
200000	3078.01	2933.60	2875.59	2851.35	2841.05	2836.65
300000	4617.01	4400.40	4313.39	4277.03	4261.58	4254.97
400000	6156.02	5867.20	5751.19	5702.70	5682.10	5673.29
500000	7695.02	7334.00	7188.98	7128.38	7102.63	7091.62

MONTHLY PAYMENT

Necessary to amortize a loan

17.5%

TERM / AMOUNT	1 YEARS	2 YEARS	3 YEARS	4 YEARS	5 YEARS	6 YEARS
500	45.72	24.84	17.95	14.56	12.56	11.26
600	54.87	29.81	21.54	17.47	15.07	13.52
700	64.01	34.78	25.13	20.38	17.59	15.77
800	73.15	39.75	28.72	23.29	20.10	18.02
900	82.30	44.71	32.31	26.20	22.61	20.27
1000	91.44	49.68	35.90	29.11	25.12	22.53
2000	182.88	99.37	71.80	58.23	50.24	45.05
3000	274.33	149.05	107.71	87.34	75.37	67.58
4000	365.77	198.73	143.61	116.46	100.49	90.10
5000	457.21	248.41	179.51	145.57	125.61	112.63
6000	548.65	298.10	215.41	174.69	150.73	135.16
7000	640.10	347.78	251.31	203.80	175.86	157.68
8000	731.54	397.46	287.22	232.91	200.98	180.21
9000	822.98	447.15	323.12	262.03	226.10	202.73
10000	914.42	496.83	359.02	291.14	251.22	225.26
11000	1005.86	546.51	394.92	320.26	276.34	247.79
12000	1097.31	596.19	430.82	349.37	301.47	270.31
13000	1188.75	645.88	466.73	378.49	326.59	292.84
14000	1280.19	695.56	502.63	407.60	351.71	315.36
15000	1371.63	745.24	538.53	436.72	376.83	337.89
16000	1463.08	794.93	574.43	465.83	401.96	360.42
17000	1554.52	844.61	610.34	494.94	427.08	382.94
18000	1645.96	894.29	646.24	524.06	452.20	405.47
19000	1737.40	943.97	682.14	553.17	477.32	427.99
20000	1828.84	993.66	718.04	582.29	502.44	450.52
21000	1920.29	1043.34	753.94	611.40	527.57	473.05
22000	2011.73	1093.02	789.85	640.52	552.69	495.57
23000	2103.17	1142.71	825.75	669.63	577.81	518.10
24000	2194.61	1192.39	861.65	698.74	602.93	540.63
25000	2286.06	1242.07	897.55	727.86	628.06	563.15
30000	2743.27	1490.49	1077.06	873.43	753.67	675.78
35000	3200.48	1738.90	1256.57	1019.00	879.28	788.41
40000	3657.69	1987.31	1436.08	1164.57	1004.89	901.04
45000	4114.90	2235.73	1615.59	1310.15	1130.50	1013.67
50000	4572.11	2484.14	1795.10	1455.72	1256.11	1126.30
55000	5029.32	2732.56	1974.61	1601.29	1381.72	1238.93
60000	5486.53	2980.97	2154.12	1746.86	1507.33	1351.56
65000	5943.74	3229.39	2333.63	1892.43	1632.94	1464.19
70000	6400.95	3477.80	2513.14	2038.01	1758.55	1576.82
75000	6858.17	3726.21	2692.65	2183.58	1884.17	1689.45
80000	7315.38	3974.63	2872.17	2329.15	2009.78	1802.08
85000	7772.59	4223.04	3051.68	2474.72	2135.39	1914.71
90000	8229.80	4471.46	3231.19	2620.29	2261.00	2027.34
95000	8687.01	4719.87	3410.70	2765.87	2386.61	2139.97
100000	9144.22	4968.28	3590.21	2911.44	2512.22	2252.60
200000	18288.44	9936.57	7180.41	5822.87	5024.44	4505.21
300000	27432.66	14904.85	10770.62	8734.31	7536.66	6757.81
400000	36576.88	19873.14	14360.83	11645.75	10048.89	9010.42
500000	45721.10	24841.42	17951.03	14557.19	12561.11	11263.02

17.5% MONTHLY PAYMENT

Necessary to amortize a loan

TERM / AMOUNT	7 YEARS	8 YEARS	9 YEARS	10 YEARS	11 YEARS	12 YEARS
500	10.36	9.71	9.22	8.85	8.56	8.33
600	12.44	11.65	11.07	10.62	10.27	9.99
700	14.51	13.59	12.91	12.39	11.98	11.66
800	16.58	15.54	14.76	14.16	13.69	13.32
900	18.65	17.48	16.60	15.93	15.40	14.99
1000	20.73	19.42	18.45	17.70	17.11	16.65
2000	41.45	38.84	36.89	35.40	34.23	33.31
3000	62.18	58.26	55.34	53.09	51.34	49.96
4000	82.90	77.68	73.78	70.79	68.46	66.62
5000	103.63	97.11	92.23	88.49	85.57	83.27
6000	124.35	116.53	110.67	106.19	102.69	99.92
7000	145.08	135.95	129.12	123.89	119.80	116.58
8000	165.81	155.37	147.56	141.58	136.92	133.23
9000	186.53	174.79	166.01	159.28	154.03	149.88
10000	207.26	194.21	184.45	176.98	171.15	166.54
11000	227.98	213.63	202.90	194.68	188.26	183.19
12000	248.71	233.05	221.34	212.37	205.38	199.85
13000	269.44	252.48	239.79	230.07	222.49	216.50
14000	290.16	271.90	258.23	247.77	239.61	233.15
15000	310.89	291.32	276.68	265.47	256.72	249.81
16000	331.61	310.74	295.13	283.17	273.84	266.46
17000	352.34	330.16	313.57	300.86	290.95	283.12
18000	373.06	349.58	332.02	318.56	308.07	299.77
19000	393.79	369.00	350.46	336.26	325.18	316.42
20000	414.52	388.42	368.91	353.96	342.30	333.08
21000	435.24	407.85	387.35	371.66	359.41	349.73
22000	455.97	427.27	405.80	389.35	376.53	366.39
23000	476.69	446.69	424.24	407.05	393.64	383.04
24000	497.42	466.11	442.69	424.75	410.76	399.69
25000	518.14	485.53	461.13	442.45	427.87	416.35
30000	621.77	582.64	553.36	530.94	513.45	499.62
35000	725.40	679.74	645.59	619.43	599.02	582.89
40000	829.03	776.85	737.81	707.92	684.60	666.15
45000	932.66	873.95	830.04	796.40	770.17	749.42
50000	1036.29	971.06	922.27	884.89	855.75	832.69
55000	1139.92	1068.17	1014.49	973.38	941.32	915.96
60000	1243.55	1165.27	1106.72	1061.87	1026.90	999.23
65000	1347.18	1262.38	1198.95	1150.36	1112.47	1082.50
70000	1450.81	1359.48	1291.17	1238.85	1198.05	1165.77
75000	1554.43	1456.59	1383.40	1327.34	1283.62	1249.04
80000	1658.06	1553.70	1475.63	1415.83	1369.19	1332.31
85000	1761.69	1650.80	1567.85	1504.32	1454.77	1415.58
90000	1865.32	1747.91	1660.08	1592.81	1540.34	1498.85
95000	1968.95	1845.01	1752.31	1681.30	1625.92	1582.12
100000	2072.58	1942.12	1844.53	1769.79	1711.49	1665.39
200000	4145.16	3884.24	3689.07	3539.58	3422.99	3330.77
300000	6217.74	5826.36	5533.60	5309.36	5134.48	4996.16
400000	8290.32	7768.48	7378.13	7079.15	6845.97	6661.55
500000	10362.90	9710.61	9222.67	8848.94	8557.47	8326.94

MONTHLY PAYMENT

Necessary to amortize a loan

17.5%

TERM / AMOUNT	15 YEARS	20 YEARS	25 YEARS	30 YEARS	35 YEARS	40 YEARS
500	7.87	7.52	7.39	7.33	7.31	7.30
600	9.45	9.03	8.87	8.80	8.77	8.76
700	11.02	10.53	10.34	10.26	10.23	10.22
800	12.60	12.04	11.82	11.73	11.69	11.68
900	14.17	13.54	13.30	13.20	13.16	13.14
1000	15.75	15.05	14.78	14.66	14.62	14.60
2000	31.49	30.10	29.55	29.33	29.23	29.19
3000	47.24	45.15	44.33	43.99	43.85	43.79
4000	62.98	60.20	59.10	58.65	58.47	58.39
5000	78.73	75.25	73.88	73.32	73.08	72.99
6000	94.47	90.30	88.65	87.98	87.70	87.58
7000	110.22	105.35	103.43	102.64	102.32	102.18
8000	125.97	120.40	118.20	117.31	116.93	116.78
9000	141.71	135.44	132.98	131.97	131.55	131.38
10000	157.46	150.49	147.75	146.63	146.17	145.97
11000	173.20	165.54	162.53	161.30	160.78	160.57
12000	188.95	180.59	177.30	175.96	175.40	175.17
13000	204.70	195.64	192.08	190.62	190.02	189.77
14000	220.44	210.69	206.85	205.29	204.63	204.36
15000	236.19	225.74	221.63	219.95	219.25	218.96
16000	251.93	240.79	236.40	234.61	233.87	233.56
17000	267.68	255.84	251.18	249.28	248.48	248.15
18000	283.42	270.89	265.96	263.94	263.10	262.75
19000	299.17	285.94	280.73	278.60	277.72	277.35
20000	314.92	300.99	295.51	293.27	292.34	291.95
21000	330.66	316.04	310.28	307.93	306.95	306.54
22000	346.41	331.09	325.06	322.59	321.57	321.14
23000	362.15	346.14	339.83	337.25	336.19	335.74
24000	377.90	361.19	354.61	351.92	350.80	350.34
25000	393.64	376.24	369.38	366.58	365.42	364.93
30000	472.37	451.48	443.26	439.90	438.50	437.92
35000	551.10	526.73	517.14	513.21	511.59	510.91
40000	629.83	601.98	591.01	586.53	584.67	583.89
45000	708.56	677.22	664.89	659.85	657.75	656.88
50000	787.29	752.47	738.76	733.16	730.84	729.87
55000	866.02	827.72	812.64	806.48	803.92	802.85
60000	944.75	902.97	886.52	879.80	877.01	875.84
65000	1023.48	978.21	960.39	953.11	950.09	948.83
70000	1102.20	1053.46	1034.27	1026.43	1023.17	1021.81
75000	1180.93	1128.71	1108.15	1099.74	1096.26	1094.80
80000	1259.66	1203.95	1182.02	1173.06	1169.34	1167.79
85000	1338.39	1279.20	1255.90	1246.38	1242.42	1240.77
90000	1417.12	1354.45	1329.78	1319.69	1315.51	1313.76
95000	1495.85	1429.69	1403.65	1393.01	1388.59	1386.75
100000	1574.58	1504.94	1477.53	1466.33	1461.68	1459.73
200000	3149.16	3009.88	2955.06	2932.65	2923.35	2919.47
300000	4723.73	4514.83	4432.59	4398.98	4385.03	4379.20
400000	6298.31	6019.77	5910.12	5865.30	5846.70	5838.93
500000	7872.89	7524.71	7387.65	7331.63	7308.38	7298.67

18%

MONTHLY PAYMENT

Necessary to amortize a loan

TERM / AMOUNT	1 YEARS	2 YEARS	3 YEARS	4 YEARS	5 YEARS	6 YEARS
500	45.84	24.96	18.08	14.69	12.70	11.40
600	55.01	29.95	21.69	17.62	15.24	13.68
700	64.18	34.95	25.31	20.56	17.78	15.97
800	73.34	39.94	28.92	23.50	20.31	18.25
900	82.51	44.93	32.54	26.44	22.85	20.53
1000	91.68	49.92	36.15	29.37	25.39	22.81
2000	183.36	99.85	72.30	58.75	50.79	45.62
3000	275.04	149.77	108.46	88.12	76.18	68.42
4000	366.72	199.70	144.61	117.50	101.57	91.23
5000	458.40	249.62	180.76	146.87	126.97	114.04
6000	550.08	299.54	216.91	176.25	152.36	136.85
7000	641.76	349.47	253.07	205.62	177.75	159.65
8000	733.44	399.39	289.22	235.00	203.15	182.46
9000	825.12	449.32	325.37	264.37	228.54	205.27
10000	916.80	499.24	361.52	293.75	253.93	228.08
11000	1008.48	549.17	397.68	323.12	279.33	250.89
12000	1100.16	599.09	433.83	352.50	304.72	273.69
13000	1191.84	649.01	469.98	381.87	330.11	296.50
14000	1283.52	698.94	506.13	411.25	355.51	319.31
15000	1375.20	748.86	542.29	440.62	380.90	342.12
16000	1466.88	798.79	578.44	470.00	406.29	364.92
17000	1558.56	848.71	614.59	499.37	431.69	387.73
18000	1650.24	898.63	650.74	528.75	457.08	410.54
19000	1741.92	948.56	686.90	558.12	482.48	433.35
20000	1833.60	998.48	723.05	587.50	507.87	456.16
21000	1925.28	1048.41	759.20	616.87	533.26	478.96
22000	2016.96	1098.33	795.35	646.25	558.66	501.77
23000	2108.64	1148.25	831.51	675.62	584.05	524.58
24000	2200.32	1198.18	867.66	705.00	609.44	547.39
25000	2292.00	1248.10	903.81	734.37	634.84	570.19
30000	2750.40	1497.72	1084.57	881.25	761.80	684.23
35000	3208.80	1747.34	1265.33	1028.12	888.77	798.27
40000	3667.20	1996.96	1446.10	1175.00	1015.74	912.31
45000	4125.60	2246.58	1626.86	1321.87	1142.70	1026.35
50000	4584.00	2496.21	1807.62	1468.75	1269.67	1140.39
55000	5042.40	2745.83	1988.38	1615.62	1396.64	1254.43
60000	5500.80	2995.45	2169.14	1762.50	1523.61	1368.47
65000	5959.20	3245.07	2349.91	1909.37	1650.57	1482.51
70000	6417.60	3494.69	2530.67	2056.25	1777.54	1596.55
75000	6876.00	3744.31	2711.43	2203.12	1904.51	1710.58
80000	7334.40	3993.93	2892.19	2350.00	2031.47	1824.62
85000	7792.80	4243.55	3072.95	2496.87	2158.44	1938.66
90000	8251.20	4493.17	3253.72	2643.75	2285.41	2052.70
95000	8709.60	4742.79	3434.48	2790.62	2412.38	2166.74
100000	9168.00	4992.41	3615.24	2937.50	2539.34	2280.78
200000	18336.00	9984.82	7230.48	5875.00	5078.69	4561.56
300000	27504.00	14977.23	10845.72	8812.50	7618.03	6842.34
400000	36672.00	19969.64	14460.96	11750.00	10157.37	9123.12
500000	45840.00	24962.05	18076.20	14687.50	12696.71	11403.90

MONTHLY PAYMENT

Necessary to amortize a loan

18%

TERM / AMOUNT	7 YEARS	8 YEARS	9 YEARS	10 YEARS	11 YEARS	12 YEARS
500	10.51	9.86	9.38	9.01	8.72	8.50
600	12.61	11.83	11.25	10.81	10.47	10.19
700	14.71	13.81	13.13	12.61	12.21	11.89
800	16.81	15.78	15.01	14.41	13.96	13.59
900	18.92	17.75	16.88	16.22	15.70	15.29
1000	21.02	19.72	18.76	18.02	17.44	16.99
2000	42.04	39.45	37.51	36.04	34.89	33.98
3000	63.05	59.17	56.27	54.06	52.33	50.97
4000	84.07	78.89	75.03	72.07	69.78	67.96
5000	105.09	98.62	93.78	90.09	87.22	84.96
6000	126.11	118.34	112.54	108.11	104.67	101.95
7000	147.12	138.06	131.30	126.13	122.11	118.94
8000	168.14	157.79	150.06	144.15	139.55	135.93
9000	189.16	177.51	168.81	162.17	157.00	152.92
10000	210.18	197.23	187.57	180.19	174.44	169.91
11000	231.20	216.96	206.33	198.20	191.89	186.90
12000	252.21	236.68	225.08	216.22	209.33	203.89
13000	273.23	256.40	243.84	234.24	226.77	220.89
14000	294.25	276.12	262.60	252.26	244.22	237.88
15000	315.27	295.85	281.35	270.28	261.66	254.87
16000	336.29	315.57	300.11	288.30	279.11	271.86
17000	357.30	335.29	318.87	306.31	296.55	288.85
18000	378.32	355.02	337.62	324.33	314.00	305.84
19000	399.34	374.74	356.38	342.35	331.44	322.83
20000	420.36	394.46	375.14	360.37	348.88	339.82
21000	441.37	414.19	393.89	378.39	366.33	356.82
22000	462.39	433.91	412.65	396.41	383.77	373.81
23000	483.41	453.63	431.41	414.43	401.22	390.80
24000	504.43	473.36	450.17	432.44	418.66	407.79
25000	525.45	493.08	468.92	450.46	436.10	424.78
30000	630.54	591.70	562.71	540.56	523.33	509.74
35000	735.62	690.31	656.49	630.65	610.55	594.69
40000	840.71	788.93	750.28	720.74	697.77	679.65
45000	945.80	887.54	844.06	810.83	784.99	764.60
50000	1050.89	986.16	937.84	900.93	872.21	849.56
55000	1155.98	1084.78	1031.63	991.02	959.43	934.52
60000	1261.07	1183.39	1125.41	1081.11	1046.65	1019.47
65000	1366.16	1282.01	1219.20	1171.20	1133.87	1104.43
70000	1471.25	1380.62	1312.98	1261.30	1221.09	1189.38
75000	1576.34	1479.24	1406.77	1351.39	1308.31	1274.34
80000	1681.43	1577.86	1500.55	1441.48	1395.53	1359.30
85000	1786.52	1676.47	1594.34	1531.57	1482.76	1444.25
90000	1891.61	1775.09	1688.12	1621.67	1569.98	1529.21
95000	1996.69	1873.71	1781.90	1711.76	1657.20	1614.16
100000	2101.78	1972.32	1875.69	1801.85	1744.42	1699.12
200000	4203.57	3944.64	3751.38	3603.70	3488.84	3398.24
300000	6305.35	5916.96	5627.07	5405.56	5233.25	5097.36
400000	8407.14	7889.29	7502.76	7207.41	6977.67	6796.48
500000	10508.92	9861.61	9378.44	9009.26	8722.09	8495.60

18%

MONTHLY PAYMENT

Necessary to amortize a loan

TERM / AMOUNT	15 YEARS	20 YEARS	25 YEARS	30 YEARS	35 YEARS	40 YEARS
500	8.05	7.72	7.59	7.54	7.51	7.51
600	9.66	9.26	9.10	9.04	9.02	9.01
700	11.27	10.80	10.62	10.55	10.52	10.51
800	12.88	12.35	12.14	12.06	12.02	12.01
900	14.49	13.89	13.66	13.56	13.53	13.51
1000	16.10	15.43	15.17	15.07	15.03	15.01
2000	32.21	30.87	30.35	30.14	30.06	30.02
3000	48.31	46.30	45.52	45.21	45.09	45.04
4000	64.42	61.73	60.70	60.28	60.12	60.05
5000	80.52	77.17	75.87	75.35	75.14	75.06
6000	96.63	92.60	91.05	90.43	90.17	90.07
7000	112.73	108.03	106.22	105.50	105.20	105.08
8000	128.83	123.46	121.39	120.57	120.23	120.09
9000	144.94	138.90	136.57	135.64	135.26	135.11
10000	161.04	154.33	151.74	150.71	150.29	150.12
11000	177.15	169.76	166.92	165.78	165.32	165.13
12000	193.25	185.20	182.09	180.85	180.35	180.14
13000	209.35	200.63	197.27	195.92	195.38	195.15
14000	225.46	216.06	212.44	210.99	210.40	210.17
15000	241.56	231.50	227.61	226.06	225.43	225.18
16000	257.67	246.93	242.79	241.13	240.46	240.19
17000	273.77	262.36	257.96	256.20	255.49	255.20
18000	289.88	277.80	273.14	271.28	270.52	270.21
19000	305.98	293.23	288.31	286.35	285.55	285.22
20000	322.08	308.66	303.49	301.42	300.58	300.24
21000	338.19	324.10	318.66	316.49	315.61	315.25
22000	354.29	339.53	333.83	331.56	330.64	330.26
23000	370.40	354.96	349.01	346.63	345.67	345.27
24000	386.50	370.39	364.18	361.70	360.69	360.28
25000	402.61	385.83	379.36	376.77	375.72	375.30
30000	483.13	462.99	455.23	452.13	450.87	450.35
35000	563.65	540.16	531.10	527.48	526.01	525.41
40000	644.17	617.32	606.97	602.83	601.16	600.47
45000	724.69	694.49	682.84	678.19	676.30	675.53
50000	805.21	771.66	758.71	753.54	751.45	750.59
55000	885.73	848.82	834.59	828.90	826.59	825.65
60000	966.25	925.99	910.46	904.25	901.74	900.71
65000	1046.77	1003.15	986.33	979.61	976.88	975.77
70000	1127.29	1080.32	1062.20	1054.96	1052.02	1050.83
75000	1207.82	1157.48	1138.07	1130.31	1127.17	1125.89
80000	1288.34	1234.65	1213.94	1205.67	1202.31	1200.95
85000	1368.86	1311.81	1289.82	1281.02	1277.46	1276.00
90000	1449.38	1388.98	1365.69	1356.38	1352.60	1351.06
95000	1529.90	1466.15	1441.56	1431.73	1427.75	1426.12
100000	1610.42	1543.31	1517.43	1507.09	1502.89	1501.18
200000	3220.84	3086.62	3034.86	3014.17	3005.78	3002.36
300000	4831.26	4629.93	4552.29	4521.26	4508.68	4503.55
400000	6441.68	6173.25	6069.72	6028.34	6011.57	6004.73
500000	8052.11	7716.56	7587.15	7535.43	7514.46	7505.91

MONTHLY PAYMENT

Necessary to amortize a loan

18.5%

TERM / AMOUNT	1 YEARS	2 YEARS	3 YEARS	4 YEARS	5 YEARS	6 YEARS
500	45.96	25.08	18.20	14.82	12.83	11.55
600	55.15	30.10	21.84	17.78	15.40	13.85
700	64.34	35.12	25.48	20.75	17.97	16.16
800	73.53	40.13	29.12	23.71	20.53	18.47
900	82.73	45.15	32.76	26.67	23.10	20.78
1000	91.92	50.17	36.40	29.64	25.67	23.09
2000	183.84	100.33	72.81	59.27	51.33	46.18
3000	275.75	150.50	109.21	88.91	77.00	69.27
4000	367.67	200.66	145.61	118.55	102.66	92.37
5000	459.59	250.83	182.02	148.18	128.33	115.46
6000	551.51	301.00	218.42	177.82	154.00	138.55
7000	643.43	351.16	254.83	207.46	179.66	161.64
8000	735.34	401.33	291.23	237.10	205.33	184.73
9000	827.26	451.49	327.63	266.73	231.00	207.82
10000	919.18	501.66	364.04	296.37	256.66	230.91
11000	1011.10	551.83	400.44	326.01	282.33	254.00
12000	1103.02	601.99	436.84	355.64	307.99	277.10
13000	1194.94	652.16	473.25	385.28	333.66	300.19
14000	1286.85	702.32	509.65	414.92	359.33	323.28
15000	1378.77	752.49	546.06	444.55	384.99	346.37
16000	1470.69	802.66	582.46	474.19	410.66	369.46
17000	1562.61	852.82	618.86	503.83	436.33	392.55
18000	1654.53	902.99	655.27	533.46	461.99	415.64
19000	1746.44	953.15	691.67	563.10	487.66	438.74
20000	1838.36	1003.32	728.07	592.74	513.32	461.83
21000	1930.28	1053.49	764.48	622.38	538.99	484.92
22000	2022.20	1103.65	800.88	652.01	564.66	508.01
23000	2114.12	1153.82	837.29	681.65	590.32	531.10
24000	2206.03	1203.98	873.69	711.29	615.99	554.19
25000	2297.95	1254.15	910.09	740.92	641.66	577.28
30000	2757.54	1504.98	1092.11	889.11	769.99	692.74
35000	3217.13	1755.81	1274.13	1037.29	898.32	808.20
40000	3676.72	2006.64	1456.15	1185.48	1026.65	923.65
45000	4136.32	2257.47	1638.17	1333.66	1154.98	1039.11
50000	4595.91	2508.30	1820.19	1481.85	1283.31	1154.57
55000	5055.50	2759.13	2002.20	1630.03	1411.64	1270.02
60000	5515.09	3009.96	2184.22	1778.21	1539.97	1385.48
65000	5974.68	3260.79	2366.24	1926.40	1668.30	1500.94
70000	6434.27	3511.62	2548.26	2074.58	1796.63	1616.39
75000	6893.86	3762.45	2730.28	2222.77	1924.97	1731.85
80000	7353.45	4013.28	2912.30	2370.95	2053.30	1847.31
85000	7813.04	4264.11	3094.32	2519.14	2181.63	1962.77
90000	8272.63	4514.94	3276.33	2667.32	2309.96	2078.22
95000	8732.22	4765.77	3458.35	2815.51	2438.29	2193.68
100000	9191.81	5016.60	3640.37	2963.69	2566.62	2309.14
200000	18383.62	10033.21	7280.74	5927.38	5133.24	4618.27
300000	27575.44	15049.81	10921.11	8891.07	7699.86	6927.41
400000	36767.25	20066.41	14561.49	11854.77	10266.48	9236.54
500000	45959.06	25083.01	18201.86	14818.46	12833.10	11545.68

18.5% MONTHLY PAYMENT

Necessary to amortize a loan

TERM / AMOUNT	7 YEARS	8 YEARS	9 YEARS	10 YEARS	11 YEARS	12 YEARS
500	10.66	10.01	9.54	9.17	8.89	8.67
600	12.79	12.02	11.44	11.00	10.67	10.40
700	14.92	14.02	13.35	12.84	12.44	12.13
800	17.05	16.02	15.26	14.67	14.22	13.86
900	19.18	18.02	17.16	16.51	16.00	15.60
1000	21.31	20.03	19.07	18.34	17.78	17.33
2000	42.62	40.05	38.14	36.68	35.55	34.66
3000	63.94	60.08	57.21	55.02	53.33	51.99
4000	85.25	80.11	76.28	73.37	71.10	69.32
5000	106.56	100.14	95.35	91.71	88.88	86.66
6000	127.87	120.16	114.42	110.05	106.66	103.99
7000	149.18	140.19	133.50	128.39	124.43	121.32
8000	170.50	160.22	152.57	146.73	142.21	138.65
9000	191.81	180.25	171.64	165.07	159.98	155.98
10000	213.12	200.27	190.71	183.42	177.76	173.31
11000	234.43	220.30	209.78	201.76	195.54	190.64
12000	255.74	240.33	228.85	220.10	213.31	207.97
13000	277.05	260.36	247.92	238.44	231.09	225.30
14000	298.37	280.38	266.99	256.78	248.86	242.64
15000	319.68	300.41	286.06	275.12	266.64	259.97
16000	340.99	320.44	305.13	293.47	284.42	277.30
17000	362.30	340.47	324.20	311.81	302.19	294.63
18000	383.61	360.49	343.27	330.15	319.97	311.96
19000	404.93	380.52	362.35	348.49	337.74	329.29
20000	426.24	400.55	381.42	366.83	355.52	346.62
21000	447.55	420.58	400.49	385.17	373.30	363.95
22000	468.86	440.60	419.56	403.52	391.07	381.29
23000	490.17	460.63	438.63	421.86	408.85	398.62
24000	511.49	480.66	457.70	440.20	426.62	415.95
25000	532.80	500.69	476.77	458.54	444.40	433.28
30000	639.36	600.82	572.12	550.25	533.28	519.93
35000	745.92	700.96	667.48	641.96	622.16	606.59
40000	852.48	801.10	762.83	733.67	711.04	693.25
45000	959.04	901.23	858.19	825.37	799.92	779.90
50000	1065.60	1001.37	953.54	917.08	888.80	866.56
55000	1172.16	1101.51	1048.89	1008.79	977.68	953.21
60000	1278.72	1201.65	1144.25	1100.50	1066.56	1039.87
65000	1385.27	1301.78	1239.60	1192.21	1155.44	1126.52
70000	1491.83	1401.92	1334.96	1283.92	1244.32	1213.18
75000	1598.39	1502.06	1430.31	1375.62	1333.20	1299.84
80000	1704.95	1602.20	1525.67	1467.33	1422.08	1386.49
85000	1811.51	1702.33	1621.02	1559.04	1510.96	1473.15
90000	1918.07	1802.47	1716.37	1650.75	1599.84	1559.80
95000	2024.63	1902.61	1811.73	1742.46	1688.72	1646.46
100000	2131.19	2002.74	1907.08	1834.17	1777.60	1733.11
200000	4262.38	4005.49	3814.16	3668.33	3555.20	3466.23
300000	6393.58	6008.23	5721.24	5502.50	5332.80	5199.34
400000	8524.77	8010.98	7628.33	7336.66	7110.40	6932.46
500000	10655.96	10013.72	9535.41	9170.83	8888.00	8665.57

MONTHLY PAYMENT

Necessary to amortize a loan

18.5%

TERM / AMOUNT	15 YEARS	20 YEARS	25 YEARS	30 YEARS	35 YEARS	40 YEARS
500	8.23	7.91	7.79	7.74	7.72	7.71
600	9.88	9.49	9.34	9.29	9.27	9.26
700	11.53	11.07	10.90	10.84	10.81	10.80
800	13.17	12.66	12.46	12.38	12.35	12.34
900	14.82	14.24	14.02	13.93	13.90	13.88
1000	16.47	15.82	15.57	15.48	15.44	15.43
2000	32.93	31.64	31.15	30.96	30.88	30.85
3000	49.40	47.46	46.72	46.44	46.33	46.28
4000	65.86	63.28	62.30	61.92	61.77	61.71
5000	82.33	79.09	77.87	77.40	77.21	77.13
6000	98.79	94.91	93.45	92.88	92.65	92.56
7000	115.26	110.73	109.02	108.36	108.09	107.99
8000	131.72	126.55	124.60	123.84	123.53	123.41
9000	148.19	142.37	140.17	139.32	138.98	138.84
10000	164.65	158.19	155.75	154.79	154.42	154.27
11000	181.12	174.01	171.32	170.27	169.86	169.69
12000	197.58	189.83	186.90	185.75	185.30	185.12
13000	214.05	205.65	202.47	201.23	200.74	200.55
14000	230.51	221.47	218.05	216.71	216.18	215.97
15000	246.98	237.28	233.62	232.19	231.63	231.40
16000	263.44	253.10	249.20	247.67	247.07	246.83
17000	279.91	268.92	264.77	263.15	262.51	262.25
18000	296.37	284.74	280.35	278.63	277.95	277.68
19000	312.84	300.56	295.92	294.11	293.39	293.11
20000	329.30	316.38	311.50	309.59	308.83	308.53
21000	345.77	332.20	327.07	325.07	324.28	323.96
22000	362.24	348.02	342.65	340.55	339.72	339.39
23000	378.70	363.84	358.22	356.03	355.16	354.81
24000	395.17	379.66	373.80	371.51	370.60	370.24
25000	411.63	395.47	389.37	386.99	386.04	385.67
30000	493.96	474.57	467.25	464.38	463.25	462.80
35000	576.28	553.66	545.12	541.78	540.46	539.93
40000	658.61	632.76	622.99	619.18	617.67	617.07
45000	740.94	711.85	700.87	696.58	694.88	694.20
50000	823.26	790.95	778.74	773.97	772.08	771.33
55000	905.59	870.04	856.62	851.37	849.29	848.47
60000	987.91	949.14	934.49	928.77	926.50	925.60
65000	1070.24	1028.23	1012.36	1006.16	1003.71	1002.73
70000	1152.57	1107.33	1090.24	1083.56	1080.92	1079.87
75000	1234.89	1186.42	1168.11	1160.96	1158.13	1157.00
80000	1317.22	1265.52	1245.99	1238.36	1235.33	1234.13
85000	1399.54	1344.61	1323.86	1315.75	1312.54	1311.26
90000	1481.87	1423.71	1401.74	1393.15	1389.75	1388.40
95000	1564.20	1502.80	1479.61	1470.55	1466.96	1465.53
100000	1646.52	1581.90	1557.48	1547.94	1544.17	1542.66
200000	3293.05	3163.79	3114.97	3095.89	3088.34	3085.33
300000	4939.57	4745.69	4672.45	4643.83	4632.50	4627.99
400000	6586.09	6327.59	6229.94	6191.78	6176.67	6170.66
500000	8232.62	7909.48	7787.42	7739.72	7720.84	7713.32

19% MONTHLY PAYMENT

Necessary to amortize a loan

TERM / AMOUNT	1 YEARS	2 YEARS	3 YEARS	4 YEARS	5 YEARS	6 YEARS
500	46.08	25.20	18.33	14.95	12.97	11.69
600	55.29	30.25	21.99	17.94	15.56	14.03
700	64.51	35.29	25.66	20.93	18.16	16.36
800	73.73	40.33	29.32	23.92	20.75	18.70
900	82.94	45.37	32.99	26.91	23.35	21.04
1000	92.16	50.41	36.66	29.90	25.94	23.38
2000	184.31	100.82	73.31	59.80	51.88	46.75
3000	276.47	151.23	109.97	89.70	77.82	70.13
4000	368.63	201.63	146.62	119.60	103.76	93.51
5000	460.78	252.04	183.28	149.50	129.70	116.88
6000	552.94	302.45	219.94	179.40	155.64	140.26
7000	645.10	352.86	256.59	209.30	181.58	163.64
8000	737.25	403.27	293.25	239.20	207.52	187.01
9000	829.41	453.68	329.90	269.10	233.46	210.39
10000	921.57	504.09	366.56	299.00	259.41	233.77
11000	1013.72	554.49	403.22	328.90	285.35	257.14
12000	1105.88	604.90	439.87	358.80	311.29	280.52
13000	1198.04	655.31	476.53	388.70	337.23	303.90
14000	1290.19	705.72	513.18	418.60	363.17	327.27
15000	1382.35	756.13	549.84	448.50	389.11	350.65
16000	1474.51	806.54	586.50	478.40	415.05	374.03
17000	1566.66	856.95	623.15	508.30	440.99	397.40
18000	1658.82	907.36	659.81	538.20	466.93	420.78
19000	1750.97	957.76	696.46	568.10	492.87	444.16
20000	1843.13	1008.17	733.12	598.00	518.81	467.53
21000	1935.29	1058.58	769.78	627.90	544.75	490.91
22000	2027.44	1108.99	806.43	657.80	570.69	514.29
23000	2119.60	1159.40	843.09	687.70	596.63	537.66
24000	2211.76	1209.81	879.74	717.60	622.57	561.04
25000	2303.91	1260.22	916.40	747.50	648.51	584.42
30000	2764.70	1512.26	1099.68	897.00	778.22	701.30
35000	3225.48	1764.30	1282.96	1046.50	907.92	818.19
40000	3686.26	2016.34	1466.24	1196.00	1037.62	935.07
45000	4147.05	2268.39	1649.52	1345.51	1167.32	1051.95
50000	4607.83	2520.43	1832.80	1495.01	1297.03	1168.84
55000	5068.61	2772.47	2016.08	1644.51	1426.73	1285.72
60000	5529.39	3024.52	2199.36	1794.01	1556.43	1402.60
65000	5990.18	3276.56	2382.64	1943.51	1686.14	1519.49
70000	6450.96	3528.60	2565.92	2093.01	1815.84	1636.37
75000	6911.74	3780.65	2749.20	2242.51	1945.54	1753.25
80000	7372.53	4032.69	2932.48	2392.01	2075.24	1870.14
85000	7833.31	4284.73	3115.76	2541.51	2204.95	1987.02
90000	8294.09	4536.78	3299.04	2691.01	2334.65	2103.91
95000	8754.87	4788.82	3482.32	2840.51	2464.35	2220.79
100000	9215.66	5040.86	3665.60	2990.01	2594.06	2337.67
200000	18431.32	10081.72	7331.20	5980.02	5188.11	4675.34
300000	27646.97	15122.59	10996.81	8970.04	7782.17	7013.02
400000	36862.63	20163.45	14662.41	11960.05	10376.22	9350.69
500000	46078.29	25204.31	18328.01	14950.06	12970.28	11688.36

MONTHLY PAYMENT

Necessary to amortize a loan

19%

TERM AMOUNT	7 YEARS	8 YEARS	9 YEARS	10 YEARS	11 YEARS	12 YEARS
500	10.80	10.17	9.69	9.33	9.06	8.84
600	12.96	12.20	11.63	11.20	10.87	10.60
700	15.13	14.23	13.57	13.07	12.68	12.37
800	17.29	16.27	15.51	14.93	14.49	14.14
900	19.45	18.30	17.45	16.80	16.30	15.91
1000	21.61	20.33	19.39	18.67	18.11	17.67
2000	43.22	40.67	38.77	37.33	36.22	35.35
3000	64.82	61.00	58.16	56.00	54.33	53.02
4000	86.43	81.34	77.55	74.67	72.44	70.69
5000	108.04	101.67	96.94	93.34	90.55	88.37
6000	129.65	122.00	116.32	112.00	108.66	106.04
7000	151.26	142.34	135.71	130.67	126.77	123.72
8000	172.86	162.67	155.10	149.34	144.88	141.39
9000	194.47	183.00	174.48	168.01	162.99	159.06
10000	216.08	203.34	193.87	186.67	181.10	176.74
11000	237.69	223.67	213.26	205.34	199.21	194.41
12000	259.30	244.01	232.64	224.01	217.32	212.08
13000	280.90	264.34	252.03	242.67	235.43	229.76
14000	302.51	284.67	271.42	261.34	253.54	247.43
15000	324.12	305.01	290.81	280.01	271.65	265.10
16000	345.73	325.34	310.19	298.68	289.77	282.78
17000	367.34	345.68	329.58	317.34	307.88	300.45
18000	388.94	366.01	348.97	336.01	325.99	318.13
19000	410.55	386.34	368.35	354.68	344.10	335.80
20000	432.16	406.68	387.74	373.34	362.21	353.47
21000	453.77	427.01	407.13	392.01	380.32	371.15
22000	475.38	447.35	426.52	410.68	398.43	388.82
23000	496.98	467.68	445.90	429.35	416.54	406.49
24000	518.59	488.01	465.29	448.01	434.65	424.17
25000	540.20	508.35	484.68	466.68	452.76	441.84
30000	648.24	610.02	581.61	560.02	543.31	530.21
35000	756.28	711.69	678.55	653.35	633.86	618.58
40000	864.32	813.35	775.48	746.69	724.41	706.95
45000	972.36	915.02	872.42	840.03	814.96	795.31
50000	1080.40	1016.69	969.35	933.36	905.52	883.68
55000	1188.44	1118.36	1066.29	1026.70	996.07	972.05
60000	1296.48	1220.03	1163.22	1120.03	1086.62	1060.42
65000	1404.52	1321.70	1260.16	1213.37	1177.17	1148.79
70000	1512.56	1423.37	1357.10	1306.71	1267.72	1237.16
75000	1620.60	1525.04	1454.03	1400.04	1358.27	1325.52
80000	1728.64	1626.71	1550.97	1493.38	1448.83	1413.89
85000	1836.68	1728.38	1647.90	1586.72	1539.38	1502.26
90000	1944.72	1830.05	1744.84	1680.05	1629.93	1590.63
95000	2052.76	1931.72	1841.77	1773.39	1720.48	1679.00
100000	2160.80	2033.39	1938.71	1866.72	1811.03	1767.36
200000	4321.60	4066.77	3877.42	3733.45	3622.07	3534.73
300000	6482.41	6100.16	5816.12	5600.17	5433.10	5302.09
400000	8643.21	8133.55	7754.83	7466.89	7244.13	7069.46
500000	10804.01	10166.93	9693.54	9333.62	9055.16	8836.82

19%

MONTHLY PAYMENT

Necessary to amortize a loan

TERM / AMOUNT	15 YEARS	20 YEARS	25 YEARS	30 YEARS	35 YEARS	40 YEARS
500	8.41	8.10	7.99	7.94	7.93	7.92
600	10.10	9.72	9.59	9.53	9.51	9.51
700	11.78	11.34	11.18	11.12	11.10	11.09
800	13.46	12.97	12.78	12.71	12.68	12.67
900	15.15	14.59	14.38	14.30	14.27	14.26
1000	16.83	16.21	15.98	15.89	15.85	15.84
2000	33.66	32.41	31.95	31.78	31.71	31.68
3000	50.49	48.62	47.93	47.67	47.56	47.53
4000	67.32	64.83	63.91	63.56	63.42	63.37
5000	84.14	81.03	79.88	79.44	79.27	79.21
6000	100.97	97.24	95.86	95.33	95.13	95.05
7000	117.80	113.45	111.84	111.22	110.98	110.89
8000	134.63	129.65	127.81	127.11	126.84	126.73
9000	151.46	145.86	143.79	143.00	142.69	142.58
10000	168.29	162.07	159.77	158.89	158.55	158.42
11000	185.12	178.28	175.74	174.78	174.40	174.26
12000	201.95	194.48	191.72	190.67	190.26	190.10
13000	218.77	210.69	207.70	206.56	206.11	205.94
14000	235.60	226.90	223.68	222.44	221.97	221.78
15000	252.43	243.10	239.65	238.33	237.82	237.63
16000	269.26	259.31	255.63	254.22	253.68	253.47
17000	286.09	275.52	271.61	270.11	269.53	269.31
18000	302.92	291.72	287.58	286.00	285.39	285.15
19000	319.75	307.93	303.56	301.89	301.24	300.99
20000	336.58	324.14	319.54	317.78	317.10	316.83
21000	353.40	340.34	335.51	333.67	332.95	332.68
22000	370.23	356.55	351.49	349.56	348.81	348.52
23000	387.06	372.76	367.47	365.45	364.66	364.36
24000	403.89	388.96	383.44	381.33	380.52	380.20
25000	420.72	405.17	399.42	397.22	396.37	396.04
30000	504.86	486.21	479.30	476.67	475.65	475.25
35000	589.01	567.24	559.19	556.11	554.92	554.46
40000	673.15	648.27	639.07	635.56	634.20	633.67
45000	757.29	729.31	718.96	715.00	713.47	712.88
50000	841.44	810.34	798.84	794.45	792.75	792.09
55000	925.58	891.38	878.72	873.89	872.02	871.30
60000	1009.73	972.41	958.61	953.34	951.30	950.50
65000	1093.87	1053.45	1038.49	1032.78	1030.57	1029.71
70000	1178.01	1134.48	1118.38	1112.22	1109.85	1108.92
75000	1262.16	1215.51	1198.26	1191.67	1189.12	1188.13
80000	1346.30	1296.55	1278.14	1271.11	1268.40	1267.34
85000	1430.44	1377.58	1358.03	1350.56	1347.67	1346.55
90000	1514.59	1458.62	1437.91	1430.00	1426.95	1425.76
95000	1598.73	1539.65	1517.80	1509.45	1506.22	1504.97
100000	1682.88	1620.68	1597.68	1588.89	1585.49	1584.17
200000	3365.75	3241.37	3195.36	3177.78	3170.99	3168.35
300000	5048.63	4862.05	4793.04	4766.68	4756.48	4752.52
400000	6731.50	6482.74	6390.72	6355.57	6341.98	6336.70
500000	8414.38	8103.42	7988.40	7944.46	7927.47	7920.87

MONTHLY PAYMENT

Necessary to amortize a loan

19.5%

TERM / AMOUNT	1 YEARS	2 YEARS	3 YEARS	4 YEARS	5 YEARS	6 YEARS
500	46.20	25.33	18.45	15.08	13.11	11.83
600	55.44	30.39	22.15	18.10	15.73	14.20
700	64.68	35.46	25.84	21.12	18.35	16.56
800	73.92	40.52	29.53	24.13	20.97	18.93
900	83.16	45.59	33.22	27.15	23.59	21.30
1000	92.40	50.65	36.91	30.16	26.22	23.66
2000	184.79	101.30	73.82	60.33	52.43	47.33
3000	277.19	151.96	110.73	90.49	78.65	70.99
4000	369.58	202.61	147.64	120.66	104.87	94.66
5000	461.98	253.26	184.55	150.82	131.08	118.32
6000	554.37	303.91	221.46	180.99	157.30	141.98
7000	646.77	354.56	258.37	211.15	183.52	165.65
8000	739.16	405.22	295.27	241.32	209.73	189.31
9000	831.56	455.87	332.18	271.48	235.95	212.97
10000	923.95	506.52	369.09	301.65	262.16	236.64
11000	1016.35	557.17	406.00	331.81	288.38	260.30
12000	1108.74	607.82	442.91	361.98	314.60	283.97
13000	1201.14	658.47	479.82	392.14	340.81	307.63
14000	1293.54	709.13	516.73	422.30	367.03	331.29
15000	1385.93	759.78	553.64	452.47	393.25	354.96
16000	1478.33	810.43	590.55	482.63	419.46	378.62
17000	1570.72	861.08	627.46	512.80	445.68	402.29
18000	1663.12	911.73	664.37	542.96	471.90	425.95
19000	1755.51	962.39	701.28	573.13	498.11	449.61
20000	1847.91	1013.04	738.19	603.29	524.33	473.28
21000	1940.30	1063.69	775.10	633.46	550.55	496.94
22000	2032.70	1114.34	812.00	663.62	576.76	520.61
23000	2125.09	1164.99	848.91	693.79	602.98	544.27
24000	2217.49	1215.65	885.82	723.95	629.19	567.93
25000	2309.88	1266.30	922.73	754.12	655.41	591.60
30000	2771.86	1519.56	1107.28	904.94	786.49	709.92
35000	3233.84	1772.82	1291.83	1055.76	917.58	828.24
40000	3695.81	2026.08	1476.37	1206.58	1048.66	946.56
45000	4157.79	2279.33	1660.92	1357.41	1179.74	1064.87
50000	4619.77	2532.59	1845.47	1508.23	1310.82	1183.19
55000	5081.75	2785.85	2030.01	1659.05	1441.90	1301.51
60000	5543.72	3039.11	2214.56	1809.88	1572.99	1419.83
65000	6005.70	3292.37	2399.11	1960.70	1704.07	1538.15
70000	6467.68	3545.63	2583.65	2111.52	1835.15	1656.47
75000	6929.65	3798.89	2768.20	2262.35	1966.23	1774.79
80000	7391.63	4052.15	2952.74	2413.17	2097.32	1893.11
85000	7853.61	4305.41	3137.29	2563.99	2228.40	2011.43
90000	8315.58	4558.67	3321.84	2714.81	2359.48	2129.75
95000	8777.56	4811.93	3506.38	2865.64	2490.56	2248.07
100000	9239.54	5065.19	3690.93	3016.46	2621.64	2366.39
200000	18479.07	10130.38	7381.86	6032.92	5243.29	4732.78
300000	27718.61	15195.56	11072.79	9049.38	7864.93	7099.17
400000	36958.15	20260.75	14763.72	12065.84	10486.58	9465.55
500000	46197.69	25325.94	18454.66	15082.30	13108.22	11831.94

19.5%

MONTHLY PAYMENT

Necessary to amortize a loan

TERM / AMOUNT	7 YEARS	8 YEARS	9 YEARS	10 YEARS	11 YEARS	12 YEARS
500	10.95	10.32	9.85	9.50	9.22	9.01
600	13.14	12.39	11.82	11.40	11.07	10.81
700	15.33	14.45	13.79	13.30	12.91	12.61
800	17.52	16.51	15.76	15.20	14.76	14.41
900	19.72	18.58	17.74	17.10	16.60	16.22
1000	21.91	20.64	19.71	19.00	18.45	18.02
2000	43.81	41.28	39.41	37.99	36.89	36.04
3000	65.72	61.93	59.12	56.99	55.34	54.06
4000	87.62	82.57	78.82	75.98	73.79	72.07
5000	109.53	103.21	98.53	94.98	92.24	90.09
6000	131.44	123.85	118.23	113.97	110.68	108.11
7000	153.34	144.50	137.94	132.97	129.13	126.13
8000	175.25	165.14	157.65	151.96	147.58	144.15
9000	197.16	185.78	177.35	170.96	166.02	162.17
10000	219.06	206.42	197.06	189.95	184.47	180.19
11000	240.97	227.07	216.76	208.95	202.92	198.21
12000	262.87	247.71	236.47	227.94	221.37	216.22
13000	284.78	268.35	256.17	246.94	239.81	234.24
14000	306.69	288.99	275.88	265.93	258.26	252.26
15000	328.59	309.64	295.58	284.93	276.71	270.28
16000	350.50	330.28	315.29	303.92	295.15	288.30
17000	372.40	350.92	335.00	322.92	313.60	306.32
18000	394.31	371.56	354.70	341.91	332.05	324.34
19000	416.22	392.21	374.41	360.91	350.50	342.35
20000	438.12	412.85	394.11	379.90	368.94	360.37
21000	460.03	433.49	413.82	398.90	387.39	378.39
22000	481.93	454.13	433.52	417.89	405.84	396.41
23000	503.84	474.78	453.23	436.89	424.28	414.43
24000	525.75	495.42	472.94	455.89	442.73	432.45
25000	547.65	516.06	492.64	474.88	461.18	450.47
30000	657.18	619.27	591.17	569.86	553.41	540.56
35000	766.71	722.49	689.70	664.83	645.65	630.65
40000	876.24	825.70	788.23	759.81	737.89	720.75
45000	985.78	928.91	886.75	854.78	830.12	810.84
50000	1095.31	1032.12	985.28	949.76	922.36	900.93
55000	1204.84	1135.34	1083.81	1044.74	1014.59	991.03
60000	1314.37	1238.55	1182.34	1139.71	1106.83	1081.12
65000	1423.90	1341.76	1280.87	1234.69	1199.06	1171.21
70000	1533.43	1444.97	1379.40	1329.67	1291.30	1261.31
75000	1642.96	1548.18	1477.92	1424.64	1383.53	1351.40
80000	1752.49	1651.40	1576.45	1519.62	1475.77	1441.49
85000	1862.02	1754.61	1674.98	1614.59	1568.01	1531.59
90000	1971.55	1857.82	1773.51	1709.57	1660.24	1621.68
95000	2081.08	1961.03	1872.04	1804.55	1752.48	1711.77
100000	2190.61	2064.25	1970.57	1899.52	1844.71	1801.86
200000	4381.22	4128.49	3941.13	3799.04	3689.43	3603.73
300000	6571.84	6192.74	5911.70	5698.57	5534.14	5405.59
400000	8762.45	8256.98	7882.26	7598.09	7378.85	7207.46
500000	10953.06	10321.23	9852.83	9497.61	9223.56	9009.32

MONTHLY PAYMENT

Necessary to amortize a loan

19.5%

TERM / AMOUNT	15 YEARS	20 YEARS	25 YEARS	30 YEARS	35 YEARS	40 YEARS
500	8.60	8.30	8.19	8.15	8.13	8.13
600	10.32	9.96	9.83	9.78	9.76	9.75
700	12.04	11.62	11.47	11.41	11.39	11.38
800	13.76	13.28	13.10	13.04	13.01	13.01
900	15.48	14.94	14.74	14.67	14.64	14.63
1000	17.19	16.60	16.38	16.30	16.27	16.26
2000	34.39	33.19	32.76	32.60	32.54	32.51
3000	51.58	49.79	49.14	48.90	48.81	48.77
4000	68.78	66.39	65.52	65.20	65.07	65.03
5000	85.97	82.98	81.90	81.50	81.34	81.29
6000	103.17	99.58	98.28	97.80	97.61	97.54
7000	120.36	116.18	114.66	114.09	113.88	113.80
8000	137.56	132.77	131.04	130.39	130.15	130.06
9000	154.75	149.37	147.42	146.69	146.42	146.31
10000	171.95	165.97	163.80	162.99	162.69	162.57
11000	189.14	182.56	180.18	179.29	178.96	178.83
12000	206.34	199.16	196.56	195.59	195.22	195.09
13000	223.53	215.76	212.94	211.89	211.49	211.34
14000	240.73	232.35	229.32	228.19	227.76	227.60
15000	257.92	248.95	245.70	244.49	244.03	243.86
16000	275.12	265.55	262.08	260.79	260.30	260.11
17000	292.31	282.14	278.46	277.09	276.57	276.37
18000	309.50	298.74	294.84	293.39	292.84	292.63
19000	326.70	315.34	311.22	309.68	309.10	308.88
20000	343.89	331.93	327.60	325.98	325.37	325.14
21000	361.09	348.53	343.98	342.28	341.64	341.40
22000	378.28	365.13	360.36	358.58	357.91	357.66
23000	395.48	381.72	376.74	374.88	374.18	373.91
24000	412.67	398.32	393.12	391.18	390.45	390.17
25000	429.87	414.92	409.50	407.48	406.72	406.43
30000	515.84	497.90	491.40	488.98	488.06	487.71
35000	601.81	580.88	573.30	570.47	569.40	569.00
40000	687.79	663.87	655.20	651.97	650.75	650.28
45000	773.76	746.85	737.10	733.46	732.09	731.57
50000	859.74	829.83	819.00	814.96	813.43	812.85
55000	945.71	912.82	900.90	896.46	894.78	894.14
60000	1031.68	995.80	982.80	977.95	976.12	975.43
65000	1117.66	1078.78	1064.70	1059.45	1057.46	1056.71
70000	1203.63	1161.77	1146.60	1140.94	1138.81	1138.00
75000	1289.60	1244.75	1228.50	1222.44	1220.15	1219.28
80000	1375.58	1327.73	1310.40	1303.94	1301.49	1300.57
85000	1461.55	1410.71	1392.31	1385.43	1382.84	1381.85
90000	1547.52	1493.70	1474.21	1466.93	1464.18	1463.14
95000	1633.50	1576.68	1556.11	1548.42	1545.52	1544.42
100000	1719.47	1659.66	1638.01	1629.92	1626.87	1625.71
200000	3438.94	3319.33	3276.01	3259.84	3253.73	3251.42
300000	5158.41	4978.99	4914.02	4889.76	4880.60	4877.13
400000	6877.88	6638.66	6552.02	6519.68	6507.47	6502.84
500000	8597.35	8298.32	8190.03	8149.60	8134.33	8128.55

20%

MONTHLY PAYMENT

Necessary to amortize a loan

TERM / AMOUNT	1 YEARS	2 YEARS	3 YEARS	4 YEARS	5 YEARS	6 YEARS
500	46.32	25.45	18.58	15.22	13.25	11.98
600	55.58	30.54	22.30	18.26	15.90	14.37
700	64.84	35.63	26.01	21.30	18.55	16.77
800	74.11	40.72	29.73	24.34	21.20	19.16
900	83.37	45.81	33.45	27.39	23.84	21.56
1000	92.63	50.90	37.16	30.43	26.49	23.95
2000	185.27	101.79	74.33	60.86	52.99	47.91
3000	277.90	152.69	111.49	91.29	79.48	71.86
4000	370.54	203.58	148.65	121.72	105.98	95.81
5000	463.17	254.48	185.82	152.15	132.47	119.76
6000	555.81	305.37	222.98	182.58	158.96	143.72
7000	648.44	356.27	260.15	213.01	185.46	167.67
8000	741.08	407.17	297.31	243.44	211.95	191.62
9000	833.71	458.06	334.47	273.87	238.44	215.58
10000	926.35	508.96	371.64	304.30	264.94	239.53
11000	1018.98	559.85	408.80	334.73	291.43	263.48
12000	1111.61	610.75	445.96	365.16	317.93	287.43
13000	1204.25	661.65	483.13	395.59	344.42	311.39
14000	1296.88	712.54	520.29	426.03	370.91	335.34
15000	1389.52	763.44	557.45	456.46	397.41	359.29
16000	1482.15	814.33	594.62	486.89	423.90	383.25
17000	1574.79	865.23	631.78	517.32	450.40	407.20
18000	1667.42	916.12	668.94	547.75	476.89	431.15
19000	1760.06	967.02	706.11	578.18	503.38	455.10
20000	1852.69	1017.92	743.27	608.61	529.88	479.06
21000	1945.32	1068.81	780.44	639.04	556.37	503.01
22000	2037.96	1119.71	817.60	669.47	582.87	526.96
23000	2130.59	1170.60	854.76	699.90	609.36	550.91
24000	2223.23	1221.50	891.93	730.33	635.85	574.87
25000	2315.86	1272.40	929.09	760.76	662.35	598.82
30000	2779.04	1526.87	1114.91	912.91	794.82	718.58
35000	3242.21	1781.35	1300.73	1065.06	927.29	838.35
40000	3705.38	2035.83	1486.54	1217.21	1059.76	958.11
45000	4168.55	2290.31	1672.36	1369.37	1192.22	1077.88
50000	4631.73	2544.79	1858.18	1521.52	1324.69	1197.64
55000	5094.90	2799.27	2044.00	1673.67	1457.16	1317.41
60000	5558.07	3053.75	2229.82	1825.82	1589.63	1437.17
65000	6021.24	3308.23	2415.63	1977.97	1722.10	1556.93
70000	6484.42	3562.71	2601.45	2130.13	1854.57	1676.70
75000	6947.59	3817.19	2787.27	2282.28	1987.04	1796.46
80000	7410.76	4071.66	2973.09	2434.43	2119.51	1916.23
85000	7873.93	4326.14	3158.90	2586.58	2251.98	2035.99
90000	8337.11	4580.62	3344.72	2738.73	2384.45	2155.75
95000	8800.28	4835.10	3530.54	2890.88	2516.92	2275.52
100000	9263.45	5089.58	3716.36	3043.04	2649.39	2395.28
200000	18526.90	10179.16	7432.72	6086.07	5298.78	4790.57
300000	27790.35	15268.74	11149.08	9129.11	7948.17	7185.85
400000	37053.80	20358.32	14865.43	12172.14	10597.55	9581.13
500000	46317.25	25447.90	18581.79	15215.18	13246.94	11976.41

MONTHLY PAYMENT

Necessary to amortize a loan

20%

TERM / AMOUNT	7 YEARS	8 YEARS	9 YEARS	10 YEARS	11 YEARS	12 YEARS
500	11.10	10.48	10.01	9.66	9.39	9.18
600	13.32	12.57	12.02	11.60	11.27	11.02
700	15.54	14.67	14.02	13.53	13.15	12.86
800	17.76	16.76	16.02	15.46	15.03	14.69
900	19.99	18.86	18.02	17.39	16.91	16.53
1000	22.21	20.95	20.03	19.33	18.79	18.37
2000	44.41	41.91	40.05	38.65	37.57	36.73
3000	66.62	62.86	60.08	57.98	56.36	55.10
4000	88.82	83.81	80.11	77.30	75.15	73.46
5000	111.03	104.77	100.13	96.63	93.93	91.83
6000	133.24	125.72	120.16	115.95	112.72	110.20
7000	155.44	146.67	140.19	135.28	131.50	128.56
8000	177.65	167.63	160.21	154.60	150.29	146.93
9000	199.86	188.58	180.24	173.93	169.08	165.29
10000	222.06	209.53	200.27	193.26	187.86	183.66
11000	244.27	230.49	220.29	212.58	206.65	202.03
12000	266.47	251.44	240.32	231.91	225.44	220.39
13000	288.68	272.39	260.34	251.23	244.22	238.76
14000	310.89	293.34	280.37	270.56	263.01	257.13
15000	333.09	314.30	300.40	289.88	281.80	275.49
16000	355.30	335.25	320.42	309.21	300.58	293.86
17000	377.51	356.20	340.45	328.53	319.37	312.22
18000	399.71	377.16	360.48	347.86	338.15	330.59
19000	421.92	398.11	380.50	367.19	356.94	348.96
20000	444.12	419.06	400.53	386.51	375.73	367.32
21000	466.33	440.02	420.56	405.84	394.51	385.69
22000	488.54	460.97	440.58	425.16	413.30	404.05
23000	510.74	481.92	460.61	444.49	432.09	422.42
24000	532.95	502.88	480.64	463.81	450.87	440.79
25000	555.15	523.83	500.66	483.14	469.66	459.15
30000	666.19	628.60	600.80	579.77	563.59	550.98
35000	777.22	733.36	700.93	676.39	657.52	642.81
40000	888.25	838.13	801.06	773.02	751.45	734.64
45000	999.28	942.89	901.19	869.65	845.39	826.47
50000	1110.31	1047.66	1001.33	966.28	939.32	918.30
55000	1221.34	1152.43	1101.46	1062.91	1033.25	1010.13
60000	1332.37	1257.19	1201.59	1159.53	1127.18	1101.97
65000	1443.40	1361.96	1301.72	1256.16	1221.11	1193.80
70000	1554.43	1466.72	1401.86	1352.79	1315.04	1285.63
75000	1665.46	1571.49	1501.99	1449.42	1408.98	1377.46
80000	1776.50	1676.26	1602.12	1546.05	1502.91	1469.29
85000	1887.53	1781.02	1702.25	1642.67	1596.84	1561.12
90000	1998.56	1885.79	1802.39	1739.30	1690.77	1652.95
95000	2109.59	1990.55	1902.52	1835.93	1784.70	1744.78
100000	2220.62	2095.32	2002.65	1932.56	1878.63	1836.61
200000	4441.24	4190.64	4005.30	3865.11	3757.27	3673.22
300000	6661.86	6285.96	6007.95	5797.67	5635.90	5509.83
400000	8882.48	8381.28	8010.60	7730.23	7514.54	7346.43
500000	11103.10	10476.60	10013.25	9662.78	9393.17	9183.04

20%

MONTHLY PAYMENT

Necessary to amortize a loan

TERM / AMOUNT	15 YEARS	20 YEARS	25 YEARS	30 YEARS	35 YEARS	40 YEARS
500	8.78	8.49	8.39	8.36	8.34	8.34
600	10.54	10.19	10.07	10.03	10.01	10.00
700	12.29	11.89	11.75	11.70	11.68	11.67
800	14.05	13.59	13.43	13.37	13.35	13.34
900	15.81	15.29	15.11	15.04	15.01	15.01
1000	17.56	16.99	16.78	16.71	16.68	16.67
2000	35.13	33.98	33.57	33.42	33.37	33.35
3000	52.69	50.96	50.35	50.13	50.05	50.02
4000	70.25	67.95	67.14	66.84	66.73	66.69
5000	87.81	84.94	83.92	83.55	83.41	83.36
6000	105.38	101.93	100.71	100.26	100.10	100.04
7000	122.94	118.92	117.49	116.97	116.78	116.71
8000	140.50	135.91	134.28	133.68	133.46	133.38
9000	158.07	152.89	151.06	150.39	150.15	150.05
10000	175.63	169.88	167.85	167.10	166.83	166.73
11000	193.19	186.87	184.63	183.81	183.51	183.40
12000	210.76	203.86	201.41	200.52	200.19	200.07
13000	228.32	220.85	218.20	217.23	216.88	216.74
14000	245.88	237.84	234.98	233.94	233.56	233.42
15000	263.44	254.82	251.77	250.65	250.24	250.09
16000	281.01	271.81	268.55	267.36	266.92	266.76
17000	298.57	288.80	285.34	284.07	283.61	283.43
18000	316.13	305.79	302.12	300.78	300.29	300.11
19000	333.70	322.78	318.91	317.49	316.97	316.78
20000	351.26	339.76	335.69	334.20	333.66	333.45
21000	368.82	356.75	352.47	350.91	350.34	350.13
22000	386.39	373.74	369.26	367.62	367.02	366.80
23000	403.95	390.73	386.04	384.33	383.70	383.47
24000	421.51	407.72	402.83	401.04	400.39	400.14
25000	439.07	424.71	419.61	417.75	417.07	416.82
30000	526.89	509.65	503.54	501.31	500.48	500.18
35000	614.70	594.59	587.46	584.86	583.90	583.54
40000	702.52	679.53	671.38	668.41	667.31	666.91
45000	790.33	764.47	755.30	751.96	750.73	750.27
50000	878.15	849.41	839.23	835.51	834.14	833.63
55000	965.96	934.35	923.15	919.06	917.55	917.00
60000	1053.78	1019.29	1007.07	1002.61	1000.97	1000.36
65000	1141.59	1104.24	1090.99	1086.16	1084.38	1083.72
70000	1229.41	1189.18	1174.92	1169.71	1167.79	1167.08
75000	1317.22	1274.12	1258.84	1253.26	1251.21	1250.45
80000	1405.04	1359.06	1342.76	1336.81	1334.62	1333.81
85000	1492.85	1444.00	1426.68	1420.37	1418.04	1417.17
90000	1580.67	1528.94	1510.61	1503.92	1501.45	1500.54
95000	1668.48	1613.88	1594.53	1587.47	1584.86	1583.90
100000	1756.30	1698.82	1678.45	1671.02	1668.28	1667.26
200000	3512.59	3397.65	3356.90	3342.04	3336.56	3334.53
300000	5268.89	5096.47	5035.36	5013.06	5004.83	5001.79
400000	7025.19	6795.30	6713.81	6684.07	6673.11	6669.06
500000	8781.48	8494.12	8392.26	8355.09	8341.39	8336.32

MONTHLY PAYMENT

Necessary to amortize a loan

20.5%

TERM / AMOUNT	1 YEARS	2 YEARS	3 YEARS	4 YEARS	5 YEARS	6 YEARS
500	46.44	25.57	18.71	15.35	13.39	12.12
600	55.72	30.68	22.45	18.42	16.06	14.55
700	65.01	35.80	26.19	21.49	18.74	16.97
800	74.30	40.91	29.94	24.56	21.42	19.39
900	83.59	46.03	33.68	27.63	24.10	21.82
1000	92.87	51.14	37.42	30.70	26.77	24.24
2000	185.75	102.28	74.84	61.39	53.55	48.49
3000	278.62	153.42	112.26	92.09	80.32	72.73
4000	371.50	204.56	149.68	122.79	107.09	96.97
5000	464.37	255.70	187.09	153.49	133.86	121.22
6000	557.24	306.84	224.51	184.18	160.64	145.46
7000	650.12	357.98	261.93	214.88	187.41	169.70
8000	742.99	409.12	299.35	245.58	214.18	193.95
9000	835.87	460.26	336.77	276.28	240.96	218.19
10000	928.74	511.40	374.19	306.97	267.73	242.44
11000	1021.61	562.54	411.61	337.67	294.50	266.68
12000	1114.49	613.68	449.03	368.37	321.27	290.92
13000	1207.36	664.83	486.44	399.07	348.05	315.17
14000	1300.24	715.97	523.86	429.76	374.82	339.41
15000	1393.11	767.11	561.28	460.46	401.59	363.65
16000	1485.98	818.25	598.70	491.16	428.37	387.90
17000	1578.86	869.39	636.12	521.86	455.14	412.14
18000	1671.73	920.53	673.54	552.55	481.91	436.38
19000	1764.61	971.67	710.96	583.25	508.68	460.63
20000	1857.48	1022.81	748.38	613.95	535.46	484.87
21000	1950.35	1073.95	785.80	644.65	562.23	509.11
22000	2043.23	1125.09	823.21	675.34	589.00	533.36
23000	2136.10	1176.23	860.63	706.04	615.78	557.60
24000	2228.98	1227.37	898.05	736.74	642.55	581.84
25000	2321.85	1278.51	935.47	767.43	669.32	606.09
30000	2786.22	1534.21	1122.57	920.92	803.19	727.31
35000	3250.59	1789.91	1309.66	1074.41	937.05	848.52
40000	3714.96	2045.62	1496.75	1227.90	1070.91	969.74
45000	4179.33	2301.32	1683.85	1381.38	1204.78	1090.96
50000	4643.70	2557.02	1870.94	1534.87	1338.64	1212.18
55000	5108.07	2812.72	2058.04	1688.36	1472.51	1333.39
60000	5572.44	3068.42	2245.13	1841.84	1606.37	1454.61
65000	6036.81	3324.13	2432.22	1995.33	1740.24	1575.83
70000	6501.18	3579.83	2619.32	2148.82	1874.10	1697.05
75000	6965.55	3835.53	2806.41	2302.30	2007.96	1818.27
80000	7429.92	4091.23	2993.51	2455.79	2141.83	1939.48
85000	7894.29	4346.93	3180.60	2609.28	2275.69	2060.70
90000	8358.66	4602.64	3367.70	2762.77	2409.56	2181.92
95000	8823.03	4858.34	3554.79	2916.25	2543.42	2303.14
100000	9287.40	5114.04	3741.88	3069.74	2677.29	2424.35
200000	18574.79	10228.08	7483.77	6139.48	5354.57	4848.71
300000	27862.19	15342.12	11225.65	9209.22	8031.86	7273.06
400000	37149.59	20456.16	14967.53	12278.96	10709.14	9697.41
500000	46436.99	25570.20	18709.42	15348.70	13386.43	12121.77

20.5% **MONTHLY PAYMENT**

Necessary to amortize a loan

TERM / AMOUNT	7 YEARS	8 YEARS	9 YEARS	10 YEARS	11 YEARS	12 YEARS
500	11.25	10.63	10.17	9.83	9.56	9.36
600	13.50	12.76	12.21	11.79	11.48	11.23
700	15.76	14.89	14.24	13.76	13.39	13.10
800	18.01	17.01	16.28	15.73	15.30	14.97
900	20.26	19.14	18.31	17.69	17.22	16.84
1000	22.51	21.27	20.35	19.66	19.13	18.72
2000	45.02	42.53	40.70	39.32	38.26	37.43
3000	67.52	63.80	61.05	58.97	57.38	56.15
4000	90.03	85.06	81.40	78.63	76.51	74.86
5000	112.54	106.33	101.75	98.29	95.64	93.58
6000	135.05	127.60	122.10	117.95	114.77	112.30
7000	157.56	148.86	142.45	137.61	133.90	131.01
8000	180.07	170.13	162.80	157.27	153.02	149.73
9000	202.57	191.39	183.15	176.92	172.15	168.44
10000	225.08	212.66	203.50	196.58	191.28	187.16
11000	247.59	233.93	223.85	216.24	210.41	205.87
12000	270.10	255.19	244.20	235.90	229.53	224.59
13000	292.61	276.46	264.54	255.56	248.66	243.31
14000	315.12	297.72	284.89	275.22	267.79	262.02
15000	337.62	318.99	305.24	294.87	286.92	280.74
16000	360.13	340.26	325.59	314.53	306.05	299.45
17000	382.64	361.52	345.94	334.19	325.17	318.17
18000	405.15	382.79	366.29	353.85	344.30	336.89
19000	427.66	404.06	386.64	373.51	363.43	355.60
20000	450.16	425.32	406.99	393.16	382.56	374.32
21000	472.67	446.59	427.34	412.82	401.69	393.03
22000	495.18	467.85	447.69	432.48	420.81	411.75
23000	517.69	489.12	468.04	452.14	439.94	430.47
24000	540.20	510.39	488.39	471.80	459.07	449.18
25000	562.71	531.65	508.74	491.46	478.20	467.90
30000	675.25	637.98	610.49	589.75	573.84	561.48
35000	787.79	744.31	712.24	688.04	669.48	655.06
40000	900.33	850.64	813.98	786.33	765.12	748.64
45000	1012.87	956.97	915.73	884.62	860.76	842.22
50000	1125.41	1063.30	1017.48	982.91	956.40	935.79
55000	1237.95	1169.63	1119.23	1081.20	1052.04	1029.37
60000	1350.49	1275.96	1220.98	1179.49	1147.67	1122.95
65000	1463.04	1382.29	1322.72	1277.78	1243.31	1216.53
70000	1575.58	1488.62	1424.47	1376.08	1338.95	1310.11
75000	1688.12	1594.95	1526.22	1474.37	1434.59	1403.69
80000	1800.66	1701.28	1627.97	1572.66	1530.23	1497.27
85000	1913.20	1807.62	1729.71	1670.95	1625.87	1590.85
90000	2025.74	1913.95	1831.46	1769.24	1721.51	1684.43
95000	2138.28	2020.28	1933.21	1867.53	1817.15	1778.01
100000	2250.82	2126.61	2034.96	1965.82	1912.79	1871.59
200000	4501.65	4253.21	4069.92	3931.65	3825.58	3743.18
300000	6752.47	6379.82	6104.88	5897.47	5738.37	5614.77
400000	9003.30	8506.42	8139.83	7863.29	7651.17	7486.36
500000	11254.12	10633.03	10174.79	9829.12	9563.96	9357.95

MONTHLY PAYMENT

Necessary to amortize a loan

20.5%

TERM / AMOUNT	15 YEARS	20 YEARS	25 YEARS	30 YEARS	35 YEARS	40 YEARS
500	8.97	8.69	8.60	8.56	8.55	8.54
600	10.76	10.43	10.31	10.27	10.26	10.25
700	12.55	12.17	12.03	11.99	11.97	11.96
800	14.35	13.91	13.75	13.70	13.68	13.67
900	16.14	15.64	15.47	15.41	15.39	15.38
1000	17.93	17.38	17.19	17.12	17.10	17.09
2000	35.87	34.76	34.38	34.24	34.19	34.18
3000	53.80	52.14	51.57	51.37	51.29	51.27
4000	71.73	69.53	68.76	68.49	68.39	68.35
5000	89.67	86.91	85.95	85.61	85.49	85.44
6000	107.60	104.29	103.14	102.73	102.58	102.53
7000	125.53	121.67	120.33	119.85	119.68	119.62
8000	143.47	139.05	137.52	136.97	136.78	136.71
9000	161.40	156.43	154.71	154.10	153.88	153.80
10000	179.33	173.82	171.90	171.22	170.97	170.88
11000	197.27	191.20	189.09	188.34	188.07	187.97
12000	215.20	208.58	206.28	205.46	205.17	205.06
13000	233.14	225.96	223.47	222.58	222.26	222.15
14000	251.07	243.34	240.66	239.71	239.36	239.24
15000	269.00	260.72	257.85	256.83	256.46	256.33
16000	286.94	278.10	275.04	273.95	273.56	273.41
17000	304.87	295.49	292.23	291.07	290.65	290.50
18000	322.80	312.87	309.42	308.19	307.75	307.59
19000	340.74	330.25	326.61	325.31	324.85	324.68
20000	358.67	347.63	343.80	342.44	341.94	341.77
21000	376.60	365.01	360.99	359.56	359.04	358.86
22000	394.54	382.39	378.18	376.68	376.14	375.94
23000	412.47	399.78	395.37	393.80	393.24	393.03
24000	430.40	417.16	412.56	410.92	410.33	410.12
25000	448.34	434.54	429.75	428.05	427.43	427.21
30000	538.00	521.45	515.70	513.65	512.92	512.65
35000	627.67	608.35	601.65	599.26	598.40	598.09
40000	717.34	695.26	687.60	684.87	683.89	683.53
45000	807.01	782.17	773.55	770.48	769.38	768.98
50000	896.67	869.08	859.50	856.09	854.86	854.42
55000	986.34	955.98	945.45	941.70	940.35	939.86
60000	1076.01	1042.89	1031.40	1027.31	1025.83	1025.30
65000	1165.68	1129.80	1117.35	1112.92	1111.32	1110.74
70000	1255.34	1216.71	1203.30	1198.53	1196.81	1196.19
75000	1345.01	1303.62	1289.26	1284.14	1282.29	1281.63
80000	1434.68	1390.52	1375.21	1369.74	1367.78	1367.07
85000	1524.34	1477.43	1461.16	1455.35	1453.27	1452.51
90000	1614.01	1564.34	1547.11	1540.96	1538.75	1537.95
95000	1703.68	1651.25	1633.06	1626.57	1624.24	1623.39
100000	1793.35	1738.15	1719.01	1712.18	1709.72	1708.84
200000	3586.69	3476.31	3438.01	3424.36	3419.45	3417.67
300000	5380.04	5214.46	5157.02	5136.54	5129.17	5126.51
400000	7173.39	6952.62	6876.03	6848.72	6838.90	6835.35
500000	8966.73	8690.77	8595.04	8560.90	8548.62	8544.18

21%

MONTHLY PAYMENT

Necessary to amortize a loan

TERM / AMOUNT	1 YEARS	2 YEARS	3 YEARS	4 YEARS	5 YEARS	6 YEARS
500	46.56	25.69	18.84	15.48	13.53	12.27
600	55.87	30.83	22.61	18.58	16.23	14.72
700	65.18	35.97	26.37	21.68	18.94	17.18
800	74.49	41.11	30.14	24.77	21.64	19.63
900	83.80	46.25	33.91	27.87	24.35	22.08
1000	93.11	51.39	37.68	30.97	27.05	24.54
2000	186.23	102.77	75.35	61.93	54.11	49.07
3000	279.34	154.16	113.03	92.90	81.16	73.61
4000	372.46	205.54	150.70	123.86	108.21	98.14
5000	465.57	256.93	188.38	154.83	135.27	122.68
6000	558.68	308.31	226.05	185.79	162.32	147.22
7000	651.80	359.70	263.73	216.76	189.37	171.75
8000	744.91	411.09	301.40	247.73	216.43	196.29
9000	838.02	462.47	339.08	278.69	243.48	220.82
10000	931.14	513.86	376.75	309.66	270.53	245.36
11000	1024.25	565.24	414.43	340.62	297.59	269.90
12000	1117.37	616.63	452.10	371.59	324.64	294.43
13000	1210.48	668.01	489.78	402.55	351.69	318.97
14000	1303.59	719.40	527.45	433.52	378.75	343.50
15000	1396.71	770.78	565.13	464.49	405.80	368.04
16000	1489.82	822.17	602.80	495.45	432.85	392.58
17000	1582.93	873.56	640.48	526.42	459.91	417.11
18000	1676.05	924.94	678.15	557.38	486.96	441.65
19000	1769.16	976.33	715.83	588.35	514.01	466.18
20000	1862.28	1027.71	753.50	619.31	541.07	490.72
21000	1955.39	1079.10	791.18	650.28	568.12	515.26
22000	2048.50	1130.48	828.85	681.25	595.17	539.79
23000	2141.62	1181.87	866.53	712.21	622.23	564.33
24000	2234.73	1233.26	904.20	743.18	649.28	588.86
25000	2327.84	1284.64	941.88	774.14	676.33	613.40
30000	2793.41	1541.57	1130.25	928.97	811.60	736.08
35000	3258.98	1798.50	1318.63	1083.80	946.87	858.76
40000	3724.55	2055.43	1507.00	1238.63	1082.13	981.44
45000	4190.12	2312.35	1695.38	1393.46	1217.40	1104.12
50000	4655.69	2569.28	1883.75	1548.28	1352.67	1226.80
55000	5121.26	2826.21	2072.13	1703.11	1487.93	1349.48
60000	5586.83	3083.14	2260.50	1857.94	1623.20	1472.16
65000	6052.40	3340.07	2448.88	2012.77	1758.47	1594.84
70000	6517.96	3597.00	2637.25	2167.60	1893.74	1717.52
75000	6983.53	3853.92	2825.63	2322.43	2029.00	1840.20
80000	7449.10	4110.85	3014.01	2477.26	2164.27	1962.88
85000	7914.67	4367.78	3202.38	2632.08	2299.54	2085.56
90000	8380.24	4624.71	3390.76	2786.91	2434.80	2208.24
95000	8845.81	4881.64	3579.13	2941.74	2570.07	2330.92
100000	9311.38	5138.57	3767.51	3096.57	2705.34	2453.60
200000	18622.75	10277.13	7535.01	6193.14	5410.67	4907.20
300000	27934.13	15415.70	11302.52	9289.71	8116.01	7360.80
400000	37245.51	20554.26	15070.03	12386.28	10821.34	9814.40
500000	46556.89	25692.83	18837.53	15482.85	13526.68	12268.00

MONTHLY PAYMENT

Necessary to amortize a loan

21%

TERM / AMOUNT	7 YEARS	8 YEARS	9 YEARS	10 YEARS	11 YEARS	12 YEARS
500	11.41	10.79	10.34	10.00	9.74	9.53
600	13.69	12.95	12.40	12.00	11.68	11.44
700	15.97	15.11	14.47	14.00	13.63	13.35
800	18.25	17.26	16.54	15.99	15.58	15.25
900	20.53	19.42	18.61	17.99	17.52	17.16
1000	22.81	21.58	20.67	19.99	19.47	19.07
2000	45.62	43.16	41.35	39.99	38.94	38.14
3000	68.44	64.74	62.02	59.98	58.42	57.20
4000	91.25	86.32	82.70	79.97	77.89	76.27
5000	114.06	107.91	103.37	99.97	97.36	95.34
6000	136.87	129.49	124.05	119.96	116.83	114.41
7000	159.69	151.07	144.72	139.95	136.30	133.48
8000	182.50	172.65	165.40	159.95	155.77	152.54
9000	205.31	194.23	186.07	179.94	175.25	171.61
10000	228.12	215.81	206.75	199.93	194.72	190.68
11000	250.93	237.39	227.42	219.92	214.19	209.75
12000	273.75	258.97	248.10	239.92	233.66	228.82
13000	296.56	280.55	268.77	259.91	253.13	247.88
14000	319.37	302.13	289.45	279.90	272.61	266.95
15000	342.18	323.72	310.12	299.90	292.08	286.02
16000	365.00	345.30	330.80	319.89	311.55	305.09
17000	387.81	366.88	351.47	339.88	331.02	324.16
18000	410.62	388.46	372.15	359.88	350.49	343.22
19000	433.43	410.04	392.82	379.87	369.96	362.29
20000	456.24	431.62	413.50	399.86	389.44	381.36
21000	479.06	453.20	434.17	419.86	408.91	400.43
22000	501.87	474.78	454.85	439.85	428.38	419.50
23000	524.68	496.36	475.52	459.84	447.85	438.56
24000	547.49	517.94	496.20	479.84	467.32	457.63
25000	570.31	539.53	516.87	499.83	486.80	476.70
30000	684.37	647.43	620.25	599.80	584.15	572.04
35000	798.43	755.34	723.62	699.76	681.51	667.38
40000	912.49	863.24	826.99	799.73	778.87	762.72
45000	1026.55	971.15	930.37	899.69	876.23	858.06
50000	1140.61	1079.05	1033.74	999.66	973.59	953.40
55000	1254.67	1186.96	1137.12	1099.62	1070.95	1048.74
60000	1368.73	1294.86	1240.49	1199.59	1168.31	1144.08
65000	1482.79	1402.77	1343.87	1299.56	1265.67	1239.42
70000	1596.86	1510.67	1447.24	1399.52	1363.03	1334.76
75000	1710.92	1618.58	1550.62	1499.49	1460.39	1430.10
80000	1824.98	1726.48	1653.99	1599.45	1557.74	1525.44
85000	1939.04	1834.39	1757.36	1699.42	1655.10	1620.78
90000	2053.10	1942.29	1860.74	1799.39	1752.46	1716.12
95000	2167.16	2050.20	1964.11	1899.35	1849.82	1811.46
100000	2281.22	2158.10	2067.49	1999.32	1947.18	1906.80
200000	4562.45	4316.20	4134.97	3998.63	3894.36	3813.60
300000	6843.67	6474.30	6202.46	5997.95	5841.54	5720.40
400000	9124.89	8632.40	8269.95	7997.27	7788.72	7627.20
500000	11406.11	10790.50	10337.43	9996.58	9735.90	9534.01

21%

MONTHLY PAYMENT

Necessary to amortize a loan

TERM / AMOUNT	15 YEARS	20 YEARS	25 YEARS	30 YEARS	35 YEARS	40 YEARS
500	9.15	8.89	8.80	8.77	8.76	8.75
600	10.98	10.67	10.56	10.52	10.51	10.50
700	12.81	12.44	12.32	12.27	12.26	12.25
800	14.64	14.22	14.08	14.03	14.01	14.00
900	16.48	16.00	15.84	15.78	15.76	15.75
1000	18.31	17.78	17.60	17.53	17.51	17.50
2000	36.61	35.55	35.19	35.07	35.02	35.01
3000	54.92	53.33	52.79	52.60	52.54	52.51
4000	73.22	71.11	70.39	70.14	70.05	70.02
5000	91.53	88.88	87.98	87.67	87.56	87.52
6000	109.84	106.66	105.58	105.20	105.07	105.03
7000	128.14	124.44	123.18	122.74	122.58	122.53
8000	146.45	142.21	140.77	140.27	140.10	140.03
9000	164.76	159.99	158.37	157.81	157.61	157.54
10000	183.06	177.76	175.97	175.34	175.12	175.04
11000	201.37	195.54	193.56	192.87	192.63	192.55
12000	219.67	213.32	211.16	210.41	210.14	210.05
13000	237.98	231.09	228.76	227.94	227.66	227.56
14000	256.29	248.87	246.35	245.48	245.17	245.06
15000	274.59	266.65	263.95	263.01	262.68	262.56
16000	292.90	284.42	281.55	280.54	280.19	280.07
17000	311.20	302.20	299.14	298.08	297.70	297.57
18000	329.51	319.98	316.74	315.61	315.22	315.08
19000	347.82	337.75	334.34	333.15	332.73	332.58
20000	366.12	355.53	351.93	350.68	350.24	350.08
21000	384.43	373.31	369.53	368.21	367.75	367.59
22000	402.73	391.08	387.13	385.75	385.26	385.09
23000	421.04	408.86	404.72	403.28	402.78	402.60
24000	439.35	426.63	422.32	420.82	420.29	420.10
25000	457.65	444.41	439.92	438.35	437.80	437.61
30000	549.18	533.29	527.90	526.02	525.36	525.13
35000	640.71	622.18	615.88	613.69	612.92	612.65
40000	732.24	711.06	703.87	701.36	700.48	700.17
45000	823.78	799.94	791.85	789.03	788.04	787.69
50000	915.31	888.82	879.83	876.70	875.60	875.21
55000	1006.84	977.70	967.81	964.37	963.16	962.73
60000	1098.37	1066.59	1055.80	1052.04	1050.72	1050.25
65000	1189.90	1155.47	1143.78	1139.71	1138.28	1137.78
70000	1281.43	1244.35	1231.76	1227.38	1225.84	1225.30
75000	1372.96	1333.23	1319.75	1315.05	1313.40	1312.82
80000	1464.49	1422.11	1407.73	1402.72	1400.96	1400.34
85000	1556.02	1511.00	1495.71	1490.39	1488.52	1487.86
90000	1647.55	1599.88	1583.70	1578.06	1576.08	1575.38
95000	1739.08	1688.76	1671.68	1665.73	1663.64	1662.90
100000	1830.61	1777.64	1759.66	1753.40	1751.20	1750.42
200000	3661.22	3555.29	3519.33	3506.80	3502.40	3500.85
300000	5491.84	5332.93	5278.99	5260.20	5253.60	5251.27
400000	7322.45	7110.57	7038.65	7013.60	7004.80	7001.69
500000	9153.06	8888.21	8798.31	8767.00	8756.00	8752.12

MONTHLY PAYMENT

Necessary to amortize a loan

21.5%

TERM / AMOUNT	1 YEARS	2 YEARS	3 YEARS	4 YEARS	5 YEARS	6 YEARS
500	46.68	25.82	18.97	15.62	13.67	12.42
600	56.01	30.98	22.76	18.74	16.40	14.90
700	65.35	36.14	26.55	21.86	19.13	17.38
800	74.68	41.31	30.35	24.99	21.87	19.86
900	84.02	46.47	34.14	28.11	24.60	22.35
1000	93.35	51.63	37.93	31.24	27.34	24.83
2000	186.71	103.26	75.86	62.47	54.67	49.66
3000	280.06	154.89	113.80	93.71	82.01	74.49
4000	373.42	206.53	151.73	124.94	109.34	99.32
5000	466.77	258.16	189.66	156.18	136.68	124.15
6000	560.12	309.79	227.59	187.41	164.01	148.98
7000	653.48	361.42	265.53	218.65	191.35	173.81
8000	746.83	413.05	303.46	249.88	218.68	198.64
9000	840.19	464.68	341.39	281.12	246.02	223.47
10000	933.54	516.32	379.32	312.35	273.35	248.30
11000	1026.89	567.95	417.26	343.59	300.69	273.13
12000	1120.25	619.58	455.19	374.82	328.02	297.96
13000	1213.60	671.21	493.12	406.06	355.36	322.79
14000	1306.95	722.84	531.05	437.29	382.70	347.62
15000	1400.31	774.47	568.98	468.53	410.03	372.45
16000	1493.66	826.11	606.92	499.76	437.37	397.28
17000	1587.02	877.74	644.85	531.00	464.70	422.11
18000	1680.37	929.37	682.78	562.23	492.04	446.94
19000	1773.72	981.00	720.71	593.47	519.37	471.77
20000	1867.08	1032.63	758.65	624.71	546.71	496.60
21000	1960.43	1084.26	796.58	655.94	574.04	521.43
22000	2053.79	1135.89	834.51	687.18	601.38	546.26
23000	2147.14	1187.53	872.44	718.41	628.71	571.09
24000	2240.49	1239.16	910.37	749.65	656.05	595.92
25000	2333.85	1290.79	948.31	780.88	683.38	620.75
30000	2800.62	1548.95	1137.97	937.06	820.06	744.91
35000	3267.39	1807.10	1327.63	1093.23	956.74	869.06
40000	3734.16	2065.26	1517.29	1249.41	1093.42	993.21
45000	4200.93	2323.42	1706.95	1405.59	1230.09	1117.36
50000	4667.70	2581.58	1896.61	1561.76	1366.77	1241.51
55000	5134.47	2839.74	2086.28	1717.94	1503.45	1365.66
60000	5601.23	3097.89	2275.94	1874.12	1640.12	1489.81
65000	6068.00	3356.05	2465.60	2030.29	1776.80	1613.96
70000	6534.77	3614.21	2655.26	2186.47	1913.48	1738.11
75000	7001.54	3872.37	2844.92	2342.64	2050.15	1862.26
80000	7468.31	4130.53	3034.58	2498.82	2186.83	1986.42
85000	7935.08	4388.68	3224.24	2655.00	2323.51	2110.57
90000	8401.85	4646.84	3413.90	2811.17	2460.18	2234.72
95000	8868.62	4905.00	3603.57	2967.35	2596.86	2358.87
100000	9335.39	5163.16	3793.23	3123.53	2733.54	2483.02
200000	18670.78	10326.31	7586.45	6247.05	5467.08	4966.04
300000	28006.17	15489.47	11379.68	9370.58	8200.61	7449.06
400000	37341.56	20652.63	15172.91	12494.10	10934.15	9932.08
500000	46676.95	25815.79	18966.14	15617.63	13667.69	12415.10

21.5%

MONTHLY PAYMENT

Necessary to amortize a loan

TERM / AMOUNT	7 YEARS	8 YEARS	9 YEARS	10 YEARS	11 YEARS	12 YEARS
500	11.56	10.95	10.50	10.17	9.91	9.71
600	13.87	13.14	12.60	12.20	11.89	11.65
700	16.18	15.33	14.70	14.23	13.87	13.60
800	18.49	17.52	16.80	16.26	15.85	15.54
900	20.81	19.71	18.90	18.30	17.84	17.48
1000	23.12	21.90	21.00	20.33	19.82	19.42
2000	46.24	43.80	42.00	40.66	39.64	38.84
3000	69.35	65.69	63.01	60.99	59.45	58.27
4000	92.47	87.59	84.01	81.32	79.27	77.69
5000	115.59	109.49	105.01	101.65	99.09	97.11
6000	138.71	131.39	126.01	121.98	118.91	116.53
7000	161.83	153.29	147.02	142.31	138.73	135.96
8000	184.95	175.18	168.02	162.64	158.54	155.38
9000	208.06	197.08	189.02	182.97	178.36	174.80
10000	231.18	218.98	210.02	203.30	198.18	194.22
11000	254.30	240.88	231.03	223.63	218.00	213.65
12000	277.42	262.78	252.03	243.96	237.82	233.07
13000	300.54	284.67	273.03	264.29	257.63	252.49
14000	323.65	306.57	294.03	284.62	277.45	271.91
15000	346.77	328.47	315.03	304.96	297.27	291.34
16000	369.89	350.37	336.04	325.29	317.09	310.76
17000	393.01	372.27	357.04	345.62	336.90	330.18
18000	416.13	394.16	378.04	365.95	356.72	349.60
19000	439.24	416.06	399.04	386.28	376.54	369.03
20000	462.36	437.96	420.05	406.61	396.36	388.45
21000	485.48	459.86	441.05	426.94	416.18	407.87
22000	508.60	481.76	462.05	447.27	435.99	427.29
23000	531.72	503.65	483.05	467.60	455.81	446.71
24000	554.84	525.55	504.06	487.93	475.63	466.14
25000	577.95	547.45	525.06	508.26	495.45	485.56
30000	693.54	656.94	630.07	609.91	594.54	582.67
35000	809.13	766.43	735.08	711.56	693.63	679.78
40000	924.73	875.92	840.09	813.21	792.72	776.90
45000	1040.32	985.41	945.10	914.87	891.81	874.01
50000	1155.91	1094.90	1050.12	1016.52	990.90	971.12
55000	1271.50	1204.39	1155.13	1118.17	1089.99	1068.23
60000	1387.09	1313.88	1260.14	1219.82	1189.08	1165.34
65000	1502.68	1423.37	1365.15	1321.47	1288.17	1262.45
70000	1618.27	1532.86	1470.16	1423.12	1387.26	1359.57
75000	1733.86	1642.35	1575.17	1524.78	1486.35	1456.68
80000	1849.45	1751.84	1680.19	1626.43	1585.44	1553.79
85000	1965.04	1861.33	1785.20	1728.08	1684.52	1650.90
90000	2080.63	1970.82	1890.21	1829.73	1783.61	1748.01
95000	2196.22	2080.31	1995.22	1931.38	1882.70	1845.13
100000	2311.81	2189.80	2100.23	2033.03	1981.79	1942.24
200000	4623.63	4379.61	4200.46	4066.07	3963.59	3884.48
300000	6935.44	6569.41	6300.70	6099.10	5945.38	5826.71
400000	9247.25	8759.21	8400.93	8132.13	7927.18	7768.95
500000	11559.07	10949.01	10501.16	10165.17	9908.97	9711.19

MONTHLY PAYMENT

Necessary to amortize a loan

21.5%

TERM / AMOUNT	15 YEARS	20 YEARS	25 YEARS	30 YEARS	35 YEARS	40 YEARS
500	9.34	9.09	9.00	8.97	8.96	8.96
600	11.21	10.90	10.80	10.77	10.76	10.75
700	13.08	12.72	12.60	12.56	12.55	12.54
800	14.94	14.54	14.40	14.36	14.34	14.34
900	16.81	16.36	16.20	16.15	16.13	16.13
1000	18.68	18.17	18.00	17.95	17.93	17.92
2000	37.36	36.35	36.01	35.89	35.85	35.84
3000	56.04	54.52	54.01	53.84	53.78	53.76
4000	74.72	72.69	72.02	71.79	71.71	71.68
5000	93.40	90.86	90.02	89.73	89.64	89.60
6000	112.09	109.04	108.02	107.68	107.56	107.52
7000	130.77	127.21	126.03	125.63	125.49	125.44
8000	149.45	145.38	144.03	143.57	143.42	143.36
9000	168.13	163.56	162.04	161.52	161.34	161.28
10000	186.81	181.73	180.04	179.47	179.27	179.20
11000	205.49	199.90	198.05	197.41	197.20	197.12
12000	224.17	218.07	216.05	215.36	215.12	215.04
13000	242.85	236.25	234.05	233.31	233.05	232.96
14000	261.53	254.42	252.06	251.25	250.98	250.88
15000	280.21	272.59	270.06	269.20	268.91	268.80
16000	298.89	290.77	288.07	287.15	286.83	286.72
17000	317.57	308.94	306.07	305.09	304.76	304.64
18000	336.26	327.11	324.07	323.04	322.69	322.56
19000	354.94	345.28	342.08	340.99	340.61	340.48
20000	373.62	363.46	360.08	358.93	358.54	358.40
21000	392.30	381.63	378.09	376.88	376.47	376.32
22000	410.98	399.80	396.09	394.83	394.39	394.24
23000	429.66	417.97	414.09	412.77	412.32	412.17
24000	448.34	436.15	432.10	430.72	430.25	430.09
25000	467.02	454.32	450.10	448.67	448.18	448.01
30000	560.43	545.18	540.12	538.40	537.81	537.61
35000	653.83	636.05	630.14	628.13	627.45	627.21
40000	747.23	726.91	720.16	717.87	717.08	716.81
45000	840.64	817.78	810.18	807.60	806.72	806.41
50000	934.04	908.64	900.21	897.33	896.35	896.01
55000	1027.45	999.50	990.23	987.07	985.99	985.61
60000	1120.85	1090.37	1080.25	1076.80	1075.62	1075.21
65000	1214.26	1181.23	1170.27	1166.54	1165.26	1164.81
70000	1307.66	1272.10	1260.29	1256.27	1254.89	1254.42
75000	1401.06	1362.96	1350.31	1346.00	1344.53	1344.02
80000	1494.47	1453.83	1440.33	1435.74	1434.16	1433.62
85000	1587.87	1544.69	1530.35	1525.47	1523.80	1523.22
90000	1681.28	1635.55	1620.37	1615.20	1613.43	1612.82
95000	1774.68	1726.42	1710.39	1704.94	1703.07	1702.42
100000	1868.08	1817.28	1800.41	1794.67	1792.70	1792.02
200000	3736.17	3634.56	3600.82	3589.34	3585.40	3584.05
300000	5604.25	5451.84	5401.23	5384.01	5378.10	5376.07
400000	7472.34	7269.13	7201.64	7178.68	7170.80	7168.09
500000	9340.42	9086.41	9002.05	8973.35	8963.50	8960.11

22%

MONTHLY PAYMENT

Necessary to amortize a loan

TERM / AMOUNT	1 YEARS	2 YEARS	3 YEARS	4 YEARS	5 YEARS	6 YEARS
500	46.80	25.94	19.10	15.75	13.81	12.56
600	56.16	31.13	22.91	18.90	16.57	15.08
700	65.52	36.31	26.73	22.05	19.33	17.59
800	74.88	41.50	30.55	25.20	22.10	20.10
900	84.23	46.69	34.37	28.36	24.86	22.61
1000	93.59	51.88	38.19	31.51	27.62	25.13
2000	187.19	103.76	76.38	63.01	55.24	50.25
3000	280.78	155.63	114.57	94.52	82.86	75.38
4000	374.38	207.51	152.76	126.02	110.48	100.50
5000	467.97	259.39	190.95	157.53	138.09	125.63
6000	561.57	311.27	229.14	189.04	165.71	150.76
7000	655.16	363.15	267.33	220.54	193.33	175.88
8000	748.76	415.03	305.52	252.05	220.95	201.01
9000	842.35	466.90	343.71	283.55	248.57	226.14
10000	935.94	518.78	381.90	315.06	276.19	251.26
11000	1029.54	570.66	420.09	346.57	303.81	276.39
12000	1123.13	622.54	458.29	378.07	331.43	301.51
13000	1216.73	674.42	496.48	409.58	359.05	326.64
14000	1310.32	726.29	534.67	441.09	386.66	351.77
15000	1403.92	778.17	572.86	472.59	414.28	376.89
16000	1497.51	830.05	611.05	504.10	441.90	402.02
17000	1591.10	881.93	649.24	535.60	469.52	427.14
18000	1684.70	933.81	687.43	567.11	497.14	452.27
19000	1778.29	985.68	725.62	598.62	524.76	477.40
20000	1871.89	1037.56	763.81	630.12	552.38	502.52
21000	1965.48	1089.44	802.00	661.63	580.00	527.65
22000	2059.08	1141.32	840.19	693.13	607.62	552.77
23000	2152.67	1193.20	878.38	724.64	635.23	577.90
24000	2246.27	1245.08	916.57	756.15	662.85	603.03
25000	2339.86	1296.95	954.76	787.65	690.47	628.15
30000	2807.83	1556.34	1145.71	945.18	828.57	753.78
35000	3275.80	1815.74	1336.67	1102.71	966.66	879.41
40000	3743.78	2075.13	1527.62	1260.24	1104.76	1005.05
45000	4211.75	2334.52	1718.57	1417.77	1242.85	1130.68
50000	4679.72	2593.91	1909.52	1575.30	1380.95	1256.31
55000	5147.69	2853.30	2100.47	1732.83	1519.04	1381.94
60000	5615.66	3112.69	2291.43	1890.36	1657.13	1507.57
65000	6083.63	3372.08	2482.38	2047.90	1795.23	1633.20
70000	6551.61	3631.47	2673.33	2205.43	1933.32	1758.83
75000	7019.58	3890.86	2864.28	2362.96	2071.42	1884.46
80000	7487.55	4150.25	3055.24	2520.49	2209.51	2010.09
85000	7955.52	4409.64	3246.19	2678.02	2347.61	2135.72
90000	8423.49	4669.03	3437.14	2835.55	2485.70	2261.35
95000	8891.47	4928.42	3628.09	2993.08	2623.80	2386.98
100000	9359.44	5187.82	3819.05	3150.61	2761.89	2512.61
200000	18718.88	10375.63	7638.09	6301.22	5523.78	5025.23
300000	28078.31	15563.45	11457.14	9451.82	8285.67	7537.84
400000	37437.75	20751.26	15276.18	12602.43	11047.56	10050.45
500000	46797.19	25939.08	19095.23	15753.04	13809.46	12563.06

MONTHLY PAYMENT

Necessary to amortize a loan

22%

TERM / AMOUNT	7 YEARS	8 YEARS	9 YEARS	10 YEARS	11 YEARS	12 YEARS
500	11.71	11.11	10.67	10.33	10.08	9.89
600	14.06	13.33	12.80	12.40	12.10	11.87
700	16.40	15.55	14.93	14.47	14.12	13.85
800	18.74	17.77	17.07	16.54	16.13	15.82
900	21.08	20.00	19.20	18.60	18.15	17.80
1000	23.43	22.22	21.33	20.67	20.17	19.78
2000	46.85	44.43	42.66	41.34	40.33	39.56
3000	70.28	66.65	64.00	62.01	60.50	59.34
4000	93.70	88.87	85.33	82.68	80.67	79.12
5000	117.13	111.09	106.66	103.35	100.83	98.89
6000	140.56	133.30	127.99	124.02	121.00	118.67
7000	163.98	155.52	149.32	144.69	141.16	138.45
8000	187.41	177.74	170.66	165.36	161.33	158.23
9000	210.83	199.95	191.99	186.03	181.50	178.01
10000	234.26	222.17	213.32	206.70	201.66	197.79
11000	257.69	244.39	234.65	227.37	221.83	217.57
12000	281.11	266.60	255.98	248.04	242.00	237.35
13000	304.54	288.82	277.31	268.71	262.16	257.13
14000	327.96	311.04	298.65	289.38	282.33	276.91
15000	351.39	333.26	319.98	310.05	302.49	296.68
16000	374.82	355.47	341.31	330.72	322.66	316.46
17000	398.24	377.69	362.64	351.38	342.83	336.24
18000	421.67	399.91	383.97	372.05	362.99	356.02
19000	445.09	422.12	405.31	392.72	383.16	375.80
20000	468.52	444.34	426.64	413.39	403.33	395.58
21000	491.94	466.56	447.97	434.06	423.49	415.36
22000	515.37	488.78	469.30	454.73	443.66	435.14
23000	538.80	510.99	490.63	475.40	463.82	454.92
24000	562.22	533.21	511.97	496.07	483.99	474.69
25000	585.65	555.43	533.30	516.74	504.16	494.47
30000	702.78	666.51	639.96	620.09	604.99	593.37
35000	819.91	777.60	746.62	723.44	705.82	692.26
40000	937.04	888.68	853.28	826.79	806.65	791.16
45000	1054.17	999.77	959.94	930.14	907.48	890.05
50000	1171.30	1110.85	1066.60	1033.48	1008.31	988.95
55000	1288.43	1221.94	1173.25	1136.83	1109.15	1087.84
60000	1405.56	1333.02	1279.91	1240.18	1209.98	1186.74
65000	1522.69	1444.11	1386.57	1343.53	1310.81	1285.63
70000	1639.82	1555.20	1493.23	1446.88	1411.64	1384.53
75000	1756.95	1666.28	1599.89	1550.23	1512.47	1483.42
80000	1874.08	1777.37	1706.55	1653.58	1613.30	1582.31
85000	1991.21	1888.45	1813.21	1756.92	1714.13	1681.21
90000	2108.33	1999.54	1919.87	1860.27	1814.97	1780.10
95000	2225.46	2110.62	2026.53	1963.62	1915.80	1879.00
100000	2342.59	2221.71	2133.19	2066.97	2016.63	1977.89
200000	4685.19	4443.42	4266.38	4133.94	4033.26	3955.79
300000	7027.78	6665.12	6399.57	6200.91	6049.89	5933.68
400000	9370.38	8886.83	8532.76	8267.88	8066.51	7911.57
500000	11712.97	11108.54	10665.95	10334.84	10083.14	9889.47

22%

MONTHLY PAYMENT

Necessary to amortize a loan

TERM / AMOUNT	15 YEARS	20 YEARS	25 YEARS	30 YEARS	35 YEARS	40 YEARS
500	9.53	9.29	9.21	9.18	9.17	9.17
600	11.43	11.14	11.05	11.02	11.01	11.00
700	13.34	13.00	12.89	12.85	12.84	12.84
800	15.25	14.86	14.73	14.69	14.67	14.67
900	17.15	16.71	16.57	16.52	16.51	16.50
1000	19.06	18.57	18.41	18.36	18.34	18.34
2000	38.12	37.14	36.82	36.72	36.68	36.67
3000	57.17	55.71	55.24	55.08	55.03	55.01
4000	76.23	74.28	73.65	73.44	73.37	73.35
5000	95.29	92.85	92.06	91.80	91.71	91.68
6000	114.35	111.42	110.47	110.16	110.05	110.02
7000	133.40	129.99	128.89	128.52	128.40	128.35
8000	152.46	148.56	147.30	146.88	146.74	146.69
9000	171.52	167.14	165.71	165.24	165.08	165.03
10000	190.58	185.71	184.12	183.60	183.42	183.36
11000	209.63	204.28	202.54	201.96	201.76	201.70
12000	228.69	222.85	220.95	220.32	220.11	220.04
13000	247.75	241.42	239.36	238.68	238.45	238.37
14000	266.81	259.99	257.77	257.04	256.79	256.71
15000	285.86	278.56	276.19	275.40	275.13	275.04
16000	304.92	297.13	294.60	293.76	293.48	293.38
17000	323.98	315.70	313.01	312.12	311.82	311.72
18000	343.04	334.27	331.42	330.48	330.16	330.05
19000	362.09	352.84	349.84	348.84	348.50	348.39
20000	381.15	371.41	368.25	367.20	366.84	366.73
21000	400.21	389.98	386.66	385.56	385.19	385.06
22000	419.27	408.55	405.07	403.92	403.53	403.40
23000	438.32	427.12	423.49	422.28	421.87	421.74
24000	457.38	445.69	441.90	440.64	440.21	440.07
25000	476.44	464.26	460.31	459.00	458.56	458.41
30000	571.73	557.12	552.37	550.80	550.27	550.09
35000	667.01	649.97	644.43	642.59	641.98	641.77
40000	762.30	742.82	736.50	734.39	733.69	733.45
45000	857.59	835.68	828.56	826.19	825.40	825.13
50000	952.88	928.53	920.62	917.99	917.11	916.82
55000	1048.17	1021.38	1012.68	1009.79	1008.82	1008.50
60000	1143.45	1114.24	1104.75	1101.59	1100.53	1100.18
65000	1238.74	1207.09	1196.81	1193.39	1192.25	1191.86
70000	1334.03	1299.94	1288.87	1285.19	1283.96	1283.54
75000	1429.32	1392.79	1380.93	1376.99	1375.67	1375.22
80000	1524.60	1485.65	1472.99	1468.79	1467.38	1466.91
85000	1619.89	1578.50	1565.06	1560.59	1559.09	1558.59
90000	1715.18	1671.35	1657.12	1652.39	1650.80	1650.27
95000	1810.47	1764.21	1749.18	1744.19	1742.51	1741.95
100000	1905.76	1857.06	1841.24	1835.98	1834.22	1833.63
200000	3811.51	3714.12	3682.48	3671.97	3668.45	3667.27
300000	5717.27	5571.18	5523.73	5507.95	5502.67	5500.90
400000	7623.02	7428.24	7364.97	7343.94	7336.90	7334.53
500000	9528.78	9285.30	9206.21	9179.92	9171.12	9168.16

MONTHLY PAYMENT

Necessary to amortize a loan

22.5%

TERM / AMOUNT	1 YEARS	2 YEARS	3 YEARS	4 YEARS	5 YEARS	6 YEARS
500	46.92	26.06	19.22	15.89	13.95	12.71
600	56.30	31.28	23.07	19.07	16.74	15.25
700	65.68	36.49	26.91	22.24	19.53	17.80
800	75.07	41.70	30.76	25.42	22.32	20.34
900	84.45	46.91	34.60	28.60	25.11	22.88
1000	93.84	52.13	38.45	31.78	27.90	25.42
2000	187.67	104.25	76.90	63.56	55.81	50.85
3000	281.51	156.38	115.35	95.33	83.71	76.27
4000	375.34	208.50	153.80	127.11	111.62	101.70
5000	469.18	260.63	192.25	158.89	139.52	127.12
6000	563.01	312.75	230.70	190.67	167.42	152.54
7000	656.85	364.88	269.15	222.45	195.33	177.97
8000	750.68	417.00	307.60	254.23	223.23	203.39
9000	844.52	469.13	346.05	286.00	251.14	228.81
10000	938.35	521.25	384.50	317.78	279.04	254.24
11000	1032.19	573.38	422.95	349.56	306.94	279.66
12000	1126.02	625.50	461.40	381.34	334.85	305.09
13000	1219.86	677.63	499.84	413.12	362.75	330.51
14000	1313.69	729.76	538.29	444.89	390.66	355.93
15000	1407.53	781.88	576.74	476.67	418.56	381.36
16000	1501.36	834.01	615.19	508.45	446.46	406.78
17000	1595.20	886.13	653.64	540.23	474.37	432.20
18000	1689.03	938.26	692.09	572.01	502.27	457.63
19000	1782.87	990.38	730.54	603.78	530.17	483.05
20000	1876.70	1042.51	768.99	635.56	558.08	508.48
21000	1970.54	1094.63	807.44	667.34	585.98	533.90
22000	2064.37	1146.76	845.89	699.12	613.89	559.32
23000	2158.21	1198.88	884.34	730.90	641.79	584.75
24000	2252.04	1251.01	922.79	762.68	669.69	610.17
25000	2345.88	1303.13	961.24	794.45	697.60	635.59
30000	2815.06	1563.76	1153.49	953.34	837.12	762.71
35000	3284.23	1824.39	1345.74	1112.24	976.64	889.83
40000	3753.41	2085.02	1537.98	1271.13	1116.16	1016.95
45000	4222.58	2345.64	1730.23	1430.02	1255.68	1144.07
50000	4691.76	2606.27	1922.48	1588.91	1395.20	1271.19
55000	5160.94	2866.90	2114.73	1747.80	1534.72	1398.31
60000	5630.11	3127.52	2306.98	1906.69	1674.24	1525.43
65000	6099.29	3388.15	2499.22	2065.58	1813.76	1652.54
70000	6568.46	3648.78	2691.47	2224.47	1953.28	1779.66
75000	7037.64	3909.40	2883.72	2383.36	2092.80	1906.78
80000	7506.81	4170.03	3075.97	2542.25	2232.32	2033.90
85000	7975.99	4430.66	3268.22	2701.14	2371.84	2161.02
90000	8445.17	4691.29	3460.46	2860.03	2511.36	2288.14
95000	8914.34	4951.91	3652.71	3018.92	2650.87	2415.26
100000	9383.52	5212.54	3844.96	3177.82	2790.39	2542.38
200000	18767.04	10425.08	7689.92	6355.63	5580.79	5084.75
300000	28150.56	15637.62	11534.88	9533.45	8371.18	7627.13
400000	37534.07	20850.16	15379.84	12711.26	11161.58	10169.51
500000	46917.59	26062.70	19224.80	15889.08	13951.97	12711.88

22.5%

MONTHLY PAYMENT

Necessary to amortize a loan

TERM / AMOUNT	7 YEARS	8 YEARS	9 YEARS	10 YEARS	11 YEARS	12 YEARS
500	11.87	11.27	10.83	10.51	10.26	10.07
600	14.24	13.52	13.00	12.61	12.31	12.08
700	16.61	15.78	15.16	14.71	14.36	14.10
800	18.99	18.03	17.33	16.81	16.41	16.11
900	21.36	20.28	19.50	18.91	18.47	18.12
1000	23.74	22.54	21.66	21.01	20.52	20.14
2000	47.47	45.08	43.33	42.02	41.03	40.28
3000	71.21	67.61	64.99	63.03	61.55	60.41
4000	94.94	90.15	86.65	84.04	82.07	80.55
5000	118.68	112.69	108.32	105.06	102.58	100.69
6000	142.41	135.23	129.98	126.07	123.10	120.83
7000	166.15	157.77	151.65	147.08	143.62	140.96
8000	189.89	180.31	173.31	168.09	164.13	161.10
9000	213.62	202.84	194.97	189.10	184.65	181.24
10000	237.36	225.38	216.64	210.11	205.17	201.38
11000	261.09	247.92	238.30	231.12	225.68	221.51
12000	284.83	270.46	259.96	252.13	246.20	241.65
13000	308.56	293.00	281.63	273.15	266.72	261.79
14000	332.30	315.53	303.29	294.16	287.23	281.93
15000	356.03	338.07	324.95	315.17	307.75	302.06
16000	379.77	360.61	346.62	336.18	328.27	322.20
17000	403.51	383.15	368.28	357.19	348.79	342.34
18000	427.24	405.69	389.94	378.20	369.30	362.48
19000	450.98	428.22	411.61	399.21	389.82	382.61
20000	474.71	450.76	433.27	420.22	410.34	402.75
21000	498.45	473.30	454.94	441.23	430.85	422.89
22000	522.18	495.84	476.60	462.25	451.37	443.03
23000	545.92	518.38	498.26	483.26	471.89	463.17
24000	569.66	540.92	519.93	504.27	492.40	483.30
25000	593.39	563.45	541.59	525.28	512.92	503.44
30000	712.07	676.14	649.91	630.34	615.50	604.13
35000	830.75	788.84	758.23	735.39	718.09	704.82
40000	949.43	901.53	866.54	840.45	820.67	805.50
45000	1068.10	1014.22	974.86	945.50	923.26	906.19
50000	1186.78	1126.91	1083.18	1050.56	1025.84	1006.88
55000	1305.46	1239.60	1191.50	1155.62	1128.42	1107.57
60000	1424.14	1352.29	1299.81	1260.67	1231.01	1208.26
65000	1542.82	1464.98	1408.13	1365.73	1333.59	1308.95
70000	1661.49	1577.67	1516.45	1470.78	1436.17	1409.63
75000	1780.17	1690.36	1624.77	1575.84	1538.76	1510.32
80000	1898.85	1803.05	1733.09	1680.89	1641.34	1611.01
85000	2017.53	1915.74	1841.40	1785.95	1743.93	1711.70
90000	2136.21	2028.43	1949.72	1891.01	1846.51	1812.39
95000	2254.89	2141.12	2058.04	1996.06	1949.09	1913.07
100000	2373.56	2253.81	2166.36	2101.12	2051.68	2013.76
200000	4747.13	4507.63	4332.72	4202.24	4103.36	4027.52
300000	7120.69	6761.44	6499.07	6303.36	6155.03	6041.29
400000	9494.25	9015.26	8665.43	8404.47	8206.71	8055.05
500000	11867.82	11269.07	10831.79	10505.59	10258.39	10068.81

MONTHLY PAYMENT
Necessary to amortize a loan

22.5%

TERM / AMOUNT	15 YEARS	20 YEARS	25 YEARS	30 YEARS	35 YEARS	40 YEARS
500	9.72	9.48	9.41	9.39	9.38	9.38
600	11.66	11.38	11.29	11.26	11.25	11.25
700	13.61	13.28	13.18	13.14	13.13	13.13
800	15.55	15.18	15.06	15.02	15.01	15.00
900	17.49	17.07	16.94	16.90	16.88	16.88
1000	19.44	18.97	18.82	18.77	18.76	18.75
2000	38.87	37.94	37.64	37.55	37.52	37.51
3000	58.31	56.91	56.46	56.32	56.27	56.26
4000	77.74	75.88	75.29	75.09	75.03	75.01
5000	97.18	94.85	94.11	93.87	93.79	93.76
6000	116.62	113.82	112.93	112.64	112.55	112.52
7000	136.05	132.79	131.75	131.41	131.30	131.27
8000	155.49	151.76	150.57	150.19	150.06	150.02
9000	174.93	170.73	169.39	168.96	168.82	168.77
10000	194.36	189.70	188.22	187.73	187.58	187.53
11000	213.80	208.67	207.04	206.51	206.33	206.28
12000	233.23	227.64	225.86	225.28	225.09	225.03
13000	252.67	246.61	244.68	244.05	243.85	243.78
14000	272.11	265.58	263.50	262.83	262.61	262.54
15000	291.54	284.55	282.32	281.60	281.37	281.29
16000	310.98	303.52	301.14	300.37	300.12	300.04
17000	330.42	322.48	319.97	319.15	318.88	318.79
18000	349.85	341.45	338.79	337.92	337.64	337.55
19000	369.29	360.42	357.61	356.69	356.40	356.30
20000	388.72	379.39	376.43	375.47	375.15	375.05
21000	408.16	398.36	395.25	394.24	393.91	393.80
22000	427.60	417.33	414.07	413.01	412.67	412.56
23000	447.03	436.30	432.89	431.79	431.43	431.31
24000	466.47	455.27	451.72	450.56	450.18	450.06
25000	485.90	474.24	470.54	469.33	468.94	468.81
30000	583.09	569.09	564.65	563.20	562.73	562.58
35000	680.27	663.94	658.75	657.07	656.52	656.34
40000	777.45	758.79	752.86	750.94	750.31	750.10
45000	874.63	853.64	846.97	844.80	844.10	843.86
50000	971.81	948.49	941.08	938.67	937.88	937.63
55000	1068.99	1043.33	1035.18	1032.54	1031.67	1031.39
60000	1166.17	1138.18	1129.29	1126.40	1125.46	1125.15
65000	1263.35	1233.03	1223.40	1220.27	1219.25	1218.91
70000	1360.53	1327.88	1317.51	1314.14	1313.04	1312.68
75000	1457.71	1422.73	1411.61	1408.00	1406.83	1406.44
80000	1554.89	1517.58	1505.72	1501.87	1500.61	1500.20
85000	1652.08	1612.42	1599.83	1595.74	1594.40	1593.96
90000	1749.26	1707.27	1693.94	1689.61	1688.19	1687.73
95000	1846.44	1802.12	1788.04	1783.47	1781.98	1781.49
100000	1943.62	1896.97	1882.15	1877.34	1875.77	1875.25
200000	3887.24	3793.94	3764.30	3754.68	3751.53	3750.50
300000	5830.85	5690.91	5646.45	5632.02	5627.30	5625.75
400000	7774.47	7587.88	7528.60	7509.36	7503.07	7501.01
500000	9718.09	9484.85	9410.76	9386.70	9378.83	9376.26

23%

MONTHLY PAYMENT

Necessary to amortize a loan

TERM / AMOUNT	1 YEARS	2 YEARS	3 YEARS	4 YEARS	5 YEARS	6 YEARS
500	47.04	26.19	19.35	16.03	14.10	12.86
600	56.45	31.42	23.23	19.23	16.91	15.43
700	65.85	36.66	27.10	22.44	19.73	18.01
800	75.26	41.90	30.97	25.64	22.55	20.58
900	84.67	47.14	34.84	28.85	25.37	23.15
1000	94.08	52.37	38.71	32.05	28.19	25.72
2000	188.15	104.75	77.42	64.10	56.38	51.45
3000	282.23	157.12	116.13	96.15	84.57	77.17
4000	376.31	209.49	154.84	128.21	112.76	102.89
5000	470.38	261.87	193.55	160.26	140.95	128.62
6000	564.46	314.24	232.26	192.31	169.14	154.34
7000	658.53	366.61	270.97	224.36	197.33	180.06
8000	752.61	418.99	309.68	256.41	225.52	205.78
9000	846.69	471.36	348.39	288.46	253.71	231.51
10000	940.76	523.73	387.10	320.51	281.90	257.23
11000	1034.84	576.11	425.81	352.57	310.10	282.95
12000	1128.92	628.48	464.52	384.62	338.29	308.68
13000	1222.99	680.85	503.23	416.67	366.48	334.40
14000	1317.07	733.23	541.94	448.72	394.67	360.12
15000	1411.14	785.60	580.65	480.77	422.86	385.85
16000	1505.22	837.97	619.36	512.82	451.05	411.57
17000	1599.30	890.35	658.07	544.88	479.24	437.29
18000	1693.37	942.72	696.77	576.93	507.43	463.02
19000	1787.45	995.09	735.48	608.98	535.62	488.74
20000	1881.53	1047.47	774.19	641.03	563.81	514.46
21000	1975.60	1099.84	812.90	673.08	592.00	540.19
22000	2069.68	1152.21	851.61	705.13	620.19	565.91
23000	2163.76	1204.59	890.32	737.18	648.38	591.63
24000	2257.83	1256.96	929.03	769.24	676.57	617.35
25000	2351.91	1309.33	967.74	801.29	704.76	643.08
30000	2822.29	1571.20	1161.29	961.54	845.71	771.69
35000	3292.67	1833.07	1354.84	1121.80	986.67	900.31
40000	3763.05	2094.93	1548.39	1282.06	1127.62	1028.92
45000	4233.43	2356.80	1741.94	1442.32	1268.57	1157.54
50000	4703.82	2618.67	1935.49	1602.57	1409.52	1286.16
55000	5174.20	2880.53	2129.03	1762.83	1550.48	1414.77
60000	5644.58	3142.40	2322.58	1923.09	1691.43	1543.39
65000	6114.96	3404.26	2516.13	2083.35	1832.38	1672.00
70000	6585.34	3666.13	2709.68	2243.60	1973.33	1800.62
75000	7055.72	3928.00	2903.23	2403.86	2114.29	1929.23
80000	7526.11	4189.86	3096.78	2564.12	2255.24	2057.85
85000	7996.49	4451.73	3290.33	2724.38	2396.19	2186.46
90000	8466.87	4713.60	3483.87	2884.63	2537.14	2315.08
95000	8937.25	4975.46	3677.42	3044.89	2678.09	2443.70
100000	9407.63	5237.33	3870.97	3205.15	2819.05	2572.31
200000	18815.26	10474.66	7741.94	6410.29	5638.09	5144.62
300000	28222.90	15711.99	11612.92	9615.44	8457.14	7716.93
400000	37630.53	20949.32	15483.89	12820.59	11276.19	10289.24
500000	47038.16	26186.65	19354.86	16025.74	14095.24	12861.55

MONTHLY PAYMENT

Necessary to amortize a loan

23%

TERM / AMOUNT	7 YEARS	8 YEARS	9 YEARS	10 YEARS	11 YEARS	12 YEARS
500	12.02	11.43	11.00	10.68	10.43	10.25
600	14.43	13.72	13.20	12.81	12.52	12.30
700	16.83	16.00	15.40	14.95	14.61	14.35
800	19.24	18.29	17.60	17.08	16.70	16.40
900	21.64	20.58	19.80	19.22	18.78	18.45
1000	24.05	22.86	22.00	21.35	20.87	20.50
2000	48.09	45.72	43.99	42.71	41.74	41.00
3000	72.14	68.58	65.99	64.06	62.61	61.50
4000	96.19	91.44	87.99	85.42	83.48	81.99
5000	120.24	114.31	109.99	106.77	104.35	102.49
6000	144.28	137.17	131.98	128.13	125.22	122.99
7000	168.33	160.03	153.98	149.48	146.09	143.49
8000	192.38	182.89	175.98	170.84	166.96	163.99
9000	216.42	205.75	197.98	192.19	187.82	184.49
10000	240.47	228.61	219.97	213.55	208.69	204.98
11000	264.52	251.47	241.97	234.90	229.56	225.48
12000	288.57	274.33	263.97	256.26	250.43	245.98
13000	312.61	297.20	285.97	277.61	271.30	266.48
14000	336.66	320.06	307.96	298.97	292.17	286.98
15000	360.71	342.92	329.96	320.32	313.04	307.48
16000	384.76	365.78	351.96	341.68	333.91	327.97
17000	408.80	388.64	373.95	363.03	354.78	348.47
18000	432.85	411.50	395.95	384.39	375.65	368.97
19000	456.90	434.36	417.95	405.74	396.52	389.47
20000	480.94	457.22	439.95	427.10	417.39	409.97
21000	504.99	480.09	461.94	448.45	438.26	430.47
22000	529.04	502.95	483.94	469.81	459.13	450.96
23000	553.09	525.81	505.94	491.16	480.00	471.46
24000	577.13	548.67	527.94	512.51	500.87	491.96
25000	601.18	571.53	549.93	533.87	521.73	512.46
30000	721.42	685.84	659.92	640.64	626.08	614.95
35000	841.65	800.14	769.91	747.42	730.43	717.44
40000	961.89	914.45	879.89	854.19	834.78	819.93
45000	1082.12	1028.75	989.88	960.97	939.12	922.43
50000	1202.36	1143.06	1099.87	1067.74	1043.47	1024.92
55000	1322.60	1257.37	1209.85	1174.51	1147.82	1127.41
60000	1442.83	1371.67	1319.84	1281.29	1252.16	1229.90
65000	1563.07	1485.98	1429.83	1388.06	1356.51	1332.39
70000	1683.30	1600.28	1539.81	1494.83	1460.86	1434.89
75000	1803.54	1714.59	1649.80	1601.61	1565.20	1537.38
80000	1923.78	1828.90	1759.79	1708.38	1669.55	1639.87
85000	2044.01	1943.20	1869.77	1815.16	1773.90	1742.36
90000	2164.25	2057.51	1979.76	1921.93	1878.24	1844.85
95000	2284.48	2171.81	2089.75	2028.70	1982.59	1947.35
100000	2404.72	2286.12	2199.73	2135.48	2086.94	2049.84
200000	4809.44	4572.24	4399.46	4270.96	4173.88	4099.67
300000	7214.16	6858.36	6599.20	6406.43	6260.81	6149.51
400000	9618.88	9144.48	8798.93	8541.91	8347.75	8199.35
500000	12023.60	11430.60	10998.66	10677.39	10434.69	10249.19

23%

MONTHLY PAYMENT

Necessary to amortize a loan

TERM / AMOUNT	15 YEARS	20 YEARS	25 YEARS	30 YEARS	35 YEARS	40 YEARS
500	9.91	9.69	9.62	9.59	9.59	9.58
600	11.89	11.62	11.54	11.51	11.50	11.50
700	13.87	13.56	13.46	13.43	13.42	13.42
800	15.85	15.50	15.39	15.35	15.34	15.34
900	17.83	17.43	17.31	17.27	17.26	17.25
1000	19.82	19.37	19.23	19.19	19.17	19.17
2000	39.63	38.74	38.46	38.37	38.35	38.34
3000	59.45	58.11	57.69	57.56	57.52	57.51
4000	79.27	77.48	76.93	76.75	76.69	76.68
5000	99.08	96.85	96.16	95.94	95.87	95.84
6000	118.90	116.22	115.39	115.12	115.04	115.01
7000	138.72	135.59	134.62	134.31	134.21	134.18
8000	158.53	154.96	153.85	153.50	153.39	153.35
9000	178.35	174.33	173.08	172.69	172.56	172.52
10000	198.17	193.70	192.31	191.87	191.73	191.69
11000	217.98	213.07	211.54	211.06	210.91	210.86
12000	237.80	232.44	230.78	230.25	230.08	230.03
13000	257.62	251.81	250.01	249.44	249.25	249.19
14000	277.43	271.18	269.24	268.62	268.43	268.36
15000	297.25	290.55	288.47	287.81	287.60	287.53
16000	317.07	309.92	307.70	307.00	306.77	306.70
17000	336.88	329.29	326.93	326.18	325.95	325.87
18000	356.70	348.66	346.16	345.37	345.12	345.04
19000	376.52	368.03	365.39	364.56	364.29	364.21
20000	396.33	387.40	384.63	383.75	383.47	383.38
21000	416.15	406.77	403.86	402.93	402.64	402.54
22000	435.97	426.14	423.09	422.12	421.81	421.71
23000	455.78	445.51	442.32	441.31	440.99	440.88
24000	475.60	464.88	461.55	460.50	460.16	460.05
25000	495.42	484.25	480.78	479.68	479.33	479.22
30000	594.50	581.10	576.94	575.62	575.20	575.06
35000	693.58	677.95	673.10	671.56	671.06	670.91
40000	792.67	774.80	769.25	767.49	766.93	766.75
45000	891.75	871.65	865.41	863.43	862.80	862.60
50000	990.83	968.50	961.56	959.37	958.66	958.44
55000	1089.91	1065.35	1057.72	1055.30	1054.53	1054.28
60000	1189.00	1162.20	1153.88	1151.24	1150.40	1150.13
65000	1288.08	1259.05	1250.03	1247.18	1246.26	1245.97
70000	1387.16	1355.90	1346.19	1343.11	1342.13	1341.81
75000	1486.25	1452.75	1442.35	1439.05	1438.00	1437.66
80000	1585.33	1549.60	1538.50	1534.98	1533.86	1533.50
85000	1684.41	1646.45	1634.66	1630.92	1629.73	1629.35
90000	1783.50	1743.30	1730.82	1726.86	1725.59	1725.19
95000	1882.58	1840.15	1826.97	1822.79	1821.46	1821.03
100000	1981.66	1937.00	1923.13	1918.73	1917.33	1916.88
200000	3963.33	3874.01	3846.26	3837.46	3834.65	3833.76
300000	5944.99	5811.01	5769.39	5756.19	5751.98	5750.63
400000	7926.65	7748.01	7692.52	7674.92	7669.31	7667.51
500000	9908.32	9685.02	9615.65	9593.65	9586.63	9584.39

MONTHLY PAYMENT

Necessary to amortize a loan

23.5%

TERM / AMOUNT	1 YEARS	2 YEARS	3 YEARS	4 YEARS	5 YEARS	6 YEARS
500	47.16	26.31	19.49	16.16	14.24	13.01
600	56.59	31.57	23.38	19.40	17.09	15.61
700	66.02	36.84	27.28	22.63	19.93	18.22
800	75.45	42.10	31.18	25.86	22.78	20.82
900	84.89	47.36	35.07	29.09	25.63	23.42
1000	94.32	52.62	38.97	32.33	28.48	26.02
2000	188.64	105.24	77.94	64.65	56.96	52.05
3000	282.95	157.87	116.91	96.98	85.44	78.07
4000	377.27	210.49	155.88	129.30	113.91	104.10
5000	471.59	263.11	194.85	161.63	142.39	130.12
6000	565.91	315.73	233.82	193.96	170.87	156.14
7000	660.22	368.35	272.80	226.28	199.35	182.17
8000	754.54	420.97	311.77	258.61	227.83	208.19
9000	848.86	473.60	350.74	290.93	256.31	234.22
10000	943.18	526.22	389.71	323.26	284.78	260.24
11000	1037.50	578.84	428.68	355.59	313.26	286.27
12000	1131.81	631.46	467.65	387.91	341.74	312.29
13000	1226.13	684.08	506.62	420.24	370.22	338.31
14000	1320.45	736.71	545.59	452.56	398.70	364.34
15000	1414.77	789.33	584.56	484.89	427.18	390.36
16000	1509.08	841.95	623.53	517.22	455.66	416.39
17000	1603.40	894.57	662.50	549.54	484.13	442.41
18000	1697.72	947.19	701.47	581.87	512.61	468.43
19000	1792.04	999.82	740.45	614.19	541.09	494.46
20000	1886.36	1052.44	779.42	646.52	569.57	520.48
21000	1980.67	1105.06	818.39	678.85	598.05	546.51
22000	2074.99	1157.68	857.36	711.17	626.53	572.53
23000	2169.31	1210.30	896.33	743.50	655.01	598.56
24000	2263.63	1262.92	935.30	775.82	683.48	624.58
25000	2357.94	1315.55	974.27	808.15	711.96	650.60
30000	2829.53	1578.66	1169.12	969.78	854.35	780.72
35000	3301.12	1841.77	1363.98	1131.41	996.75	910.84
40000	3772.71	2104.87	1558.83	1293.04	1139.14	1040.97
45000	4244.30	2367.98	1753.69	1454.67	1281.53	1171.09
50000	4715.89	2631.09	1948.54	1616.30	1423.92	1301.21
55000	5187.48	2894.20	2143.39	1777.93	1566.32	1431.33
60000	5659.07	3157.31	2338.25	1939.56	1708.71	1561.45
65000	6130.66	3420.42	2533.10	2101.19	1851.10	1691.57
70000	6602.25	3683.53	2727.96	2262.82	1993.49	1821.69
75000	7073.83	3946.64	2922.81	2424.45	2135.89	1951.81
80000	7545.42	4209.75	3117.66	2586.08	2278.28	2081.93
85000	8017.01	4472.86	3312.52	2747.71	2420.67	2212.05
90000	8488.60	4735.97	3507.37	2909.34	2563.06	2342.17
95000	8960.19	4999.08	3702.23	3070.97	2705.46	2472.29
100000	9431.78	5262.19	3897.08	3232.60	2847.85	2602.41
200000	18863.56	10524.37	7794.16	6465.21	5695.70	5204.83
300000	28295.34	15786.56	11691.24	9697.81	8543.54	7807.24
400000	37727.12	21048.75	15588.32	12930.41	11391.39	10409.65
500000	47158.90	26310.94	19485.40	16163.02	14239.24	13012.07

23.5%

MONTHLY PAYMENT

Necessary to amortize a loan

TERM / AMOUNT	7 YEARS	8 YEARS	9 YEARS	10 YEARS	11 YEARS	12 YEARS
500	12.18	11.59	11.17	10.85	10.61	10.43
600	14.62	13.91	13.40	13.02	12.73	12.52
700	17.05	16.23	15.63	15.19	14.86	14.60
800	19.49	18.55	17.87	17.36	16.98	16.69
900	21.92	20.87	20.10	19.53	19.10	18.78
1000	24.36	23.19	22.33	21.70	21.22	20.86
2000	48.72	46.37	44.67	43.40	42.45	41.72
3000	73.08	69.56	67.00	65.10	63.67	62.58
4000	97.44	92.74	89.33	86.80	84.90	83.44
5000	121.80	115.93	111.67	108.50	106.12	104.31
6000	146.16	139.12	134.00	130.20	127.34	125.17
7000	170.52	162.30	156.33	151.90	148.57	146.03
8000	194.88	185.49	178.66	173.60	169.79	166.89
9000	219.25	208.68	201.00	195.30	191.02	187.75
10000	243.61	231.86	223.33	217.00	212.24	208.61
11000	267.97	255.05	245.66	238.70	233.46	229.47
12000	292.33	278.23	268.00	260.41	254.69	250.33
13000	316.69	301.42	290.33	282.11	275.91	271.19
14000	341.05	324.61	312.66	303.81	297.14	292.06
15000	365.41	347.79	335.00	325.51	318.36	312.92
16000	389.77	370.98	357.33	347.21	339.58	333.78
17000	414.13	394.17	379.66	368.91	360.81	354.64
18000	438.49	417.35	402.00	390.61	382.03	375.50
19000	462.85	440.54	424.33	412.31	403.26	396.36
20000	487.21	463.72	446.66	434.01	424.48	417.22
21000	511.57	486.91	468.99	455.71	445.70	438.08
22000	535.93	510.10	491.33	477.41	466.93	458.95
23000	560.29	533.28	513.66	499.11	488.15	479.81
24000	584.65	556.47	535.99	520.81	509.38	500.67
25000	609.01	579.65	558.33	542.51	530.60	521.53
30000	730.82	695.59	669.99	651.01	636.72	625.83
35000	852.62	811.52	781.66	759.52	742.84	730.14
40000	974.42	927.45	893.32	868.02	848.96	834.45
45000	1096.23	1043.38	1004.99	976.52	955.08	938.75
50000	1218.03	1159.31	1116.65	1085.02	1061.20	1043.06
55000	1339.83	1275.24	1228.32	1193.52	1167.32	1147.36
60000	1461.64	1391.17	1339.99	1302.03	1273.44	1251.67
65000	1583.44	1507.10	1451.65	1410.53	1379.56	1355.97
70000	1705.24	1623.03	1563.32	1519.03	1485.68	1460.28
75000	1827.04	1738.96	1674.98	1627.53	1591.80	1564.59
80000	1948.85	1854.90	1786.65	1736.03	1697.92	1668.89
85000	2070.65	1970.83	1898.31	1844.54	1804.04	1773.20
90000	2192.45	2086.76	2009.98	1953.04	1910.16	1877.50
95000	2314.26	2202.69	2121.64	2061.54	2016.28	1981.81
100000	2436.06	2318.62	2233.31	2170.04	2122.40	2086.11
200000	4872.12	4637.24	4466.62	4340.09	4244.81	4172.23
300000	7308.18	6955.86	6699.93	6510.13	6367.21	6258.34
400000	9744.24	9274.48	8933.24	8680.17	8489.61	8344.46
500000	12180.30	11593.10	11166.54	10850.22	10612.01	10430.57

MONTHLY PAYMENT

Necessary to amortize a loan

23.5%

TERM / AMOUNT	15 YEARS	20 YEARS	25 YEARS	30 YEARS	35 YEARS	40 YEARS
500	10.10	9.89	9.82	9.80	9.79	9.79
600	12.12	11.86	11.79	11.76	11.75	11.75
700	14.14	13.84	13.75	13.72	13.71	13.71
800	16.16	15.82	15.71	15.68	15.67	15.67
900	18.18	17.79	17.68	17.64	17.63	17.63
1000	20.20	19.77	19.64	19.60	19.59	19.59
2000	40.40	39.54	39.28	39.20	39.18	39.17
3000	60.60	59.31	58.93	58.80	58.77	58.76
4000	80.80	79.09	78.57	78.41	78.36	78.34
5000	100.99	98.86	98.21	98.01	97.95	97.93
6000	121.19	118.63	117.85	117.61	117.53	117.51
7000	141.39	138.40	137.49	137.21	137.12	137.10
8000	161.59	158.17	157.13	156.81	156.71	156.68
9000	181.79	177.94	176.78	176.41	176.30	176.27
10000	201.99	197.72	196.42	196.02	195.89	195.85
11000	222.19	217.49	216.06	215.62	215.48	215.44
12000	242.39	237.26	235.70	235.22	235.07	235.02
13000	262.58	257.03	255.34	254.82	254.66	254.61
14000	282.78	276.80	274.98	274.42	274.25	274.19
15000	302.98	296.57	294.63	294.02	293.84	293.78
16000	323.18	316.34	314.27	313.62	313.42	313.36
17000	343.38	336.12	333.91	333.23	333.01	332.95
18000	363.58	355.89	353.55	352.83	352.60	352.53
19000	383.78	375.66	373.19	372.43	372.19	372.12
20000	403.98	395.43	392.83	392.03	391.78	391.70
21000	424.18	415.20	412.48	411.63	411.37	411.29
22000	444.37	434.97	432.12	431.23	430.96	430.87
23000	464.57	454.74	451.76	450.84	450.55	450.46
24000	484.77	474.52	471.40	470.44	470.14	470.04
25000	504.97	494.29	491.04	490.04	489.73	489.63
30000	605.97	593.15	589.25	588.05	587.67	587.55
35000	706.96	692.00	687.46	686.05	685.62	685.48
40000	807.95	790.86	785.67	784.06	783.56	783.40
45000	908.95	889.72	883.88	882.07	881.51	881.33
50000	1009.94	988.58	982.09	980.08	979.45	979.26
55000	1110.94	1087.43	1080.29	1078.08	1077.40	1077.18
60000	1211.93	1186.29	1178.50	1176.09	1175.34	1175.11
65000	1312.92	1285.15	1276.71	1274.10	1273.29	1273.03
70000	1413.92	1384.01	1374.92	1372.11	1371.23	1370.96
75000	1514.91	1482.86	1473.13	1470.12	1469.18	1468.88
80000	1615.91	1581.72	1571.34	1568.12	1567.12	1566.81
85000	1716.90	1680.58	1669.55	1666.13	1665.07	1664.73
90000	1817.90	1779.44	1767.76	1764.14	1763.01	1762.66
95000	1918.89	1878.29	1865.96	1862.15	1860.96	1860.59
100000	2019.88	1977.15	1964.17	1960.15	1958.90	1958.51
200000	4039.77	3954.30	3928.35	3920.31	3917.80	3917.02
300000	6059.65	5931.46	5892.52	5880.46	5876.70	5875.53
400000	8079.54	7908.61	7856.69	7840.61	7835.61	7834.04
500000	10099.42	9885.76	9820.86	9800.77	9794.51	9792.55

24%

MONTHLY PAYMENT

Necessary to amortize a loan

TERM / AMOUNT	1 YEARS	2 YEARS	3 YEARS	4 YEARS	5 YEARS	6 YEARS
500	47.28	26.44	19.62	16.30	14.38	13.16
600	56.74	31.72	23.54	19.56	17.26	15.80
700	66.19	37.01	27.46	22.82	20.14	18.43
800	75.65	42.30	31.39	26.08	23.01	21.06
900	85.10	47.58	35.31	29.34	25.89	23.69
1000	94.56	52.87	39.23	32.60	28.77	26.33
2000	189.12	105.74	78.47	65.20	57.54	52.65
3000	283.68	158.61	117.70	97.81	86.30	78.98
4000	378.24	211.48	156.93	130.41	115.07	105.31
5000	472.80	264.36	196.16	163.01	143.84	131.63
6000	567.36	317.23	235.40	195.61	172.61	157.96
7000	661.92	370.10	274.63	228.21	201.38	184.29
8000	756.48	422.97	313.86	260.81	230.14	210.61
9000	851.04	475.84	353.10	293.42	258.91	236.94
10000	945.60	528.71	392.33	326.02	287.68	263.27
11000	1040.16	581.58	431.56	358.62	316.45	289.60
12000	1134.72	634.45	470.79	391.22	345.22	315.92
13000	1229.27	687.32	510.03	423.82	373.98	342.25
14000	1323.83	740.20	549.26	456.43	402.75	368.58
15000	1418.39	793.07	588.49	489.03	431.52	394.90
16000	1512.95	845.94	627.73	521.63	460.29	421.23
17000	1607.51	898.81	666.96	554.23	489.06	447.56
18000	1702.07	951.68	706.19	586.83	517.82	473.88
19000	1796.63	1004.55	745.42	619.43	546.59	500.21
20000	1891.19	1057.42	784.66	652.04	575.36	526.54
21000	1985.75	1110.29	823.89	684.64	604.13	552.86
22000	2080.31	1163.16	863.12	717.24	632.90	579.19
23000	2174.87	1216.04	902.36	749.84	661.66	605.52
24000	2269.43	1268.91	941.59	782.44	690.43	631.84
25000	2363.99	1321.78	980.82	815.05	719.20	658.17
30000	2836.79	1586.13	1176.99	978.06	863.04	789.80
35000	3309.59	1850.49	1373.15	1141.06	1006.88	921.44
40000	3782.38	2114.84	1569.31	1304.07	1150.72	1053.07
45000	4255.18	2379.20	1765.48	1467.08	1294.56	1184.71
50000	4727.98	2643.55	1961.64	1630.09	1438.40	1316.34
55000	5200.78	2907.91	2157.81	1793.10	1582.24	1447.98
60000	5673.58	3172.27	2353.97	1956.11	1726.08	1579.61
65000	6146.37	3436.62	2550.14	2119.12	1869.92	1711.24
70000	6619.17	3700.98	2746.30	2282.13	2013.76	1842.88
75000	7091.97	3965.33	2942.46	2445.14	2157.60	1974.51
80000	7564.77	4229.69	3138.63	2608.15	2301.44	2106.15
85000	8037.57	4494.04	3334.79	2771.16	2445.28	2237.78
90000	8510.36	4758.40	3530.96	2934.17	2589.12	2369.41
95000	8983.16	5022.75	3727.12	3097.17	2732.96	2501.05
100000	9455.96	5287.11	3923.29	3260.18	2876.80	2632.68
200000	18911.92	10574.22	7846.57	6520.37	5753.59	5265.37
300000	28367.88	15861.33	11769.86	9780.55	8630.39	7898.05
400000	37823.84	21148.44	15693.14	13040.73	11507.19	10530.73
500000	47279.80	26435.55	19616.43	16300.92	14383.98	13163.42

MONTHLY PAYMENT

Necessary to amortize a loan

24%

TERM / AMOUNT	7 YEARS	8 YEARS	9 YEARS	10 YEARS	11 YEARS	12 YEARS
500	12.34	11.76	11.34	11.02	10.79	10.61
600	14.81	14.11	13.60	13.23	12.95	12.74
700	17.27	16.46	15.87	15.43	15.11	14.86
800	19.74	18.81	18.14	17.64	17.26	16.98
900	22.21	21.16	20.40	19.84	19.42	19.10
1000	24.68	23.51	22.67	22.05	21.58	21.23
2000	49.35	47.03	45.34	44.10	43.16	42.45
3000	74.03	70.54	68.01	66.14	64.74	63.68
4000	98.70	94.05	90.68	88.19	86.32	84.90
5000	123.38	117.57	113.35	110.24	107.90	106.13
6000	148.05	141.08	136.03	132.29	129.48	127.36
7000	172.73	164.59	158.70	154.34	151.06	148.58
8000	197.41	188.11	181.37	176.38	172.65	169.81
9000	222.08	211.62	204.04	198.43	194.23	191.03
10000	246.76	235.13	226.71	220.48	215.81	212.26
11000	271.43	258.64	249.38	242.53	237.39	233.48
12000	296.11	282.16	272.05	264.58	258.97	254.71
13000	320.79	305.67	294.72	286.63	280.55	275.94
14000	345.46	329.18	317.39	308.67	302.13	297.16
15000	370.14	352.70	340.06	330.72	323.71	318.39
16000	394.81	376.21	362.73	352.77	345.29	339.61
17000	419.49	399.72	385.40	374.82	366.87	360.84
18000	444.16	423.24	408.08	396.87	388.45	382.07
19000	468.84	446.75	430.75	418.91	410.03	403.29
20000	493.52	470.26	453.42	440.96	431.61	424.52
21000	518.19	493.78	476.09	463.01	453.19	445.74
22000	542.87	517.29	498.76	485.06	474.77	466.97
23000	567.54	540.80	521.43	507.11	496.36	488.19
24000	592.22	564.32	544.10	529.15	517.94	509.42
25000	616.90	587.83	566.77	551.20	539.52	530.65
30000	740.27	705.39	680.13	661.44	647.42	636.78
35000	863.65	822.96	793.48	771.68	755.32	742.91
40000	987.03	940.53	906.83	881.92	863.23	849.03
45000	1110.41	1058.09	1020.19	992.16	971.13	955.16
50000	1233.79	1175.66	1133.54	1102.40	1079.03	1061.29
55000	1357.17	1293.22	1246.90	1212.65	1186.94	1167.42
60000	1480.55	1410.79	1360.25	1322.89	1294.84	1273.55
65000	1603.93	1528.35	1473.61	1433.13	1402.74	1379.68
70000	1727.31	1645.92	1586.96	1543.37	1510.65	1485.81
75000	1850.69	1763.48	1700.31	1653.61	1618.55	1591.94
80000	1974.06	1881.05	1813.67	1763.85	1726.45	1698.07
85000	2097.44	1998.62	1927.02	1874.09	1834.36	1804.20
90000	2220.82	2116.18	2040.38	1984.33	1942.26	1910.33
95000	2344.20	2233.75	2153.73	2094.57	2050.16	2016.46
100000	2467.58	2351.31	2267.08	2204.81	2158.07	2122.59
200000	4935.16	4702.63	4534.17	4409.62	4316.13	4245.17
300000	7402.74	7053.94	6801.25	6614.43	6474.20	6367.76
400000	9870.32	9405.25	9068.34	8819.24	8632.27	8490.34
500000	12337.91	11756.56	11335.42	11024.05	10790.34	10612.93

24%

MONTHLY PAYMENT

Necessary to amortize a loan

TERM / AMOUNT	15 YEARS	20 YEARS	25 YEARS	30 YEARS	35 YEARS	40 YEARS
500	10.29	10.09	10.03	10.01	10.00	10.00
600	12.35	12.10	12.03	12.01	12.00	12.00
700	14.41	14.12	14.04	14.01	14.00	14.00
800	16.47	16.14	16.04	16.01	16.00	16.00
900	18.52	18.16	18.05	18.01	18.00	18.00
1000	20.58	20.17	20.05	20.02	20.00	20.00
2000	41.17	40.35	40.11	40.03	40.01	40.00
3000	61.75	60.52	60.16	60.05	60.01	60.00
4000	82.33	80.70	80.21	80.06	80.02	80.01
5000	102.91	100.87	100.26	100.08	100.02	100.01
6000	123.50	121.04	120.32	120.10	120.03	120.01
7000	144.08	141.22	140.37	140.11	140.03	140.01
8000	164.66	161.39	160.42	160.13	160.04	160.01
9000	185.24	181.57	180.47	180.14	180.04	180.01
10000	205.83	201.74	200.53	200.16	200.05	200.01
11000	226.41	221.91	220.58	220.18	220.05	220.02
12000	246.99	242.09	240.63	240.19	240.06	240.02
13000	267.58	262.26	260.69	260.21	260.06	260.02
14000	288.16	282.44	280.74	280.22	280.07	280.02
15000	308.74	302.61	300.79	300.24	300.07	300.02
16000	329.32	322.79	320.84	320.26	320.08	320.02
17000	349.91	342.96	340.90	340.27	340.08	340.03
18000	370.49	363.13	360.95	360.29	360.09	360.03
19000	391.07	383.31	381.00	380.30	380.09	380.03
20000	411.65	403.48	401.05	400.32	400.10	400.03
21000	432.24	423.66	421.11	420.34	420.10	420.03
22000	452.82	443.83	441.16	440.35	440.11	440.03
23000	473.40	464.00	461.21	460.37	460.11	460.03
24000	493.99	484.18	481.27	480.39	480.12	480.04
25000	514.57	504.35	501.32	500.40	500.12	500.04
30000	617.48	605.22	601.58	600.48	600.15	600.04
35000	720.40	706.09	701.85	700.56	700.17	700.05
40000	823.31	806.96	802.11	800.64	800.20	800.06
45000	926.22	907.83	902.37	900.72	900.22	900.07
50000	1029.14	1008.70	1002.64	1000.80	1000.24	1000.07
55000	1132.05	1109.57	1102.90	1100.88	1100.27	1100.08
60000	1234.96	1210.44	1203.16	1200.96	1200.29	1200.09
65000	1337.88	1311.32	1303.43	1301.04	1300.32	1300.10
70000	1440.79	1412.19	1403.69	1401.12	1400.34	1400.10
75000	1543.71	1513.06	1503.96	1501.20	1500.37	1500.11
80000	1646.62	1613.93	1604.22	1601.28	1600.39	1600.12
85000	1749.53	1714.80	1704.48	1701.36	1700.42	1700.13
90000	1852.45	1815.67	1804.75	1801.44	1800.44	1800.13
95000	1955.36	1916.54	1905.01	1901.52	1900.46	1900.14
100000	2058.27	2017.41	2005.27	2001.60	2000.49	2000.15
200000	4116.55	4034.82	4010.55	4003.21	4000.98	4000.30
300000	6174.82	6052.22	6015.82	6004.81	6001.47	6000.45
400000	8233.09	8069.63	8021.10	8006.42	8001.95	8000.60
500000	10291.37	10087.04	10026.37	10008.02	10002.44	10000.74

MONTHLY PAYMENT

Necessary to amortize a loan

24.5%

TERM / AMOUNT	1 YEARS	2 YEARS	3 YEARS	4 YEARS	5 YEARS	6 YEARS
500	47.40	26.56	19.75	16.44	14.53	13.32
600	56.88	31.87	23.70	19.73	17.44	15.98
700	66.36	37.18	27.65	23.02	20.34	18.64
800	75.84	42.50	31.60	26.30	23.25	21.30
900	85.32	47.81	35.55	29.59	26.15	23.97
1000	94.80	53.12	39.50	32.88	29.06	26.63
2000	189.60	106.24	78.99	65.76	58.12	53.26
3000	284.41	159.36	118.49	98.64	87.18	79.89
4000	379.21	212.48	157.98	131.52	116.24	106.52
5000	474.01	265.60	197.48	164.39	145.29	133.16
6000	568.81	318.73	236.98	197.27	174.35	159.79
7000	663.61	371.85	276.47	230.15	203.41	186.42
8000	758.41	424.97	315.97	263.03	232.47	213.05
9000	853.22	478.09	355.46	295.91	261.53	239.68
10000	948.02	531.21	394.96	328.79	290.59	266.31
11000	1042.82	584.33	434.45	361.67	319.65	292.94
12000	1137.62	637.45	473.95	394.55	348.71	319.57
13000	1232.42	690.57	513.45	427.43	377.77	346.21
14000	1327.22	743.69	552.94	460.30	406.82	372.84
15000	1422.03	796.81	592.44	493.18	435.88	399.47
16000	1516.83	849.94	631.93	526.06	464.94	426.10
17000	1611.63	903.06	671.43	558.94	494.00	452.73
18000	1706.43	956.18	710.93	591.82	523.06	479.36
19000	1801.23	1009.30	750.42	624.70	552.12	505.99
20000	1896.03	1062.42	789.92	657.58	581.18	532.62
21000	1990.84	1115.54	829.41	690.46	610.24	559.25
22000	2085.64	1168.66	868.91	723.34	639.30	585.89
23000	2180.44	1221.78	908.40	756.21	668.36	612.52
24000	2275.24	1274.90	947.90	789.09	697.41	639.15
25000	2370.04	1328.02	987.40	821.97	726.47	665.78
30000	2844.05	1593.63	1184.88	986.37	871.77	798.94
35000	3318.06	1859.23	1382.36	1150.76	1017.06	932.09
40000	3792.07	2124.84	1579.83	1315.15	1162.36	1065.25
45000	4266.08	2390.44	1777.31	1479.55	1307.65	1198.40
50000	4740.09	2656.05	1974.79	1643.94	1452.95	1331.56
55000	5214.10	2921.65	2172.27	1808.34	1598.24	1464.72
60000	5688.10	3187.26	2369.75	1972.73	1743.53	1597.87
65000	6162.11	3452.86	2567.23	2137.13	1888.83	1731.03
70000	6636.12	3718.47	2764.71	2301.52	2034.12	1864.18
75000	7110.13	3984.07	2962.19	2465.92	2179.42	1997.34
80000	7584.14	4249.68	3159.67	2630.31	2324.71	2130.49
85000	8058.15	4515.28	3357.15	2794.70	2470.01	2263.65
90000	8532.16	4780.89	3554.63	2959.10	2615.30	2396.81
95000	9006.16	5046.49	3752.11	3123.49	2760.60	2529.96
100000	9480.17	5312.10	3949.59	3287.89	2905.89	2663.12
200000	18960.35	10624.20	7899.17	6575.77	5811.78	5326.24
300000	28440.52	15936.29	11848.76	9863.66	8717.67	7989.35
400000	37920.69	21248.39	15798.34	13151.55	11623.57	10652.47
500000	47400.87	26560.49	19747.93	16439.43	14529.46	13315.59

24.5%

MONTHLY PAYMENT

Necessary to amortize a loan

TERM / AMOUNT	7 YEARS	8 YEARS	9 YEARS	10 YEARS	11 YEARS	12 YEARS
500	12.50	11.92	11.51	11.20	10.97	10.80
600	15.00	14.31	13.81	13.44	13.16	12.96
700	17.49	16.69	16.11	15.68	15.36	15.11
800	19.99	19.07	18.41	17.92	17.55	17.27
900	22.49	21.46	20.71	20.16	19.75	19.43
1000	24.99	23.84	23.01	22.40	21.94	21.59
2000	49.99	47.68	46.02	44.80	43.88	43.18
3000	74.98	71.53	69.03	67.19	65.82	64.78
4000	99.97	95.37	92.04	89.59	87.76	86.37
5000	124.96	119.21	115.05	111.99	109.70	107.96
6000	149.96	143.05	138.06	134.39	131.64	129.55
7000	174.95	166.89	161.07	156.78	153.57	151.15
8000	199.94	190.74	184.08	179.18	175.51	172.74
9000	224.94	214.58	207.10	201.58	197.45	194.33
10000	249.93	238.42	230.11	223.98	219.39	215.92
11000	274.92	262.26	253.12	246.38	241.33	237.52
12000	299.91	286.10	276.13	268.77	263.27	259.11
13000	324.91	309.95	299.14	291.17	285.21	280.70
14000	349.90	333.79	322.15	313.57	307.15	302.29
15000	374.89	357.63	345.16	335.97	329.09	323.89
16000	399.89	381.47	368.17	358.36	351.03	345.48
17000	424.88	405.31	391.18	380.76	372.97	367.07
18000	449.87	429.16	414.19	403.16	394.91	388.66
19000	474.86	453.00	437.20	425.56	416.85	410.26
20000	499.86	476.84	460.21	447.95	438.79	431.85
21000	524.85	500.68	483.22	470.35	460.72	453.44
22000	549.84	524.52	506.23	492.75	482.66	475.03
23000	574.84	548.37	529.24	515.15	504.60	496.63
24000	599.83	572.21	552.25	537.55	526.54	518.22
25000	624.82	596.05	575.26	559.94	548.48	539.81
30000	749.79	715.26	690.32	671.93	658.18	647.77
35000	874.75	834.47	805.37	783.92	767.87	755.74
40000	999.71	953.68	920.42	895.91	877.57	863.70
45000	1124.68	1072.89	1035.48	1007.90	987.27	971.66
50000	1249.64	1192.10	1150.53	1119.89	1096.96	1079.62
55000	1374.61	1311.31	1265.58	1231.88	1206.66	1187.59
60000	1499.57	1430.52	1380.63	1343.86	1316.36	1295.55
65000	1624.53	1549.73	1495.69	1455.85	1426.05	1403.51
70000	1749.50	1668.94	1610.74	1567.84	1535.75	1511.47
75000	1874.46	1788.15	1725.79	1679.83	1645.45	1619.44
80000	1999.43	1907.36	1840.85	1791.82	1755.14	1727.40
85000	2124.39	2026.57	1955.90	1903.81	1864.84	1835.36
90000	2249.36	2145.78	2070.95	2015.80	1974.53	1943.32
95000	2374.32	2264.99	2186.00	2127.78	2084.23	2051.29
100000	2499.28	2384.20	2301.06	2239.77	2193.93	2159.25
200000	4998.57	4768.39	4602.11	4479.55	4387.85	4318.49
300000	7497.85	7152.59	6903.17	6719.32	6581.78	6477.74
400000	9997.13	9536.78	9204.23	8959.09	8775.71	8636.99
500000	12496.42	11920.98	11505.28	11198.87	10969.63	10796.24

MONTHLY PAYMENT

Necessary to amortize a loan

24.5%

TERM / AMOUNT	15 YEARS	20 YEARS	25 YEARS	30 YEARS	35 YEARS	40 YEARS
500	10.48	10.29	10.23	10.22	10.21	10.21
600	12.58	12.35	12.28	12.26	12.25	12.25
700	14.68	14.40	14.32	14.30	14.29	14.29
800	16.77	16.46	16.37	16.34	16.34	16.33
900	18.87	18.52	18.42	18.39	18.38	18.38
1000	20.97	20.58	20.46	20.43	20.42	20.42
2000	41.94	41.16	40.93	40.86	40.84	40.84
3000	62.90	61.73	61.39	61.29	61.26	61.25
4000	83.87	82.31	81.86	81.72	81.68	81.67
5000	104.84	102.89	102.32	102.15	102.10	102.09
6000	125.81	123.47	122.79	122.58	122.53	122.51
7000	146.78	144.04	143.25	143.02	142.95	142.93
8000	167.75	164.62	163.71	163.45	163.37	163.34
9000	188.71	185.20	184.18	183.88	183.79	183.76
10000	209.68	205.78	204.64	204.31	204.21	204.18
11000	230.65	226.35	225.11	224.74	224.63	224.60
12000	251.62	246.93	245.57	245.17	245.05	245.01
13000	272.59	267.51	266.04	265.60	265.47	265.43
14000	293.56	288.09	286.50	286.03	285.89	285.85
15000	314.52	308.66	306.96	306.46	306.31	306.27
16000	335.49	329.24	327.43	326.89	326.73	326.69
17000	356.46	349.82	347.89	347.32	347.15	347.10
18000	377.43	370.40	368.36	367.75	367.58	367.52
19000	398.40	390.98	388.82	388.19	388.00	387.94
20000	419.36	411.55	409.29	408.62	408.42	408.36
21000	440.33	432.13	429.75	429.05	428.84	428.78
22000	461.30	452.71	450.21	449.48	449.26	449.19
23000	482.27	473.29	470.68	469.91	469.68	469.61
24000	503.24	493.86	491.14	490.34	490.10	490.03
25000	524.21	514.44	511.61	510.77	510.52	510.45
30000	629.05	617.33	613.93	612.92	612.63	612.54
35000	733.89	720.22	716.25	715.08	714.73	714.63
40000	838.73	823.11	818.57	817.23	816.83	816.72
45000	943.57	925.99	920.89	919.39	918.94	918.81
50000	1048.41	1028.88	1023.21	1021.54	1021.04	1020.90
55000	1153.25	1131.77	1125.54	1123.69	1123.15	1122.99
60000	1258.09	1234.66	1227.86	1225.85	1225.25	1225.07
65000	1362.94	1337.55	1330.18	1328.00	1327.36	1327.16
70000	1467.78	1440.44	1432.50	1430.16	1429.46	1429.25
75000	1572.62	1543.32	1534.82	1532.31	1531.57	1531.34
80000	1677.46	1646.21	1637.14	1634.46	1633.67	1633.43
85000	1782.30	1749.10	1739.46	1736.62	1735.77	1735.52
90000	1887.14	1851.99	1841.79	1838.77	1837.88	1837.61
95000	1991.98	1954.88	1944.11	1940.93	1939.98	1939.70
100000	2096.82	2057.77	2046.43	2043.08	2042.09	2041.79
200000	4193.65	4115.53	4092.86	4086.16	4084.17	4083.58
300000	6290.47	6173.30	6139.28	6129.24	6126.26	6125.37
400000	8387.30	8231.06	8185.71	8172.32	8168.35	8167.17
500000	10484.12	10288.83	10232.14	10215.40	10210.43	10208.96

25%

MONTHLY PAYMENT

Necessary to amortize a loan

TERM / AMOUNT	1 YEARS	2 YEARS	3 YEARS	4 YEARS	5 YEARS	6 YEARS
500	47.52	26.69	19.88	16.58	14.68	13.47
600	57.03	32.02	23.86	19.89	17.61	16.16
700	66.53	37.36	27.83	23.21	20.55	18.86
800	76.04	42.70	31.81	26.53	23.48	21.55
900	85.54	48.03	35.78	29.84	26.42	24.24
1000	95.04	53.37	39.76	33.16	29.35	26.94
2000	190.09	106.74	79.52	66.31	58.70	53.87
3000	285.13	160.11	119.28	99.47	88.05	80.81
4000	380.18	213.49	159.04	132.63	117.41	107.75
5000	475.22	266.86	198.80	165.79	146.76	134.69
6000	570.27	320.23	238.56	198.94	176.11	161.62
7000	665.31	373.60	278.32	232.10	205.46	188.56
8000	760.35	426.97	318.08	265.26	234.81	215.50
9000	855.40	480.34	357.84	298.41	264.16	242.43
10000	950.44	533.72	397.60	331.57	293.51	269.37
11000	1045.49	587.09	437.36	364.73	322.86	296.31
12000	1140.53	640.46	477.12	397.89	352.22	323.25
13000	1235.57	693.83	516.88	431.04	381.57	350.18
14000	1330.62	747.20	556.64	464.20	410.92	377.12
15000	1425.66	800.57	596.40	497.36	440.27	404.06
16000	1520.71	853.94	636.16	530.51	469.62	430.99
17000	1615.75	907.32	675.92	563.67	498.97	457.93
18000	1710.80	960.69	715.68	596.83	528.32	484.87
19000	1805.84	1014.06	755.44	629.99	557.68	511.81
20000	1900.88	1067.43	795.20	663.14	587.03	538.74
21000	1995.93	1120.80	834.96	696.30	616.38	565.68
22000	2090.97	1174.17	874.72	729.46	645.73	592.62
23000	2186.02	1227.54	914.48	762.61	675.08	619.56
24000	2281.06	1280.92	954.24	795.77	704.43	646.49
25000	2376.11	1334.29	994.00	828.93	733.78	673.43
30000	2851.33	1601.15	1192.79	994.71	880.54	808.12
35000	3326.55	1868.00	1391.59	1160.50	1027.30	942.80
40000	3801.77	2134.86	1590.39	1326.29	1174.05	1077.49
45000	4276.99	2401.72	1789.19	1492.07	1320.81	1212.17
50000	4752.21	2668.58	1987.99	1657.86	1467.57	1346.86
55000	5227.43	2935.43	2186.79	1823.64	1614.32	1481.54
60000	5702.65	3202.29	2385.59	1989.43	1761.08	1616.23
65000	6177.87	3469.15	2584.39	2155.21	1907.84	1750.92
70000	6653.09	3736.01	2783.19	2321.00	2054.59	1885.60
75000	7128.32	4002.86	2981.99	2486.78	2201.35	2020.29
80000	7603.54	4269.72	3180.79	2652.57	2348.11	2154.97
85000	8078.76	4536.58	3379.59	2818.36	2494.86	2289.66
90000	8553.98	4803.44	3578.38	2984.14	2641.62	2424.35
95000	9029.20	5070.29	3777.18	3149.93	2788.38	2559.03
100000	9504.42	5337.15	3975.98	3315.71	2935.13	2693.72
200000	19008.84	10674.30	7951.97	6631.43	5870.26	5387.44
300000	28513.26	16011.46	11927.95	9947.14	8805.40	8081.15
400000	38017.68	21348.61	15903.93	13262.85	11740.53	10774.87
500000	47522.10	26685.76	19879.91	16578.56	14675.66	13468.59

MONTHLY PAYMENT

Necessary to amortize a loan

25%

TERM AMOUNT	7 YEARS	8 YEARS	9 YEARS	10 YEARS	11 YEARS	12 YEARS
500	12.66	12.09	11.68	11.37	11.15	10.98
600	15.19	14.50	14.01	13.65	13.38	13.18
700	17.72	16.92	16.35	15.92	15.61	15.37
800	20.25	19.34	18.68	18.20	17.84	17.57
900	22.78	21.76	21.02	20.47	20.07	19.76
1000	25.31	24.17	23.35	22.75	22.30	21.96
2000	50.62	48.35	46.70	45.50	44.60	43.92
3000	75.93	72.52	70.06	68.25	66.90	65.88
4000	101.25	96.69	93.41	91.00	89.20	87.84
5000	126.56	120.86	116.76	113.75	111.50	109.80
6000	151.87	145.04	140.11	136.50	133.80	131.77
7000	177.18	169.21	163.47	159.25	156.10	153.73
8000	202.49	193.38	186.82	181.99	178.40	175.69
9000	227.80	217.55	210.17	204.74	200.70	197.65
10000	253.12	241.73	233.52	227.49	223.00	219.61
11000	278.43	265.90	256.87	250.24	245.30	241.57
12000	303.74	290.07	280.23	272.99	267.60	263.53
13000	329.05	314.24	303.58	295.74	289.90	285.49
14000	354.36	338.42	326.93	318.49	312.20	307.45
15000	379.67	362.59	350.28	341.24	334.50	329.41
16000	404.99	386.76	373.64	363.99	356.80	351.37
17000	430.30	410.94	396.99	386.74	379.10	373.34
18000	455.61	435.11	420.34	409.49	401.40	395.30
19000	480.92	459.28	443.69	432.24	423.70	417.26
20000	506.23	483.45	467.04	454.99	446.00	439.22
21000	531.54	507.63	490.40	477.74	468.30	461.18
22000	556.86	531.80	513.75	500.48	490.59	483.14
23000	582.17	555.97	537.10	523.23	512.89	505.10
24000	607.48	580.14	560.45	545.98	535.19	527.06
25000	632.79	604.32	583.80	568.73	557.49	549.02
30000	759.35	725.18	700.57	682.48	668.99	658.83
35000	885.91	846.04	817.33	796.23	780.49	768.63
40000	1012.47	966.91	934.09	909.97	891.99	878.44
45000	1139.02	1087.77	1050.85	1023.72	1003.49	988.24
50000	1265.58	1208.63	1167.61	1137.46	1114.99	1098.05
55000	1392.14	1329.50	1284.37	1251.21	1226.49	1207.85
60000	1518.70	1450.36	1401.13	1364.96	1337.99	1317.66
65000	1645.26	1571.22	1517.89	1478.70	1449.48	1427.46
70000	1771.81	1692.09	1634.65	1592.45	1560.98	1537.27
75000	1898.37	1812.95	1751.41	1706.20	1672.48	1647.07
80000	2024.93	1933.81	1868.18	1819.94	1783.98	1756.87
85000	2151.49	2054.68	1984.94	1933.69	1895.48	1866.68
90000	2278.05	2175.54	2101.70	2047.44	2006.98	1976.48
95000	2404.61	2296.40	2218.46	2161.18	2118.48	2086.29
100000	2531.16	2417.27	2335.22	2274.93	2229.98	2196.09
200000	5062.33	4834.53	4670.44	4549.86	4459.95	4392.19
300000	7593.49	7251.80	7005.66	6824.79	6689.93	6588.28
400000	10124.65	9669.07	9340.88	9099.72	8919.90	8784.37
500000	12655.82	12086.33	11676.10	11374.65	11149.88	10980.46

25%

MONTHLY PAYMENT

Necessary to amortize a loan

TERM / AMOUNT	15 YEARS	20 YEARS	25 YEARS	30 YEARS	35 YEARS	40 YEARS
500	10.68	10.49	10.44	10.42	10.42	10.42
600	12.81	12.59	12.53	12.51	12.50	12.50
700	14.95	14.69	14.61	14.59	14.59	14.58
800	17.08	16.79	16.70	16.68	16.67	16.67
900	19.22	18.88	18.79	18.76	18.75	18.75
1000	21.36	20.98	20.88	20.85	20.84	20.83
2000	42.71	41.96	41.75	41.69	41.67	41.67
3000	64.07	62.95	62.63	62.54	62.51	62.50
4000	85.42	83.93	83.51	83.38	83.35	83.34
5000	106.78	104.91	104.38	104.23	104.18	104.17
6000	128.13	125.89	125.26	125.07	125.02	125.01
7000	149.49	146.88	146.13	145.92	145.86	145.84
8000	170.84	167.86	167.01	166.77	166.70	166.68
9000	192.20	188.84	187.89	187.61	187.53	187.51
10000	213.55	209.82	208.76	208.46	208.37	208.34
11000	234.91	230.80	229.64	229.30	229.21	229.18
12000	256.26	251.79	250.52	250.15	250.04	250.01
13000	277.62	272.77	271.39	271.00	270.88	270.85
14000	298.97	293.75	292.27	291.84	291.72	291.68
15000	320.33	314.73	313.14	312.69	312.55	312.52
16000	341.68	335.71	334.02	333.53	333.39	333.35
17000	363.04	356.70	354.90	354.38	354.23	354.18
18000	384.40	377.68	375.77	375.22	375.07	375.02
19000	405.75	398.66	396.65	396.07	395.90	395.85
20000	427.11	419.64	417.53	416.92	416.74	416.69
21000	448.46	440.63	438.40	437.76	437.58	437.52
22000	469.82	461.61	459.28	458.61	458.41	458.36
23000	491.17	482.59	480.16	479.45	479.25	479.19
24000	512.53	503.57	501.03	500.30	500.09	500.03
25000	533.88	524.55	521.91	521.14	520.92	520.86
30000	640.66	629.46	626.29	625.37	625.11	625.03
35000	747.44	734.38	730.67	729.60	729.29	729.20
40000	854.21	839.29	835.05	833.83	833.48	833.38
45000	960.99	944.20	939.43	938.06	937.66	937.55
50000	1067.76	1049.11	1043.82	1042.29	1041.85	1041.72
55000	1174.54	1154.02	1148.20	1146.52	1146.03	1145.89
60000	1281.32	1258.93	1252.58	1250.75	1250.22	1250.06
65000	1388.09	1363.84	1356.96	1354.98	1354.40	1354.23
70000	1494.87	1468.75	1461.34	1459.21	1458.59	1458.41
75000	1601.65	1573.66	1565.72	1563.43	1562.77	1562.58
80000	1708.42	1678.57	1670.10	1667.66	1666.96	1666.75
85000	1815.20	1783.48	1774.49	1771.89	1771.14	1770.92
90000	1921.98	1888.39	1878.87	1876.12	1875.33	1875.09
95000	2028.75	1993.31	1983.25	1980.35	1979.51	1979.27
100000	2135.53	2098.22	2087.63	2084.58	2083.69	2083.44
200000	4271.06	4196.43	4175.26	4169.16	4167.39	4166.88
300000	6406.59	6294.65	6262.89	6253.74	6251.08	6250.31
400000	8542.12	8392.86	8350.52	8338.31	8334.78	8333.75
500000	10677.64	10491.08	10438.15	10422.89	10418.47	10417.19

SECTION TWO

Payment Required to Amortize a $1,000 Loan

EXAMPLE

These charts reflect the interest and principal paid during any given year during the term of the loan and the remaining mortgage.

EXAMPLE: You have a $50,000 loan for 10% interest. What amount of interest and principal will you pay in the 15th year of the loan and what will the mortgage balance be at the end of the 15th year?

Turn to the chart entitled "Annual Amortization" based upon $1,000 at the 10% interest mortgage page. There are columns across the top of the page showing interest paid during year, principal paid during the year and mortgage balance at year end. Going down the page are the years. At the year 15 line go across and the columns read as follows: Interest—$82.90, Principal—$22.41 and mortgage balance $816.62. Simply take these figures and multiply them by 50. Therefore, at the end of the 15th year you will have paid interest for the previous 12 months of $4,145.00 and principal of $1,120.50. To determine the mortgage balance simply multiply 816.62 x 50. The remaining balance is $40,831.00.

8% ANNUAL AMORTIZATION

Based on a mortgage of $1,000

30-YEAR TERM
Monthly Payment: $ 7.34
Annual Payment: $88.06

YEAR	INTEREST PAID DURING YEAR	PRINCIPAL PAID DURING YEAR	MORTGAGE BALANCE AT YEAR END
1	$79.71	$ 8.35	$986.91
2	$79.01	$ 9.05	$977.86
3	$78.26	$ 9.80	$968.06
4	$77.45	$10.61	$957.45
5	$76.57	$11.49	$945.96
6	$75.61	$12.45	$933.51
7	$74.58	$13.48	$920.03
8	$73.46	$14.60	$905.43
9	$72.97	$15.09	$890.34
10	$70.94	$17.12	$873.22
11	$69.52	$18.54	$854.68
12	$67.97	$20.09	$834.59
13	$66.31	$21.75	$812.84
14	$64.51	$23.55	$789.29
15	$62.55	$25.51	$763.78
16	$60.43	$27.63	$736.15
17	$58.14	$29.92	$706.23
18	$55.66	$32.40	$673.83
19	$52.97	$35.09	$638.74
20	$50.06	$38.00	$600.74
21	$46.90	$41.16	$559.58
22	$43.49	$44.57	$515.01
23	$39.79	$48.27	$466.74
24	$35.76	$52.30	$414.44
25	$31.44	$56.62	$357.82
26	$26.74	$61.32	$296.50
27	$21.66	$66.40	$230.10
28	$16.14	$71.92	$158.18
29	$10.17	$77.89	$ 80.29
30	$ 7.77	$80.29	$ 0.00

ANNUAL AMORTIZATION

Based on a mortgage of $1,000

9%

30-YEAR TERM
Monthly Payment: $ 8.05
Annual Payment: $96.55

YEAR	INTEREST PAID DURING YEAR	PRINCIPAL PAID DURING YEAR	MORTGAGE BALANCE AT YEAR END
1	$89.73	$ 6.82	$993.17
2	$89.08	$ 7.47	$985.70
3	$88.37	$ 8.18	$977.52
4	$87.61	$ 8.94	$968.58
5	$86.77	$ 9.78	$958.80
6	$85.85	$10.70	$948.10
7	$84.85	$11.70	$936.40
8	$83.56	$12.99	$923.41
9	$82.55	$14.00	$909.41
10	$81.24	$15.31	$894.10
11	$79.80	$16.75	$877.35
12	$78.23	$18.32	$859.03
13	$76.51	$20.04	$838.99
14	$74.63	$21.92	$817.07
15	$72.58	$23.97	$793.10
16	$70.33	$26.22	$766.88
17	$67.87	$28.68	$738.20
18	$65.18	$31.37	$706.83
19	$62.24	$34.31	$672.52
20	$59.02	$37.53	$634.99
21	$55.50	$41.05	$593.94
22	$51.65	$44.90	$549.04
23	$47.44	$49.11	$499.93
24	$42.83	$53.72	$446.21
25	$37.78	$58.77	$387.44
26	$32.27	$64.28	$323.16
27	$26.24	$70.31	$252.85
28	$19.65	$76.90	$175.95
29	$12.44	$84.11	$ 91.84
30	$ 4.71	$91.84	$ .00

10% ANNUAL AMORTIZATION

Based on a mortgage of $1,000

30-YEAR TERM
Monthly Payment: $ 8.78
Annual Payment: $105.31

YEAR	INTEREST PAID DURING YEAR	PRINCIPAL PAID DURING YEAR	MORTGAGE BALANCE AT YEAR END
1	$99.71	$ 5.60	$994.40
2	$99.17	$ 6.14	$988.26
3	$98.53	$ 6.78	$981.48
4	$97.82	$ 7.49	$973.99
5	$97.03	$ 8.28	$965.71
6	$96.16	$ 9.15	$956.56
7	$95.21	$10.10	$946.46
8	$94.15	$11.16	$935.30
9	$92.98	$12.33	$922.97
10	$91.69	$13.62	$909.35
11	$90.26	$15.05	$894.30
12	$88.69	$16.62	$877.68
13	$86.95	$18.36	$859.32
14	$85.02	$20.29	$839.03
15	$82.90	$22.41	$816.62
16	$80.55	$24.76	$791.86
17	$77.96	$27.35	$764.51
18	$75.09	$30.22	$734.29
19	$71.93	$33.38	$700.91
20	$68.44	$36.87	$664.04
21	$64.57	$40.74	$623.30
22	$60.31	$45.00	$578.30
23	$55.60	$49.71	$528.59
24	$50.39	$54.92	$473.67
25	$44.64	$60.67	$413.00
26	$38.29	$67.02	$345.98
27	$31.27	$74.04	$271.94
28	$23.52	$81.79	$190.15
29	$14.95	$90.36	$ 99.79
30	$ 5.52	$99.79	$ 0.00

ANNUAL AMORTIZATION

Based on a mortgage of $1,000

11%

30-YEAR TERM
Monthly Payment: $ 9.52
Annual Payment: $114.27

YEAR	INTEREST PAID DURING YEAR	PRINCIPAL PAID DURING YEAR	MORTGAGE BALANCE AT YEAR END
1	$109.77	$ 4.50	$995.50
2	$109.25	$ 5.02	$990.48
3	$108.67	$ 5.60	$984.88
4	$108.02	$ 6.25	$978.63
5	$107.29	$ 6.98	$971.65
6	$106.49	$ 7.78	$963.87
7	$105.59	$ 8.68	$955.19
8	$104.58	$ 9.69	$945.50
9	$103.46	$ 10.81	$934.69
10	$102.21	$ 12.06	$922.63
11	$100.81	$ 13.46	$909.17
12	$ 99.26	$ 15.01	$894.16
13	$ 97.52	$ 16.75	$877.41
14	$ 95.58	$ 18.69	$858.72
15	$ 93.42	$ 20.85	$837.87
16	$ 91.05	$ 23.22	$814.65
17	$ 88.32	$ 25.95	$788.70
18	$ 85.31	$ 28.96	$759.74
19	$ 81.97	$ 32.30	$727.44
20	$ 78.22	$ 36.05	$691.39
21	$ 74.05	$ 40.22	$651.17
22	$ 69.40	$ 44.87	$606.30
23	$ 64.21	$ 50.06	$556.24
24	$ 58.41	$ 55.86	$500.38
25	$ 51.95	$ 62.32	$438.06
26	$ 44.71	$ 69.56	$368.50
27	$ 36.69	$ 77.58	$290.92
28	$ 27.71	$ 86.56	$204.36
29	$ 17.70	$ 96.57	$107.79
30	$ 6.48	$107.79	$ .00

12% ANNUAL AMORTIZATION

Based on a mortgage of $1,000

30-YEAR TERM
Monthly Payment: $ 10.29
Annual Payment: $123.43

YEAR	INTEREST PAID DURING YEAR	PRINCIPAL PAID DURING YEAR	MORTGAGE BALANCE AT YEAR END
1	$119.80	$ 3.63	$996.37
2	$119.34	$ 4.09	$992.28
3	$118.83	$ 4.60	$987.68
4	$118.24	$ 5.19	$982.49
5	$117.58	$ 5.85	$976.64
6	$116.84	$ 6.59	$970.05
7	$116.00	$ 7.43	$962.62
8	$114.70	$ 8.73	$953.89
9	$114.00	$ 9.43	$944.45
10	$112.80	$ 10.63	$933.83
11	$111.45	$ 11.98	$921.85
12	$109.94	$ 13.49	$908.36
13	$108.23	$ 15.20	$893.16
14	$106.29	$ 17.14	$876.02
15	$104.13	$ 19.30	$856.72
16	$101.67	$ 21.76	$834.95
17	$ 98.91	$ 24.52	$810.44
18	$ 95.80	$ 27.63	$782.81
19	$ 92.30	$ 31.13	$751.68
20	$ 88.35	$ 35.08	$716.60
21	$ 83.90	$ 39.53	$677.07
22	$ 78.89	$ 44.54	$632.53
23	$ 73.24	$ 50.19	$582.34
24	$ 66.88	$ 56.55	$525.79
25	$ 59.70	$ 63.73	$462.06
26	$ 51.63	$ 71.80	$390.26
27	$ 42.51	$ 80.92	$309.34
28	$ 32.25	$ 91.18	$218.16
29	$ 20.69	$102.74	$115.42
30	$ 8.01	$115.42	$ .00

ANNUAL AMORTIZATION

Based on a mortgage of $1,000

13%

30-YEAR TERM
Monthly Payment: $ 11.06
Annual Payment: $132.74

YEAR	INTEREST PAID DURING YEAR	PRINCIPAL PAID DURING YEAR	MORTGAGE BALANCE AT YEAR END
1	$129.83	$ 2.91	$997.09
2	$129.43	$ 3.31	$993.78
3	$128.97	$ 3.77	$990.01
4	$128.45	$ 4.29	$985.72
5	$127.86	$ 4.88	$980.84
6	$127.18	$ 5.56	$975.28
7	$126.41	$ 6.33	$968.95
8	$125.54	$ 7.20	$961.75
9	$124.54	$ 8.20	$953.55
10	$123.41	$ 9.33	$944.22
11	$122.57	$ 10.17	$934.05
12	$120.66	$ 12.08	$921.97
13	$118.99	$ 13.75	$908.22
14	$117.09	$ 15.65	$892.57
15	$114.94	$ 17.80	$874.77
16	$112.48	$ 20.26	$854.51
17	$109.68	$ 23.06	$831.45
18	$106.49	$ 26.25	$805.20
19	$102.87	$ 29.87	$775.33
20	$ 98.75	$ 33.99	$741.34
21	$ 94.06	$ 38.68	$702.66
22	$ 88.72	$ 44.02	$658.64
23	$ 82.65	$ 50.09	$608.55
24	$ 75.73	$ 57.01	$551.54
25	$ 67.86	$ 64.88	$486.66
26	$ 58.90	$ 73.84	$412.82
27	$ 48.71	$ 84.03	$328.79
28	$ 37.11	$ 95.63	$233.16
29	$ 23.91	$108.83	$124.33
30	$ 8.41	$124.33	$ .00

14% ANNUAL AMORTIZATION

Based on a mortgage of $1,000

30-YEAR TERM
Monthly Payment: $ 11.85
Annual Payment: $142.19

YEAR	INTEREST PAID DURING YEAR	PRINCIPAL PAID DURING YEAR	MORTGAGE BALANCE AT YEAR END
1	$139.86	$ 2.33	$997.67
2	$139.51	$ 2.68	$994.99
3	$139.11	$ 3.08	$991.91
4	$138.65	$ 3.54	$988.37
5	$138.12	$ 4.07	$984.30
6	$137.52	$ 4.67	$979.63
7	$136.87	$ 5.32	$974.31
8	$136.05	$ 6.14	$968.17
9	$135.11	$ 7.08	$961.09
10	$134.03	$ 8.16	$952.93
11	$132.82	$ 9.37	$943.56
12	$131.42	$ 10.77	$932.79
13	$129.81	$ 12.38	$920.41
14	$127.96	$ 14.23	$906.18
15	$125.83	$ 16.36	$889.82
16	$123.39	$ 18.80	$871.02
17	$120.58	$ 21.61	$849.41
18	$117.36	$ 24.83	$824.58
19	$113.65	$ 28.54	$796.04
20	$109.38	$ 32.81	$763.23
21	$104.48	$ 37.71	$725.52
22	$ 98.82	$ 43.37	$682.15
23	$ 92.38	$ 49.81	$632.34
24	$ 84.94	$ 57.25	$575.09
25	$ 76.39	$ 65.80	$509.29
26	$ 66.57	$ 75.62	$433.67
27	$ 55.27	$ 86.92	$346.75
28	$ 42.29	$ 99.90	$246.85
29	$ 27.37	$114.82	$132.03
30	$ 10.16	$132.03	$ 0.00

ANNUAL AMORTIZATION

Based on a mortgage of $1,000

15%

30-YEAR TERM
Monthly Payment: $ 12.64
Annual Payment: $151.73

YEAR	INTEREST PAID DURING YEAR	PRINCIPAL PAID DURING YEAR	MORTGAGE BALANCE AT YEAR END
1	$149.87	$ 1.86	$998.14
2	$149.57	$ 2.16	$995.98
3	$149.23	$ 2.50	$993.48
4	$148.82	$ 2.91	$990.57
5	$148.36	$ 3.37	$987.20
6	$147.82	$ 3.91	$983.29
7	$147.19	$ 4.54	$978.75
8	$146.46	$ 5.27	$973.48
9	$145.61	$ 6.12	$967.36
10	$144.62	$ 7.11	$960.25
11	$143.48	$ 8.25	$952.00
12	$142.16	$ 9.57	$942.43
13	$140.62	$ 11.11	$931.32
14	$138.83	$ 12.90	$918.42
15	$136.76	$ 14.97	$903.45
16	$134.35	$ 17.38	$886.07
17	$131.56	$ 20.17	$865.90
18	$128.31	$ 23.42	$842.48
19	$124.55	$ 27.18	$815.30
20	$120.18	$ 31.55	$783.75
21	$115.11	$ 36.62	$747.13
22	$109.22	$ 42.51	$704.62
23	$102.39	$ 49.34	$655.28
24	$ 94.45	$ 57.28	$598.00
25	$ 85.25	$ 66.48	$531.52
26	$ 74.56	$ 77.17	$454.35
27	$ 62.15	$ 89.58	$364.77
28	$ 47.75	$103.98	$260.79
29	$ 31.04	$120.69	$140.10
30	$ 11.63	$140.10	$ .00

16% ANNUAL AMORTIZATION

Based on a mortgage of $1,000

30-YEAR TERM
Monthly Payment: $ 13.45
Annual Payment: $161.38

YEAR	INTEREST PAID DURING YEAR	PRINCIPAL PAID DURING YEAR	MORTGAGE BALANCE AT YEAR END
1	$159.90	$ 1.48	$998.52
2	$159.65	$ 1.73	$996.79
3	$159.35	$ 2.03	$994.76
4	$159.00	$ 2.38	$992.38
5	$158.59	$ 2.79	$989.59
6	$158.11	$ 3.27	$986.32
7	$157.55	$ 3.83	$982.49
8	$156.89	$ 4.49	$978.00
9	$156.12	$ 5.26	$972.74
10	$155.21	$ 6.17	$966.57
11	$154.15	$ 7.23	$959.34
12	$152.90	$ 8.48	$950.86
13	$151.44	$ 9.94	$940.92
14	$149.73	$ 11.65	$929.27
15	$147.72	$ 13.66	$915.61
16	$145.37	$ 16.01	$899.60
17	$142.61	$ 18.77	$880.83
18	$139.38	$ 22.00	$858.83
19	$135.58	$ 25.80	$833.03
20	$131.14	$ 30.24	$802.79
21	$125.93	$ 35.45	$767.34
22	$119.82	$ 41.56	$725.78
23	$112.59	$ 48.79	$676.99
24	$104.27	$ 57.11	$619.88
25	$ 94.43	$ 66.95	$552.93
26	$ 82.90	$ 78.48	$474.45
27	$ 69.38	$ 92.00	$382.45
28	$ 53.53	$107.85	$274.60
29	$ 34.95	$126.43	$148.17
30	$ 13.21	$148.17	$ .00

ANNUAL AMORTIZATION

Based on a mortgage of $1,000

17%

30-YEAR TERM
Monthly Payment: $ 14.26
Annual Payment: $171.08

YEAR	INTEREST PAID DURING YEAR	PRINCIPAL PAID DURING YEAR	MORTGAGE BALANCE AT YEAR END
1	$169.91	$ 1.17	$998.83
2	$169.70	$ 1.38	$997.45
3	$169.44	$ 1.64	$995.81
4	$169.14	$ 1.94	$993.87
5	$168.78	$ 2.30	$991.57
6	$168.36	$ 2.72	$988.85
7	$167.86	$ 3.22	$985.63
8	$167.27	$ 3.81	$981.82
9	$166.57	$ 4.51	$977.31
10	$165.74	$ 5.34	$971.97
11	$164.75	$ 6.33	$965.64
12	$163.59	$ 7.49	$958.15
13	$162.22	$ 8.86	$949.29
14	$160.58	$ 10.50	$938.79
15	$158.65	$ 12.43	$926.36
16	$156.37	$ 14.71	$911.65
17	$153.66	$ 17.42	$894.23
18	$150.46	$ 20.62	$873.61
19	$146.67	$ 24.41	$849.20
20	$142.18	$ 28.90	$820.30
21	$136.87	$ 34.21	$786.09
22	$130.58	$ 40.50	$745.59
23	$123.13	$ 47.95	$697.64
24	$114.31	$ 56.77	$640.87
25	$103.87	$ 67.21	$573.66
26	$ 91.33	$ 79.75	$493.91
27	$ 76.88	$ 94.20	$399.71
28	$ 59.55	$111.53	$288.18
29	$ 39.04	$132.04	$156.14
30	$ 14.94	$156.14	$ .00

ANNUAL AMORTIZATION

Based on a mortgage of $1,000

30-YEAR TERM
Monthly Payment: $ 15.07
Annual Payment: $180.85

YEAR	INTEREST PAID DURING YEAR	PRINCIPAL PAID DURING YEAR	MORTGAGE BALANCE AT YEAR END
1	$179.93	$ 0.92	$999.08
2	$179.75	$ 1.10	$997.98
3	$179.53	$ 1.32	$996.66
4	$179.27	$ 1.58	$995.08
5	$178.96	$ 1.89	$993.19
6	$178.59	$ 2.26	$990.93
7	$178.15	$ 2.70	$988.23
8	$177.62	$ 3.23	$985.00
9	$176.99	$ 3.86	$981.14
10	$176.24	$ 4.61	$976.53
11	$175.33	$ 5.52	$971.01
12	$174.25	$ 6.60	$964.41
13	$172.97	$ 7.88	$956.53
14	$171.42	$ 9.43	$947.10
15	$169.58	$ 11.27	$935.83
16	$167.37	$ 13.48	$922.35
17	$164.74	$ 16.11	$906.24
18	$161.59	$ 19.26	$886.98
19	$157.82	$ 23.03	$863.95
20	$153.31	$ 27.54	$836.41
21	$147.92	$ 32.93	$803.48
22	$141.48	$ 39.37	$764.11
23	$133.77	$ 47.08	$717.03
24	$124.61	$ 56.24	$660.79
25	$113.57	$ 67.28	$593.51
26	$100.41	$ 80.44	$513.07
27	$ 84.67	$ 96.18	$416.89
28	$ 65.86	$114.99	$301.90
29	$ 43.36	$137.49	$164.41
30	$ 16.44	$164.41	$ .00

ANNUAL AMORTIZATION

Based on a mortgage of $1,000

19%

30-YEAR TERM
Monthly Payment: $ 15.89
Annual Payment: $190.67

YEAR	INTEREST PAID DURING YEAR	PRINCIPAL PAID DURING YEAR	MORTGAGE BALANCE AT YEAR END
1	$189.94	$ 0.73	$999.27
2	$189.79	$ 0.88	$998.39
3	$189.61	$ 1.06	$997.33
4	$189.39	$ 1.28	$996.05
5	$189.12	$ 1.55	$994.50
6	$188.80	$ 1.87	$992.63
7	$188.41	$ 2.26	$990.37
8	$187.95	$ 2.72	$987.65
9	$187.38	$ 3.29	$984.36
10	$186.70	$ 3.97	$980.39
11	$185.87	$ 4.80	$975.59
12	$184.88	$ 5.79	$969.80
13	$183.68	$ 6.99	$962.81
14	$182.22	$ 8.45	$954.36
15	$180.47	$ 10.20	$944.15
16	$178.36	$ 12.31	$931.85
17	$175.80	$ 14.87	$916.98
18	$172.72	$ 17.95	$899.03
19	$168.99	$ 21.68	$877.35
20	$164.50	$ 26.17	$851.18
21	$159.07	$ 31.60	$819.58
22	$152.51	$ 38.16	$781.42
23	$144.59	$ 46.08	$735.34
24	$135.01	$ 55.66	$679.68
25	$123.49	$ 67.18	$612.50
26	$109.56	$ 81.11	$531.39
27	$ 92.73	$ 97.94	$433.45
28	$ 72.41	$118.26	$315.19
29	$ 47.88	$142.79	$172.40
30	$ 18.27	$172.40	$ .00

20% ANNUAL AMORTIZATION

Based on a mortgage of $1,000

30-YEAR TERM
Monthly Payment: $ 16.71
Annual Payment: $200.52

YEAR	INTEREST PAID DURING YEAR	PRINCIPAL PAID DURING YEAR	MORTGAGE BALANCE AT YEAR END
1	$199.95	$ 0.57	$999.43
2	$199.82	$ 0.70	$998.73
3	$199.67	$ 0.85	$997.88
4	$199.48	$ 1.04	$996.84
5	$199.25	$ 1.27	$995.57
6	$198.98	$ 1.54	$994.03
7	$198.64	$ 1.80	$992.15
8	$198.22	$ 2.30	$989.85
9	$197.72	$ 2.80	$987.05
10	$197.11	$ 3.41	$983.64
11	$196.36	$ 4.16	$979.48
12	$195.45	$ 5.07	$974.41
13	$194.33	$ 6.19	$968.22
14	$192.97	$ 7.55	$960.67
15	$191.32	$ 9.20	$951.47
16	$189.29	$ 11.23	$940.24
17	$186.83	$ 13.69	$926.55
18	$183.83	$ 16.69	$909.86
19	$180.17	$ 20.35	$889.51
20	$175.70	$ 24.82	$864.69
21	$170.25	$ 30.27	$834.42
22	$163.62	$ 36.90	$797.52
23	$155.52	$ 45.00	$752.52
24	$145.65	$ 54.87	$697.65
25	$133.61	$ 66.91	$630.74
26	$118.93	$ 81.59	$549.15
27	$101.03	$ 99.49	$449.66
28	$ 79.20	$121.32	$328.34
29	$ 52.59	$147.93	$180.41
30	$ 20.11	$180.41	($ .00)

ANNUAL AMORTIZATION

Based on a mortgage of $1,000

21%

30-YEAR TERM
Monthly Payment: $ 17.53
Annual Payment: $210.41

YEAR	INTEREST PAID DURING YEAR	PRINCIPAL PAID DURING YEAR	MORTGAGE BALANCE AT YEAR END
1	$209.96	$ 0.45	$999.55
2	$209.86	$ 0.55	$999.00
3	$209.73	$ 0.68	$998.32
4	$209.57	$ 0.84	$997.48
5	$209.38	$ 1.03	$996.45
6	$209.14	$ 1.27	$995.18
7	$208.84	$ 1.57	$993.61
8	$208.48	$ 1.93	$991.68
9	$208.03	$ 2.38	$989.30
10	$207.48	$ 2.93	$986.37
11	$206.80	$ 3.61	$982.76
12	$205.97	$ 4.44	$978.32
13	$204.94	$ 5.47	$972.85
14	$203.68	$ 6.73	$966.12
15	$201.49	$ 8.92	$957.20
16	$200.20	$ 10.21	$946.99
17	$197.84	$ 12.57	$934.42
18	$194.93	$ 15.48	$918.94
19	$191.31	$ 19.10	$899.84
20	$186.93	$ 23.48	$876.36
21	$181.49	$ 28.92	$847.44
22	$174.80	$ 35.61	$811.83
23	$166.56	$ 43.85	$767.98
24	$156.41	$ 54.00	$713.98
25	$143.91	$ 66.50	$647.48
26	$128.52	$ 81.89	$565.59
27	$109.57	$100.84	$464.75
28	$ 86.24	$124.17	$340.58
29	$ 57.50	$152.91	$187.67
30	$ 22.74	$187.67	($ .00)

22% ANNUAL AMORTIZATION

Based on a mortgage of $1,000

30-YEAR TERM
Monthly Payment: $ 18.36
Annual Payment: $220.32

YEAR	INTEREST PAID DURING YEAR	PRINCIPAL PAID DURING YEAR	MORTGAGE BALANCE AT YEAR END
1	$219.97	$ 0.35	$999.65
2	$219.88	$ 0.44	$999.21
3	$219.77	$ 0.55	$998.66
4	$219.64	$ 0.68	$997.98
5	$219.48	$ 0.84	$997.14
6	$219.27	$ 1.05	$996.09
7	$219.02	$ 1.30	$994.79
8	$218.70	$ 1.62	$993.17
9	$218.31	$ 2.01	$991.16
10	$217.82	$ 2.50	$988.66
11	$217.21	$ 3.11	$985.55
12	$216.44	$ 3.88	$981.67
13	$215.50	$ 4.82	$976.85
14	$214.33	$ 5.99	$970.86
15	$212.87	$ 7.45	$963.41
16	$211.05	$ 9.27	$954.14
17	$208.79	$ 11.53	$942.61
18	$205.99	$ 14.33	$928.28
19	$202.49	$ 17.83	$910.45
20	$198.15	$ 22.17	$888.28
21	$192.75	$ 27.57	$860.71
22	$186.03	$ 34.29	$826.42
23	$177.68	$ 42.64	$783.78
24	$167.29	$ 53.03	$730.75
25	$154.37	$ 65.95	$664.80
26	$138.31	$ 82.01	$582.79
27	$118.32	$102.00	$480.79
28	$ 93.48	$126.84	$353.95
29	$ 62.58	$157.74	$196.21
30	$ 24.11	$196.21	($ .00)

ANNUAL AMORTIZATION

Based on a mortgage of $1,000

23%

30-YEAR TERM
Monthly Payment: $ 19.19
Annual Payment: $230.24

YEAR	INTEREST PAID DURING YEAR	PRINCIPAL PAID DURING YEAR	MORTGAGE BALANCE AT YEAR END
1	$229.97	$ 0.27	$999.72
2	$229.89	$ 0.35	$999.37
3	$229.81	$ 0.43	$998.94
4	$229.69	$ 0.55	$998.39
5	$229.56	$ 0.68	$997.71
6	$229.38	$ 0.86	$996.85
7	$229.16	$ 1.08	$995.77
8	$228.88	$ 1.36	$994.41
9	$228.54	$ 1.70	$992.71
10	$228.10	$ 2.14	$990.57
11	$227.55	$ 2.69	$987.88
12	$226.86	$ 3.38	$984.50
13	$226.00	$ 4.24	$980.26
14	$224.92	$ 5.32	$974.94
15	$223.55	$ 6.69	$968.25
16	$221.84	$ 8.40	$959.85
17	$219.69	$ 10.55	$949.30
18	$216.99	$ 13.25	$936.05
19	$213.60	$ 16.64	$919.41
20	$209.34	$ 20.90	$898.51
21	$203.99	$ 26.25	$872.26
22	$197.28	$ 32.96	$839.30
23	$188.85	$ 41.39	$797.91
24	$178.26	$ 51.98	$745.93
25	$164.96	$ 65.28	$680.65
26	$148.24	$ 82.00	$598.65
27	$127.28	$102.96	$495.69
28	$100.93	$129.31	$366.38
29	$ 67.84	$162.40	$203.98
30	$ 26.26	$203.98	$ 0.00

24% ANNUAL AMORTIZATION

Based on a mortgage of $1,000

30-YEAR TERM
Monthly Payment: $ 20.02
Annual Payment: $240.19

YEAR	INTEREST PAID DURING YEAR	PRINCIPAL PAID DURING YEAR	MORTGAGE BALANCE AT YEAR END
1	$239.98	$ 0.21	$999.79
2	$239.92	$ 0.27	$999.52
3	$239.85	$ 0.34	$999.18
4	$239.75	$ 0.44	$998.74
5	$239.64	$ 0.55	$998.19
6	$239.48	$ 0.71	$997.48
7	$239.29	$ 0.90	$996.58
8	$239.05	$ 1.14	$995.44
9	$238.75	$ 1.44	$994.00
10	$238.37	$ 1.82	$992.18
11	$237.87	$ 2.32	$989.86
12	$237.25	$ 2.94	$986.92
13	$236.47	$ 3.72	$983.20
14	$235.47	$ 4.72	$978.48
15	$234.19	$ 6.00	$972.48
16	$232.59	$ 7.60	$964.88
17	$230.55	$ 9.64	$955.24
18	$227.97	$ 12.22	$943.02
19	$224.69	$ 15.50	$927.52
20	$220.53	$ 19.66	$907.86
21	$215.25	$ 24.94	$882.92
22	$208.56	$ 31.63	$851.29
23	$200.08	$ 40.11	$811.18
24	$189.32	$ 50.87	$760.31
25	$175.67	$ 64.52	$695.79
26	$158.37	$ 81.82	$613.97
27	$136.42	$103.77	$510.20
28	$108.59	$131.60	$378.60
29	$ 73.29	$166.90	$211.70
30	$ 28.49	$211.70	($ .00)

SECTION THREE
Loan Progress Charts

5% LOAN PROGRESS CHART

Showing dollar balance remaining on a $1000 loan

AGE OF LOAN	ORIGINAL TERM IN YEARS										
	5	8	10	12	15	16	17	18	19	20	21
1	819	896	921	938	954	959	962	965	967	970	973
2	630	786	838	872	906	914	922	928	933	939	944
3	430	671	751	803	855	868	880	889	897	906	913
4	220	550	659	731	802	820	835	848	860	871	881
5		422	562	654	746	768	788	805	820	835	847
6		289	461	574	687	715	739	760	779	796	812
7		148	354	490	625	658	687	713	735	756	775
8			242	402	560	599	633	663	689	714	735
9			124	309	491	536	576	610	641	669	694
10				211	419	471	516	555	590	622	651
11				108	343	402	453	497	537	573	605
12					264	329	386	437	481	521	557
13					180	253	317	373	422	467	507
14					92	173	243	305	360	410	454
15						89	166	235	295	350	399
16							85	160	227	287	340
17								82	155	220	279
18									79	150	214
19										77	146
20											75

AGE OF LOAN	ORIGINAL TERM IN YEARS										
	22	23	24	25	26	27	28	29	30	35	40
1	974	976	978	980	980	982	984	985	986	990	992
2	947	951	955	958	960	963	966	968	970	978	983
3	919	924	930	936	939	943	948	951	954	966	974
4	889	897	905	912	916	922	928	932	937	954	965
5	858	868	878	886	893	900	908	913	919	941	955
6	825	837	849	860	868	877	886	893	900	927	945
7	790	805	819	832	842	853	863	872	880	912	934
8	754	771	788	803	815	828	839	849	859	897	922
9	716	736	755	772	786	801	814	826	837	881	910
10	676	699	720	740	756	773	788	801	814	864	898
11	634	660	684	706	725	743	760	775	789	846	885
12	589	618	645	670	691	712	731	748	764	827	871
13	543	575	605	633	656	679	701	719	737	808	856
14	494	530	563	593	620	645	668	689	709	787	841
15	442	482	518	552	581	609	635	658	679	765	825
16	388	432	472	508	540	571	599	624	648	742	808
17	331	379	422	462	498	531	562	589	615	718	790
18	271	323	371	414	453	489	522	552	581	693	771
19	209	265	316	363	405	445	481	514	544	667	751
20	142	204	259	310	356	398	438	473	506	639	730
21	73	139	199	254	304	350	392	430	466	609	709
22		71	136	195	249	298	344	386	424	578	686
23			70	133	191	244	294	338	380	546	661
24				68	131	188	241	289	333	512	636
25					67	128	185	237	285	476	610
26						66	126	182	233	438	582
27							65	124	179	399	552
28								64	122	357	521
29									63	314	489
30										268	454
31										219	419
32										168	381
33										115	341
34										59	299
35											255

LOAN PROGRESS CHART 5.5%

Showing dollar balance remaining on a $1000 loan

ORIGINAL TERM IN YEARS											AGE
5	8	10	12	15	16	17	18	19	20	21	OF LOAN
821	898	923	939	956	960	964	966	969	972	974	1
633	790	841	875	909	917	925	931	937	942	946	2
433	675	755	808	860	872	884	893	903	911	917	3
223	555	664	736	808	825	841	854	866	877	887	4
	427	568	661	753	775	796	812	828	842	854	5
	293	467	581	695	722	747	768	788	805	820	6
	150	359	497	633	667	697	722	745	766	784	7
		246	408	569	608	643	673	700	724	746	8
		126	315	500	546	586	621	652	680	705	9
			215	428	480	526	566	602	634	662	10
			111	351	410	463	508	549	585	617	11
				271	337	396	447	493	533	570	12
				185	260	325	382	433	479	519	13
				95	178	250	314	371	421	466	14
					91	171	242	304	360	410	15
						88	166	234	296	351	16
							85	161	228	288	17
								82	156	222	18
									80	152	19
										78	20

ORIGINAL TERM IN YEARS											AGE
22	23	24	25	26	27	28	29	30	35	40	OF LOAN
976	977	979	981	982	983	985	986	987	990	993	1
951	954	957	960	963	966	968	971	973	980	986	2
924	929	934	939	943	947	951	955	958	969	978	3
896	903	910	916	922	928	933	938	942	958	970	4
866	875	884	893	900	907	914	920	925	946	961	5
834	846	857	867	877	885	893	901	907	933	952	6
800	815	828	841	852	862	872	881	888	920	942	7
765	782	798	813	826	838	849	860	869	905	931	8
728	748	766	783	798	812	825	837	848	890	920	9
688	711	732	751	769	785	800	814	826	874	909	10
647	673	697	718	738	756	773	789	802	858	897	11
603	632	659	683	705	726	745	762	778	840	884	12
556	589	619	646	671	694	715	734	752	821	870	13
507	543	577	607	635	660	683	705	724	802	856	14
455	495	532	566	596	624	650	674	695	781	840	15
400	445	485	522	556	586	615	641	664	759	824	16
342	391	436	476	513	546	577	606	632	735	807	17
281	335	383	427	467	504	538	570	598	711	789	18
217	275	328	376	420	460	497	531	562	685	770	19
148	212	269	321	369	413	453	490	523	657	750	20
76	145	207	264	316	363	406	447	483	628	729	21
	74	142	203	259	310	357	401	440	598	707	22
		73	139	200	255	306	353	395	565	683	23
			72	137	196	251	302	348	531	658	24
				70	134	193	248	297	495	632	25
					69	132	191	244	457	604	26
						68	131	188	416	574	27
							67	129	374	543	28
								66	329	510	29
									281	475	30
									231	439	31
									178	400	32
									122	359	33
									63	316	34
										270	35

6% LOAN PROGRESS CHART

Showing dollar balance remaining on a $1000 loan

AGE OF LOAN	ORIGINAL TERM IN YEARS										
	5	8	10	12	15	16	17	18	19	20	21
1	823	899	925	941	958	961	965	968	971	973	976
2	635	793	845	879	913	920	928	934	940	944	950
3	436	680	760	813	865	877	889	898	907	914	922
4	225	560	670	743	814	831	847	860	872	882	893
5		432	574	668	760	782	802	820	835	848	861
6		296	473	589	703	730	755	777	796	812	828
7		153	365	505	642	676	705	731	754	774	793
8			250	416	578	617	652	683	710	734	756
9			129	321	509	555	596	631	663	691	716
10				220	437	489	536	577	613	645	674
11				113	359	419	472	519	560	596	630
12					277	345	405	457	504	545	582
13					190	267	333	392	444	490	532
14					98	183	257	323	381	432	478
15						94	177	249	313	370	422
16							91	171	242	305	362
17								88	166	235	298
18									86	162	230
19										83	158
20											81

AGE OF LOAN	ORIGINAL TERM IN YEARS										
	22	23	24	25	26	27	28	29	30	35	40
1	977	979	981	982	984	985	986	987	988	991	993
2	953	957	960	963	966	968	971	973	975	982	987
3	928	934	939	943	948	951	955	958	962	972	980
4	901	909	916	922	928	933	938	942	947	962	972
5	872	882	891	899	907	914	919	925	931	951	965
6	842	854	865	875	885	893	900	908	915	939	956
7	809	824	838	849	861	871	880	889	897	927	947
8	775	793	808	822	836	848	858	869	878	913	938
9	739	759	777	794	810	823	836	847	859	900	928
10	700	723	744	763	781	797	811	825	837	885	917
11	659	686	709	731	751	769	785	801	815	869	906
12	615	645	672	696	719	739	758	775	791	852	894
13	569	603	633	660	686	708	729	748	766	834	881
14	520	557	591	621	650	675	698	719	739	816	868
15	468	509	546	580	612	639	665	689	711	796	854
16	412	458	499	536	571	602	630	656	681	774	838
17	353	404	449	490	528	562	593	622	649	752	822
18	291	346	396	441	482	520	554	586	615	728	805
19	225	285	339	389	434	475	512	547	579	702	787
20	154	220	279	333	383	427	468	506	540	675	768
21	79	151	216	274	328	377	421	462	500	647	747
22		78	148	212	270	323	371	416	457	616	725
23			76	145	208	266	318	366	411	584	702
24				75	143	205	262	314	362	550	678
25					74	141	202	258	310	513	652
26						73	139	200	255	475	624
27							71	137	197	434	595
28								71	135	390	564
29									70	344	531
30										295	495
31										243	458
32										187	419
33										129	376
34										66	332
35											284

LOAN PROGRESS CHART **6.5%**

Showing dollar balance remaining on a $1000 loan

ORIGINAL TERM IN YEARS 5	8	10	12	15	16	17	18	19	20	21	AGE OF LOAN
825	902	926	943	959	963	967	970	973	975	976	**1**
639	797	848	882	916	924	931	938	943	948	952	**2**
439	684	764	818	869	882	893	903	912	920	926	**3**
227	565	675	749	820	837	853	867	878	889	898	**4**
	437	580	675	767	790	809	827	842	856	868	**5**
	301	479	596	711	739	763	785	804	821	836	**6**
	155	370	512	651	685	714	741	764	784	802	**7**
		255	423	587	627	662	693	720	745	765	**8**
		132	327	518	565	606	642	674	702	727	**9**
			225	445	499	546	588	624	657	685	**10**
			116	367	429	482	530	571	609	641	**11**
				284	354	414	468	515	557	594	**12**
				196	274	342	402	455	502	544	**13**
				101	188	265	332	391	444	490	**14**
					97	182	257	323	381	433	**15**
						94	177	250	315	372	**16**
							91	172	243	307	**17**
								89	167	238	**18**
									86	163	**19**
										84	**20**

ORIGINAL TERM IN YEARS 22	23	24	25	26	27	28	29	30	35	40	AGE OF LOAN
979	980	983	983	985	987	987	988	989	992	994	**1**
956	960	964	966	969	972	973	975	977	984	988	**2**
932	938	943	947	951	956	958	961	964	975	982	**3**
906	914	921	927	933	938	942	946	950	966	975	**4**
879	889	898	905	913	920	926	931	936	956	968	**5**
850	862	873	883	892	901	908	914	921	945	961	**6**
818	833	847	858	869	880	888	896	904	934	953	**7**
785	802	819	832	845	858	868	877	886	921	944	**8**
750	770	789	804	820	834	846	857	868	908	935	**9**
712	735	757	775	793	809	823	835	848	895	926	**10**
671	698	722	743	763	782	798	812	826	880	915	**11**
628	658	686	710	732	753	771	788	803	864	904	**12**
582	616	647	674	699	722	743	762	779	847	892	**13**
533	570	605	635	664	690	712	734	753	829	880	**14**
480	522	561	594	626	655	680	704	726	810	866	**15**
424	471	513	551	586	617	646	672	696	790	852	**16**
364	416	463	504	543	578	609	638	664	768	837	**17**
301	357	409	455	497	535	570	601	631	745	821	**18**
233	295	351	402	448	490	528	563	595	720	803	**19**
160	228	290	345	396	442	483	521	557	693	785	**20**
83	157	224	285	340	390	436	477	516	665	765	**21**
	81	154	220	280	335	385	430	472	635	744	**22**
		80	152	217	277	331	380	426	603	721	**23**
			78	149	214	273	327	376	569	697	**24**
				77	147	211	269	323	532	672	**25**
					76	145	208	266	493	644	**26**
						75	143	206	451	615	**27**
							74	142	407	584	**28**
								73	359	551	**29**
									309	515	**30**
									255	477	**31**
									197	437	**32**
									136	394	**33**
									70	348	**34**
										299	**35**

7% LOAN PROGRESS CHART

Showing dollar balance remaining on a $1000 loan

AGE OF LOAN	ORIGINAL TERM IN YEARS 5	8	10	12	15	16	17	18	19	20	21
1	827	903	928	944	961	965	969	972	974	976	978
2	641	799	852	885	919	927	935	941	946	950	954
3	442	688	769	822	874	886	898	908	916	923	929
4	229	569	681	754	826	843	859	872	883	894	903
5		441	586	681	774	797	817	834	849	862	874
6		304	485	603	719	747	772	793	812	829	843
7		158	376	519	659	693	723	750	772	792	810
8			259	429	596	636	672	703	730	754	775
9			134	333	527	574	616	652	684	712	737
10				230	454	509	557	599	635	667	696
11				119	375	438	493	541	582	620	653
12					291	362	424	479	526	568	606
13					201	281	351	412	466	513	556
14					104	194	272	341	401	455	502
15						100	188	264	332	391	445
16							97	182	257	324	383
17								94	177	251	317
18									92	173	245
19										90	169
20											88

AGE OF LOAN	ORIGINAL TERM IN YEARS 22	23	24	25	26	27	28	29	30	35	40
1	980	982	984	985	986	987	989	989	989	993	995
2	958	962	966	969	971	973	976	977	979	986	990
3	936	942	947	951	955	959	962	964	967	978	984
4	911	919	926	932	938	943	947	951	954	970	978
5	885	895	904	912	919	925	932	936	941	960	972
6	857	869	880	890	899	907	915	921	926	951	965
7	827	842	855	867	878	887	897	904	911	940	958
8	794	812	828	842	855	866	877	886	895	929	950
9	760	780	799	815	830	844	856	867	877	917	942
10	722	746	768	787	804	819	834	846	858	904	933
11	683	710	734	756	775	793	810	824	837	890	924
12	640	671	698	723	745	765	784	800	815	875	914
13	594	629	660	687	713	736	757	775	792	860	903
14	545	584	618	650	678	703	727	748	767	842	891
15	492	535	574	609	640	669	695	718	740	824	879
16	436	484	527	565	600	632	661	687	711	805	865
17	375	428	476	519	557	593	625	653	680	784	851
18	310	369	421	468	511	550	586	617	647	761	835
19	241	305	363	415	462	505	544	579	611	737	819
20	166	236	300	357	409	456	499	537	573	711	801
21	86	163	233	295	352	404	451	493	532	683	782
22		84	160	229	291	347	399	445	488	653	761
23			83	158	226	287	343	394	441	621	740
24				82	156	223	284	339	390	587	716
25					81	154	220	281	336	550	691
26						80	152	218	278	511	664
27							79	150	215	469	635
28								78	149	423	604
29									77	375	571
30										323	535
31										267	497
32										207	455
33										143	411
34										74	364
35											314

LOAN PROGRESS CHART **7.5%**

Showing dollar balance remaining on a $1000 loan

ORIGINAL TERM IN YEARS 5	8	10	12	15	16	17	18	19	20	21	AGE OF LOAN
829	905	930	946	962	967	970	973	975	978	979	**1**
644	803	855	889	922	930	937	943	949	954	957	**2**
445	693	774	827	878	891	902	912	920	928	934	**3**
231	574	687	760	832	849	864	877	889	900	908	**4**
	446	592	688	781	804	824	840	856	869	881	**5**
	308	491	610	726	755	780	801	820	837	851	**6**
	160	382	527	668	702	732	758	781	802	819	**7**
		264	436	604	645	681	712	739	764	785	**8**
		137	339	536	584	626	662	694	723	748	**9**
			234	463	518	567	609	646	679	708	**10**
			122	383	447	503	551	593	632	665	**11**
				298	371	434	489	537	581	618	**12**
				206	288	359	422	477	525	568	**13**
				107	199	279	349	411	466	514	**14**
					103	193	272	341	402	456	**15**
						100	188	265	333	394	**16**
							97	183	259	326	**17**
								95	179	254	**18**
									93	175	**19**
										91	**20**

ORIGINAL TERM IN YEARS 22	23	24	25	26	27	28	29	30	35	40	AGE OF LOAN
982	983	985	986	986	988	989	990	990	994	996	**1**
962	964	968	971	973	976	978	980	981	987	991	**2**
940	945	950	954	957	962	965	968	970	980	987	**3**
917	923	931	936	941	947	951	955	958	972	981	**4**
892	901	910	917	924	931	936	942	946	964	976	**5**
865	876	888	897	905	914	921	927	932	955	970	**6**
836	849	863	875	885	895	903	912	918	945	964	**7**
805	821	837	851	863	875	885	895	903	935	957	**8**
771	790	809	825	839	853	865	876	886	924	949	**9**
734	757	779	797	814	830	844	857	868	912	941	**10**
695	721	746	767	786	805	821	836	848	899	932	**11**
653	683	711	735	757	778	796	813	827	885	923	**12**
607	641	673	700	725	749	769	788	805	870	913	**13**
558	596	632	663	691	717	740	762	780	854	902	**14**
505	548	588	623	654	683	709	733	754	837	890	**15**
448	496	540	579	614	647	676	702	726	818	878	**16**
387	440	489	532	571	607	640	669	695	798	864	**17**
321	380	434	482	525	565	601	633	662	776	850	**18**
249	315	374	427	475	519	559	595	627	752	834	**19**
172	245	310	369	422	470	514	553	589	727	817	**20**
89	169	241	306	364	417	465	509	548	700	798	**21**
	88	167	238	302	360	412	460	503	670	779	**22**
		86	164	234	298	356	408	456	639	757	**23**
			85	162	232	295	352	404	605	735	**24**
				84	160	229	292	349	568	710	**25**
					83	158	227	289	528	683	**26**
						82	157	225	485	654	**27**
							81	155	439	624	**28**
								81	390	590	**29**
									336	554	**30**
									279	516	**31**
									217	474	**32**
									150	429	**33**
									78	381	**34**
										328	**35**

8% LOAN PROGRESS CHART

Showing dollar balance remaining on a $1000 loan

AGE OF LOAN	5	8	10	12	15	16	17	18	19	20	21
	ORIGINAL TERM IN YEARS										
1	831	907	932	948	964	968	971	974	977	978	980
2	647	806	858	892	925	933	940	946	952	955	960
3	448	697	778	831	883	895	906	916	924	931	937
4	233	579	692	765	837	855	869	883	895	904	913
5		451	598	694	788	810	830	847	862	875	887
6		313	497	617	734	762	787	808	828	843	858
7		163	387	534	676	711	740	767	790	809	827
8			268	443	613	654	690	721	749	772	794
9			139	345	545	593	635	672	705	732	758
10				239	471	528	576	619	657	689	718
11				124	392	456	512	561	605	642	676
12					305	379	443	499	549	591	630
13					211	295	368	432	488	536	580
14					110	205	287	358	422	477	526
15						106	199	279	350	412	468
16							103	193	273	342	404
17								101	189	267	336
18									98	185	262
19										96	181
20											94

AGE OF LOAN	22	23	24	25	26	27	28	29	30	35	40
	ORIGINAL TERM IN YEARS										
1	982	984	986	987	989	989	990	991	992	994	996
2	964	967	970	973	976	977	980	981	983	988	992
3	943	948	953	958	962	964	968	970	973	982	988
4	921	928	935	941	946	950	955	959	962	975	983
5	897	906	915	923	930	935	941	946	951	968	979
6	871	883	894	903	912	919	927	933	939	960	973
7	843	857	871	882	893	901	911	918	925	951	967
8	813	830	845	859	872	882	893	902	910	941	961
9	780	800	818	835	849	862	874	885	895	931	954
10	745	768	789	808	825	839	854	866	878	920	947
11	706	733	757	779	798	815	832	846	859	908	939
12	664	695	722	747	770	789	808	824	839	895	931
13	619	654	685	713	739	761	782	800	817	881	921
14	570	609	645	676	705	730	754	774	794	865	911
15	517	561	601	636	668	697	723	746	768	849	900
16	460	509	553	593	629	661	690	716	740	831	889
17	398	452	502	546	586	621	654	684	711	811	876
18	330	391	446	495	540	579	616	648	678	790	862
19	257	325	386	440	490	533	574	610	643	768	847
20	178	253	320	381	435	484	528	568	605	743	831
21	93	175	250	316	376	430	479	523	564	716	813
22		91	173	246	313	372	426	475	519	687	794
23			90	171	243	309	368	422	471	656	774
24				89	169	241	306	365	419	622	751
25					88	167	238	303	362	585	727
26						87	165	236	301	545	701
27							86	164	234	502	673
28								85	162	456	642
29									84	405	609
30										350	573
31										291	534
32										227	492
33										157	446
34										82	396
35											343

LOAN PROGRESS CHART 8.5%

Showing dollar balance remaining on a $1000 loan

ORIGINAL TERM IN YEARS											
5	8	10	12	15	16	17	18	19	20	21	AGE OF LOAN
833	909	934	950	966	969	972	975	977	980	982	1
650	809	862	895	928	935	942	948	953	959	962	2
451	701	783	836	887	899	910	919	927	935	941	3
235	584	697	771	843	859	874	887	899	909	918	4
	456	604	701	794	816	836	853	868	881	893	5
	317	503	624	742	769	794	815	834	851	865	6
	165	393	541	684	718	748	774	797	818	835	7
		273	450	622	663	699	730	757	782	803	8
		142	352	554	602	645	682	714	743	768	9
			244	480	537	586	629	666	700	729	10
			127	400	465	522	571	615	654	687	11
				312	387	452	509	559	603	642	12
				217	302	376	441	498	548	592	13
				113	210	294	367	431	488	538	14
					109	204	287	359	423	479	15
						106	199	280	352	415	16
							104	195	275	346	17
								101	191	270	18
									100	187	19
										98	20

ORIGINAL TERM IN YEARS											
22	23	24	25	26	27	28	29	30	35	40	AGE OF LOAN
983	985	987	988	989	989	991	992	993	995	997	1
966	969	972	974	977	979	981	983	984	990	993	2
946	952	956	960	964	967	970	973	975	984	990	3
925	933	939	945	949	954	958	962	966	978	986	4
903	912	920	928	934	940	945	951	955	972	981	5
878	890	900	909	917	925	932	938	943	964	977	6
851	865	878	889	899	908	916	924	931	956	972	7
822	839	854	867	879	890	900	909	917	947	966	8
790	810	828	843	857	870	882	893	902	938	960	9
755	778	799	817	834	849	863	875	886	928	953	10
717	744	768	789	808	826	841	856	868	916	946	11
676	707	734	759	780	800	818	835	849	904	938	12
631	666	697	725	750	773	793	812	828	891	930	13
582	622	657	689	717	743	766	787	806	877	920	14
529	574	614	649	681	710	736	760	781	861	910	15
471	522	566	606	642	674	704	730	754	844	899	16
408	465	515	559	599	636	668	698	725	825	887	17
340	403	458	508	553	593	630	663	693	805	874	18
265	335	397	453	503	548	588	625	658	783	860	19
184	262	331	392	448	498	543	584	620	759	845	20
96	182	258	327	388	443	493	538	579	732	828	21
	95	179	255	323	384	439	489	534	704	810	22
		93	177	252	320	381	436	486	673	790	23
			92	175	250	317	378	433	639	768	24
				91	173	247	314	375	602	744	25
					90	172	246	312	563	719	26
						90	170	244	519	691	27
							89	169	472	660	28
								88	420	627	29
									364	591	30
									303	552	31
									237	509	32
									164	463	33
									86	412	34
										357	35

9% LOAN PROGRESS CHART

Showing dollar balance remaining on a $1000 loan

AGE OF LOAN	ORIGINAL TERM IN YEARS 5	8	10	12	15	16	17	18	19	20	21
1	834	911	936	951	967	971	974	976	979	982	984
2	653	813	865	898	931	939	946	951	956	961	965
3	454	706	787	840	891	904	914	923	931	939	945
4	237	589	703	777	848	866	880	892	904	914	923
5		461	610	707	800	824	843	859	874	887	899
6		321	509	631	749	778	802	822	842	858	873
7		168	398	548	692	727	757	783	806	826	844
8			277	457	630	672	708	739	767	791	812
9			145	358	563	612	655	691	724	752	778
10				249	488	546	596	639	677	710	740
11				130	407	475	532	582	626	665	699
12					319	396	462	519	570	614	653
13					222	310	385	451	509	559	604
14					116	216	302	376	442	499	550
15						113	210	294	368	434	491
16							110	205	288	362	426
17								107	201	283	356
18									105	197	278
19										103	194
20											101

AGE OF LOAN	ORIGINAL TERM IN YEARS 22	23	24	25	26	27	28	29	30	35	40
1	985	986	988	989	990	991	991	992	994	996	997
2	968	971	975	976	979	981	982	984	986	991	994
3	950	955	960	963	967	970	972	975	978	986	991
4	930	937	944	948	954	958	962	965	969	980	987
5	908	917	926	933	939	945	950	954	959	974	983
6	885	896	907	915	924	930	937	943	949	968	979
7	859	873	885	896	906	915	922	930	937	960	975
8	830	847	862	875	887	898	907	916	924	952	970
9	799	819	837	852	867	879	890	900	910	944	964
10	765	788	809	827	844	858	871	883	895	934	958
11	728	755	779	800	819	836	851	865	878	924	952
12	688	718	746	770	792	811	829	845	860	912	945
13	643	678	710	737	763	785	805	823	840	900	937
14	595	634	670	701	730	755	778	799	818	886	928
15	541	586	627	662	695	723	749	772	794	871	919
16	483	534	580	620	656	688	717	743	767	855	908
17	420	477	528	573	614	650	682	712	739	837	897
18	350	414	471	521	567	608	644	677	707	818	885
19	274	345	409	465	516	562	603	639	673	796	872
20	191	270	341	404	461	512	557	598	635	773	857
21	100	188	267	337	400	457	507	553	594	747	841
22		98	186	264	334	396	453	503	549	719	823
23			97	184	261	331	393	449	500	689	804
24				96	182	259	328	390	447	655	783
25					95	180	257	325	388	619	760
26						94	179	255	323	579	735
27							93	177	253	535	708
28								93	176	487	677
29									92	435	645
30										378	609
31										315	569
32										247	526
33										172	479
34										90	428
35											371

LOAN PROGRESS CHART 9.5%

Showing dollar balance remaining on a $1000 loan

ORIGINAL TERM IN YEARS											
5	8	10	12	15	16	17	18	19	20	21	AGE OF LOAN
836	912	937	953	968	972	975	978	980	982	984	1
656	816	868	901	933	941	948	954	959	963	966	2
457	710	792	844	895	907	918	927	935	942	947	3
239	593	708	782	853	870	885	898	909	918	926	4
	465	616	713	807	829	849	865	880	893	903	5
	325	515	638	756	784	809	830	848	864	878	6
	170	404	555	700	735	765	791	814	833	850	7
		282	464	639	681	717	748	775	799	820	8
		148	364	571	621	664	701	733	762	786	9
			254	497	555	606	649	687	720	749	10
			133	416	483	542	592	636	675	709	11
				326	404	471	530	581	625	664	12
				227	317	394	461	519	570	615	13
				119	221	309	385	452	510	561	14
					116	216	302	378	444	502	15
						113	211	296	371	437	16
							110	207	291	365	17
								108	203	286	18
									106	200	19
										105	20

ORIGINAL TERM IN YEARS											
22	23	24	25	26	27	28	29	30	35	40	AGE OF LOAN
985	987	989	990	991	991	993	993	994	997	998	1
970	973	976	979	981	982	984	986	987	993	995	2
953	958	962	966	970	972	975	977	980	988	992	3
934	941	947	953	957	961	965	968	972	983	989	4
913	923	931	938	944	949	954	958	963	978	986	5
891	902	912	921	929	935	942	947	953	972	982	6
866	880	892	903	913	920	929	935	942	965	978	7
838	855	870	883	895	904	914	922	930	958	974	8
808	828	846	861	875	886	898	908	917	950	969	9
775	798	819	837	853	867	880	892	902	941	963	10
739	766	789	810	829	845	861	874	886	931	957	11
699	730	757	781	803	822	839	855	869	921	951	12
655	690	721	749	774	796	816	834	850	909	944	13
606	647	682	714	742	767	790	810	829	896	936	14
553	599	639	675	708	736	762	785	805	882	927	15
495	546	592	633	669	701	730	756	780	866	918	16
430	489	540	586	627	663	696	725	752	849	907	17
360	425	483	535	581	621	658	691	721	830	896	18
282	355	420	478	530	575	617	654	687	810	883	19
197	279	351	416	474	525	571	613	650	787	869	20
103	194	276	348	412	470	521	567	609	762	854	21
	102	192	273	345	409	466	518	564	735	837	22
		101	190	270	342	406	463	515	705	818	23
			100	189	268	339	403	460	672	798	24
				99	187	266	337	400	635	776	25
					98	186	264	335	595	751	26
						97	184	263	551	724	27
							96	183	503	694	28
								96	450	662	29
									391	626	30
									327	587	31
									257	543	32
									179	496	33
									94	443	34
										386	35

10% LOAN PROGRESS CHART

Showing dollar balance remaining on a $1000 loan

AGE OF LOAN	ORIGINAL TERM IN YEARS 5	8	10	12	15	16	17	18	19	20	21
1	838	914	939	954	970	973	976	979	981	983	985
2	659	819	871	904	937	944	950	956	961	965	969
3	461	714	796	849	900	911	921	931	938	945	951
4	242	598	714	788	859	875	889	902	913	923	931
5		470	622	720	813	835	854	871	885	898	909
6		329	521	645	764	792	816	837	855	871	885
7		173	410	562	708	743	773	799	821	841	858
8			286	471	648	689	725	757	784	807	829
9			150	370	580	630	673	710	742	771	796
10				259	506	565	615	659	697	730	760
11				136	424	492	551	602	646	685	720
12					333	412	481	540	591	636	675
13					233	324	403	471	530	581	627
14					122	227	316	394	462	521	573
15						119	221	310	387	454	513
16							116	217	304	380	448
17								114	213	299	375
18									112	209	295
19										110	206
20											108

AGE OF LOAN	ORIGINAL TERM IN YEARS 22	23	24	25	26	27	28	29	30	35	40
1	987	988	989	991	992	992	993	993	995	997	998
2	972	975	977	980	982	984	986	986	989	993	996
3	956	961	964	969	972	975	977	979	982	989	993
4	938	945	950	956	960	964	968	971	974	985	991
5	919	927	935	942	948	953	958	961	966	980	988
6	897	908	917	926	934	940	946	951	957	975	984
7	873	886	898	909	918	926	934	940	947	969	981
8	846	863	877	890	901	911	920	928	936	962	977
9	817	836	853	869	882	894	905	914	923	955	972
10	785	808	827	846	861	875	888	899	910	946	967
11	749	776	799	820	838	855	870	882	895	937	962
12	710	740	767	792	813	832	849	864	878	928	956
13	666	701	732	761	785	807	826	843	860	917	950
14	618	658	694	726	754	779	801	821	839	905	942
15	565	611	651	688	720	748	774	796	817	891	934
16	506	558	604	646	682	714	743	768	792	876	925
17	441	500	552	599	640	677	709	738	765	860	916
18	370	436	495	548	594	635	672	704	735	842	905
19	291	365	432	491	543	589	631	667	701	822	893
20	203	287	362	428	486	539	585	626	664	800	880
21	107	201	284	358	424	483	535	581	624	776	865
22		105	199	282	355	421	479	531	579	749	849
23			104	197	279	352	418	476	529	720	831
24				103	195	277	350	415	474	687	812
25					102	194	275	348	413	651	790
26						102	192	273	346	611	766
27							101	191	272	567	740
28								100	190	518	710
29									100	464	678
30										405	642
31										339	603
32										267	560
33										186	511
34										98	458
35											400

LOAN PROGRESS CHART **10.5%**

Showing dollar balance remaining on a $1000 loan

ORIGINAL TERM IN YEARS											AGE
5	**8**	**10**	**12**	**15**	**16**	**17**	**18**	**19**	**20**	**21**	**OF LOAN**
839	916	940	956	971	974	977	980	982	984	987	**1**
661	822	874	907	938	946	953	958	963	967	971	**2**
463	718	800	853	903	915	925	934	941	948	954	**3**
244	603	718	793	863	880	894	907	917	926	935	**4**
	475	628	726	819	841	860	876	891	903	914	**5**
	333	527	652	770	798	822	843	861	877	891	**6**
	175	415	569	716	750	780	806	828	848	865	**7**
		291	478	655	698	734	765	792	815	837	**8**
		153	377	588	639	682	719	751	779	805	**9**
			264	514	574	625	668	707	740	769	**10**
			139	432	501	561	612	657	695	730	**11**
				340	421	490	550	601	646	686	**12**
				238	331	411	480	540	592	638	**13**
				125	232	324	403	472	531	584	**14**
					122	227	318	396	464	525	**15**
						119	223	312	390	458	**16**
							117	219	307	385	**17**
								115	215	303	**18**
									113	212	**19**
										112	**20**

ORIGINAL TERM IN YEARS											AGE
22	**23**	**24**	**25**	**26**	**27**	**28**	**29**	**30**	**35**	**40**	**OF LOAN**
988	989	990	991	992	993	994	994	995	997	999	**1**
975	977	979	981	984	985	987	988	990	994	997	**2**
959	964	967	971	974	976	980	981	984	990	995	**3**
943	949	954	959	963	967	971	973	977	986	992	**4**
924	932	939	946	952	956	962	965	969	982	990	**5**
903	914	922	931	939	945	951	955	961	977	987	**6**
880	893	904	915	924	932	939	945	951	971	984	**7**
855	870	884	896	908	917	927	933	941	965	980	**8**
826	845	861	876	890	901	912	920	929	959	976	**9**
795	817	836	854	870	883	896	906	916	951	972	**10**
760	786	808	829	848	863	878	890	902	943	967	**11**
721	751	778	802	823	841	859	873	886	934	962	**12**
678	713	743	771	796	817	837	853	869	923	956	**13**
630	670	706	737	765	790	813	831	849	912	949	**14**
577	623	663	700	732	760	786	807	828	899	942	**15**
518	571	617	658	694	726	756	780	804	885	933	**16**
453	512	565	611	653	689	722	751	777	870	924	**17**
380	448	507	560	607	648	686	718	747	853	914	**18**
299	376	443	503	556	602	645	681	715	834	903	**19**
210	296	372	439	499	552	599	640	678	812	890	**20**
110	207	293	369	436	495	549	595	638	789	877	**21**
	109	205	290	366	433	493	545	593	763	861	**22**
		108	204	288	363	430	489	543	734	844	**23**
			107	202	286	361	428	487	701	825	**24**
				106	201	285	359	426	666	804	**25**
					106	199	283	357	626	781	**26**
						105	198	282	582	755	**27**
							104	197	533	726	**28**
								104	478	694	**29**
									418	659	**30**
									351	619	**31**
									276	576	**32**
									194	527	**33**
									102	473	**34**
										414	**35**

11% LOAN PROGRESS CHART

Showing dollar balance remaining on a $1000 loan

AGE OF LOAN	ORIGINAL TERM IN YEARS										
	5	8	10	12	15	16	17	18	19	20	21
1	841	918	942	958	973	976	978	981	983	985	987
2	664	825	877	910	942	949	955	960	965	969	973
3	466	723	805	857	907	918	928	937	944	951	957
4	246	608	724	798	868	885	899	911	921	931	939
5		480	634	732	825	847	866	882	896	908	919
6		337	533	659	777	805	829	850	867	883	897
7		178	421	577	724	758	788	813	835	855	872
8			296	485	664	706	742	773	800	823	844
9			156	383	597	648	691	728	760	788	813
10				269	523	583	634	678	716	749	778
11				142	440	510	570	622	667	706	740
12					347	429	499	560	611	657	697
13					244	339	420	490	550	603	649
14					129	238	331	412	482	542	595
15						125	233	325	405	475	535
16							123	229	320	399	469
17								121	225	315	394
18									118	221	311
19										117	219
20											115

AGE OF LOAN	ORIGINAL TERM IN YEARS										
	22	23	24	25	26	27	28	29	30	35	40
1	988	990	991	992	993	994	994	995	995	997	998
2	976	979	981	983	985	987	988	990	990	995	997
3	961	966	970	973	976	979	980	983	985	991	995
4	945	952	957	962	966	970	973	976	978	988	993
5	928	936	943	949	955	960	964	969	971	984	990
6	908	919	928	936	943	949	954	960	964	979	988
7	886	899	910	920	929	937	943	950	955	975	985
8	861	877	891	903	914	923	931	939	945	969	982
9	834	853	869	884	896	908	917	927	934	963	978
10	803	826	845	862	877	891	902	914	922	956	974
11	769	795	818	838	856	872	885	899	909	948	970
12	731	762	788	812	832	851	867	882	894	940	965
13	689	724	755	782	806	827	846	863	877	930	960
14	641	682	717	749	776	801	822	842	858	920	954
15	588	635	676	711	743	771	796	819	838	908	947
16	529	582	629	670	706	739	767	793	814	895	939
17	463	524	577	624	665	702	734	763	788	880	931
18	390	459	519	572	619	661	698	731	759	863	921
19	308	386	454	515	568	616	657	695	727	845	911
20	216	305	382	451	511	565	612	654	691	824	899
21	114	214	302	379	448	508	561	609	651	802	886
22		113	212	299	376	445	505	559	606	776	871
23			112	210	297	374	442	503	556	747	855
24				111	209	295	372	440	500	716	837
25					110	207	294	370	438	680	816
26						109	206	292	368	641	794
27							109	205	291	596	769
28								108	204	547	740
29									108	492	709
30										431	674
31										363	634
32										286	591
33										201	542
34										106	488
35											427

LOAN PROGRESS CHART 11.5%

Showing dollar balance remaining on a $1000 loan

ORIGINAL TERM IN YEARS											AGE OF LOAN
5	**8**	**10**	**12**	**15**	**16**	**17**	**18**	**19**	**20**	**21**	
843	919	943	959	973	977	980	982	984	986	988	**1**
667	828	880	913	944	951	957	962	967	971	975	**2**
469	727	809	861	910	922	932	940	947	953	960	**3**
248	613	729	803	873	889	903	915	925	934	943	**4**
	485	639	738	831	853	871	887	901	913	924	**5**
	341	539	665	784	812	835	856	873	888	902	**6**
	180	426	583	731	766	795	820	842	861	878	**7**
		300	492	672	714	750	781	808	831	851	**8**
		159	389	605	656	700	737	769	797	821	**9**
			274	531	591	643	687	725	758	788	**10**
			145	448	519	580	632	676	715	750	**11**
				354	437	508	569	622	667	707	**12**
				249	346	429	499	560	613	660	**13**
				132	244	339	421	492	553	606	**14**
					129	239	333	414	485	546	**15**
						126	234	328	409	479	**16**
							124	231	323	404	**17**
								122	228	320	**18**
									120	225	**19**
										119	**20**

ORIGINAL TERM IN YEARS											AGE OF LOAN
22	**23**	**24**	**25**	**26**	**27**	**28**	**29**	**30**	**35**	**40**	
989	991	992	992	994	994	995	995	996	998	998	**1**
977	980	982	984	986	988	989	990	991	995	997	**2**
964	969	972	975	978	980	983	984	986	992	995	**3**
949	955	960	964	969	972	976	978	980	989	994	**4**
932	941	947	953	959	963	967	971	974	986	992	**5**
913	924	932	940	947	953	958	963	967	982	989	**6**
892	905	916	925	934	941	948	954	959	977	987	**7**
868	884	897	909	920	929	937	943	950	972	984	**8**
842	861	877	890	903	914	924	932	940	966	981	**9**
812	834	853	870	885	898	910	919	928	960	977	**10**
779	805	827	847	865	880	893	905	916	953	974	**11**
741	772	798	821	842	859	875	889	901	945	969	**12**
699	735	765	792	816	837	855	871	885	936	964	**13**
652	693	728	759	787	811	832	851	868	926	959	**14**
599	646	687	723	755	782	807	828	847	915	952	**15**
540	594	641	682	718	750	778	803	825	903	945	**16**
474	535	589	636	678	714	746	775	800	889	937	**17**
399	470	531	584	632	674	711	743	771	873	929	**18**
316	396	466	527	581	628	670	707	740	855	919	**19**
222	313	393	462	524	577	625	667	704	835	908	**20**
118	221	311	389	459	520	575	622	664	813	895	**21**
	117	219	308	387	457	518	572	620	788	881	**22**
		116	217	306	385	454	515	569	761	866	**23**
			115	216	304	383	452	513	729	848	**24**
				114	214	303	381	450	694	829	**25**
					113	213	301	379	655	807	**26**
						113	212	300	611	782	**27**
							112	211	561	754	**28**
								112	506	723	**29**
									444	689	**30**
									374	650	**31**
									296	606	**32**
									208	557	**33**
									110	502	**34**
										440	**35**

12% LOAN PROGRESS CHART

Showing dollar balance remaining on a $1000 loan

AGE OF LOAN	5	8	10	12	15	16	17	18	19	20	21
	ORIGINAL TERM IN YEARS										
1	845	921	945	960	974	978	981	983	985	987	989
2	670	831	883	915	946	953	959	964	969	973	976
3	472	731	813	865	914	925	935	943	950	956	962
4	250	617	734	808	877	894	907	919	929	938	946
5		489	645	744	836	858	876	892	905	917	928
6		345	545	672	790	818	842	862	879	894	907
7		183	432	590	738	773	802	828	849	868	884
8			305	499	680	722	758	789	815	838	858
9			162	395	614	665	708	746	777	805	829
10				279	539	601	652	696	734	767	796
11				148	456	528	589	641	686	725	759
12					361	446	517	579	632	677	717
13					255	353	437	509	570	624	670
14					135	249	347	430	501	563	617
15						132	245	341	423	495	557
16							130	240	336	418	490
17								127	237	331	414
18									125	234	328
19										124	231
20											123

AGE OF LOAN	22	23	24	25	26	27	28	29	30	35	40
	ORIGINAL TERM IN YEARS										
1	990	992	992	993	994	994	996	996	997	998	998
2	979	982	983	985	987	988	990	991	993	996	997
3	966	971	974	977	980	982	985	986	988	994	996
4	952	958	963	967	971	974	978	980	983	991	994
5	936	944	950	956	962	966	970	973	977	988	993
6	918	929	936	944	951	956	962	966	970	984	991
7	898	911	921	930	939	945	953	957	963	980	988
8	875	891	903	915	925	933	942	948	955	976	986
9	850	868	883	897	909	920	930	937	945	970	983
10	821	843	861	877	892	904	916	925	935	965	980
11	788	814	836	855	872	887	901	912	923	958	976
12	751	782	807	830	850	867	884	896	909	951	972
13	710	745	775	802	825	845	864	879	894	943	968
14	663	704	739	770	797	821	842	860	877	933	963
15	611	658	698	734	765	793	817	838	857	923	957
16	551	606	652	693	730	761	790	813	836	911	951
17	485	547	600	648	690	726	758	786	811	898	943
18	409	481	542	597	644	686	723	755	783	883	935
19	325	406	477	539	593	641	683	719	752	866	926
20	229	322	403	473	536	590	638	680	717	847	915
21	121	227	319	400	471	532	587	635	678	825	904
22		120	225	317	398	468	530	585	633	801	890
23			119	224	315	395	466	528	583	774	876
24				119	222	313	394	464	526	743	859
25					118	221	312	392	463	708	840
26						117	220	311	391	669	819
27							117	219	310	625	795
28								116	219	576	767
29									116	520	737
30										457	703
31										386	664
32										306	620
33										216	571
34										114	516
35											453

LOAN PROGRESS CHART **12.5%**

Showing dollar balance remaining on a $1000 loan

ORIGINAL TERM IN YEARS											AGE
5	**8**	**10**	**12**	**15**	**16**	**17**	**18**	**19**	**20**	**21**	**OF LOAN**
847	922	946	962	976	979	982	984	986	988	989	**1**
673	834	886	918	949	956	961	966	971	974	977	**2**
476	735	817	869	918	929	938	946	953	959	964	**3**
253	622	739	813	882	898	912	923	933	941	949	**4**
	494	651	750	842	864	882	897	910	922	931	**5**
	349	551	678	797	825	848	868	885	899	912	**6**
	186	438	597	746	780	810	834	856	874	890	**7**
		309	506	688	730	766	797	823	845	865	**8**
		164	402	622	674	717	754	786	813	836	**9**
			284	548	609	661	705	743	776	804	**10**
			151	464	536	598	651	696	734	768	**11**
				369	454	527	589	642	687	727	**12**
				261	361	446	518	580	634	680	**13**
				138	255	354	439	511	573	627	**14**
					135	250	349	433	505	567	**15**
						133	246	344	427	500	**16**
							131	243	340	423	**17**
								129	240	336	**18**
									128	238	**19**
										126	**20**

ORIGINAL TERM IN YEARS											AGE
22	**23**	**24**	**25**	**26**	**27**	**28**	**29**	**30**	**35**	**40**	**OF LOAN**
991	992	993	993	994	995	996	997	997	998	999	**1**
981	983	985	986	988	990	991	992	993	996	998	**2**
969	973	976	979	981	983	986	988	989	994	997	**3**
955	961	966	970	973	977	980	982	984	991	996	**4**
940	948	954	959	964	969	973	976	979	989	994	**5**
923	933	941	948	954	960	965	969	973	985	992	**6**
904	916	926	935	943	950	956	961	966	982	990	**7**
882	897	909	920	930	938	946	953	958	978	988	**8**
857	875	890	903	915	925	935	943	949	973	986	**9**
829	850	868	884	898	911	922	931	939	968	983	**10**
797	822	844	863	879	894	907	919	928	962	980	**11**
761	791	816	839	858	875	891	904	915	955	976	**12**
720	755	785	811	834	854	872	888	901	947	972	**13**
674	714	749	780	807	830	851	869	884	938	967	**14**
622	669	709	745	776	803	827	848	866	929	962	**15**
562	617	664	705	741	772	800	824	845	917	956	**16**
495	558	612	659	701	737	769	797	821	905	949	**17**
419	491	554	608	656	698	734	766	794	891	942	**18**
333	416	488	550	605	653	695	732	763	874	933	**19**
235	330	413	484	547	602	650	692	729	856	923	**20**
125	234	328	410	482	545	600	648	690	835	912	**21**
	124	232	326	408	480	543	598	646	812	900	**22**
		123	230	324	406	478	541	595	785	885	**23**
			122	229	323	404	476	539	755	869	**24**
				122	228	321	403	474	721	851	**25**
					121	227	320	401	682	830	**26**
						121	226	319	638	807	**27**
							120	226	589	781	**28**
								120	533	751	**29**
									469	717	**30**
									397	678	**31**
									315	635	**32**
									223	585	**33**
									118	529	**34**
										466	**35**

13% LOAN PROGRESS CHART

Showing dollar balance remaining on a $1000 loan

AGE OF LOAN	ORIGINAL TERM IN YEARS 5	8	10	12	15	16	17	18	19	20	21
1	848	924	948	963	977	980	983	985	987	989	990
2	675	837	888	921	950	957	963	968	972	976	979
3	479	739	821	873	920	931	941	948	956	962	966
4	255	627	744	818	886	902	916	926	937	945	952
5		499	656	756	847	869	887	901	915	926	935
6		354	557	685	803	830	854	873	890	905	917
7		188	443	604	753	787	816	841	862	880	896
8			314	513	695	738	774	804	830	853	871
9			167	408	630	682	725	762	794	821	844
10				289	556	618	670	714	752	785	813
11				154	472	545	607	660	705	744	777
12					375	462	536	598	651	697	736
13					266	368	454	527	590	644	690
14					142	261	362	447	521	584	638
15						139	256	356	442	515	578
16							136	252	352	437	510
17								134	249	348	432
18									133	247	344
19										131	244
20											130

AGE OF LOAN	ORIGINAL TERM IN YEARS 22	23	24	25	26	27	28	29	30	35	40
1	991	993	993	994	995	995	996	996	997	998	1000
2	982	984	986	988	989	990	992	993	994	997	999
3	971	975	977	981	983	985	987	988	990	995	998
4	958	964	968	972	975	978	981	983	986	992	997
5	944	951	957	963	967	971	975	978	981	990	995
6	927	937	945	952	958	963	968	971	975	987	994
7	909	921	931	940	947	953	959	964	969	984	992
8	888	903	915	926	935	943	950	956	962	980	990
9	864	882	896	910	921	930	939	947	953	976	988
10	837	858	875	892	905	917	927	936	944	971	985
11	806	831	852	871	887	901	913	924	933	965	982
12	770	800	825	847	866	883	898	910	921	959	979
13	730	765	794	821	843	862	880	894	908	952	975
14	684	725	759	790	816	839	859	877	892	944	971
15	632	679	720	755	786	813	836	856	874	935	966
16	573	628	675	716	751	782	810	833	854	924	961
17	505	569	623	671	712	748	780	807	831	912	955
18	429	502	565	620	668	709	745	777	805	899	948
19	341	426	498	562	617	665	707	743	775	883	940
20	242	339	423	496	559	614	662	704	741	865	930
21	129	240	337	420	493	556	612	660	702	845	920
22		128	239	335	418	491	554	610	658	823	908
23			127	237	333	416	489	552	608	797	894
24				126	236	332	415	487	551	767	879
25					126	235	330	413	486	733	861
26						125	234	329	412	695	842
27							125	233	328	652	819
28								124	233	602	793
29									124	545	764
30										481	730
31										408	692
32										325	649
33										230	599
34										123	543
35											479

LOAN PROGRESS CHART 13.5%

Showing dollar balance remaining on a $1000 loan

ORIGINAL TERM IN YEARS											AGE
5	8	10	12	15	16	17	18	19	20	21	OF LOAN
850	926	949	964	978	981	984	986	988	989	991	1
678	840	891	923	952	960	965	970	974	977	980	2
482	743	825	876	923	935	944	951	958	963	968	3
257	631	749	823	890	906	919	930	940	948	955	4
	504	662	761	852	874	891	906	919	930	939	5
	358	562	691	809	837	859	879	895	909	921	6
	191	449	611	760	794	823	847	868	886	901	7
		319	519	703	746	781	811	837	859	877	8
		170	414	638	690	733	770	801	828	851	9
			294	564	626	679	723	760	793	820	10
			157	479	554	616	669	714	752	785	11
				382	471	545	607	661	706	746	12
				272	375	463	537	600	654	700	13
				145	267	369	456	530	593	648	14
					142	262	364	451	525	588	15
						140	258	360	446	520	16
							138	255	356	442	17
								136	253	352	18
									135	250	19
										134	20

ORIGINAL TERM IN YEARS											AGE
22	23	24	25	26	27	28	29	30	35	40	OF LOAN
992	993	994	995	995	996	997	997	997	998	999	1
983	985	987	989	990	992	993	993	994	997	998	2
973	976	980	982	984	987	988	989	991	995	997	3
961	966	971	975	977	981	983	985	987	993	996	4
947	954	960	966	970	974	977	980	982	991	995	5
932	941	949	956	961	966	971	974	977	988	994	6
914	926	935	944	951	957	963	967	971	985	992	7
894	908	920	931	939	947	954	960	965	982	991	8
871	888	903	915	926	936	944	951	957	978	989	9
844	865	883	898	911	923	933	941	948	974	987	10
814	839	860	878	893	908	919	929	938	969	984	11
780	809	834	855	874	890	904	916	927	963	981	12
740	774	804	829	851	871	887	901	914	956	978	13
695	735	770	800	825	848	868	884	899	949	974	14
643	690	731	766	796	822	845	865	882	940	969	15
584	639	686	727	762	793	820	842	862	930	964	16
516	580	635	682	723	759	790	817	840	919	959	17
438	512	576	631	679	721	757	787	815	906	952	18
350	435	509	573	628	676	718	754	785	891	945	19
248	347	433	507	570	626	674	716	752	874	936	20
133	247	345	431	504	568	624	672	714	855	926	21
	132	245	344	428	502	566	622	670	833	915	22
		131	244	342	427	501	564	620	807	902	23
			130	243	341	425	499	563	778	887	24
				130	242	339	424	498	745	870	25
					129	241	338	423	708	851	26
						129	240	337	664	829	27
							128	240	615	804	28
								128	558	775	29
									493	742	30
									419	704	31
									334	661	32
									238	612	33
									127	556	34
										491	35

14% LOAN PROGRESS CHART

Showing dollar balance remaining on a $1000 loan

AGE OF LOAN	ORIGINAL TERM IN YEARS 5	8	10	12	15	16	17	18	19	20	21
1	852	927	951	965	979	982	984	986	989	991	992
2	681	843	894	926	955	961	966	971	976	979	982
3	485	747	829	880	927	938	946	954	960	966	971
4	259	636	754	827	895	910	923	933	943	951	958
5		508	667	767	858	879	896	910	923	934	943
6		362	568	697	815	842	865	884	900	914	926
7		193	454	618	767	801	829	853	874	892	906
8			323	526	711	753	788	818	844	866	884
9			173	420	646	698	741	778	809	836	858
10				299	572	635	687	731	769	801	828
11				160	487	562	625	678	723	762	794
12					390	479	553	616	670	716	755
13					277	383	471	546	610	664	710
14					148	272	377	465	540	604	658
15						146	268	372	460	535	598
16							143	265	367	455	530
17								141	262	364	451
18									140	259	361
19										139	257
20											137

AGE OF LOAN	ORIGINAL TERM IN YEARS 22	23	24	25	26	27	28	29	30	35	40
1	993	994	995	995	996	997	997	998	998	999	999
2	984	986	989	990	991	993	993	995	995	998	999
3	975	978	981	984	986	988	989	991	992	996	998
4	963	968	973	977	980	983	985	987	988	995	997
5	951	957	963	968	972	976	979	982	984	993	996
6	936	944	952	959	964	969	973	977	980	990	995
7	919	930	940	948	955	961	966	971	974	988	994
8	900	913	925	935	944	952	958	964	968	984	992
9	877	894	909	921	931	941	948	955	961	981	990
10	852	872	889	904	917	928	938	946	953	977	988
11	822	846	867	885	900	914	925	935	944	972	986
12	788	817	842	863	881	897	911	923	933	967	983
13	749	783	813	838	859	878	894	908	920	961	980
14	705	744	779	809	834	857	875	892	906	954	977
15	653	700	741	775	805	832	854	873	890	946	973
16	594	649	697	737	772	803	829	852	871	936	968
17	526	590	646	693	734	770	800	827	849	926	963
18	448	523	587	642	690	732	767	798	825	913	957
19	358	445	520	584	640	688	729	765	796	899	950
20	255	356	443	517	582	638	686	727	763	883	942
21	136	253	354	441	515	580	636	684	725	864	932
22		135	252	352	439	514	578	634	682	843	922
23			135	251	351	437	512	577	632	818	910
24				134	250	350	436	511	575	790	895
25					134	249	348	435	509	757	879
26						133	248	348	434	720	861
27							133	247	347	677	839
28								132	247	628	815
29									132	571	787
30										505	754
31										430	717
32										344	674
33										245	625
34										131	568
35											503

LOAN PROGRESS CHART **14.5%**

Showing dollar balance remaining on a $1000 loan

ORIGINAL TERM IN YEARS											
5	8	10	12	15	16	17	18	19	20	21	AGE OF LOAN
853	929	952	967	980	983	985	988	989	991	992	1
684	846	897	928	957	963	968	973	977	980	983	2
488	751	832	883	930	940	949	956	963	968	973	3
261	640	758	832	899	914	926	937	946	954	960	4
	513	673	772	863	883	900	915	927	937	946	5
	366	574	704	822	848	870	889	905	918	930	6
	196	460	624	774	807	835	859	880	897	911	7
		328	533	718	760	795	825	850	871	890	8
		176	427	654	706	749	785	816	842	865	9
			304	581	643	695	740	777	809	836	10
			163	495	570	633	687	732	770	802	11
				397	487	562	626	679	725	764	12
				283	390	479	555	619	673	719	13
				152	278	384	474	549	613	668	14
					149	274	379	468	544	608	15
						147	271	375	464	540	16
							145	268	372	461	17
								144	265	369	18
									142	263	19
										141	20

ORIGINAL TERM IN YEARS											
22	23	24	25	26	27	28	29	30	35	40	AGE OF LOAN
993	994	995	996	997	997	997	998	998	999	999	1
985	987	989	991	992	993	994	995	996	998	999	2
976	980	983	985	987	989	990	992	993	996	998	3
966	971	975	978	982	984	986	988	990	995	997	4
954	960	966	970	975	978	981	984	986	993	997	5
940	948	956	961	967	972	975	979	982	991	996	6
923	934	944	951	958	964	969	973	977	989	994	7
905	918	930	939	948	955	961	966	971	986	993	8
883	900	914	925	936	945	952	959	965	983	992	9
858	878	896	910	922	933	942	950	957	979	990	10
830	854	874	891	907	919	930	940	948	975	988	11
797	825	850	870	888	904	916	928	938	970	985	12
758	792	821	846	867	885	901	914	926	964	983	13
714	754	788	817	843	864	883	899	913	958	979	14
663	710	751	785	815	840	862	880	897	950	976	15
604	659	707	747	782	812	837	860	879	941	971	16
536	601	656	703	745	780	809	835	858	931	967	17
457	533	598	653	701	742	777	807	834	920	961	18
366	455	530	595	651	699	740	775	806	906	954	19
261	364	453	528	593	649	697	738	774	891	947	20
140	260	363	450	526	591	647	695	737	873	938	21
	139	259	361	449	524	589	645	694	852	928	22
		139	257	360	447	523	588	644	828	916	23
			138	257	359	446	522	587	800	903	24
				138	256	357	445	521	768	888	25
					137	255	356	444	731	870	26
						137	254	356	689	849	27
							136	254	639	825	28
								136	583	798	29
									517	766	30
									441	729	31
									353	686	32
									252	637	33
									135	581	34
										515	35

15% LOAN PROGRESS CHART

Showing dollar balance remaining on a $1000 loan

AGE OF LOAN	ORIGINAL TERM IN YEARS										
	5	8	10	12	15	16	17	18	19	20	21
1	855	930	953	968	981	984	986	988	990	992	993
2	686	849	899	930	959	965	970	975	978	982	984
3	491	755	836	887	933	943	952	959	965	970	974
4	264	645	763	836	903	917	930	940	949	957	963
5		518	678	778	868	888	905	919	931	941	949
6		370	580	710	827	854	876	894	909	923	934
7		199	465	631	780	814	842	865	885	902	916
8			333	539	726	767	802	832	856	877	895
9			179	433	662	714	757	793	823	849	871
10				310	588	651	704	748	785	816	843
11				166	503	579	642	695	740	778	810
12					404	495	571	635	688	734	772
13					289	397	488	564	628	682	728
14					155	284	392	482	558	623	677
15						153	280	387	477	554	618
16							150	277	383	473	549
17								149	274	380	470
18									147	272	377
19										146	270
20											145

AGE OF LOAN	ORIGINAL TERM IN YEARS										
	22	23	24	25	26	27	28	29	30	35	40
1	994	995	995	996	996	997	998	998	998	999	999
2	986	988	990	992	992	994	995	995	996	998	999
3	978	981	984	986	988	990	992	993	993	997	998
4	968	973	977	980	982	985	988	989	990	996	998
5	957	963	968	973	976	980	983	985	987	994	997
6	944	952	958	964	969	974	978	981	983	992	996
7	928	938	947	955	961	967	972	975	978	990	995
8	910	923	934	944	951	958	964	969	973	988	994
9	890	905	919	930	940	949	956	962	967	985	993
10	865	885	901	915	927	938	947	954	960	981	991
11	838	861	881	898	912	925	935	944	952	978	989
12	805	833	857	877	894	910	922	933	942	973	987
13	768	801	829	854	874	892	907	920	931	968	984
14	724	763	797	826	850	872	890	905	918	962	982
15	673	720	760	794	823	848	870	888	903	955	978
16	614	670	717	757	791	821	846	868	886	946	974
17	546	611	666	714	754	789	819	844	866	937	970
18	467	543	608	664	711	752	787	817	842	926	965
19	375	464	541	606	661	709	750	785	815	913	959
20	268	373	462	538	603	660	708	749	783	898	952
21	144	266	371	460	536	602	658	706	747	881	943
22		143	265	370	458	535	601	657	704	861	934
23			142	264	368	457	534	599	655	838	923
24				142	263	367	456	533	598	810	910
25					141	263	366	455	531	779	895
26						141	262	365	454	743	878
27							141	261	365	700	858
28								140	261	651	835
29									140	594	808
30										528	777
31										452	740
32										363	698
33										259	649
34										139	593
35											527

LOAN PROGRESS CHART 15.5%

Showing dollar balance remaining on a $1000 loan

ORIGINAL TERM IN YEARS											AGE
5	8	10	12	15	16	17	18	19	20	21	OF LOAN
856	932	955	969	982	985	987	989	991	992	993	1
689	852	902	932	960	967	971	976	980	983	985	2
494	758	840	890	935	946	954	961	967	972	976	3
266	649	768	841	906	921	933	943	952	959	965	4
	522	683	783	872	892	909	923	934	944	953	5
	374	585	716	833	859	880	899	914	927	938	6
	202	471	637	786	820	847	871	890	907	921	7
		337	546	732	774	809	838	863	883	901	8
		182	439	670	721	764	800	830	856	877	9
			315	596	659	712	756	793	824	850	10
			169	511	587	650	704	749	786	818	11
				411	503	579	643	697	742	781	12
				294	404	496	573	637	692	738	13
				158	290	399	491	567	632	687	14
					156	286	395	486	563	628	15
						154	283	391	482	559	16
							152	280	388	479	17
								151	278	385	18
									150	276	19
										149	20

ORIGINAL TERM IN YEARS											AGE
22	23	24	25	26	27	28	29	30	35	40	OF LOAN
994	995	996	997	997	997	998	998	999	1000	999	1
988	989	991	992	994	994	995	996	997	999	999	2
980	982	985	987	989	991	992	993	995	998	998	3
970	974	979	982	984	986	988	990	992	996	998	4
960	965	971	975	979	981	984	987	989	995	997	5
947	955	962	967	972	976	979	983	985	993	996	6
932	942	951	958	964	969	973	978	981	991	996	7
915	927	939	947	955	961	967	972	976	989	995	8
895	910	924	935	945	952	959	965	971	987	993	9
872	891	907	921	932	942	950	958	964	984	992	10
845	867	887	904	918	929	940	949	956	980	990	11
813	840	864	884	901	915	927	938	947	976	988	12
776	809	837	861	881	898	913	926	937	971	986	13
733	772	806	834	858	879	896	911	924	965	984	14
683	729	769	803	832	856	877	895	910	959	980	15
624	679	727	766	800	829	854	875	893	951	977	16
556	621	677	724	764	798	827	852	874	942	973	17
476	553	619	674	722	762	796	826	851	932	968	18
383	474	551	616	672	719	760	795	825	919	962	19
274	381	472	549	614	670	718	759	794	905	956	20
148	273	380	470	547	613	669	717	758	889	948	21
	147	272	378	469	545	611	668	716	869	939	22
		146	271	377	467	544	610	667	847	929	23
			146	270	376	466	543	609	820	917	24
				145	269	375	465	543	789	902	25
					145	269	374	465	754	886	26
						145	268	374	712	867	27
							144	268	663	844	28
								144	606	818	29
									540	787	30
									462	751	31
									372	710	32
									266	661	33
									143	604	34
										538	35

16%

LOAN PROGRESS CHART

Showing dollar balance remaining on a $1000 loan

AGE OF LOAN	ORIGINAL TERM IN YEARS 5	8	10	12	15	16	17	18	19	20	21
1	858	933	956	970	983	985	987	989	991	992	993
2	692	854	904	935	962	968	973	977	981	984	986
3	497	762	843	894	938	948	956	963	969	973	977
4	268	654	772	845	910	924	936	946	955	961	967
5		527	689	788	877	896	913	926	938	947	955
6		378	591	722	838	864	885	903	918	931	941
7		204	476	644	793	826	853	876	895	911	925
8			342	553	740	781	815	844	868	888	905
9			185	445	677	729	771	807	837	862	883
10				320	604	667	719	763	800	830	856
11				173	518	595	659	712	757	794	825
12					418	511	588	652	706	751	789
13					300	412	504	581	646	700	746
14					162	296	406	499	577	641	696
15						159	292	402	495	572	637
16							157	289	399	491	568
17								156	286	396	488
18									155	284	393
19										153	282
20											152

AGE OF LOAN	ORIGINAL TERM IN YEARS 22	23	24	25	26	27	28	29	30	35	40
1	995	996	996	997	997	998	998	998	999	999	1000
2	988	990	991	993	994	995	996	996	997	998	1000
3	981	984	986	988	990	992	993	994	995	997	999
4	972	977	980	983	985	988	989	991	993	996	999
5	962	968	972	977	980	983	986	988	990	995	998
6	950	958	964	970	974	978	981	984	987	994	997
7	936	946	954	961	967	972	976	980	983	992	997
8	920	932	942	951	958	965	970	974	978	990	996
9	901	916	928	939	948	956	962	968	973	987	995
10	878	897	912	925	936	946	954	961	967	985	993
11	852	874	893	909	923	934	944	952	960	981	992
12	821	848	870	890	906	921	932	942	951	978	990
13	785	817	844	868	888	904	918	931	941	973	988
14	742	781	814	842	865	886	902	917	929	968	986
15	692	739	778	811	839	863	884	901	916	962	983
16	634	689	736	775	809	838	862	882	900	955	980
17	565	631	686	733	773	807	836	860	881	946	976
18	485	563	628	684	731	771	805	834	859	936	972
19	391	483	560	627	682	730	770	804	833	925	966
20	281	389	481	559	625	681	728	769	803	911	960
21	152	280	388	480	557	623	679	727	767	895	953
22		151	278	387	478	556	622	678	726	876	945
23			150	278	385	477	555	621	677	855	935
24				150	277	385	476	554	620	829	923
25					149	276	384	475	553	799	910
26						149	276	383	475	763	894
27							149	275	383	722	875
28								148	275	674	853
29									148	617	828
30										550	798
31										472	762
32										381	721
33										273	673
34										147	616
35											549

LOAN PROGRESS CHART **16.5%**

Showing dollar balance remaining on a $1000 loan

ORIGINAL TERM IN YEARS											AGE
5	8	10	12	15	16	17	18	19	20	21	OF LOAN
860	934	957	971	984	986	988	990	992	993	994	1
694	857	906	937	964	970	974	979	982	985	987	2
500	766	847	897	941	950	958	965	971	975	979	3
270	658	777	849	913	928	939	949	957	964	969	4
	532	694	794	881	901	916	930	941	950	958	5
	383	597	728	844	869	890	908	922	934	944	6
	207	482	650	799	832	859	881	900	916	929	7
		347	559	746	788	822	850	874	894	910	8
		188	452	685	736	778	814	843	868	888	9
			325	612	675	727	771	807	837	862	10
			176	526	603	667	720	764	801	832	11
				425	519	596	661	714	759	796	12
				306	419	512	590	655	709	754	13
				165	301	414	507	585	650	705	14
					163	298	410	503	581	646	15
						161	295	406	500	578	16
							160	292	404	497	17
								158	290	401	18
									157	289	19
										156	20

ORIGINAL TERM IN YEARS											AGE
22	23	24	25	26	27	28	29	30	35	40	OF LOAN
995	995	996	997	998	998	998	998	999	999	1000	1
989	991	992	993	995	996	996	997	997	998	999	2
982	985	987	989	991	993	993	994	995	998	999	3
974	978	981	984	987	989	990	992	993	997	999	4
964	970	974	978	982	985	987	989	991	996	998	5
953	960	966	972	976	980	983	985	988	994	998	6
940	949	957	963	969	974	978	981	984	993	997	7
924	936	946	954	961	967	972	976	980	991	996	8
906	920	932	943	952	959	965	971	975	989	995	9
884	902	917	930	941	950	957	964	969	986	994	10
858	880	899	914	928	939	948	956	963	983	993	11
828	855	877	896	912	926	937	947	955	980	991	12
793	825	852	874	894	910	924	935	945	976	989	13
751	789	822	849	873	892	908	922	934	971	987	14
701	747	786	819	847	871	890	907	921	965	985	15
643	698	745	784	817	845	869	889	906	958	982	16
575	640	696	743	782	816	844	868	888	950	978	17
494	572	638	694	741	781	814	842	866	941	974	18
399	492	570	636	692	739	779	813	841	930	969	19
287	397	490	569	635	691	738	778	812	917	964	20
155	286	396	489	567	634	689	737	777	902	957	21
	155	285	395	488	566	632	688	736	884	949	22
		154	284	394	487	565	631	687	863	940	23
			154	284	393	486	564	630	838	929	24
				153	283	392	485	563	808	916	25
					153	282	392	484	773	900	26
						153	282	391	733	882	27
							152	281	684	861	28
								152	628	836	29
									561	807	30
									482	772	31
									389	732	32
									280	683	33
									152	627	34
										560	35

17% LOAN PROGRESS CHART

Showing dollar balance remaining on a $1000 loan

AGE OF LOAN	ORIGINAL TERM IN YEARS 5	8	10	12	15	16	17	18	19	20	21
1	861	936	958	972	984	987	989	991	992	994	995
2	697	859	909	939	965	971	976	980	983	986	988
3	503	769	850	900	943	953	960	967	972	977	981
4	272	663	781	853	917	931	942	952	959	966	971
5		536	699	799	886	905	920	933	944	953	961
6		387	602	734	849	874	895	912	926	938	948
7		210	487	657	805	838	864	886	904	920	933
8			352	566	753	794	828	856	879	899	915
9			191	458	692	743	786	820	849	874	894
10				330	619	683	735	778	814	844	869
11				179	533	611	675	728	772	809	839
12					432	526	604	669	722	767	804
13					311	426	521	599	663	718	763
14					169	307	421	516	594	659	714
15						167	304	417	512	590	656
16							165	301	414	508	587
17								163	299	411	506
18									162	297	409
19										161	295
20											160

AGE OF LOAN	ORIGINAL TERM IN YEARS 22	23	24	25	26	27	28	29	30	35	40
1	995	996	997	997	997	998	998	998	999	1000	1000
2	990	991	993	994	995	996	996	997	998	999	999
3	983	986	988	990	991	993	994	995	996	999	999
4	976	979	983	986	988	990	991	992	994	998	999
5	967	972	977	980	983	986	988	990	992	997	998
6	956	963	969	974	978	982	984	987	989	996	998
7	943	952	960	966	971	976	980	983	986	994	997
8	928	940	950	957	964	970	974	978	982	993	996
9	911	925	937	947	955	962	968	973	978	991	996
10	890	907	922	934	944	953	960	967	972	988	995
11	865	886	904	920	932	943	951	959	966	986	993
12	835	861	884	902	917	930	941	950	958	982	992
13	801	832	859	881	899	916	929	940	949	979	990
14	759	797	830	857	879	898	914	927	939	974	989
15	711	756	795	827	854	877	896	912	927	969	986
16	653	708	754	793	825	853	876	895	912	962	984
17	584	650	706	752	791	824	851	874	894	955	980
18	503	582	648	704	750	790	822	850	874	946	977
19	407	501	580	646	702	749	788	821	849	936	972
20	294	406	500	579	645	701	747	787	820	923	967
21	159	292	404	498	577	644	699	746	786	909	960
22		159	292	403	497	576	642	698	746	891	953
23			158	291	402	496	575	641	698	871	944
24				158	290	402	495	574	641	846	934
25					157	290	401	495	574	818	921
26						157	289	400	494	784	907
27							157	289	400	743	889
28								156	288	695	869
29									156	639	845
30										572	816
31										492	782
32										399	742
33										287	694
34										156	637
35											571

LOAN PROGRESS CHART **17.5%**

Showing dollar balance remaining on a $1000 loan

ORIGINAL TERM IN YEARS											AGE OF LOAN
5	**8**	**10**	**12**	**15**	**16**	**17**	**18**	**19**	**20**	**21**	
863	937	960	973	985	988	990	991	993	994	995	**1**
700	862	911	941	967	973	977	981	984	987	989	**2**
506	773	854	903	946	955	963	969	974	978	982	**3**
275	667	786	857	920	934	945	954	962	968	973	**4**
	541	705	803	890	909	924	936	947	956	963	**5**
	391	608	739	854	879	899	916	930	941	951	**6**
	212	493	663	811	843	870	891	909	924	936	**7**
		356	572	760	801	834	862	885	904	919	**8**
		194	464	699	750	792	827	855	879	899	**9**
			335	627	690	743	785	821	850	875	**10**
			182	541	619	683	736	780	816	846	**11**
				439	534	613	677	730	775	812	**12**
				317	433	529	607	672	726	771	**13**
				172	313	429	524	603	668	722	**14**
					170	310	425	520	599	665	**15**
						168	307	422	517	596	**16**
							167	305	419	514	**17**
								166	303	417	**18**
									165	301	**19**
										164	**20**

ORIGINAL TERM IN YEARS											AGE OF LOAN
22	**23**	**24**	**25**	**26**	**27**	**28**	**29**	**30**	**35**	**40**	
996	997	997	998	998	998	999	999	999	1000	1000	**1**
991	992	993	995	995	996	997	997	998	999	1000	**2**
985	987	989	991	992	994	995	996	996	999	1000	**3**
978	981	984	987	989	991	992	994	994	998	999	**4**
969	974	978	982	984	987	989	991	992	997	999	**5**
959	966	971	976	979	983	986	988	990	996	998	**6**
947	956	963	969	974	978	982	985	987	995	998	**7**
933	944	953	961	966	972	977	980	983	993	997	**8**
916	929	941	951	958	965	971	975	979	992	997	**9**
895	912	926	939	948	957	964	970	974	989	996	**10**
871	892	909	924	936	947	955	962	968	987	995	**11**
842	868	889	908	922	935	945	954	961	984	993	**12**
808	840	865	887	905	921	934	944	953	981	992	**13**
768	806	837	864	885	904	919	932	943	976	990	**14**
719	765	803	835	861	884	903	918	931	971	988	**15**
662	717	763	801	833	860	883	901	917	966	986	**16**
593	660	715	761	799	832	859	881	900	959	983	**17**
512	592	657	713	759	798	831	858	880	950	979	**18**
415	510	590	656	711	758	797	829	857	940	975	**19**
300	414	509	588	654	710	757	796	828	929	970	**20**
163	299	413	508	587	653	709	756	795	914	964	**21**
	163	298	412	506	586	653	708	755	898	957	**22**
		162	297	411	506	585	652	707	878	949	**23**
			162	297	410	505	584	651	854	939	**24**
				161	296	409	504	584	826	927	**25**
					161	296	409	504	793	913	**26**
						161	295	408	753	897	**27**
							161	295	705	877	**28**
								160	649	853	**29**
									582	825	**30**
									502	792	**31**
									407	752	**32**
									294	704	**33**
									160	648	**34**
										581	**35**

18% LOAN PROGRESS CHART

Showing dollar balance remaining on a $1000 loan

AGE OF LOAN	ORIGINAL TERM IN YEARS										
	5	8	10	12	15	16	17	18	19	20	21
1	864	938	961	974	985	988	990	992	993	994	995
2	702	865	914	943	968	974	979	982	985	987	990
3	509	777	857	906	948	957	965	971	975	979	983
4	277	671	790	861	923	936	948	957	964	970	975
5		545	710	808	894	912	928	940	950	958	965
6		395	613	745	858	883	903	920	933	944	954
7		215	498	669	816	848	875	896	913	928	940
8			361	578	766	807	840	867	890	908	924
9			197	470	706	757	799	833	861	885	904
10				340	634	698	750	792	827	856	881
11				185	548	627	691	744	787	823	852
12					445	542	621	685	738	782	819
13					322	440	537	616	680	734	779
14					176	319	436	532	611	677	731
15						174	316	432	528	608	673
16							172	313	429	525	605
17								170	311	427	523
18									169	309	425
19										168	308
20											168

AGE OF LOAN	ORIGINAL TERM IN YEARS										
	22	23	24	25	26	27	28	29	30	35	40
1	996	997	997	997	998	998	999	999	999	1000	1000
2	991	993	994	995	996	996	997	997	998	999	1000
3	986	988	990	991	993	994	995	996	997	999	999
4	979	983	986	988	990	991	993	994	995	998	999
5	971	976	980	983	986	988	990	992	993	997	999
6	962	968	973	977	982	984	987	989	991	996	998
7	950	958	965	971	976	980	983	986	988	995	998
8	936	947	956	963	969	974	978	982	985	994	997
9	920	933	944	953	962	968	973	977	981	992	997
10	900	917	931	942	952	960	966	972	976	990	996
11	877	898	915	928	941	950	958	965	971	988	995
12	849	874	895	912	927	939	949	957	964	986	994
13	816	846	872	893	911	925	938	948	956	982	993
14	776	813	844	870	892	909	924	936	947	978	991
15	728	773	811	842	868	890	908	923	936	974	989
16	671	726	771	809	841	867	889	907	922	968	987
17	603	669	724	769	808	839	866	888	906	962	984
18	521	601	667	722	768	806	838	864	887	954	981
19	423	519	599	665	721	767	805	837	864	945	977
20	306	422	518	597	664	719	766	804	836	933	973
21	167	305	421	516	597	663	718	765	803	920	967
22		166	305	420	516	595	662	717	764	904	961
23			166	304	419	515	595	661	717	885	953
24				165	303	418	514	594	661	862	943
25					165	303	418	513	593	834	932
26						165	302	417	513	801	919
27							165	302	417	762	903
28								164	302	715	883
29									164	659	860
30										592	833
31										512	800
32										416	761
33										301	714
34										164	658
35											591

LOAN PROGRESS CHART **18.5%**

Showing dollar balance remaining on a $1000 loan

ORIGINAL TERM IN YEARS											AGE OF LOAN
5	**8**	**10**	**12**	**15**	**16**	**17**	**18**	**19**	**20**	**21**	
866	940	962	975	987	989	991	992	993	995	996	**1**
705	867	916	945	970	975	980	983	986	988	990	**2**
512	780	861	909	950	959	966	972	977	981	984	**3**
279	676	794	865	927	939	950	958	966	972	977	**4**
	550	715	813	898	916	931	942	952	961	967	**5**
	399	619	750	864	888	907	923	937	948	957	**6**
	218	504	675	822	854	879	900	917	932	943	**7**
		366	585	773	813	846	872	894	913	928	**8**
		200	476	713	764	805	839	867	890	909	**9**
			345	642	705	757	799	834	863	886	**10**
			189	556	634	699	751	794	830	859	**11**
				452	549	628	693	746	790	826	**12**
				328	447	544	623	689	742	786	**13**
				179	325	443	540	619	685	739	**14**
					177	322	440	536	616	682	**15**
						175	319	437	534	614	**16**
							174	317	435	531	**17**
								173	315	433	**18**
									172	314	**19**
										171	**20**

ORIGINAL TERM IN YEARS											AGE OF LOAN
22	**23**	**24**	**25**	**26**	**27**	**28**	**29**	**30**	**35**	**40**	
996	997	998	998	998	999	999	999	999	1000	1000	**1**
992	994	995	995	996	997	998	998	998	999	1000	**2**
987	989	991	992	994	995	996	996	997	999	1000	**3**
980	984	987	989	991	993	994	995	996	998	1000	**4**
973	978	982	984	987	990	991	992	994	997	999	**5**
964	970	975	979	983	986	988	990	992	997	999	**6**
953	961	968	973	978	982	985	987	989	996	999	**7**
940	950	959	965	972	977	980	983	986	994	998	**8**
924	937	948	956	964	970	975	979	983	993	997	**9**
905	922	935	946	955	963	969	974	979	991	997	**10**
883	903	919	933	944	954	962	968	973	989	996	**11**
855	880	901	917	931	943	953	960	967	987	995	**12**
823	853	878	898	916	930	942	952	960	984	994	**13**
783	821	851	876	897	915	929	941	951	980	992	**14**
736	781	819	849	875	896	914	928	940	976	991	**15**
679	734	779	816	848	874	895	912	927	971	989	**16**
611	678	732	777	815	847	873	894	912	965	986	**17**
529	610	676	731	776	814	846	871	893	957	983	**18**
431	528	608	674	730	775	813	845	871	948	980	**19**
313	430	527	607	673	729	774	812	844	938	975	**20**
171	312	429	525	606	673	728	773	812	925	970	**21**
	170	311	428	525	605	672	727	773	909	964	**22**
		170	310	427	524	604	671	726	891	957	**23**
			169	310	427	523	604	670	869	948	**24**
				169	310	426	523	603	842	937	**25**
					169	309	426	522	810	924	**26**
						169	309	425	771	909	**27**
							169	309	724	890	**28**
								168	669	868	**29**
									602	841	**30**
									521	809	**31**
									424	770	**32**
									308	724	**33**
									168	668	**34**
										601	**35**

19% LOAN PROGRESS CHART

Showing dollar balance remaining on a $1000 loan

AGE OF LOAN	5	8	10	12	15	16	17	18	19	20	21
	ORIGINAL TERM IN YEARS										
1	868	941	963	976	987	989	991	993	994	995	996
2	708	870	918	947	971	976	980	984	987	989	991
3	515	784	864	911	952	961	968	973	978	982	985
4	281	680	799	869	929	942	952	961	968	974	978
5		555	720	818	902	919	934	945	955	963	969
6		403	624	756	868	892	911	927	940	951	959
7		221	509	681	828	859	884	904	922	936	947
8			370	591	779	819	851	877	899	917	931
9			203	482	720	771	811	845	873	895	913
10				351	649	712	764	806	840	868	891
11				192	563	642	706	758	801	836	865
12					459	557	636	701	754	797	833
13					334	454	552	631	697	750	794
14					183	330	450	548	628	693	747
15						181	327	447	545	625	690
16							179	325	444	542	622
17								178	323	442	540
18									177	322	440
19										176	320
20											175

AGE OF LOAN	22	23	24	25	26	27	28	29	30	35	40
	ORIGINAL TERM IN YEARS										
1	997	997	998	998	998	999	999	999	999	999	1000
2	993	994	995	996	996	997	997	998	998	999	1000
3	988	990	992	993	994	995	996	997	997	999	999
4	982	985	988	990	991	993	994	995	996	998	999
5	975	979	983	986	988	990	992	993	995	998	999
6	966	972	977	981	984	987	989	991	993	997	999
7	956	963	970	975	979	983	986	988	990	996	998
8	944	953	962	968	974	978	982	985	988	995	998
9	929	941	951	960	966	972	977	981	984	994	998
10	910	926	939	950	958	965	971	976	980	992	997
11	888	908	924	937	948	957	964	970	976	990	996
12	862	886	906	922	935	947	956	963	970	988	995
13	830	859	884	904	920	934	945	955	963	985	994
14	791	827	858	882	902	919	933	945	954	982	993
15	745	789	826	856	881	901	918	932	944	978	991
16	688	742	787	824	854	880	900	918	932	973	990
17	620	686	741	786	823	853	879	900	917	967	987
18	538	618	685	740	784	822	852	878	899	960	985
19	439	536	617	684	738	783	821	852	877	952	981
20	319	438	535	616	682	737	782	820	851	942	977
21	175	318	437	534	615	681	736	782	820	930	973
22		174	318	436	533	614	681	736	781	915	967
23			174	317	435	533	613	680	735	897	960
24				173	316	435	532	613	680	875	951
25					173	316	434	532	613	849	941
26						173	316	434	531	818	929
27							173	315	433	779	914
28								173	315	734	896
29									172	678	875
30										611	849
31										530	817
32										432	779
33										314	733
34										172	678
35											611

LOAN PROGRESS CHART **19.5%**

Showing dollar balance remaining on a $1000 loan

ORIGINAL TERM IN YEARS: 5	8	10	12	15	16	17	18	19	20	21	AGE OF LOAN
869	942	964	977	987	990	992	993	994	996	996	1
710	872	920	949	972	978	982	985	988	990	991	2
518	787	867	914	954	963	970	975	979	983	986	3
284	684	803	873	932	945	955	963	969	975	979	4
	559	725	823	905	923	937	949	957	965	971	5
	407	630	761	872	896	915	931	943	953	961	6
	223	515	687	833	864	889	909	925	939	949	7
		375	597	785	825	857	883	904	921	935	8
		206	488	726	777	818	851	878	900	917	9
			356	656	719	771	812	846	874	896	10
			195	570	649	713	766	808	842	870	11
				466	564	644	709	761	804	839	12
				339	461	560	640	704	758	801	13
				186	336	457	556	636	701	755	14
					184	333	454	553	633	699	15
						183	331	452	550	631	16
							182	329	450	548	17
								180	328	448	18
									180	326	19
										179	20

ORIGINAL TERM IN YEARS: 22	23	24	25	26	27	28	29	30	35	40	AGE OF LOAN
997	997	998	998	999	999	999	999	999	1000	1000	1
993	994	996	996	997	998	998	998	999	1000	1000	2
988	991	992	994	995	996	996	997	998	999	1000	3
983	986	989	991	992	994	995	996	997	999	1000	4
976	981	984	987	989	991	993	994	995	998	999	5
968	974	979	982	986	988	990	992	993	998	999	6
958	966	972	977	981	985	987	989	991	997	999	7
947	956	964	970	976	980	983	986	989	996	999	8
932	944	954	962	969	975	979	983	986	995	998	9
915	930	943	953	961	968	973	978	982	993	998	10
893	912	928	941	951	960	967	973	978	992	997	11
868	891	911	926	940	950	959	966	972	990	996	12
836	865	890	909	925	939	949	958	966	987	995	13
798	834	864	888	908	924	937	949	958	984	994	14
752	796	833	862	887	907	923	937	948	980	993	15
696	750	795	831	861	886	906	923	936	976	991	16
629	695	749	794	830	860	885	905	922	970	989	17
546	627	693	748	793	829	859	884	905	964	986	18
446	545	626	692	747	792	828	859	884	956	983	19
325	445	544	625	691	746	791	828	858	946	980	20
178	325	445	543	624	691	745	790	827	934	975	21
	178	324	444	542	623	690	745	790	920	970	22
		178	323	443	542	623	689	744	903	963	23
			177	323	443	541	622	689	882	955	24
				177	323	442	541	622	857	946	25
					177	322	442	540	826	934	26
						177	322	442	788	920	27
							177	322	743	902	28
								176	688	881	29
									621	856	30
									539	825	31
									441	788	32
									321	742	33
									176	687	34
										620	35

20% LOAN PROGRESS CHART

Showing dollar balance remaining on a $1000 loan

AGE OF LOAN	ORIGINAL TERM IN YEARS 5	8	10	12	15	16	17	18	19	20	21
1	871	943	965	978	988	990	992	994	995	996	997
2	713	875	923	951	974	978	983	986	988	991	992
3	520	791	870	917	956	964	971	976	981	984	987
4	286	688	807	877	935	947	957	965	971	977	981
5		564	730	827	909	926	940	951	960	967	973
6		412	635	767	877	900	919	934	946	956	964
7		226	520	693	838	868	893	913	929	942	953
8			380	604	791	830	862	887	908	925	939
9			209	494	733	783	824	856	883	904	922
10				361	663	726	777	818	852	879	901
11				198	577	656	721	772	814	848	876
12					473	571	651	716	768	811	845
13					345	468	567	647	712	765	808
14					190	342	464	564	644	709	762
15						188	339	461	561	641	707
16							186	337	459	558	639
17								185	335	457	556
18									184	334	456
19										183	333
20											183

AGE OF LOAN	ORIGINAL TERM IN YEARS 22	23	24	25	26	27	28	29	30	35	40
1	997	998	998	998	999	999	999	999	999	1000	1000
2	994	995	996	996	997	998	998	998	999	999	1000
3	989	991	993	994	995	996	997	997	998	999	1000
4	984	987	990	991	993	995	995	996	997	999	999
5	978	982	985	988	990	992	993	995	996	998	999
6	970	976	980	984	987	989	991	993	994	998	999
7	961	968	974	978	982	986	988	990	992	997	999
8	950	959	966	972	977	982	985	988	990	996	998
9	936	948	957	965	971	977	981	984	987	995	998
10	919	934	946	955	964	971	976	980	984	994	998
11	899	917	932	944	954	963	969	975	979	992	997
12	873	896	915	930	943	954	962	969	974	990	996
13	843	871	895	914	929	942	953	961	968	988	995
14	806	841	870	893	913	929	941	952	961	985	994
15	760	804	839	868	892	912	928	941	951	982	993
16	705	758	802	838	867	892	911	927	940	978	992
17	637	703	757	801	837	867	891	910	927	973	990
18	555	636	702	756	800	836	866	890	910	966	987
19	454	553	634	701	755	799	835	865	889	959	985
20	332	453	552	633	700	754	798	835	865	950	981
21	182	331	452	551	633	699	753	798	834	939	977
22		182	330	452	551	632	698	753	797	925	972
23			181	330	451	550	631	698	752	908	966
24				181	329	451	550	631	698	888	958
25					181	329	450	549	631	863	949
26						181	329	450	549	833	938
27							181	329	450	796	924
28								180	328	751	908
29									180	696	887
30										630	863
31										548	832
32										449	796
33										328	751
34										180	696
35											629

LOAN PROGRESS CHART **20.5%**

Showing dollar balance remaining on a $1000 loan

ORIGINAL TERM IN YEARS											AGE
5	**8**	**10**	**12**	**15**	**16**	**17**	**18**	**19**	**20**	**21**	**OF LOAN**
872	945	966	979	989	991	993	994	995	996	997	**1**
715	877	924	952	975	980	984	987	989	991	993	**2**
523	794	873	920	958	966	973	978	982	985	988	**3**
288	693	811	880	937	949	959	967	973	978	982	**4**
	568	734	832	912	929	943	954	962	969	975	**5**
	416	640	772	881	904	922	937	949	958	966	**6**
	229	525	699	843	873	897	917	932	945	956	**7**
		384	610	797	836	867	892	912	929	942	**8**
		212	500	740	789	829	862	888	909	926	**9**
			366	670	733	784	825	858	884	906	**10**
			202	584	664	728	779	821	854	882	**11**
				479	579	659	723	775	817	852	**12**
				351	475	575	655	720	772	815	**13**
				193	347	471	571	652	717	770	**14**
					191	345	469	568	649	715	**15**
						190	343	466	566	647	**16**
							189	341	464	565	**17**
								188	340	463	**18**
									187	339	**19**
										187	**20**

ORIGINAL TERM IN YEARS											AGE
22	**23**	**24**	**25**	**26**	**27**	**28**	**29**	**30**	**35**	**40**	**OF LOAN**
997	998	998	999	999	999	999	999	999	1000	1000	**1**
994	995	996	997	997	998	998	999	999	1000	1000	**2**
990	992	993	995	996	996	997	998	998	999	1000	**3**
985	988	990	992	994	995	996	997	997	999	1000	**4**
980	983	986	989	991	992	994	995	996	999	1000	**5**
972	977	981	985	988	990	992	993	995	998	999	**6**
964	970	976	980	984	987	989	991	993	998	999	**7**
953	961	968	974	979	983	986	989	991	997	999	**8**
940	951	960	967	973	978	982	986	988	996	999	**9**
923	937	949	959	966	972	977	982	985	995	998	**10**
903	921	936	948	957	965	972	977	981	993	998	**11**
879	901	920	935	947	956	965	971	976	992	997	**12**
849	877	900	918	934	946	956	964	971	990	996	**13**
813	847	875	899	917	932	945	955	963	987	995	**14**
768	811	846	874	898	916	932	944	955	984	994	**15**
713	766	809	845	873	897	916	931	944	980	993	**16**
645	711	765	808	844	872	896	915	931	975	991	**17**
563	644	710	764	807	843	872	896	915	969	989	**18**
462	562	643	709	763	806	842	871	895	962	986	**19**
338	461	561	642	708	762	806	842	871	954	983	**20**
186	337	460	560	641	707	761	806	841	943	979	**21**
	186	337	459	559	641	707	761	805	930	975	**22**
		185	336	459	559	640	707	761	914	969	**23**
			185	336	458	558	640	706	894	962	**24**
				185	335	458	558	639	870	953	**25**
					185	335	458	558	840	942	**26**
						185	335	458	804	929	**27**
							184	335	760	913	**28**
								184	705	893	**29**
									639	869	**30**
									557	840	**31**
									457	804	**32**
									334	759	**33**
									184	705	**34**
										638	**35**

21% LOAN PROGRESS CHART

Showing dollar balance remaining on a $1000 loan

AGE OF LOAN	ORIGINAL TERM IN YEARS 5	8	10	12	15	16	17	18	19	20	21
1	874	946	967	979	990	991	993	994	995	997	997
2	718	880	926	954	976	981	984	987	990	992	993
3	526	798	876	922	960	968	974	979	983	986	989
4	291	697	815	884	940	952	961	968	975	980	983
5		573	739	836	916	932	945	956	964	971	976
6		420	646	777	886	908	925	940	951	961	968
7		232	531	705	848	878	901	920	936	948	958
8			389	616	803	841	872	896	916	932	945
9			215	506	746	796	835	867	892	913	929
10				371	677	740	790	830	863	889	910
11				205	591	671	734	786	827	860	886
12					486	586	666	730	782	824	857
13					356	482	582	662	727	779	821
14					197	353	478	579	659	725	777
15						195	351	476	576	657	722
16							194	349	474	574	655
17								192	347	472	572
18									192	346	470
19										191	345
20											190

AGE OF LOAN	ORIGINAL TERM IN YEARS 22	23	24	25	26	27	28	29	30	35	40
1	998	998	998	999	999	999	999	999	999	1000	1000
2	995	996	997	997	998	998	998	999	999	1000	1000
3	991	993	994	995	996	997	997	998	998	999	1000
4	986	989	991	993	994	995	996	997	997	999	999
5	981	985	988	990	992	993	995	996	996	999	999
6	974	979	983	986	989	991	993	994	995	998	999
7	966	973	978	982	985	988	990	992	993	998	999
8	956	964	971	977	981	984	987	990	991	997	999
9	943	954	963	970	975	980	984	987	989	996	998
10	927	941	952	961	969	974	979	983	986	995	998
11	908	926	940	951	960	968	974	979	983	994	998
12	884	906	924	939	950	959	967	973	978	992	997
13	855	883	905	923	937	949	959	966	973	990	996
14	819	854	881	904	922	936	948	958	966	988	996
15	775	818	852	880	903	921	936	948	958	985	995
16	721	774	816	851	879	902	920	935	947	981	993
17	654	719	772	816	850	878	901	920	935	977	992
18	571	652	718	772	815	849	878	901	919	972	990
19	469	570	651	717	771	814	849	877	900	965	987
20	344	468	569	651	716	770	813	848	877	957	984
21	190	343	468	568	650	716	769	813	848	946	981
22		190	343	467	568	649	715	769	812	934	976
23			189	343	467	567	649	715	768	918	971
24				189	342	466	567	648	714	899	964
25					189	342	466	566	648	876	956
26						189	342	466	566	847	946
27							188	341	465	811	933
28								188	341	768	918
29									188	714	899
30										647	875
31										565	846
32										465	811
33										341	767
34										188	713
35											647

LOAN PROGRESS CHART **21.5%**

Showing dollar balance remaining on a $1000 loan

ORIGINAL TERM IN YEARS											AGE
5	8	10	12	15	16	17	18	19	20	21	OF LOAN
875	947	968	980	990	992	994	995	996	996	997	1
721	882	928	955	977	982	986	988	990	992	994	2
530	801	879	925	962	969	976	980	984	987	990	3
293	701	819	887	943	954	963	970	976	981	984	4
	577	744	840	919	935	948	958	966	973	978	5
	424	651	782	889	911	929	943	954	963	970	6
	235	536	710	853	882	906	924	939	951	960	7
		394	622	808	846	877	901	920	936	948	8
		218	512	752	802	841	872	897	917	933	9
			376	683	746	796	836	868	894	914	10
			208	598	678	741	792	832	865	891	11
				492	593	673	737	789	830	863	12
				362	489	589	670	734	786	827	13
				200	359	485	586	667	732	784	14
					198	357	483	584	665	730	15
						197	355	481	582	663	16
							196	353	479	580	17
								195	352	478	18
									195	351	19
										194	20

ORIGINAL TERM IN YEARS											AGE
22	23	24	25	26	27	28	29	30	35	40	OF LOAN
998	998	998	999	999	999	999	999	1000	1000	1000	1
995	996	997	997	998	998	998	999	999	1000	1000	2
992	993	994	995	997	997	998	998	999	1000	1000	3
987	990	992	993	995	996	996	997	998	999	1000	4
982	986	988	990	993	994	995	996	997	999	1000	5
976	981	984	987	990	992	993	994	996	999	999	6
968	974	979	983	987	989	991	993	994	998	999	7
958	966	973	978	982	985	988	990	993	998	999	8
946	956	965	971	977	981	985	988	990	997	999	9
931	944	955	964	971	976	981	984	988	996	999	10
912	929	943	954	963	970	976	980	984	995	998	11
889	911	928	942	953	962	969	975	980	993	998	12
861	888	909	927	941	952	961	969	975	992	997	13
826	859	886	908	926	940	952	961	969	989	996	14
782	824	858	885	908	925	940	951	961	987	995	15
728	781	823	857	885	907	925	939	951	983	994	16
661	727	779	822	857	884	906	924	939	979	993	17
579	660	726	779	822	856	883	906	924	974	991	18
477	578	659	725	778	821	855	883	906	968	989	19
350	476	577	658	725	777	820	855	883	960	986	20
194	350	475	576	658	724	777	820	855	950	983	21
	193	349	475	576	657	723	776	820	938	979	22
		193	349	474	575	657	723	776	923	973	23
			193	348	474	575	657	723	905	967	24
				193	348	473	575	657	882	959	25
					192	348	473	575	854	950	26
						192	348	473	819	938	27
							192	348	776	923	28
								192	722	904	29
									656	881	30
									574	853	31
									473	818	32
									347	775	33
									192	722	34
										656	35

22% LOAN PROGRESS CHART

Showing dollar balance remaining on a $1000 loan

AGE OF LOAN	ORIGINAL TERM IN YEARS										
	5	8	10	12	15	16	17	18	19	20	21
1	877	949	969	981	991	992	994	995	996	997	997
2	723	884	930	957	979	983	986	989	991	993	994
3	532	805	882	927	964	971	977	981	985	988	990
4	295	705	823	890	945	956	965	972	978	982	985
5		582	748	844	922	938	951	960	968	974	979
6		428	656	787	893	915	932	945	956	965	972
7		237	541	716	858	886	910	927	942	953	962
8			398	628	814	851	881	905	924	939	951
9			221	518	759	807	846	877	901	921	936
10				381	690	753	803	842	873	898	918
11				211	605	685	748	798	839	871	896
12					499	600	681	744	795	836	868
13					367	495	597	677	741	793	834
14					204	365	492	594	675	739	791
15						202	362	490	591	672	737
16							201	360	488	589	671
17								200	359	486	588
18									199	358	485
19										198	357
20											198

AGE OF LOAN	ORIGINAL TERM IN YEARS										
	22	23	24	25	26	27	28	29	30	35	40
1	998	999	999	999	999	999	999	1000	1000	1000	1000
2	996	997	997	998	998	998	999	999	999	1000	1000
3	993	994	995	996	997	997	998	999	999	999	1000
4	989	991	992	994	995	996	997	998	998	999	1000
5	984	987	989	991	993	994	995	997	997	999	1000
6	978	982	985	988	991	992	994	995	996	999	1000
7	970	976	981	984	988	990	992	994	995	998	1000
8	961	969	975	980	984	987	989	992	993	998	999
9	949	959	967	973	979	983	986	989	991	997	999
10	935	948	958	966	973	978	982	986	989	996	999
11	917	933	946	957	965	972	977	982	986	995	999
12	895	915	932	945	956	964	971	977	982	994	998
13	867	893	914	931	945	955	964	971	977	992	998
14	832	865	892	913	930	944	955	964	971	990	997
15	789	831	864	891	912	929	943	955	963	988	996
16	736	788	830	863	890	911	929	943	954	984	995
17	669	735	787	829	863	889	911	929	943	981	994
18	587	668	733	786	828	862	889	911	928	976	992
19	484	586	667	733	785	827	861	889	910	970	990
20	356	483	585	667	732	785	827	861	888	962	988
21	198	356	483	584	666	732	784	827	861	953	984
22		197	355	482	584	665	731	784	826	942	981
23			197	355	482	583	665	731	784	927	976
24				197	355	481	583	665	731	909	970
25					197	354	481	583	665	887	962
26						196	354	481	583	860	953
27							196	354	481	825	942
28								196	354	783	927
29									196	730	909
30										664	887
31										582	860
32										480	825
33										354	783
34										196	730
35											664

LOAN PROGRESS CHART **22.5%**

Showing dollar balance remaining on a $1000 loan

ORIGINAL TERM IN YEARS											
5	**8**	**10**	**12**	**15**	**16**	**17**	**18**	**19**	**20**	**21**	**AGE OF LOAN**
878	950	970	982	991	993	994	996	997	997	998	**1**
726	887	932	959	980	984	987	990	992	993	995	**2**
535	808	885	930	965	973	978	983	986	989	991	**3**
297	709	826	894	948	958	967	974	979	983	987	**4**
	586	753	849	925	941	952	962	970	976	981	**5**
	432	661	792	897	919	935	948	959	967	974	**6**
	240	546	722	863	891	913	931	945	956	965	**7**
		403	634	819	856	885	909	928	942	954	**8**
		224	524	765	813	851	882	906	925	940	**9**
			386	697	759	808	847	878	903	923	**10**
			215	612	692	754	805	844	876	901	**11**
				506	607	687	751	802	842	874	**12**
				373	502	604	684	749	799	840	**13**
				207	370	499	601	682	746	798	**14**
					206	368	497	599	680	745	**15**
						204	366	495	597	678	**16**
							204	365	493	596	**17**
								203	364	492	**18**
									202	363	**19**
										202	**20**

ORIGINAL TERM IN YEARS											
22	**23**	**24**	**25**	**26**	**27**	**28**	**29**	**30**	**35**	**40**	**AGE OF LOAN**
998	998	999	999	999	1000	1000	1000	1000	1000	1000	**1**
996	997	997	998	998	999	999	999	999	1000	1000	**2**
993	994	995	996	997	998	998	999	999	1000	1000	**3**
989	991	993	994	996	997	997	998	998	1000	1000	**4**
985	988	990	992	994	995	996	997	997	999	1000	**5**
979	983	987	989	992	993	995	996	996	999	999	**6**
972	977	982	986	989	991	993	994	995	999	999	**7**
963	970	976	981	985	988	991	992	994	998	999	**8**
952	961	969	975	981	985	988	990	992	997	999	**9**
938	950	960	968	975	980	984	987	989	997	999	**10**
921	937	949	959	968	974	979	983	987	996	998	**11**
899	919	936	948	959	967	974	979	983	995	998	**12**
872	898	918	935	948	958	967	973	978	993	998	**13**
838	871	897	917	934	947	958	966	973	991	997	**14**
796	837	870	896	917	934	947	957	966	989	996	**15**
743	795	836	869	895	916	933	946	957	986	995	**16**
677	742	794	835	868	895	916	933	946	982	994	**17**
594	676	741	793	835	868	894	915	932	978	993	**18**
491	593	675	740	792	834	867	894	915	972	991	**19**
362	491	593	674	740	792	834	867	893	965	988	**20**
201	362	490	592	674	739	792	833	866	956	986	**21**
	201	361	489	592	674	739	791	833	945	982	**22**
		201	361	489	592	673	739	791	932	977	**23**
			201	361	489	591	673	738	914	972	**24**
				200	361	489	591	673	893	965	**25**
					200	360	488	591	866	956	**26**
						200	360	488	832	945	**27**
							200	360	790	931	**28**
								200	738	914	**29**
									672	892	**30**
									590	866	**31**
									488	832	**32**
									360	790	**33**
									200	737	**34**
										672	**35**

23% LOAN PROGRESS CHART

Showing dollar balance remaining on a $1000 loan

AGE OF LOAN	ORIGINAL TERM IN YEARS										
	5	8	10	12	15	16	17	18	19	20	21
1	880	951	971	982	991	993	994	996	996	997	998
2	728	889	934	960	981	984	988	990	992	994	995
3	538	811	888	932	967	974	979	984	987	990	992
4	300	713	830	897	950	960	968	975	980	984	988
5		591	757	852	928	943	955	964	971	977	982
6		436	666	797	901	922	938	951	961	969	975
7		243	552	727	867	895	916	934	947	958	967
8			408	640	824	861	890	913	931	945	956
9			227	530	771	818	856	886	909	928	943
10				391	703	765	814	853	883	907	926
11				218	618	698	761	810	849	881	905
12					512	614	694	758	808	847	879
13					378	508	611	691	755	805	846
14					211	376	506	608	689	753	804
15						209	374	503	606	687	751
16							208	372	502	604	686
17								207	371	500	603
18									206	370	499
19										206	369
20											205

AGE OF LOAN	ORIGINAL TERM IN YEARS										
	22	23	24	25	26	27	28	29	30	35	40
1	999	999	999	999	999	1000	1000	1000	1000	1000	1000
2	996	997	998	998	999	999	999	999	1000	1000	1000
3	994	995	996	997	997	998	998	999	999	999	1000
4	990	992	994	995	996	997	998	998	999	999	1000
5	986	989	991	993	994	996	996	997	998	999	1000
6	981	984	988	990	992	994	995	996	997	999	1000
7	974	979	983	987	990	992	993	995	996	998	1000
8	965	972	978	982	986	989	991	993	995	998	999
9	955	964	971	977	982	986	989	991	993	997	999
10	942	953	963	970	977	981	985	988	991	997	999
11	925	940	952	962	970	976	981	985	988	996	999
12	904	923	939	951	961	969	976	980	985	995	998
13	877	902	922	938	951	961	969	975	980	994	998
14	844	876	901	921	938	950	960	968	975	992	997
15	803	843	875	901	921	937	950	960	968	990	997
16	750	801	842	874	900	920	937	949	960	987	996
17	685	749	801	841	874	900	920	936	949	984	995
18	602	684	748	800	841	873	899	920	936	979	994
19	499	601	683	748	799	840	873	899	920	974	992
20	369	498	601	682	747	799	840	872	899	967	990
21	205	368	497	600	682	747	798	839	872	959	987
22		205	368	497	600	681	746	798	839	948	984
23			205	367	497	599	681	746	798	935	979
24				204	367	496	599	681	746	919	974
25					204	367	496	599	681	898	967
26						204	367	496	599	871	959
27							204	366	496	839	948
28								204	366	797	935
29									204	745	919
30										680	898
31										598	871
32										495	839
33										366	797
34										204	745
35											680

LOAN PROGRESS CHART 23.5%

Showing dollar balance remaining on a $1000 loan

ORIGINAL TERM IN YEARS											AGE
5	8	10	12	15	16	17	18	19	20	21	OF LOAN
881	952	972	983	992	994	995	996	997	997	998	1
731	891	936	961	981	985	989	991	993	994	995	2
541	814	891	934	968	975	981	984	988	990	992	3
302	717	834	900	952	962	970	976	981	985	988	4
	595	762	856	931	946	957	966	973	979	983	5
	441	671	802	904	925	941	953	963	971	977	6
	246	557	732	871	899	920	937	950	961	969	7
		412	645	829	866	894	916	934	948	959	8
		230	535	776	824	861	890	913	931	946	9
			396	709	771	820	857	887	911	930	10
			221	625	705	767	816	855	885	909	11
				518	621	701	764	814	853	883	12
				384	515	618	698	762	812	851	13
				214	381	512	615	696	760	810	14
					213	379	510	613	694	758	15
						212	378	509	612	693	16
							211	377	507	610	17
								210	376	506	18
									210	375	19
										209	20

ORIGINAL TERM IN YEARS											AGE
22	23	24	25	26	27	28	29	30	35	40	OF LOAN
998	999	999	999	999	1000	999	1000	1000	1000	1000	1
996	997	998	998	999	999	999	999	999	1000	1000	2
994	995	996	997	998	998	998	999	999	1000	1000	3
991	993	994	995	996	997	998	998	998	1000	1000	4
987	990	992	993	995	996	997	998	998	999	1000	5
982	986	989	991	993	994	995	997	997	999	1000	6
975	981	985	988	990	992	994	995	996	999	1000	7
967	974	980	984	987	990	992	994	995	998	1000	8
957	966	973	979	983	987	989	992	993	998	1000	9
944	956	965	972	978	983	986	989	991	997	999	10
928	943	955	964	972	978	982	986	989	997	999	11
908	927	942	954	964	971	977	982	986	996	999	12
882	907	926	941	954	963	971	977	982	994	998	13
850	881	906	925	941	953	963	971	977	993	998	14
809	849	880	905	925	941	953	963	970	991	997	15
757	808	848	879	905	924	940	953	962	988	997	16
692	756	807	847	879	904	924	940	952	985	996	17
609	691	755	806	847	879	904	924	940	981	994	18
506	609	690	755	806	846	878	904	923	976	993	19
374	505	608	690	754	805	846	878	903	970	991	20
209	374	504	608	689	754	805	846	878	962	988	21
	209	374	504	607	689	754	805	845	952	985	22
		208	373	504	607	689	754	805	939	981	23
			208	373	503	607	689	753	923	976	24
				208	373	503	607	688	903	970	25
					208	373	503	606	877	962	26
						208	373	503	845	952	27
							208	372	804	939	28
								208	753	923	29
									688	903	30
									606	877	31
									503	845	32
									372	804	33
									208	753	34
										688	35

24% LOAN PROGRESS CHART

Showing dollar balance remaining on a $1000 loan

AGE OF LOAN	ORIGINAL TERM IN YEARS 5	8	10	12	15	16	17	18	19	20	21
1	882	953	973	984	992	994	995	996	997	997	998
2	733	893	938	963	982	986	989	991	993	995	996
3	544	817	894	936	970	976	981	985	988	991	993
4	304	721	838	903	954	964	972	978	982	986	989
5		599	766	860	933	948	959	968	975	980	985
6		445	676	806	908	928	943	955	965	972	978
7		249	562	738	875	902	923	940	953	963	971
8			417	651	834	870	898	920	937	950	961
9			233	541	782	829	866	895	917	935	949
10				402	715	777	825	862	892	915	933
11				225	631	711	773	822	860	890	913
12					525	628	708	770	819	858	888
13					389	522	625	705	768	817	857
14					218	387	519	622	703	766	816
15						216	385	517	620	701	765
16							215	384	515	619	700
17								214	382	514	618
18									214	381	513
19										213	381
20											213

AGE OF LOAN	ORIGINAL TERM IN YEARS 22	23	24	25	26	27	28	29	30	35	40
1	999	999	999	999	999	999	1000	1000	1000	1000	1000
2	997	997	998	998	999	999	999	999	1000	1000	1000
3	994	995	997	997	998	998	999	999	999	1000	1000
4	992	993	995	996	997	997	998	998	999	999	1000
5	988	990	993	994	995	996	997	998	998	999	1000
6	983	986	990	992	993	995	996	997	998	999	1000
7	977	982	986	989	991	993	995	996	997	999	1000
8	969	976	981	985	988	991	993	994	996	998	1000
9	960	968	975	980	984	988	991	992	994	998	999
10	947	958	967	974	980	984	988	990	992	997	999
11	932	946	958	967	974	979	984	987	990	997	999
12	912	930	946	957	966	973	979	983	987	996	999
13	887	911	930	945	956	966	973	979	983	995	998
14	855	886	910	929	944	956	966	973	979	993	998
15	815	854	885	909	929	944	956	965	973	991	997
16	764	814	854	884	909	928	944	955	965	989	997
17	699	763	813	853	884	908	928	943	955	986	996
18	617	698	762	813	852	884	908	928	943	982	995
19	513	616	698	762	812	852	884	908	928	978	993
20	380	512	616	697	761	812	852	883	908	972	991
21	213	380	512	615	697	761	812	851	883	964	989
22		212	380	511	615	696	761	811	851	954	986
23			212	379	511	614	696	760	811	942	982
24				212	379	511	614	696	760	927	978
25					212	379	511	614	696	907	972
26						212	379	510	614	882	964
27							212	379	510	851	954
28								212	379	811	942
29									212	760	927
30										695	907
31										613	882
32										510	851
33										378	811
34										212	760
35											695

LOAN PROGRESS CHART **24.5%**

Showing dollar balance remaining on a $1000 loan

ORIGINAL TERM IN YEARS											AGE
5	**8**	**10**	**12**	**15**	**16**	**17**	**18**	**19**	**20**	**21**	**OF LOAN**
884	954	973	984	993	994	995	996	997	998	998	**1**
736	895	940	964	983	987	990	992	994	995	996	**2**
547	820	896	938	971	978	982	986	989	992	993	**3**
307	725	841	906	956	966	973	979	983	987	990	**4**
	604	771	864	936	950	961	970	976	981	985	**5**
	449	681	811	911	931	946	958	967	974	980	**6**
	251	567	743	880	906	926	943	955	965	972	**7**
		422	657	839	875	902	923	940	953	963	**8**
		236	547	787	834	870	899	921	938	951	**9**
			406	722	783	830	867	896	919	936	**10**
			228	638	718	779	827	865	894	917	**11**
				531	634	714	777	825	863	893	**12**
				395	528	631	712	774	823	862	**13**
				221	393	525	629	710	773	822	**14**
					220	391	524	627	708	771	**15**
						219	389	522	626	707	**16**
							218	388	521	625	**17**
								218	387	520	**18**
									217	387	**19**
										217	**20**

ORIGINAL TERM IN YEARS											AGE
22	**23**	**24**	**25**	**26**	**27**	**28**	**29**	**30**	**35**	**40**	**OF LOAN**
999	999	999	999	999	1000	1000	1000	1000	1000	1000	**1**
997	997	998	998	999	999	999	999	1000	1000	1000	**2**
995	996	997	997	998	999	999	999	999	1000	1000	**3**
992	994	995	996	997	998	998	998	999	1000	1000	**4**
989	991	993	994	995	997	997	998	998	999	1000	**5**
984	987	990	992	994	995	996	997	998	999	1000	**6**
979	983	987	989	992	994	995	996	997	999	1000	**7**
971	977	982	986	989	992	993	995	996	999	1000	**8**
962	970	977	981	985	989	991	993	995	998	1000	**9**
950	961	969	976	981	985	988	991	993	998	999	**10**
935	949	960	969	975	981	985	988	991	997	999	**11**
916	934	948	959	968	975	980	984	988	996	999	**12**
892	915	933	948	959	968	975	980	984	995	999	**13**
861	890	914	933	947	959	968	974	980	994	998	**14**
821	859	890	913	932	947	958	967	974	992	998	**15**
771	820	859	889	913	932	947	958	967	990	997	**16**
706	769	819	858	889	913	932	946	958	987	996	**17**
624	705	769	819	858	889	913	931	946	984	995	**18**
520	623	705	768	818	858	888	912	931	980	994	**19**
386	519	623	704	768	818	857	888	912	974	992	**20**
216	386	519	622	704	768	818	857	888	967	990	**21**
	216	386	518	622	704	768	817	857	957	987	**22**
		216	385	518	622	703	767	817	946	984	**23**
			216	385	518	622	703	767	931	980	**24**
				216	385	518	621	703	912	974	**25**
					216	385	517	621	887	967	**26**
						216	385	517	856	957	**27**
							216	385	817	946	**28**
								216	767	931	**29**
									703	912	**30**
									621	887	**31**
									517	856	**32**
									384	817	**33**
									215	767	**34**
										703	**35**

25% LOAN PROGRESS CHART

Showing dollar balance remaining on a $1000 loan

AGE OF LOAN	ORIGINAL TERM IN YEARS 5	8	10	12	15	16	17	18	19	20	21
1	885	955	974	985	993	995	996	997	997	998	998
2	738	897	941	965	984	988	990	993	994	995	996
3	550	823	899	940	973	979	983	987	990	992	994
4	309	729	845	908	958	967	974	980	984	988	991
5		608	775	868	939	952	963	971	977	982	986
6		453	686	815	915	934	948	960	969	976	981
7		254	572	748	884	910	930	945	957	967	974
8			426	662	844	879	906	927	943	955	965
9			239	552	793	839	875	903	924	941	954
10				411	728	789	836	872	900	922	939
11				231	644	724	785	833	870	898	921
12					537	641	721	783	830	868	897
13					400	534	638	718	780	829	867
14					225	398	532	636	716	779	828
15						223	396	530	634	715	778
16							223	395	529	633	714
17								222	394	528	632
18									221	393	527
19										221	393
20											220

AGE OF LOAN	ORIGINAL TERM IN YEARS 22	23	24	25	26	27	28	29	30	35	40
1	999	999	999	1000	1000	1000	1000	1000	1000	1000	1000
2	997	998	998	999	999	999	999	1000	1000	1000	1000
3	995	996	997	998	998	999	999	999	1000	1000	1000
4	992	994	996	997	997	998	998	999	999	1000	1000
5	989	992	994	995	996	997	997	998	999	1000	1000
6	985	988	991	993	995	996	996	997	998	1000	1000
7	980	984	988	991	993	994	995	996	997	999	1000
8	973	979	984	987	990	992	994	995	996	999	999
9	964	972	978	983	987	990	992	994	995	999	999
10	953	963	971	978	983	986	989	992	994	998	999
11	938	952	963	971	977	982	986	989	992	998	999
12	920	937	951	962	970	977	982	986	989	997	999
13	896	919	937	951	962	970	976	982	986	996	999
14	865	895	918	936	950	961	969	976	982	995	998
15	826	865	895	918	936	950	961	969	976	993	998
16	777	826	864	894	917	935	949	961	969	991	997
17	713	776	825	864	894	917	935	949	961	989	996
18	631	712	776	825	863	893	917	935	949	985	996
19	526	630	712	775	825	863	893	917	935	981	994
20	392	526	630	711	775	824	863	893	917	976	993
21	220	392	525	630	711	774	824	863	893	969	991
22		220	391	525	629	711	774	824	863	960	988
23			220	391	525	629	710	774	824	949	985
24				220	391	525	629	710	774	935	981
25					220	391	524	629	710	916	975
26						219	391	524	629	892	969
27							219	391	524	862	960
28								219	391	823	949
29									219	774	934
30										710	916
31										629	892
32										524	862
33										390	823
34										219	773
35											710

SECTION FOUR

Real Estate Section

RATIO OF LOAN TO APPRAISED VALUE

APPRAISED VALUE	50%	55%	60%	65%	70%
1,000	500	550	600	650	700
2,000	1,000	1,100	1,200	1,300	1,400
3,000	1,500	1,650	1,800	1,950	2,100
4,000	2,000	2,200	2,400	2,600	2,800
5,000	2,500	2,750	3,000	3,250	3,500
6,000	3,000	3,300	3,600	3,900	4,200
7,000	3,500	3,850	4,200	4,550	4,900
8,000	4,000	4,400	4,800	5,200	5,600
9,000	4,500	4,950	5,400	5,850	6,300
10,000	5,000	5,500	6,000	6,500	7,000
11,000	5,500	6,050	6,600	7,150	7,700
12,000	6,000	6,600	7,200	7,800	8,400
13,000	6,500	7,150	7,800	8,450	9,100
14,000	7,000	7,700	8,400	9,100	9,800
15,000	7,500	8,250	9,000	9,750	10,500
16,000	8,000	8,800	9,600	10,400	11,200
17,000	8,500	9,350	10,200	11,050	11,900
18,000	9,000	9,900	10,800	11,700	12,600
19,000	9,500	10,450	11,400	12,350	13,300
20,000	0,000	11,000	12,000	13,000	14,000
21,000	10,500	11,050	12,600	13,650	14,700
22,000	11,000	12,100	13,200	14,300	15,400
23,000	11,500	12,650	13,800	14,950	16,100
24,000	12,000	13,200	14,400	15,600	16,800
25,000	12,500	13,750	15,000	16,250	17,500
30,000	15,000	16,500	18,000	19,500	21,000
35,000	17,500	19,250	21,000	22,750	24,500
40,000	20,000	22,000	24,000	26,000	28,000
45,000	22,500	24,750	27,000	29,250	31,500
50,000	25,000	27,500	30,000	32,500	35,000
60,000	30,000	33,000	36,000	39,000	42,000
70,000	35,000	38,500	42,000	45,500	49,000
80,000	40,000	44,000	48,000	52,000	56,000
90,000	45,000	49,500	54,000	58,500	63,000
100,000	50,000	55,000	60,000	65,000	70,000
150,000	75,000	87,500	90,000	97,500	105,000
200,000	100,000	110,000	120,000	130,000	140,000
250,000	125,000	137,500	150,000	162,500	175,000
300,000	150,000	165,000	180,000	195,000	210,000
400,000	200,000	220,000	240,000	260,000	280,000
500,000	250,000	275,000	300,000	325,000	350,000

RATIO OF LOAN TO APPRAISED VALUE

75%	80%	85%	90%	95%
750	800	850	900	950
1,500	1,600	1,700	1,800	1,900
2,250	2,400	2,550	2,700	2,850
3,000	3,200	3,400	3,600	3,800
3,750	4,000	4,250	4,500	4,750
4,500	4,800	5,100	5,400	5,700
5,250	5,600	5,950	6,300	6,650
6,000	6,400	6,800	7,200	7,600
6,750	7,200	7,650	8,100	8,550
7,500	8,000	8,500	9,000	9,500
8,250	8,800	9,350	9,900	10,450
9,000	9,600	10,200	10,800	11,400
9,750	10,400	11,050	11,700	12,350
10,500	11,200	11,900	12,600	13,300
11,250	12,000	12,750	13,500	14,250
12,000	12,800	13,600	14,400	15,200
12,750	13,600	14,450	15,300	16,150
13,500	14,400	15,300	16,200	17,100
14,250	15,200	16,150	17,100	18,050
15,000	16,000	17,000	18,000	19,000
15,750	16,800	17,850	18,900	19,950
16,500	17,600	18,700	19,800	20,900
17,250	18,400	19,550	20,700	21,850
18,000	19,200	20,400	21,600	22,800
18,750	20,000	21,250	22,500	23,750
22,500	24,000	25,500	27,000	28,500
26,250	28,000	29,750	31,500	33,250
30,000	32,000	34,000	36,000	38,000
33,750	36,000	38,250	40,500	42,750
37,500	40,000	42,500	45,000	47,500
45,000	48,000	51,000	54,000	57,000
52,500	56,000	59,500	63,000	66,500
60,000	64,000	68,000	72,000	76,000
67,500	72,000	76,500	81,000	85,500
75,000	80,000	85,000	90,000	95,000
112,500	120,000	127,500	135,000	142,500
150,000	160,000	170,000	180,000	190,000
187,500	200,000	212,500	225,000	237,500
225,000	240,000	255,000	270,000	285,000
300,000	320,000	340,000	360,000	380,000
375,000	400,000	425,000	450,000	475,000

POINTS DISCOUNT TABLE

TERM

INTEREST RATE	5 YEARS	10 YEARS	15 YEARS	20 YEARS	25 YEARS	30 YEARS	35 YEARS	40 YEARS	POINTS
	7.14	6.11	5.78	5.63	5.53	5.46	5.40	5.39	5
	6.70	5.88	5.64	5.49	5.40	5.36	5.32	5.30	4
5%	6.25	5.66	5.48	5.38	5.31	5.26	5.25	5.20	3
	5.85	5.43	5.31	5.22	5.19	5.17	5.15	5.14	2
	5.42	5.21	5.15	5.11	5.10	5.09	5.08	5.07	1
	8.16	7.16	6.80	6.66	6.54	6.50	6.44	6.41	5
	7.70	6.90	6.63	6.52	6.44	6.40	6.36	6.32	4
6%	7.26	6.65	6.48	6.38	6.32	6.27	6.25	6.24	3
	6.86	6.46	6.31	6.26	6.22	6.19	6.16	6.85	2
	6.44	6.23	6.15	6.13	6.12	6.09	6.09	6.08	1
	9.19	8.19	7.83	7.69	7.58	7.50	7.47	7.46	5
	8.74	7.92	7.65	7.52	7.47	7.42	7.36	7.34	4
7%	8.30	7.70	7.50	7.40	7.33	7.30	7.27	7.25	3
	7.86	7.47	7.32	7.25	7.23	7.20	7.19	7.18	2
	7.41	7.24	7.17	7.14	7.11	7.10	7.09	7.09	1
	10.19	9.18	8.87	8.70	8.60	8.56	8.52	8.47	5
	9.75	8.95	8.66	8.54	8.47	8.44	8.41	8.37	4
8%	9.29	8.71	8.50	8.40	8.37	8.33	8.31	8.28	3
	8.86	8.46	8.35	8.26	8.25	8.22	8.21	8.18	2
	8.42	8.22	8.16	8.14	8.12	8.11	8.10	8.09	1
	11.21	10.22	9.89	9.72	9.65	9.58	9.55	9.52	5
	10.75	9.98	9.71	9.59	9.50	9.47	9.44	9.41	4
9%	10.30	9.72	9.51	9.44	9.37	9.35	9.33	9.31	3
	9.88	9.47	9.34	9.27	9.25	9.22	9.21	9.20	2
	9.42	9.25	9.16	9.15	9.12	9.11	9.11	9.09	1
	12.25	11.25	10.90	10.77	10.66	10.61	10.58	10.57	5
	11.77	10.99	10.71	10.59	10.53	10.48	10.48	10.43	4
10%	11.33	10.72	10.55	10.45	10.41	10.38	10.36	10.34	3
	10.87	10.47	10.37	10.29	10.27	10.24	10.23	10.22	2
	10.42	10.25	10.17	10.15	10.12	10.12	10.11	10.11	1
	13.27	12.25	11.94	11.78	11.72	11.65	11.62	11.61	5
	12.80	12.00	11.75	11.63	11.58	11.53	11.50	11.47	4
11%	12.34	11.74	11.58	11.48	11.43	11.38	11.36	11.35	3
	11.88	11.50	11.36	11.31	11.28	11.27	11.25	11.23	2
	11.45	11.26	11.19	11.15	11.14	11.13	11.12	11.12	1
	14.29	13.28	12.98	12.81	12.75	12.69	12.67	12.65	5
	13.80	13.02	12.78	12.65	12.60	12.55	12.53	12.52	4
12%	13.35	12.77	12.58	12.48	12.45	12.40	12.40	12.38	3
	12.88	12.51	12.38	12.33	12.28	12.27	12.26	12.25	2
	12.45	12.24	12.20	12.17	12.15	12.14	12.13	12.13	1
	15.32	14.33	14.00	13.85	13.80	13.73	13.71	13.70	5
	14.82	14.04	13.80	13.67	13.63	13.58	13.57	13.56	4
13%	14.37	13.77	13.60	13.50	13.45	13.44	13.43	13.42	3
	13.91	13.51	13.40	13.33	13.30	13.29	13.28	13.27	2
	13.45	13.27	13.20	13.16	13.15	13.14	13.14	13.14	1

POINTS DISCOUNT TABLE

TERM

INTEREST RATE	5 YEARS	10 YEARS	15 YEARS	20 YEARS	25 YEARS	30 YEARS	35 YEARS	40 YEARS	POINTS
	16.32	15.35	15.02	14.88	14.81	14.78	14.76	14.75	5
	15.86	15.06	14.81	14.70	14.66	14.63	14.60	14.60	4
14%	15.37	14.78	14.60	14.52	14.47	14.45	14.45	14.44	3
	14.90	14.51	14.39	14.34	14.33	14.31	14.30	14.29	2
	14.46	14.27	14.19	14.16	14.16	14.15	14.14	14.14	1
	17.36	16.38	16.06	15.94	15.88	15.84	15.82	15.80	5
	16.88	16.10	15.84	15.75	15.67	15.66	15.65	15.64	4
15%	16.38	15.82	15.62	15.55	15.52	15.49	15.48	15.47	3
	15.93	15.55	15.44	15.36	15.35	15.33	15.32	15.31	2
	15.46	15.28	15.22	15.18	15.17	15.17	15.16	15.15	1
	18.39	17.41	17.11	16.98	16.90	16.88	16.86	16.85	5
	17.90	17.10	16.88	16.76	16.73	16.68	16.68	16.66	4
16%	17.40	16.84	16.65	16.58	16.54	16.52	16.51	16.50	3
	16.94	16.56	16.44	16.38	16.34	16.34	16.33	16.33	2
	16.47	16.28	16.22	16.20	16.18	16.17	16.17	16.16	1
	19.40	18.43	18.14	18.02	17.96	17.93	17.92	17.91	5
	18.89	18.12	17.91	17.81	17.76	17.74	17.72	17.71	4
17%	18.43	17.85	17.68	17.60	17.57	17.55	17.53	17.43	3
	17.95	17.57	17.44	17.40	17.37	17.36	17.35	17.35	2
	17.47	17.29	17.23	17.20	17.19	17.18	17.17	17.17	1
	20.43	19.47	19.17	19.06	19.00	18.98	18.97	18.96	5
	19.93	19.17	18.94	18.84	18.80	18.77	18.76	18.75	4
18%	19.44	18.88	18.69	18.63	18.59	18.58	18.57	18.56	3
	18.96	18.57	18.46	18.42	18.39	18.38	18.37	18.37	2
	18.48	18.29	18.23	18.21	18.19	18.19	18.18	18.18	1
	21.46	20.50	20.20	20.10	20.05	20.03	20.02	20.00	5
	20.95	20.19	19.97	19.86	19.83	19.82	19.81	19.80	4
19%	20.46	19.88	19.72	19.64	19.62	19.61	19.60	19.58	3
	19.97	19.60	19.48	19.43	19.41	19.40	19.39	19.39	2
	19.48	19.30	19.24	19.22	19.20	19.20	19.19	19.19	1
	22.47	21.58	21.25	21.14	21.09	21.08	21.07	21.06	5
	21.96	21.21	20.99	20.90	20.87	20.86	20.85	20.84	4
20%	21.47	20.90	20.74	20.68	20.65	20.64	20.63	20.62	3
	20.98	20.60	20.49	20.45	20.43	20.41	20.41	20.41	2
	20.49	20.30	20.25	20.23	20.22	20.21	20.20	20.20	1
	23.50	22.55	22.28	22.19	22.14	22.12	22.11	22.10	5
	22.99	22.25	22.02	21.94	21.91	21.88	21.88	21.88	4
21%	22.49	21.90	21.75	21.70	21.68	21.67	21.66	21.65	3
	21.99	21.59	21.51	21.47	21.45	21.44	21.43	21.43	2
	21.49	21.29	21.26	21.24	21.23	21.22	21.21	21.21	1
	24.53	23.59	23.33	23.23	23.19	23.17	23.16	23.15	5
	24.00	23.27	23.05	22.98	22.95	22.92	22.92	22.92	4
22%	23.50	22.93	22.78	22.71	22.70	22.69	22.68	22.68	3
	23.00	22.61	22.51	22.46	22.46	22.45	22.45	22.45	2
	22.50	22.31	22.26	22.23	22.23	22.22	22.22	22.22	1

POINTS DISCOUNT TABLE

TERM

INTEREST RATE	5 YEARS	10 YEARS	15 YEARS	20 YEARS	25 YEARS	30 YEARS	35 YEARS	40 YEARS	POINTS
	25.56	24.61	24.37	24.28	24.23	24.22	24.22	24.21	5
	25.02	24.29	24.09	24.00	23.99	23.96	23.96	23.96	4
23%	24.52	23.95	23.81	23.76	23.73	23.72	23.71	23.71	3
	24.00	23.64	23.54	23.48	23.48	23.47	23.47	23.47	2
	23.50	23.30	23.27	23.25	23.24	23.23	23.23	23.23	1
	26.59	25.66	25.41	25.32	25.29	25.27	25.27	25.25	5
	26.05	25.31	25.12	25.05	25.00	25.00	25.00	24.99	4
24%	25.52	24.97	24.82	24.76	24.75	24.75	24.74	24.73	3
	25.00	24.65	24.55	24.50	24.50	24.49	24.48	24.48	2
	24.50	24.33	24.26	24.24	24.24	24.24	24.24	24.24	1
	27.60	26.69	26.45	26.37	26.32	26.31	26.31	26.31	5
	27.08	26.35	26.15	26.09	26.06	26.06	26.05	26.04	4
25%	26.55	26.00	25.86	25.80	25.77	25.77	25.77	25.77	3
	26.01	25.65	25.55	25.53	25.53	25.52	25.51	25.51	2
	25.50	25.35	25.27	25.27	25.26	25.25	25.25	25.25	1

A HOME BUYER'S GUIDE

In publishing a book of mortgage payment tables, it seems reasonable to include some personal financial advice on buying or building a house, as well as information on sales contracts, types of mortgages and mortgage lenders, attorney's fees, closing costs and so forth.

Many people rush into the process of buying a home with very little guidance or planning. When a poor decision is made, everyone who was involved is affected. The more an individual is informed, the more everyone will benefit in the long run.

It should be noted that there are excellent books in the field of personal finance available at the local library for anyone who wishes to spend more time researching the subject of home buying and real estate investing.

A. LOCATION

Once the decision to move, buy or build your first home has been made, the first criterion is to select a location: city, suburb or rural area; a particular community or neighborhood within that community. Avoid the frequent pitfall of impulse buying by preparing in advance. Horror stories are plentiful. For example, the couple buying a home that "had such a beautiful view" only to find out that they were two miles from the local sewage treatment plant!

Here is a list of certain factors that need to be considered:

1. Time & Mileage—How far would you be from schools, church, the office, relatives, friends' homes, shopping malls and community facilities?
2. Undesirable Places—Noisy and environmental pollution are factors that should be investigated. Is there a plant which creates unpleasant aromas at certain times? How far away is the nearest airport or expressway?
3. Community character—Is it neat and well-maintained, prosperous-appearing or run-down? Are there trees, sidewalks, lights, etc.?
4. Zoning of area—Are there strict zoning ordinances? This is extremely important. Otherwise, you may purchase a home only to find a supermarket across the street from you in three years!
5. Availability of utilities and services—Sometimes taxes are higher than you might have expected. If this is the case find out what services would justify the higher rates. Some other considerations: is there garbage collection, sewers, water, fire hydrants? Note the location of the police and fire departments.

There are numerous selection criteria based on individual tastes, economic situation and life style. Information can be obtained from many places but the important thing to remember is to plan carefully in your selection of a community before looking at houses for sale.

B. BUY OR BUILD?

Older Homes

Many people view an older home as an opportunity to find a bargain. The initial price, would make this appear so but the buyer should beware: his savings may soon disappear in repair costs, repainting, new appliances, and other general rehabilitation expenses.

On the other hand, an older home usually has storms and screen, a reasonably good lawn, and finished landscaping. They also have a warmth and charm difficult to find in new homes. For many people this is a very attractive feature worth whatever expense might be incurred in fix-up costs.

An important piece of advice in buying an older home: Be sure to have it inspected by a professional builder, appraiser or architect. He will charge between $50 and $100, but it will be money well spent. With his input you should be able to determine the cost for repairs before arranging financing.

New Homes

There are additional expenses with new homes as well. New homes settle and often the plaster will crack and doors and windows stick. In new developments the house often comes with a bare lawn, little or no shrubbery, no storm or screen windows or doors. All these cost money to buy.

Probably the greatest advantage of a new home is that it can usually be financed more easily than an older home. Thirty-year mortgages with smaller down payments are normally available.

Custom-Built Homes

The obvious advantage of a custom-built home is that it provides the family an opportunity to design a house specifically meeting their wishes, needs and life-style on a site they have selected.

The first step, after selecting a community, is to retain the services of an architect—preferably one who has been established in the local area and is knowledgeable of local contractors and builders. He will work with you in site selection, designing a house and supervision of the construction.

An architect's fee will range between 10 to 15 percent of the cost of the construction of the house. This may seem high but over a 20 to 30 year period, his fee usually will be less than 5 percent of the total cost of the project.

C. ATTORNEYS—THEY ARE IMPORTANT!

Take advantage of the various experts in their field and do not try to practice law on your own behalf. Never get involved in buying or selling land or a house without the advice of an experienced real estate agent or an attorney. Never put anything in writing; never sign anything, no matter how understandable the document seems to be.

The best practice is to have your attorney work with the seller's attorney. They can assess the legal ramifications and a sales contract can be drawn up in a very short period of time. At the time the contract is signed a down payment, usually 10 percent of the purchase price, is usually required.

Find out in advance the attorney's fee. It can run as high as 1 or 2 percent of the purchase price. Although it is possible to have one lawyer, such as the bank's, handle the complete transaction, it's preferable to have your own.

D. FINANCING THE PROPERTY

Clearly, the first consideration in purchasing a home is how much can you afford. There are many ways to calculate this. Financial planners often advise buyers not to exceed two-and-a-half times their annual income. Or be sure the sum of your monthly mortgage payment, taxes and home insurance does not exceed one-forth of your monthly take-home pay.

A down payment is usually required. On a older home it could be as much as a third of the price for an older house. The rest will be financed through what is called a mortgage.

A mortgage is a long term loan, usually covering

20, 25, or even 30 years—in which the lender, in the event you default, may foreclose on the property.

Monthly payments include interest and principle. The first few years of the mortgage payments usually go towards reducing the interest. The reverse is true in the later years of the loan at which time the majority of the payments go against the principle owed on the house.

At first glance the annual interest rate on home loans may seem lower than some other types of installment loans. But the fact is, over a 20 to 30 year period, the interest paid on a home loan is more than the cost of the house itself. However, with an amortization schedule in hand and arrangements made in advance with the lender to pay the monthly principle payments in the early years, thousands of dollars in interest can be saved.

Sources of Mortgage Money

There is a considerable selection of lenders and interest terms available. So do some shopping around before deciding where to borrow money. The usual sources are banks, savings and loan associations, mortgage banks, and life insurance companies.

There are various types of mortgage loans depending upon the kind of institution selected and the area of the country. By far the most common of these is the "conventional mortgage". The lender finances 60–95 percent of the appraised value of the home provided it meets certain financial requirements.

The other two common kinds of mortgages are FHA and VA loans. When securing a FHA loan, the risk is covered by mortgage insurance issued by the *F*ederal *H*ousing *A*dministration and paid by the borrower. If you obtain a VA mortgage, the risk is covered by the *V*eterans *A*dministration at no cost to the veteran. The chief advantage of the FHA and VA mortgages is that the down payment may be smaller. Also, the interest rate charges on these loans are a little lower than conventional loans interest rates. For this reason, bankers are reluctant to issue these types of loans without points. Points are a fee charged by the mortgagee for the granting of the loan. Each point is equal to 1 percent of the amount of the loan.

E. INSURANCE

Two types of insurance are necessary when buying a home. The first is known as a "homeowner's policy"; the bank or mortgage company requires it. It essentially covers the mortgage balance of the home and its contents. The second type of insurance is what is called "title insurance." Your deed alone, is not sufficient assurance that you are, in fact, the owner of the property purchased. Title insurance protects against the loss of real estate due to various claims and undisclosed risks, such as forged or improperly signed documents, missing heirs, and many others. Unlike most other forms of insurance, title insurance requires no monthly premiums to keep it in force. One premium covers the entire cost of protection so long as ownership of the home remains in your name.

F. CLOSING

Once the location selection, house-hunting, and arranging of financing are completed, the culmination comes at what is called the closing. The closing is attended by a number of individuals, some of whom you have never seen before and most likely will never see again. They include the buyers, sellers, attorneys or closing agents, realtors and any other parties that have a vested interest in the closing.

Your attorney should tell you an estimate of the charges you will be expected to pay at the closing. Be sure to bring your checkbook.

Typical closing costs are: 1) appraisal fee; 2) title search; 3) title insurance; 4) survey; 5) tax adjustment; 6) fuel oil adjustment; 7) deed recording fee; 8) credit report charge; 9) property insurance; 10) attorney's fees, which may be paid later.

After all the checks have been written be sure to ask for the keys to your new home—they were included in the purchase price!

GLOSSARY

ABSOLUTE TITLE. Title which is exclusive to the person who has it. No one else has any right, interest, or claim in the same property.

ACRE. 43560 square feet; 4,840 square yards; 160 square rods.

ADMINISTRATOR. A legal representative of a deceased person's estate, appointed by a court when the individual dies without a will or without naming someone as the executor of his estate in a will.

AD VALOREM. A tax or duty based on value and levied as a percentage of that value, e.g., 30 mills per dollar (3.0%) of property value.

AFFILIATE BROKER. An individual who performs any act or engages in any transaction performed by a broker except the completion of the negotiation of any agreement or transaction. He is employed by and is under the direction and supervision of a broker or a regular employer engaged in the real estate business.

AGENT. One who is employed to represent another (a principal) in business and legal affairs with third persons.

AMORTIZATION. The process of gradually extinguishing a debt by a series of periodic payments to the creditor. The usual method of amortization calls for equal periodic payments made at equal intervals of time and is used principally in the liquidation of bonded indebtedness and mortgages.

ANNUITY. An amount, especially of money, payable yearly until death of the recipient.

APPRAISAL. An estimate or opinion of the value of a property as of a specific date.

APPRAISER. A person engaged in the procedures of estimating the value of property. This definition includes the professional appraiser who devotes the bulk of his time to appraising, either as a fee appraiser or as an employee of some agency.

ASSESSMENT. The valuation of property to establish a basis for an ad valorem tax. The act of assessing, or the specific amount or value assessed.

BANKRUPTCY. A legal proceeding in which a debtor's property is taken over by a receiver or trustee for the benefit of the creditors.

BILL OF SALE. A written contract transferring personal property from one person to another.

BLANKET MORTGAGE. One mortgage on a number of parcels of Real Property.

BOND. An agreement under which a person or corporation becomes surety to pay, within the stated limits, for financial loss caused to another by the act of default of a third person or by some contingency over which the principal may have no control.

BROKER. Generally, a special agent who acts as an intermediary between other parties and assists in negotiating agreements between them.

CLOSING DATE. The date established by contractual agreement for the transferring of title.

CLOSING TITLE. The transaction in which the formalities of a sale of real property are executed.

COLLATERAL. Something of value, easily converted into cash, deposited as a pledge with a lender to secure the repayment of a loan.

COMMERICAL BANK. A bank whose principal functions include making short-term loans and term loans, maintaining checking accounts, receiving time deposits, and discounting negotiable instruments.

COMMERCIAL PROPERTY. A type of income property, as distinguished from industrial or agricultural properties, which is normally zoned for business purposes. Property held for the production of income through rental to one or more tenants is also included in the subclassification of commercial properties.

COMMISSION. The amount due to a broker for services rendered, usually figured as a percentage of the total price.

CONTINGENCY. That which is dependent on something that may or may not occur. A doubtful or uncertain future event.

CONTRACT. A promise or agreement, the performance of which is a legal duty, and the breach of which is actionable by law.

CONVENTIONAL MORTGAGE. One that is neither insured by the Federal Housing Administration nor guaranteed by the Veterans' Administration.

CORPOREAL PROPERTY. In describing real property, the actual land and all physical items affixed to it.

COVENANT. A promise in writing under seal often used as a substitute for the verb 'contract.'

COVENANTS OF TITLE. Guarantees made by a grantor when real property is conveyed by a warranty deed. These covenants are usually of seizin, quiet enjoyment, and free of encumbrances.

DEED. A formal document by which title to real property is conveyed from one person to another.

DEFAULT. Failure of a party to fulfill a contractual obligation or to perform some duty.

DELIVERY IN ESCROW. A conditional delivery of something to a third person to be held until the happening of some event or the performance of some act.

DELIVERY OF DEED. The final act by which one who has signed and sealed an instrument signifies his intention that it shall have legal operation as his deed. Delivery by the grantor is requisite to the validity of this deed.

DEPRECIATION. The decline in value of an asset due to physical deterioration, functional obsolescence, or economic obsolescence.

DOMICILE. A fixed and permanent home to which a person, if he is absent therefrom, intends to return. A person can have several residences at a time, but only one domicile. Domicile is not synonymous with residence.

EASEMENT. A right or privilege to use the Real Property of another for a specific purpose. An easement is an encumbrance against the property.

EMINENT DOMAIN. The power of the federal, state, and local governments to appropriate private property for public use or for the public welfare.

ENCROACHMENT. Illegal infringement upon the property of another. It may consist of a wall, cornice, casement windows, or garage doors that extend upon adjoining property when opened, et cetera.

ENCUMBRANCE. A lien, charge, or claim against real property which diminishes the value of the property, but does not prevent the passing of title. An existing mortgage on a property is the usual encumbrance.

EQUITY. The owner's interest in the value of real property usually reflected as the difference between the market value and the balance owed on the mortgage.

EQUITY OF REDEMPTION. The right of a borrower to redeem the property and regain legal title to it after default and before foreclosure sale by paying the amount due in full with interest. A clause in a mortgage waiving the equity of redemption has no legal effect, as this equity is extinguished only by foreclosure.

ESCHEAT. The return to the state of real or personal property if the owner dies without legal heirs.

ESCROW. A conditional delivery of something to a third person to be held until the happening of some event or the performance of some act.

ESTATE. An interest or right in the use, enjoyment, and disposition of land. The term "estate" is often used synonymously with the word "interest."

EVICTION. A forcible removal of a tenant by a landlord from possession of real property (actual eviction), or a violation by the landlord of an important provision of the lease amounting to an interference with the tenant's useful and peaceful enjoyment of the premises (constructive eviction).

FEDERAL HOUSING ADMINISTRATION (FHA). The governmental agency which insures loans on homes which meet FHA standards.

FEE SIMPLE. The absolute ownership of real property giving the owner and his heirs the unconditional power of disposition and other rights.

FIDUCIARY. One who is in a position of trust or confidence with respect to another person.
FIRST LIEN. A lien which takes priority over all other liens. A tax lien, for example, is a first lien and takes priority over all other liens . . . including the mortgage note.
FORECLOSURE. A proceeding against property which secures a debt. Foreclosure is brought upon default to cut off the mortgagor's equitable right to redeem the property.
FRAUD. Willful misrepresentation of a material fact which results in a person's assent to a contract in reliance upon it to his damage. The misrepresentation must be a statement of fact, not an opinion.
FREEHOLD. An estate in which the owner of real property retains title thereto for a period of indeterminate duration, such as an estate in fee simple or a life estate.
GRANTOR. One who conveys his real property to another by deed.
GROSS LEASE. A lease wherein all property charges regularly incurred through ownership, such as operating expenses, taxes, and insurance, are paid by landlord.
GUARANTY. A contract whereby one party agrees to answer for the debt or default of another.
HEIR. One entitled to inherit realty in the case of intestacy in accordance with the statute of descent.
INCOME PROPERTY. A broad classification of property which produces income directly (e.g., rental property) or as a factor in the production of income (e.g., commercial property used in one's trade or business).
INDEMNIFICATION CONTRACTS. Relative to insurance, indemnification contracts are designed to cover pure risks . . . risks in which there are no promises of gain.
INDEMNITY. An agreement that one party will secure another against loss or damage due to the happening of a specified event.
INDENTURE. A sealed agreement between two or more parties. Also, a deed executed by both parties as distinguished from a deed executed only by the grantor.
INDEPENDENT CONTRACTOR. A person, usually in business for himself, who contracts to do a complete job for another, being responsible to the latter for the finished product only, and not for the means by which that product is produced.
INVESTMENT PROPERTY. Investment property is real property acquired for the specific purpose of realizing a profitable return at some future date. It is property which is not held, as is income property, for the immediate and continuing production of income.
JOINT TENANCY. An estate held by two or more persons at the same time under the same title or source of ownership in which each has the same degree of interest and the same right of possession. Joint tenancy has the distinct character of survivorship.

LEASE. A contract, written or oral, between the owner of real property (the lessor, or landlord) and a tenant (the lessee) for the possession and use of lands and improvements in return for the payment of rent. In most states, a lease for more than one year must be in writing to be enforceable.

LIEN. A right, hold, or claim against specific property as security for a debt.

MARKET VALUE. The price in terms of money for which a property if exposed for a reasonable time will sell in a competitive market at a particular time by a seller to a buyer, each acting prudently and without obligation to act, with knowledge of the uses to which the property can be adapted.

MATURITY. The date on which an instrument becomes due.

MECHANIC'S LIEN. The statutory lien of a laborer, contractor, subcontractor, or material-man who performs work or furnishes material for the permanent improvement of real property. Such lien has for its purpose to subject the land of an owner to a lien for material and labor expended in the construction of buildings, which buildings having been placed on the land become a part thereof by the law of accession.

NOTARY PUBLIC. A public officer who has authority to attest and certify deeds and other writings, to take affidavits and other depositions, and to protest negotiable instruments.

OPTION. The right given by the owner to another to purchase or lease a property at a specific price within a set time for which the optionor is paid by the optionee a consideration for releasing this right.

OVER-IMPROVEMENT. An improvement not in consonance with the "highest and best use" or an improvement exceeding that justified by local conditions.

PASSAGE OF TITLE. The transfer of ownership from one to another.

PERCENTAGE LEASE. A lease wherein the amount of the rental is determined by a percentage of the business transacted on the leased property, usually a percentage of the tenant's gross sales.

PROPERTY TAX. An impersonal levy which focuses on both real and personal property. It is determined by the property's exchange value and is levied against the property owner.

PURCHASE AND SALE AGREEMENT. A written contract for consideration paid whereby one party agrees to sell and another party agrees to buy certain real estate under the provisions of the agreement.

QUITCLAIM DEED. A deed by which the grantor releases any interest he may have in the real property, without attempting to convey title. The grantor makes no warranty; if he has title, he conveys it; if he does not have title, he is not responsible for failure to convey a clear title, and the grantee has no right of action against him.

REAL ESTATE. Any and every estate or interest in land and the improvements thereon.

REAL PROPERTY. Land, buildings, minerals, and other products of the soil and the air space above the land.
REALTOR. A title which may be used only by members of an organization affiliated with the NATIONAL ASSOCIATION OF REALTORS.
RECORDING. The act of a public officer in recording an entry in a public docket, archive, or record, and by so doing, establishing evidence of a particular transaction, lien, or obligation, and in placing the general public on notice of the rights of the parties concerned.
REDEMPTION. The right of the original owner of property to reclaim his property after default, upon payment of the amount of the debt with interest and costs.
REGISTERED TITLE. A title which is certified by a Decree of the Land Court and which is usually accepted as unquestionable up to the date of the Decree.
RESTRICTIVE COVENANT. A clause in a deed placing a restriction on the use of the property conveyed for a specific period of time.
RIGHT OF WAY. A form of easement which gives one person the right to pass over the estate of another.
SEARCHING THE TITLE. The process by which a lawyer or searcher of titles investigates to determine whether the seller of property has title and if there are any claims against the property.
SECURITY DEPOSIT. A money deposit often required by the landlord as security for payment of the rent which frequently takes the form of an advance rent payment.
SUBDIVISION. The division of a parcel of land into house lots.
SUBLEASE. The transfer for a portion of the balance of the term of the lease of the whole or a part of the leased premises.
SURETY BOND. A contract to indemnify injured parties upon the failure of another to perform a particular act.
TANGIBLE. Property that is physical in character and capable of being moved.
TAX LIEN. A claim against real property from assessed taxes against the property that accrues to the taxing agency (municipality, city, et cetera). If not paid when due, the taxing agency sells the property at a tax sale.
TENANCY. The period of time that a tenant is permitted to remain in possession of real property. Also, an interest in land, e.g., joint tenancy, tenancy in common, tenancy by the entirety, and tenancy in severalty.
TITLE. Evidence of ownership and often used interchangeably with the term "ownership" to indicate a person's right to possess, use, and dispose of property.
TITLE INSURANCE. An insurance which protects the insured from loss or damage resulting from defects in title. It guarantees the authenticity

of every recorded instrument and places an absolute guarantee behind the work of the title company.

TITLE SEARCH. A circumspect review of all documents and records in the local recorder's office pertaining to a property to determine if the seller has good title to the property. This service is usually performed by a lawyer or a title insurance company.

TRUSTEE. In a trust relationship, one who holds property for the benefit of another person.

TRUST DEED. A deed which conveys real estate to a third person to be held for the benefit of a beneficiary.

V.A. MORTGAGE. A mortgage in which the repayment of the loan to the lending institution is guaranteed in part by the Veterans' Administration. Sometimes referred to as a V.A. Loan, V.A. Guaranteed Mortgage, G.I. Loan, or G.I. Mortgage.

VARIANCE. An exception to the zoning ordinances authorized by a special board of appeals in the event of unusual hardship or special circumstances.

WARRANTY DEED. A deed, upon a sale of real property, under which the grantor formally agrees that he will forever guarantee title to the conveyed real property. A warranty deed does not correct a bad title. It simply gives the grantee the right to sue the grantor for breach of warranty if someone later makes a claim against the property.

WATER RIGHTS. The rights of an owner of land adjoining a stream which is not navigable to use the stream to a reasonable extent.

ZONING ORDINANCE. An ordinance under which communities restrict the use of certain land areas and control the type, intensity, and volume of building construction in such areas.